UNEQUAL VICTIMS

Poles and Jews
During World War Two

by

**Yisrael Gutman
Shmuel Krakowski**

**Holocaust Library
New York**

Translated from the Hebrew and Polish

by

Ted Gorelick and Witold Jedlicki

Library of Congress Catalogue Card Number 86-081417

ISBN: 0-89604-055-0 (Cloth)
ISBN: 0-89604-056-9 (Paper)

Cover design by Judith L. Anderson

Printed in the United States of America

The translation and publication of this book
was made possible by a grant in memory of

Sonia Berg

1899 - 1985

whose wisdom, courage and strength
serve as an inspiration to her
family and to all who
were privileged
to know
her.

CONTENTS

The following chapters were written by Yisrael Gutman: 1, 5, 7, 9, 10.

The following chapters were written by Shmuel Krakowski: 2, 3, 4, 6, 8.

Introduction

In the long history of the Jewish people the relationship to Poland and the Polish people plays a very central part. Poland was a hospitable haven to the Jews from the Middle Ages on and until well into the early modern period. Then, with troubles and disasters befalling the Polish people themselves, an era began of Jewish suffering too. During most of that period Jews fulfilled essential socio-economic functions in Polish society—they, together with the Germans, were a largely urban element of craftsmen and traders; in the eastern marches of the kingdom they fulfilled the precarious role of the go-betweens in the relationships of feudal Polish lords to the local peasantry. The monarchy and the aristocracy viewed them with some favor; the peasantry accepted them as an essential and useful part of the scheme of things, except when poverty and natural and human-made disasters intervened to cause them to rise against those that were nearest to them. The small Polish urban element was jealous of the Jews' position; the Church, more often than not, actively hostile. But as long as social equilibrium was somehow maintained, with the aristocracy and the central government predominant, Jews could develop their culture and their society. This they did indeed do, and the result was a flourishing of Jewish learning and tradition that lasted, in effect, until the destruction of Polish Jewry during the Holocaust.

The partition of Poland brought most of Polish Jewry under the rule of the extreme anti-Semitic regime of the Muscovite Czars on the one hand, and a strict, though not malevolent Austrian regime on the other. Relationships with Poles became secondary in the struggle for existence of the impoverished and—in Russia—persecuted masses of the Jewish people. The nationalistic Polish gentry and bourgeoisie did, however, find sympathy and even identification among Jewish groups. In the heroic and tragic struggles for Polish independence in the nineteenth century there was active Jewish participation. Anti-Jewish sentiment remained the preserve of circles of the Church and some of the urban Polish elements, but a new anti-Semitism emerged in Poland as well as in other European countries in the latter half of the 19th century.

All this changed drastically after the attainment of Polish independence in the wake of World War I. The sudden violent rise of anti-Semitism, expressing itself in pogroms, especially in southeastern Poland, is often explained by the unenviable position of the Jewish minority in Eastern Galicia between Poles and Ukrainians. But the mainstream of the middle-class nationalist movement around Roman Dmowski and his National Democrats emerged as a violently anti-Semitic factor in the newly-constituted Poland. One is tempted to explain the virulent hatred of Jews by economic factors—the competition between the Jews as a middle-class population and the rising Polish bourgeoisie, and by the exigencies of a severe and permanent economic crisis as it affected the peasantry. However, one ought perhaps not to close one's eyes to traditional elements such as the long-standing opposition to Jews on the part of the Church. Nor is it possible to deny the influence of integral nationalism as such, though that affected not only Jews but also the other minorities in inter-war Poland; nevertheless, the main target was considered to be the Jew—after all, he was both foreign and familiar, supposedly strong economically and yet visibly weak, contemptible and powerful.

Prof. Yisrael Gutman and Dr. Shmuel Krakowski have taken all this as their background in order to examine in depth the story of the development of Polish-Jewish relations during the Holocaust itself. The task is vitally important because one faces, on the one hand, a united choir of historical falsification emerging from both Warsaw and the Polish exile in the West attempting to deny Polish anti-Semitism and the largely indifferent or negative attitude of the Polish population toward the Jews, and, on the other hand, Jewish anti-Polish sentiment tending to deny the heroic help extended to some Jews by what one is tempted to describe as the best elements in Polish society. The two authors pick their way carefully amid conflicting evidence. They build some of their writing on the brilliant and penetrating essay by Emmanuel Ringelblum on Polish-Jewish relations, written by the great ghetto historian while in hiding on the "Aryan" side of Warsaw, protected by a Polish worker and his family, who were to pay with their lives for their heroism. The authors have to face, in many cases, a lack of reliable materials altogether, forcing them to desist from both description and judgment. They try to analyze Polish attitudes toward Jews both regionally and by social classes. They avoid the pitfalls of facile generalizations by pointing out exceptions and contradictions to the general conclusions they reach.

The picture that finally emerges is not a very pleasant one. There were some Poles who helped; there were groups of Poles who helped, too. Some, like Mieczyslaw Wolski, who hid Ringelblum and 37 others, paid with their lives for their identification with their Jewish neighbors; some Polish forest fighters cooperated with Jews, accepted them into Polish units, or helped them when in need. But the majority, and that included the official underground movement linked to the Government-in-Exile in London and its armed forces, were either indifferent or actively hostile. Against that background, it must be remembered, the minority that helped stands out the more. The authors not only describe the situation, but they also try to explain the reasons for it. The impressive thing about their historical writing is that they stick very closely indeed to their source materials, and do not permit themselves any emotional remarks. Their dispassionate discussion of events and attitudes makes their judgment impressive indeed.

Apart from the situation in Poland itself, the authors discuss both the Government-in-Exile in London and its policies. Some of this had been made available to the English-reading public before, but here we have for the first time an attempt at a comprehensive analysis of the situation.

There is little doubt that this book will arouse controversy—as well it might. It may destroy many preconceptions and force many people to re-examine views and attitudes. But that, after all, is what historians should do. Gutman and Krakowski have done that, and we should be grateful to them for it.

Yehuda Bauer
Hebrew University of Jerusalem

Preface

The subject dealt with in this book is not only complex, warranting examination of a large amount of documentary material, but is also of an extremely delicate nature. The fact that contemporary questions and events are discussed is only one of the reasons for this sensitivity. We are attempting a thorough examination of the range of contacts, interconnections, and tensions between the two peoples, who had lived on the same land for hundreds of years and confronted a period of a very difficult historical test. These connections were shrouded by experiences and images that were the products of many generations, and especially of the difficult conflicts of the period between the world wars, the days of the Second Polish Republic, in which the clearly anti-Semitic policy and attitude toward the Jews was one of the dominant revelations.

During the period of the war itself, both the Poles and the Jews were victims of the cruel and brutal occupation regime. Moreover, in the Nazis' view, both peoples were considered inferior and, therefore, their position in the Nazi "New Order" in Europe was to be established accordingly. In fact, to an outside observer, it may seemed as if the Poles and the Jews were in similar, if not identical, situation. For example, the British historian Norman Davies, in his book *Heart of Europe* on the history of Poland in the last generations, writes:

> The Jews had been segregated since the winter 1939–1940, since when all normal intercommunal contact had been lost. The Polish population at large lived under the formal threat of instant execution for the entire family of anyone sheltering, feeding, or helping Jews. In this light it is as pointless to ask why the Poles did little to help the Jews as to enquire why the Jews did nothing to assist Poles.[1]

Of course, one cannot charge the Poles with the responsibility for the Holocaust and the Jewish tragedy during World War II. The Poles did not plan, initate, nor carry out the destruction of the Jews. There is also no solid basis for the argument that the Germans chose Poland, as the site for the establishment of the death camps because the Poles were known for their anti-Semitism and therefore could be counted on for collaboration in the process of the destruction of the Jews. The truth is that the Nazis evidently chose areas of Poland as the murder site because millions of Jews lived in that country; Poland was under an absolute occupation force; and, finally, in Poland, far from the heart of Europe, it was easier to cover up the murder and try to carry it out under conditions of secrecy. However, the question still remains to what extent the situation of the Poles was different from that of the Jews during the occupation period. Secondly, what was then the character of the relationship between the Jews and Poles.

The Nazi occupation was the most difficult experience in the history of the Polish nation. The Poles were decimated during the five years of German rule, suffering casualties reaching almost 10 percent of their pre-war population. The heaviest losses were among the intelligentsia and the Warsaw population after the tragic uprising in the summer of 1944. Hundreds of thousands were expelled from the western Polish territories which were incorporated into the Third Reich and from the Zamość region. Almost two million were sent to slave labor in Germany. Severe collective punishment was introduced for every kind of resistance. According to Nazi ideology and policies, the destiny of the Poles was to be used as cheap laborers for the Greater German Reich, while the policy towards the Jews was their total physical extermination. According to Nazi racial ideology the Poles were still a part of the Aryan race, though they constitued a lower stratum. On the contrary, the Jews were the absolute inferior elements which, according to the Nazi belief, were not even granted the elementary right to existence.

The plight of the Jews, however, was from the very beginning substantially different than that of the Poles. From the very beginning the Jews were objects of persecution and terror of special dimensions. Mass confiscations of property, mass killings, round-ups for forced labor under the reign of terror, prohibitions on the use of public transportation and the wearing of the yellow star were all introduced from the first months of the occupation. In 1940 ghettoization was instituted. The entire Jewish population was shut up inside ghettos, where they became subject to mass mortality due to hunger and disease. In many ghettos the mortality rate exceeded 10 percent—in one year. From December 1941, death camps built exclusively for murder by the use of poison gas began operation in Poland—Chelmno, Belzec, Sobibor, Treblinka and Auschwitz II-Birkenau. During the one year of 1942, most of the ghettos were liquidated, and the majority of the Jews murdered in the gas chambers. During the years 1943–1944, the German occupiers continued the mass destruction of those Jews who remain in the diminished ghettos, in concentration and slave-labor camps, and the few who escaped to the forests, villages, and the so-called "Aryan" sections of certain cities.

In their desperate situations, the Jews looked to the Poles for assistance. No matter how difficult their own situation, the Poles' plight could not be compared to the destiny of the Jews. In spite of the Nazi terror, the great majority of Poles still lived in their pre-war apartments, and worked at their pre-war jobs. Although they were subject to exploitation and terror, they never faced total extermination. Although they had lost their independence, they could still look for help to the Polish Government-in-London, the Polish Armed Forces in exile and the constant support that the Allied Powers extended to the Polish underground.

The Polish response to the Jewish request for help and salvation, therefore, was the result not only of the objective conditions created by the Nazi occupiers but also of the subjective Polish stand, the attitude of the various strata of the Polish population, and the position of the various political forces and the Church. This book is an attempt to study and define these various attitudes and positions.

Both from Jews and Poles one sometimes hears the contention that there is no sense in opening old wounds, in reviving painful questions that were the result of an inhumane period; conditions have changed, and the present situation has changed along with them. Once many Poles referred to Jews with contempt; today the tone is different, as the Jews, their country, and their position in the world is today seen in a completely different light. Many Jews once saw the Poles as extreme anti-Semites. Today Jews also refrain from these one-sited judgments. However, the period between the wars and the last wave of the Polish government's anti-Semitic campaign in 1967–1968 certainly did not ease the relationship and even added a spasm of anger to group memory.

Time and distance have separated Jews and Poles, and, in a practical sense, there are almost no direct relations between the two peoples at the present time. It is only the monuments of the Jewish past that remain on Polish soil that have to be preserved. If so, we are dealing with a historical issue, a subject to be studied as a chapter in the realm of history. But one must not assume that the memory of the past, the heritage, is without implication on our current life.

Stefan Wilkanowicz has expressed this in his preface to the anthology *Christianity and Judaism*, which was published in Poland in 1983. Wilkanowicz both queries and replies:

> Why do we raise the Jewish problem? Because it exists, because at some point is must be raised—and this answer should be a basically satisfactory one. We cannot escape from this matter and let time heal the wounds. Although time does submerge many things in the abyss of forgetfulness, sometimes this is merely an illusion (because the things continue to exist somewhere in our subconscious, ready to reveal themselves in an unexpected way). In addition, we also forget the sins, that is, the confession and penance for them. And so we have to strike a sort of balance between the national or social conscience and cleansing the wounds—and this in order that time can nurse them and heal them. This is in no way connected to the practical consequences of the subject, whether the Jewish matter is a sort of an ace in a tactical plan, or whether at this moment nothing is happening in this area.[2]

It seems to us that Mr. Wilkanowicz has touched on the basic matter. It is an illusion and mistake to think that forgetfulness itself uproots injustice and historical errors. At best one tears a page or two from a history book and tries to ignore the facts. However, just as a man cannot run away from his past, because the past lives within him, and he returns to it and it guides his actions and feelings, in the same way, the past of nations cannot be erased simply with the wave of a hand. It accompanies us in a tangible, palpable way or in a suppressed manner, but it is apt to float to the surface in critical periods.

When we deal with a range of continuous relationships that were accompanied by aspects of discrimination, hostility, and contempt, it is safe to assume that the marks that were left do not disappear when the object of hatred is removed. The true victory over weaknesses and sins is in the open, bold grappling with the past. Both the Jewish and Polish peoples are strong enough to look honestly and bravely at the past with open and probing eyes and to excise the wounds so as to be able to turn to the future with a pure heart and a bit of hope. If any single principle directed the authors— aside from responsible research and methodological criteria—this was their basic guideline.

Despite the numerous available sources, no comprehensive reseach on this subject has been written during the forty post-war years. The only comprehensive work on the subject was written by Dr. Emmanuel Ringelblum while in hiding during late 1943, and naturally could not have been based on the material available today.

Among the Jewish historians dealing with some aspects of

Polish-Jewish relations, Philip Friedman's *Their Brother's Keepers* (New York, 1957) deserves mention. Friedman deals with the aid extended to Jews by "Righteous Among the Nations" in various countries, including Poland.

Polish historiography has preferred to treat one aspect, mainly, that is, the help provided to Jews. Three of the best-known books in this field are *Righteous Among Nations: how Poles Helped the Jews, 1939–1945* (London 1963) by Wadyslaw Bartoszewski and Zofia Lewin; *He Who Saves One Life* (New York, 1971) by Kazimierz Iranek—Osmecki; and *Konspiracyjna Rada Pomocy Zydom w Warszawie* ("The Underground Council for Help to Jews in Warsaw". Warsaw, 1982) by Teresa Preker. Despite all the importance attached to these books, which reveal events concerning rescue and aid, one cannot overlook the main fact that they treat only one aspect of the relationship between the Jews and Poles and omit the other aspects. In the case of Iranek-Osmecki, there is marked exaggeration and blatant apology.

The authors of this book attempted to deal with the subject with the utmost objectivity and based their research on a wide range of documentation, mainly primary material, Polish and Jewish alike. Among the rich archival sources studied by the authors, the following were the most valuable:

— Documentation of the Polish Government-in-Exile;
— Documentation of various Polish underground organizations;
— Jewish underground archives, including the Ringelblum Archives;
— The collection of Dr. Yitzhak (Ignacy) Schwarzbart;
— Documentation of the Representation of Polish Jews;
— Polish and Jewish underground press;
— Diaries, memoirs and testimonies by Jews and Poles.

On the long road to the completion of this work, we were assisted by many people and institutions. Above all, we would like to thank our friends at Yad Vashem and the Institute of Contemporary Jewry of the Hebrew University of Jerusalem, who supported us and helped us in our work at all times. Our thanks also to the Sikorski Institute in London for the opportunity to research many documents in the Institute's archives. We would like to acknowledge the late Michael Silberberg and thank Rabbi Dr. David Kahana of Tel Aviv and Dr. Simon Frisner of London who helped us with documentary material in their possession. We would also like to acknowledge the late Alexander Donat, who took a great interest in this research, helped in the various stages of its preparation, and whose encouragement was of great assistance to the authors. We are obliged to Prof. Yehuda Bauer, who was kind enough to read the manuscript and made most useful remarks. And finally, our thanks to Mr. and Mrs. Yekutiel Federman, whose contribution in memory of Joel Reiner made this research possible.

Yisrael Gutman   Jerusalem
Shmuel Krakowski   February, 1985

NOTES

1. Norman Davies, *Heart of Europe, A Short History of Poland,* (Clarendon Press, Oxford, 1984,) p. 72.

2. Stefan Wilkanowicz, *"Antisemity-zm,* Patriotyzm, Chrześcijaństwo," published in *"Znak",* No. 339–340, Cracow, February-March 1983, p. 171.

CHAPTER ONE

Between the Wars

RENEWED POLAND AND THE JEWS

The period between the wars, two decades of the independent Polish Republic, is an era in which the relations between the Poles and the Jews were characterized by increasing tension and conflicts: the earmark of hostility which had grown ever since the end of the nineteenth century reached previously unheard of peaks during this period, having grown over the hundreds of years the Jews had lived on Polish territory.

It is customary to think that the anti-Semitism of the Poles was an endemic phenomenon, persisting in all ages. There is no way to encompass the entire complex of relations between Poles and Jews throughout the generations within the framework of a limited review. At any rate, the balance of the encounter is not always negative or even primarily so, when viewed against the background of the history of the Jews in Europe. The very fact that the Jews were concentrated in Poland, where they found over centuries a refuge when being pursued and forced to flee or to move from the West or the East, for a variety of reasons, indicates that Poland demonstrated a certain degree of tolerance. It was there that Jewish inner autonomy and economic activity developed in the cities, a desirable development from the point of view of certain strata in Polish society.

At the end of the First World War, Poland was granted renewed independence after a hundred and thirty years of partition and political subjugation. Many people in Europe and the U.S.A. viewed the resurrection of Poland as the correction of an historic injustice. The Polish question had constantly bothered Europe during the nineteenth century. The Poles proved their deeply-entrenched national tenacity, rebelled frequently and fought against the conqueror in wars already lost before they began, whereas from the point of view of the champions of social progress

1

the chaining of Poland was a sin oppressing the conscience of Europe.

The actual resurrective process did not evolve as the result of a Polish victory or a Polish decisive contribution on the battlefield, but rather as the product of an extremely propitious political constellation, from the Polish point of view, which came about as a result of the First World War. Their traditional enemies and the occupiers of their land were defeated (Imperial Germany), were in the throes of a revolution and a civil war (Russia), or completely disintergrated as a political unit (Austria-Hungary). In addition, Poland benefited from the political bargaining which followed the First World War, from France's desire to establish in the east and the south-east of Europe a set of independent states allied to her and serving to counterbalance German power, and from the strong anti-Bolshevik attitude in western Europe. This political climate aided Poland to expand borders, especially in the east, which encompassed more than just the territory inhabited by a Polish ethnic majority.

In retrospect one may wonder whether these conjunctural advantages did not over a longer period of time prove to work to Poland's disadvantage. Poland's resurgence not only was achieved at the expense of a conflict with the powers to her east and her west, but also generated border disputes with neighbors to the north (Lithuania) and the south (Czechoslovakia). Poland's firm national cohesion and pride in her glorious history contributed to the stability of the new state, but, on the other hand, they dictated political norms and ambitions unsuitable to a new state troubled by numerous difficulties. Above all, even during the period of her independence, Poland continued in its tradition of excessive political dissension, many factions and sectors applying pressure in the parliamentary and public sphere, and weak governments frequently replaced one another.

Poland between the wars was a relatively large state inhabited by over thirty million people. The division rife among the powers created considerable differences economically, socially and legally. Three quarters of the Polish population were peasants, largely without land or dependent upon a small plot of ground, while a handful of aristocratic magnates controlled vast estates. Poland was divided into two zones which differed visibly regarding economic development. The western part was the more advanced than the east. The Polish city was weak and backward in urban and industrial development. Those urban centers which did break through and achieve an impressive level of development in certain fields(textile products in Lodz and in Bialystok) were to a large extent dependent upon the huge Russian consumer market which, as a result of the war and consequent changes, was now cut off from them. Moreover, Poland had to undergo reunification and establish its economy in a Europe split by sharp political differences and in the throes of a severe economic depression.

Another significant Polish deficiency during the period between the wars stemmed from the country's national composition. Against the background of internal Polish cohesion and the Poles' pronounced claims, the problem posed by the minorities, who made up about a third of the inhabitants of the country (Ukrainians, Byelorussians, Germans and Lithuanians primarily), stood out very clearly. Most of the minorities represented national units which maintained relations with their compatriots or with the states in which their peoples lived, across the border. Ukrainians and Byelorussians constituted a majority in regions adjacent to the eastern border, and, as a result, a separatist spirit and irredentist activity in these areas became an inevitable phenomenon.

At the beginning of the period, there were in Poland two general and loosely defined trends or, more precisely, guidelines regarding policy towards the minorities. The National Democratic Party (*Endeks*), which encompassed a large segment of the Polish middle class and lower-middle class and intelligentsia, and whose influence was strongest mainly in the western provinces of Poland, maintained that the decisive principle was the basing of the state on the supremacy and control of the Poles, i.e., not a Polish state encompassing several peoples with the Poles as the majority and main nucleus, but rather "Poland for the Poles."[1] The *Endeks* wanted to follow a policy of Polonization towards the minorities in the east, assuming it would be possible to assimilate these sectors and to integrate them into the lower strata of the Polish population; whereas with regard to the Germans they were in favor of expulsion by purchasing their lands and other methods.

The position adopted by the *Endeks* with regard to the Jews was especially virulent. The Jews were, in their opinion, a foreign element which had exploited the political weakness of Poland and settled there. The Jews had served the enemies of Poland for generations, and even in the independent Polish state they tended to adopt anti-Polish positions, maintaining contacts with the rivals of Poland abroad, and constituted an obstacle to the economic development of the country.[2] In addition, the main exponent of this ideology, Roman Dmowski, claimed that Jews, except for some exceptional cases, were incapable of being assimilated into Polish society and thus should not be forced to do so. The Jewish character and mentality were foreign and dangerous to the essence of Polish-ness. Therefore "the Jewish problem in Poland should be solved". During the early years of the period they strove to arrive at such a "solution" by removing the Jews from economic life, cultural fields and professions, boycotting Jewish factories and businesses, main-taining a *numerus clausus* in the universities, and other similar steps. In this initial stage their struggle against the Jews was carried on mainly at the parliamentary level with public opinion at home and abroad having considerable influence in determining the positions and operative steps adopted by them. During the thirties, and especially the later part, the attitudes of the *Endeks* became more extreme, as did those of the splinter groups which broke away from this party or operated in secondary groupings outside it. The unambiguous demand to expel the Jews from the country was voiced, while accelerating this process of expulsion by violent means. A Polish publicist and politician from the conservative right wing, Stanislaw Mackewicz (Cat) stated later that "Dmowski held that the Jews were in more complete control over the Poles' economic life than the foreign conquerors were over their political life, and his anti-Jewish sentiments were far stronger than his feelings against the conquerors."[3]

Another attitude towards minorities was represented by Poland's prominent leader between the wars, Marshal Jozef Pilsudski, and the moderate socialist camp, together with liberal strata of the popula-tion and parts of the organized peasantry. The policy favored by this sector was the setting up of a kind of federation of peoples under the auspices of the Poles, granting far-reaching autonomy in internal affairs and education at various levels, including higher education, to the ethnic groups living in defined areas. The federa-tive idea as an alliance of Slavic peoples against the hegemony of Russia never reached fruition because of the political situation, and also because the various Slavic groups didn't discern any advantage in the superiority and precedence of the Poles over the Russians. In actual practice, autonomous rights were not granted to the Ukrainians and the Byelorussians, and those tentative steps taken in this direction were the result of a bitter parliamentary struggle and the outbursts of Ukrainian and Byelorussian groups and organizations in the eastern territories. Actually, neither of these two schemes involving the territorial minorities was ever realized in full. The Polonization plans for the minorities encountered stiff opposition; attempts to settle Poles in border regions and to alter the ethnic structures of the area led to the formation of an irredentist movement; as for autonomous rights, the system of the carrot and the stick was employed, the impression of the stick being the more apparent.

Pilsudski and the socialists showed moderation and occasionally even understanding in connection with the Jewish minority. Though this group had no consistent and explicit political policy in connection with Jews, many of them supported the idea of integrating the Jews into the economic life of Poland, opposed legislative discrimination against Jews (the socialists did, however, through a distorted interpretation of social legislation for all, support the closing of Jewish stores and the cessation of Jewish labor on Sundays, thus furthering the strong discrimination against Jewish small merchants and workmen), and some of them viewed the assimilation of the Jews as a desirable solution in the more distant future. Pilsudski himself was not anti-Semitic; at any rate, he made no use of anti-Jewish slogans or incitement in his political activity or in his methods when in power. Many Jews saw him as a friend of the Jews and as their benefactor. There is, on the other hand, no sign in the writings and speeches of Marshal Pilsudski of any attachment for the Jews. It is more likely that the Jews, accustomed to systematic hostility on the part of Polish leaders, saw in Pilsudski, who did not revile Jews and on occasion even tended to listen to their complaints with understanding, a positive personality and a benefactor in the Polish political panorama. Pilsudski's heirs adopted extreme anti-Semitic positions, raised the massive emigration of Jews to the level of a prerogative in their internal and external political activity, publicly declared their support of an economic boycott of the Jews, despite their mild dissociation from the violence introduced into the streets of the cities, the towns and villages by the Endeks, and especially the radical splinter groups of youths with fascistic overtones.

From the point of view of the regime and the forces predominant in Poland, the period between the World Wars can be divided into four secondary periods. The first stage lasted from 1918 to 1922, the formative years during which the borders stabilized, a war was fought with Communist Russia, and the basis was laid for the parliamentary regime of Poland. As we shall see, this was also the period of anti-Semitic arguments and the outburst of pogroms which served to entrench Jew-hatred as a constant element in the political and social atmosphere in Poland between the wars.

The second stage, extending from the convening of the first regular Polish sejm (Parliament) between the wars to the Pilsudski coup d'état of May 1926, is considered the era of Polish parliamentarism. It is more appropriate to speak of the dominance of the sejm, the legislature, in Polish life than it would be to talk of real democracy during the period. One of the obviously detrimental phenomena, which has roots deeply entrenched in Poland's political history, is the multiple split into parties and social strata striving to perpetuate their differences rather than to exploit whatever they had in common. The Polish Governments replaced each other every few months, the executive authority was dependent upon the unstable support of factions in the legislature, and parliamentary maneuvering used up most of the energy which was never devoted to thorough planning and continuous execution. The *Endeks* were the dominant element or partner in most of the Governments during this period. Pilsudski took no part in the Governments until 1926 but directed his darts against the exaggerated political diversity and demanded the strengthening of the authority of the President and Government at the expense of that of the Parliament. The Marshal enjoyed widespread popularity among the masses as a national hero who had established Polish independence, and was supported by the army; on the other hand, the right-wing factions, the *Endeks*, and part of the large peasant camp, who were dependent upon more electoral support, strove to maintain the strength of the Parliament in the governmental structure.

In May 1926 there came about the coup initiated by Pilsudski and his confederates, the fate of which was actually decided after the army came out in support of the Marshal. Pilsudski was also supported by liberal circles, by the socialists and by the vast majority of the Jews. At first the reforms he carried out in his capacity as sole ruler, despite the severe reduction of the authority of the *sejm* were of a calming nature, and there was even a temporary strengthening of the economy, mainly because of the helpful international situation. Concerning the Jews positive steps were taken which produced a high level of expectation. However, in 1930, a change occurred, expressed in far-reaching oppression of opposition to the left and right, in sharp attacks against the Parliament, and in signs of the economic depression, which, while becoming a worldwide phenomenon, was especially strong in Poland. In foreign policy, the non-aggression pact with Nazi Germany signed at the beginning of 1934 was the most notable and significant step. Some Polish historians claim that the Marshal suggested to France, in light of Hitler's rise to power, that Poland and France initiate a common preventive war, and that France rejected the suggestion, but no irrefutable proof of this claim has been found. On the other hand, it is clear that Pilsudski held that of the two giant powers between which Poland found itself, the German connection was preferable, for Germany was less of a threat than Soviet Russia. The non-aggression pact with Germany quickly led to firm, close relations, first developing in Pilsudski's lifetime, and steadily strengthening after his death.

The fourth and last stage in the history of Poland between the wars extended from Pilsudski's death in 1935, until the outbreak of hostilities in September 1939. Pilsudski and his supporters did not set up an organized and united political party. Pilsudski, who favored "sanacja," political resuscitation, linked up splinter parties, groups representing social strata and various organizations into a loose political bloc. It was reasonable that this leader, whose roots originated in revolution and in Polish romanticism and whose political beginnings were socialistic, acted pragmatically when in power, and preferred practical and immediate considerations to programmatic platforms. He brought together the capitalists and big landowners, on the one hand, and trade-union representatives who had abandoned socialistic ideological principles, on the other. His operative regime itself was entrusted to a group of his adherents, mostly Pilsudski's followers from the days of the "legions" during the First World War, called the "colonels." The cement which kept this checkered and variegated bloc together was the leader's own charismatic personality. After his demise, his heirs were helpless. Dissension in various fields, as well as personal frictions, surfaced immediately within the ruling faction, and these various differences were not resolved until the fall of the Republic. Basically, they constituted a group lacking vision and political understanding. Jozef Beck is known to have been especially influential as the executor of the views of the Marshal in the field of foreign policy, and he was mainly responsible for piloting the political ship during the stormy period of the late thirties in Europe and the outbreak of the conflict with Germany. Beck engaged in intrigue, becoming involved both in his relations with friends and in his contacts with opponents; and when his pro-German political conception proved groundless, he neither dared reveal the truth to his countrymen nor tried to avoid a conflict by means of limited concessions until it was too late.

THE CHARACTER OF ANTI-JEWISH OPINIONS AND POLICY

As we have already pointed out, this last stage—from the point of view of the Jews—was one of legal persecution, of ever-more-powerful attempts to force them to emigrate, and of unleashed violence.

In contrast to the Slavic minorities, the Jews lacked territorial concentration, being scattered throughout the entire country, especially in its central and eastern provinces. In this respect, the situation of the Jews was analogous to that of the German minority; however, the Germans, who made up a significant stratum of the population in some of the cities, were also firmly entrenched in agriculture and industry in the western districts, previously part of Prussia. The greatest difference was that the German minority had a patron and power outside the country, always ready to defend them—the German state.

The change that took place with the restoration of an independent Poland emphasized the demographic factor involving the Jewish minority. Earlier the Jews had been one of many minorities or ethnic sectors in the Russian Czarist State, the Prussian Empire or in Austria-Hungary. The new situation dramatically highlighted the Jewish population. According to the 1921 census, the Jews constituted some 10.5% of Poland's total population, in absolute terms—2,855,000 individuals. This quantitative aspect stands out even more in light of the fact that the Jews were a distinctly urban element. According to this same census, only 22% of the overall Polish populace lived in the cities, whereas with the Jews, the proportion was reversed, 76.4% of them were city-dwellers. In the large cities of Poland—Warsaw, Lodz, Wilno, Cracow and Lwow—there were concentrated about a quarter of Polish Jewry, their percentage of the population of these cities being between 24.8% and 36.1%, i.e., from a quarter to over a third of the residents. In numerous towns in the eastern regions the Jews made up absolute majorities, while in Lublin, which had nearly 100,000 inhabitants during the twenties, the Jews comprised around 40%, with a similar percentage in Bialystok.

In addition to the quantitative factor and the Jewish urban preponderence, their professional composition drew the most attention to Poland's Jews. According to the 1921 census, 41% of the Jewish wage-earners engaged in trade, with another 34% in industry and crafts. The 1931 census shows a certain shift—the merchants dropping to 36% with 42.2% of Jews engaged in industry and skilled labor. However, in 1931, the differences were clear between Jews and Poles with respect to their concentration in these various occupations. While only 4% of the Jews made their living from agriculture, only 6% of the Poles were engaged in trade, however, their concentration in agriculture was still over 60%.[4]

According to Jewish sources, an anti-Semitic drive began in Poland immediately following the regaining of political independence, for no specific reason whatever. Yitzhak Gruenbaum, the outstanding Zionist leader of Polish Jewry, claimed that the Polish masses were trying to express the change experienced in their new status of sovereignty, by maltreating the Jews.[5] The Jewish historian Ben-Zion Dinur states in an article about Polish Jewry, that after the Poles had achieved independence "the war against the Jews began to be waged in ways and to degrees completely different from those customary earlier. Before the Polish renaissance this war could only rely on popular forces: a movement, propaganda, an organization. However, after the First World War, the entire governmental complex was at the disposal of this persecution mania."[6]

There were two events which occurred immediately after independence which left a deep impression: a) the minorities pact, b) the wave of pogroms leveled against Polish Jewry during the Polish War against Bolshevik Russia.

The Minorities Pact, or the Little Versailles Pact, did not affect the Poles alone, but applied rather to the new and enlarged states in central, eastern and south-eastern Europe after the First World War. After it became obvious that under no conditions could the principle of national self-determination be fully realized, it appeared necessary to guarantee the rights of ethnic and religious minorities doomed to remain as such according to the new political maps. The Jews had a significant part in the political struggle for these pacts and for their actual wording. Representatives of American, English and French Jewry exercised considerable political influence for the minority rights while the Jewish populations of eastern European states set up committees, held conventions and dispatched delegations to France to safeguard their interests. The representatives of Polish Jewry viewed the very matter of the pact as tantamount to recognition of them as a national minority (in actual fact, the status of Jews as a national minority was not recognized, the emphasis being placed on religious freedom) and as a chance to organize and function in Poland with the status of a national minority. The Poles, together with others, held—and not unjustly—that the very imposition of a pact on certain kinds of states and not on all states, was a clear interference in their internal affairs and a limitation of their political sovereignty, especially since the supervision of the pact was placed in the hands of the future League of Nations. Under these circumstances, the representatives of the new and enlarged countries (especially the

Rumanians and the Poles) initiated a vigorous campaign against the pacts, and when their attempt was defeated, their anger was directed mainly against the Jews. In Polish historiography and before public opinion the pact was portrayed as a plot of international Jewry.[7] In time it became clear that the Jews had gained very little, if at all, from the pact and its meaning. The Polish authorities found ways and means to bypass the explicit paragraphs of the Pact, to frame laws and actually discriminate against the Jews. The Jews, for their part, avoided appealing to the League of Nations, as they learned very quickly that a complaint of this sort might very well worsen their plight. In actual practice it was the German and Ukrainian minorities who exploited the pact and lodged numerous complaints with the League of Nations. In 1934, on the eve of joining the League by the Soviets, Poland took advantage of the weakness of the League to cancel the Pact unilaterally, and announced from the podium of the League that she no longer saw herself as obligated to the Minorities Pact. The expectations of organizing as a separate national entity by virtue of the rights granted by the pact were not realized either. The Zionist parties, which were the main driving force in Poland behind the organization as a separate national sector, strove to change the Jewish communities into cells of the new organization, and the Federation of Communities into the supreme organ of the Jewish national minority. The Polish regime, however, restricted the authority of the community to religious services and some limited fields of welfare and education, and prevented the formation by the communities of a supreme coordinating and executive body with broad authority, encouraging, on the other hand, the orthodox circles with their adaptive approach, to run the communities. At the same time, the political organs, and especially the Zionist parties, did not forgo the political struggle on behalf of the Jewish minority, the major arenas of which were transferred to the Polish *sejm* and to the minority factions.

Not only did the Poles hold the Jews responsible for the imposition of the pacts, but also viewed this very political organization of the Jews and the raising of national political claims as insulting conduct and a breach of faith. According to Polish opinion, or at any rate, the main sectors of the Polish public, the Jews, as tolerated guests on Polish soil, were obliged to support the desires of the Polish national entity on political questions with no reservations of any kind.

The wave of pogroms sweeping Poland in 1918–1920 left a much worse impression and an undercurrent of bitterness and enmity. The anti-Jewish rioting was a kind of side-effect of the war the Poles were waging against the Bolsheviks to fix Poland's eastern border. Most of the murders were perpetrated in a whole line of cities and towns during the Polish-Soviet War of 1919–20. Jews were accused of favoring communism, of treason and of espionage. In Lwow, a city whose fate was disputed, the Jews tried to maintain their neutrality between Poles and Ukrainians, and in reaction a pogrom was held in the city under the auspices of the Polish army, in which seventy-two Jews were killed and hundreds were injured. In a long list of cities and towns in eastern Poland pogroms and riots were carried out. An incident which occurred in the city of Pinsk caused a deep shock. A group of Jews gathered in the People's Palace in the city on April 5, 1919, to divide the aid sent them by their relatives and by organizations in the U.S.A. The army broke into the building, accused those present of holding a communist conspiratorial gathering, and without conducting any sort of investigation or inquiry summarily executed thirty-five Jews.[8] The authorities tried to hush up the incident, but the wave of rioting and pogroms had severe repercussions abroad. The Poles attempted to shirk all responsibility and cynically claimed that the reports of rioting and pogroms were merely sick propaganda intended to destroy the image of the Poles in world public opinion. The Poles were especially irritated by the use of the term "pogrom", which was identified, in their opinion, with the savagery of the "inferior Russians" and which was unsuitable to describe the Polish national character. The harsh impression made by the reports of the wave of pogroms crossing Poland had significant influence on Poland's status during the discussions on the peace treaty. With the agreement of the Poles, committees from abroad were sent to Poland (one committee headed by Henry Morgenthau from the U.S.A. and one including Stewart—the brother of Herbert— Samuel of Great Britain), to check into the events in Poland on the spot. These committees became inundated in the morass of claims made by both sides, but, despite all the attempts to hide or detract from the severity of the incidents, concluded that hundreds had been murdered in the wave of libel, evil and anarchy unrestrainedly ravaging Poland.

In 1920, the rioting subsided and the regime tended to stabilize. The Polish constitution approved in March 1921 was without a doubt progressive in spirit, guaranteeing equal rights to minorities, freedom of faith and religion and the right of each minority to use its own language. However, the enforcement of these singularly democratic laws and the guarantees of the Minorities Pact was made dependent upon detailed decrees and regulations cancelling the existing rules dating from the period of the conquest, which were still in force in the various provinces. This translation of the constitution into practical terms was a long time in coming, and the courts, unfortunately, operated according to the stipulations of the Czarist constitution.

One of the bothersome questions was that of citizenship. The authorities refused to recognize the citizenship of refugees who had moved from place to place during the war and who were unable to prove with documents their permanent residence within the new established Polish borders. (One of the common claims was that a stream of Jewish masses from various parts of Russia, called "Litvaks," was flooding Poland and leading to the expansion of Russian culture and anti-Polish feeling.)

A protractive and intensive campaign was waged about the mandatory rest day on Sundays. Officially, resting on Sunday was compulsory before the war as well, but the regime did not trouble to enforce this ruling on Sabbath-observing Jews. The Polish authorities exploited the fact that the Minorities Pact made no explicit statement on this point, and even before the end of 1919 rushed to enact a law prohibiting the opening of stores (except for certain kinds of services) and enforcing a cessation of labor on Sundays. The sting of this prohibition, aimed at Jewish trade, had severe effects.

In June 1923 the Foreign Affairs Committee of the Polish sejm approved a bill enforcing a numerus clausus at the universities. This proposal aroused a wave of protest in the foreign press, and it was apparently the personal intervention of the French premier Poincaré that led the Polish government to retreat from its plan. However, shelving the bill did not mean giving up the numerus clausus in actual practice. In this case clever use was made of the autonomy granted to academic institutions to bring about a reduction or disqualification of Jewish applicants. As a result of the maneuvers within university walls, the number of Jewish students accepted and trained for the professions followed a steady decline. In the academic year 1921/22 the Jews comprised 24.6% of the students in the institutions of higher learning. From that time on their number decreased constantly so that in the last year of the Republic, 1938/39, they comprised no more than 8.2%, i.e., less than the numerus clausus. As a matter of fact, during the last stage of the period the extreme factions of the the Polish right demanded enactment of a numerus nullus. This discrimination is even more apparent since the Jews were an urban element, and the vast majority of university students in Poland came from the urban stratum.

However, the most severe discrimination, which caused

irreparable damage to Jewish livelihoods, was in the field of economic policy. Throughout the period between the wars, the extreme right wing in Poland had preached an economic boycott of the Jews and encouraged the development of Polish trade, often not along lines recommended to develop the economy but rather as competition aimed at removing the Jews. In the same way as other states which had achieved independence accompanied by a sharp change in their internal regimes, so did the Polish state have widespread authority, especially in the later phases in planning economic policy; furthermore it controlled the major financial resources and means of credit. Yitzhak Gruenbaum stated that the Polish etatism "had an anti-Semitic soul." The government nationalized a whole list of industries, such as the tobacco industry, which had previously been in the hands of the Jews. Not only were the Jewish owners in this field removed, but also Jewish laborers, and, since the tobacco and alcohol trades were handed over to people with special permits, this also served to undermine the status of the Jews. Credit sources were either closed to Jewish traders or operated with severe discrimination. The Jews made almost no inroads into the state or municipal administrations; for example, in Warsaw 16% of the Poles were employed by the state or in general public services, while the percentage of Jews so engaged was only 0.8%. The Jews made up about 40% of the population of Lublin, whereas in the municipality only 2.6% of the workers were Jews. In Warsaw two Jews worked in the City Street Car Authority which employed 4,392 workers. We shall also see that the reverse system determined taxation policy. Where collecting taxes was concerned, the heaviest burden was imposed on urban commerce, the small Jewish merchant bearing the brunt. According to Hartglas, a former member of the Jewish faction in the *sejm*, Jews paid ten times more in taxes than their Polish competitors.[9]

Paradoxically, the steps taken to improve and further the economy also were to the detriment of the Jews. Thus the organization of the cooperative movement supported by leftist elements as well, removed many burdensome intermediary units between the countryside and the cities, but at the same time wiped out many Jewish livelihoods. The widespread claim, traces of which are still found in Polish publications today, was that the Jews were extremely wealthy or lived at a level above the average, and controlled key positions in Polish economic and financial life. The truth is that only a minimal number engaged in international trade, banking and industry; between five and ten per cent of the entire Jewish population were wealthy or had above average incomes or even enjoyed average urban conditions. The vast majority of the Jews was made up of people constantly struggling to subsist and of masses living under conditions of poverty, including total destitution.[10] Visitors to Poland from abroad were stunned by the filth and poverty of the Jewish neighborhoods and the cries of distress emanating from them. The Jewish international welfare organizations, especially the Joint, that attempted to aid the needy and also to help Jews maintain their workshops and their jobs despite the economic war waged against them, were at best able to rehabilitate individuals or small groups but could not bring about any basic change in the situation. Many tried to make inroads into industry, but this proletarization process also encountered difficulties. The slow development of industry created limitations in the absorption of workers, whereas the workers in many existing factories opposed the introduction of Jews to their ranks. This situation worsened during the economic crisis, when a high degree of unemployment was characteristic of the entire economy. Jewish craftsmen were compelled to take a practical examination but the examiners were not satisfied with professional skill, using their ignorance of the Polish language, for example, as an excuse to refuse the Jews permits in their fields. The professional potential of the Jews was suppressed rather than exploited, as the Poles doggedly poured out the baby with the bath water. The professions suffered a considerable shortage of skilled manpower. Poland had fewer doctors than most of the other countries of Europe, but this did not interfere with blocking the entrance of the Jews to the medical profession or with preventing Jews who had studied medicine in foreign universities from engaging in the practice of medicine within Polish borders.

The Jewish fight against anti-Semitism and economic and social oppression was mainly parliamentary. During the first stage after the war, Jewish members of Parliament, or the Jewish faction, concentrated on fighting for the achievement of national rights and strengthening autonomous Jewish institutions.

Before the elections to the first regular *sejm* in 1922, an attempt was made to detract from the importance of the minorities by means of gerrymandering and an electoral system aimed at reducing the representation of the minorities. In response, the minorities coalesced into a single coordinated bloc for the coming elections, and because of their united front they achieved an impressive result. The faction leading the Zionist forces in the bloc together with the Zionist representatives from Galicia, who did not participate in the bloc, numbered twenty-eight members of the *sejm* and

eight senators; and after the orthodox members and those of the
Trade Center joined the national faction it came to thirty-four
members of the sejm and twelve of the Senate (only a single Jewish
representative, Prylucki, representing the Folkists, remained
outside the Jewish faction.) The large faction headed by Yitzhak
Gruenbaum left its mark on the Polish Parliament and waged
numerous stubborn struggles in defense of Jewish interests. In
certain cases the minorities succeeded in serving as the balance of
power between the right and the left in deciding vital questions in
the life of the country. In this way, for instance, Gabriel Naruto-
wicz, a liberal close to Pilsudski, was elected first President of the
state thanks to the support of the minorities. However, he was
assassinated after only a few days in office by an extreme nationalist, and following the public storm which took place.

The Jewish members of Parliament came to the conclusion that it
would be better for them not to exercise parliamentary power to
decide general questions on which the Poles were divided into
rival camps. However, in the 1928 elections the bloc and particularly the Jewish faction did not repeat its success of the previous
elections, and parliamentary minority power decreased.

In 1925, when Wladyslaw Grabski was the Polish Premier, an
attempt was made to reach an accord with the Jewish minority,
known as "Ugoda"—agreement. Since the practical results were
very limited and almost valueless, strong opposition was voiced in
the Jewish camp, claiming that in return for vague obligations the
Jewish faction had abandoned its independent oppositionary stand
and stirred up the other minorities against the Jews. Despite the
difficulties and the economic pressure affecting the Jewish masses,
there were in Poland a number of Jews holding central positions in
industry and international trade, and the Jewish representation in
the professions, such as medicine and law, was significant. The
prominent role played by Jews and people of Jewish origin in the
various branches of Polish culture was remarkable. Some of the
best known poets and authors, composers and renowned
musicians, outstanding figures in the world of theater and key
figures in the field of publishing—were Jews who had assimilated
into Polish cultural life, and into Polish society as well. However,
the Polish right wing and actually a great part of Polish society
rejected this integration even of single Jews into their cultural and
political life (some of the leading Socialists were of Jewish
descent). In the period after the war, one of Pilsudski's followers,
Pobog-Malinowski, the author of a comprehensive book on the
history of Poland in modern times, who had emigrated to London,

claimed that these assimilated Jews had two hearts—a Polish one and a Jewish one.[11] On the other hand, the great Polish poet of Jewish descent, Julian Tuwim, who did not convert, but drifted completely away from the Jewish community and its affairs, bemoaned the fate of Polish Jewry during the Holocaust, and stated that to the overwhelming majority of Poles "I am and shall remain a Jew".[12] Thus it was not the divided heart of these people that prevented them from identifying completely with their Polishness, but rather their rejection by so many of the Polish people. This applied not only to a respected artist in the Polish language, like Tuwim, but also to a poet like Antony Slonimski, who was actually the grandson of the founder of the periodical *Hatsefira*, Chaim Zelig Slonimski, but was baptized while yet a child. Nevertheless, the anti-Semites refused to accept him as a true Pole.

It should be noted that the anti-Semitism and the anti-Jewish policy between the wars were not successful in dampening the vitality and the dynamic development of the Jews. In the Jewish quarters, despite the suffering from poverty and oppression and incalculable distress, there took place variegated cultural and socio-political activity. Jews read a great deal, they wrote books, published newspapers, belonged to political parties of various stripes, were active in clubs and organizations of various kinds. They did all this out of identification and great enthusiasm stemming from their faith that by their actions they were contributing to the correction of the injustices both in Jewish life and in universal human life. There is a clear disproportion between their humble and base condition, on the one hand, and the measure of their hopes, their energy and their feeling that they were living in a period of great change, on the other. In this period, Polish Jewry dominated world Jewry in many fields. In Poland the ideological and national streams of the Zionist factions and movements and of the "Bund" and the "Folkists" were ripening and crystallizing. In Poland there was the great concentration of Orthodox Jewry, the *tzaddikim* with their faithful adherents, *yeshivoth* and numerous Torah institutions. In Poland Yiddish and Hebrew literature was blossoming, and in the cities and towns of Poland there was a widespread network of educational streams in both languages. From Poland there came the main flow of pioneers to Eretz Yisrael; the fourth Aliya was in the main composed of Polish Jewry.

The first Prime Minister after the coûp d'état by Pilsudski, Professor Kazimierz Bartel, included in his coûp d'état statement a paragraph concerning the Jewish minority. His words were published in a separate pamphlet, and, Gruenbaum, who generally tends to a severely critical approach, perceived Professor Bartel as a "progressive, energetic man", and noted that "he did not refrain from declaring that the goverenment would not operate according to an anti-Semitic economic policy, appreciating that such a policy could only cause damage to the entire state . . . This statement, so unlike any which had ever been made by a Polish Prime Minister from the day of liberation and political rebirth, could be viewed as the forerunner of a new era for the Jews, with the fulfilling of most of their demands, except for those of a national character."[13]

However, this "springtime" of Polish-Jewish relations did not last long. After a year and a half of thawed hostility and an honest attempt on the part of the government to improve the situation of the Jews, things began to slow down and to reverse direction, until the former status was once again restored. Certain matters did indeed straighten out even later, like the question of the regulation of citizenship for those Jews whose civil status had not previously been recognized by the State. The deterioration in the policy towards the Jews and in their status in various areas began as already mentioned in 1930. The most important of these was the destruction of the democratic structure of the State. The regime held elections in an atmosphere of pressure and the disqualification of rivals. In these elections the Jews lost their parliamentary power and their significant national representation. On the other hand, the Endeks who had despaired of the chance to overthrow Pilsudski's "sanation" regime by democratic means, abandoned, to a large extent, the methods of proper parliamentary struggle and began to directly incite the masses. Their strength grew among the peasants and especially among the youth and the academic sector where fascist tendencies were rife. The Endeks, in their propaganda, accused the regime of protecting the Jews and of giving in to Jewish interests. The government's attitude towards the Jews was influenced by the fear of successful Endek propaganda and of pro-fascistic radicalism penetrating Pilsudski's camp as well. However, the regime had not yet adopted an anti-Semitic line as official policy, and in certain cases, such as during the anti-Jewish riots the Endeks incited at the universities, actually rose in defense of the Jews.

THE CRITICAL YEARS 1935—1939

Immediately after the Nazis came to power in Germany, the Polish regime supported the boycott which Jewish circles initiated against German goods, and Polish consular representatives in Germany prevented harm from being done to Jews of Polish citizenship. However, drastic change occurred in 1934, after Poland signed a non-aggression pact with Germany. Prominent Nazi leaders began to visit Warsaw, and a close relationship between the two countries developed in many areas. In 1935, after the death of Pilsudski, the last obstacle preventing the adoption of an open, official anti-Semitic policy by the regime was removed. The period after the death of Pilsudski was characterized by friction and quarreling within the group of diadochs who replaced Pilsudski. He personally did not leave behind an organized, ideological testament or a clear, consistent political line. Ever since he took over the government, he had ruled and alone made political decisions, and personal appointments. Even in his weakness during his last years, illness having removed him from the center of political activity, he still kept control of foreign policy, while other fields were entrusted to people who were considered his adherents. After his demise, his pupils and heirs—people lacking the qualities of political wisdom and leadership—began to claim the right to speak and govern in his name. Finally, the rule was divided between the President of the state Moscicki and the new head of the Army Rydz-Smigly and their men. Despite the political tension and the dangers developing around Poland, the politicians did not strive to achieve a national front to unite all the citizens of the state and its political parties, including oppositionary forces, into a body fit to deal with emergency conditions. The tendency was to wipe out concrete social conflicts and problems by increasing nationalistic feeling and campaigning against minorities, especially Jews. Pobog-Malinowski, in the volume of his history dealing with the period between the wars, devotes over ninety pages to the final chapter called "Poland without Pilsudski." Over many pages Malinowski describes the gossip and intrigues in which the leaders of the state were engaged. Later on, the author devotes approximately twenty pages to Polish-Jewish affairs, and the remainder—reduced quantitatively to very little—is devoted to the political hardships and the dangers threatening Poland just before the Second World War. It seems to us that the form and the tone adopted by Malinowski accurately reflect the attention and importance ascribed by the government and public opinion to the subjects occupying the country at that time.

There were three focal points of political power in Poland during these last fateful years. The President of the State, Ignacy Moscicki, an elderly man lacking independent political insight, apparently wielded much official authority, but everyone viewed him as a transient phenomenon. Alongside him, the power of the Army Commander, the newly appointed Marshal, Rydz-Smigly, grew stronger and more entrenched. The Marshal was a narrow-minded man who, instead of devoting himself exclusively to strengthening Poland's defenses, preferred to further his own political ambitions and semi-dictatorial status. The third point of focus, a man actually lacking public support, but considered a faithful, pupil who correctly interpreted the intentions of the late leader, was the Foreign Minister, Jozef Beck.

A few members of the Government gradually realized that no substantial ideological rift separated them from the radical *Endek* right, and that mutual cooperation had been prevented in the past by the personal antagonism between Pilsudski and Dmowski. This supposition, however, was not interpreted as possible grounds for the fusion of a right-wing political bloc, but rather as an indication that the government was striving to attract and lead the rightist elements. Fascist circles, encompassing dissenters from the *Endek* camp, young people eager to gain power, accepted the overtures. It became obvious that the extreme anti-Jewish platform was one of the links between the sides. At the same time, the *Endeks* who interpreted the government's adoption of an anti-Jewish policy as an attempt to inherit the slogans and positions traditionally and legitimately held by their party, naturally leaned towards more extreme positions and incitement of the masses.

The Catholic Church in Poland played a considerable and not always calming role in the renewed, extreme anti-Semitic campaign. In Shepherds' Epistles from the heads of the Church, along with ill-concealed reservations concerning the imported racism and pious affirmations that "very many Jews are believers, decent, honest, merciful and charitable", we find emphasized that "it is a fact that Jews (and here they aren't very many, but merely Jews, in general) battle against the Church, tend towards free thinking and form the vanguard of atheism, the Bolshevik movement, and activity striving for revolution . . . In trade relations it is better to prefer our own industry to others, to skip over Jewish shops and Jewish stalls in the market, but no permission is granted to loot Jewish shops, to destroy goods belonging to Jews, to break windows, to throw bombs at their homes . . ."[15]

Among the priests, the real shepherds of the congregations, many belonged to or leaned towards the *Endeks* and did not refrain from preaching in the spirit of their party. Officially the Polish Catholic Church refrained from identifying with a specific political camp.

From the middle of the thirties, priests espoused wild incitement
in open fascist and pro-Nazi fashion, and though they were in the
minority, they clearly had a damaging influence. The priest
Stanislaw Trzeciak, who preached for years from the pulpit of one
of the important churches in the center of Warsaw, and was a
lecturer at the Theological Seminary, was especially popular. He
was an almost declared agent of a Nazi propaganda institute, the
Weltdienst; he wrote books, pamphlets and many articles, and
spoke before a crowd in praise of anti-Semitism and viewed Hitler
as "the whip of God."

In the words of an American historian, E.D. Wynot, the Polish
government adopted an anti-Jewish line as an official component
of government policy during this period, the last years before the
outbreak of war.[16] Though circles close to the government made no
claim, as the Endeks did, that the Jews were striving to conquer the
Polish state in dark and mysterious ways, they did agree that the
Jewish intelligentsia was capable of gaining control of Polish spiritual life, and above all, that there were too many Jews in the state,
who should vacate their places in favor of the excess village
population of Poland flowing to the cities. The government weakly
expressed its reservations concerning the increasing acts of
violence and the spreading atmosphere of violence, but gave its
blessing to the economic boycott, i.e., the economic war against the
Jews. The Jewish sociologist, Jacob Lestschinsky said that "it is impossible to accuse the Polish government of organizing savageries
against the Jews. But it is possible, and necessary, to accuse it of
laying the foundations for the pogroms; in their passivity towards
the propaganda which of necessity leads to pogroms; in their dismissal, without punishment, of the small attacks and riots, which
encourage the hooligans and which become, as time passes,
stabbings with knives and killings; and finally—in reducing the
punishment meted out to murderers and stabbers."[17]

There is no doubt that the mild reaction to the violent wave
engulfing Poland during the period between 1935–1939 and bringing in its wake hundreds of fatalities in the cities, villages and
university campuses, was interpreted as the government's acqui-
escence or even complicity in the situation. Moreover, the token
punishments meted out to murderers and rioters by the courts on
the one hand and the harsh treatment of Jews attempting to defend
themselves, as in the case of the pogrom in the town of Przytyk in
March 1936, on the other hand, were also interpreted as
encouragement to violence. It should be stressed that Polish liberal
groups, as well as the Socialist Party, and dissidents from

Pilsudski's camp, publicly condemned both the violence and the tactical hypocrisy of the government, and even demonstrated in protest, in certain instances declaring strikes and joining in defensive actions taken by the Jews, which were organized by the Bund and various Zionist factions. When separate benches, a sort of "bench ghetto," were introduced in the universities, the Jews refused to sit and listened to the lectures while standing. In identification with the Jewish students, a few of the professors including famed scholars decided to stand as well, an act which brought them under attack, including physical confrontations with rioters.

In 1936 the ruling team trying to stabilize their rule began to set up the OZN (Oboz Zjednoczenia Narodowego—The Camp of National Unity), a political movement in place of the former bloc headed by the "colonels" which was dissolved, aimed at letting the wind out of the sails of the opposition and establishing a body of widespread support for the regime. Although the most attractive and persuasive means at the disposal of the rulers was the economic and political power and influence in light of gradual economic improvement after the crisis, they also attempted to phrase a programmatic platform for the new bloc. The organizational and ideological crystallization processes moved forward slowly, revealing a lack of efficiency and common ideological base. The leader summoned to organize and shape the new body, Colonel Adam Koc, favored totalitarian models, and thus devoted most of his efforts to attracting the fascist youth and its leaders. The principles finally determined by this pro-government movement can be summarized in three points: a) A centralist government recognizing the supremacy of the army and guided by its commanders; b) The supremacy of the Polish nation and the rejection of the minorities, especially the Jews, as "foreigners"; c) The supremacy of the Catholic Church. In contrast to the supra-party camp which functioned in Pilsudski's time and included the assimilationists and the Jewish orthodoxy, the leaders of the new body declared that the Jews had no place in·their ranks.

The anti-Semitic policy which reached climactic expression at this stage—1938 and the beginning of 1939—concentrated on two fields: a) internal affairs—an economic boycott and gradual anti-Semitic legislation; b) external affairs—accelerated activity in both internal and external policy to force the Jews to emigrate and to seek out new places to absorb them.[18]

The Jews waged a bitter and stubborn campaign against the bill proposed to cancel the existing system of slaughtering animals in Poland, which met the requirements of Jewish *Kashruth* (dietary laws). Officially the proposers claimed to have been guided by "humanitarian" considerations, and the fact that the existing system of slaughter increased the suffering of the animals. However, everyone knew that the real intention behind the "humane" excuse was to remove tens of thousands of Jews from the meat industry, which was one of the few economic sectors where Jews still had some influence. This law, amended slightly after a rigorous campaign, greatly disappointed religious Jewry who generally supported the government and viewed independent Jewish politics as a disturbing factor harmful to the Jews.

Laws were being prepared to abrogate the formal equality of rights of the Jews. A private bill of this kind was presented by members of Parliament from the Government camp and, though at the time only a trial balloon was intended, the apparently actual comprehensive legislation was prevented only by the deterioration of the security conditions on the eve of the outbreak of war in 1939. Decisions to enact an "Aryan clause" and to expel the Jews were taken by a whole series of professional and trade unions, such as physicians and lawyers. These elements of racism penetrated the ranks by means of the Fascist youth organizations, and some youth leaders in the Endeks preached racial discrimination. It was determined that not only a religious person or one identifying himself as a Jew would be considered Jewish, but also anyone of "Jewish origin"; conversion does change a Jew into a Christian, but cannot make him a Pole. J. Giertych, the most extreme of the young Endeks demanded that converts be denied the right to vote and to be elected.

Of course, many Jews needed no Polish pressure to awaken in them the desire to leave Poland. The steep drop in emigration during the thirties was caused by the sealing of the gates to the countries where the Jewish emigres had streamed over the generations, especially the United States, by means of a "quota" a restrictive number, and by a steady decrease in permits to immigrate to Eretz (the Land of) Israel. Both by international standards and by those of Eretz Israel, Jewish institutions preferred to assist Jews to leave Germany, followed by Austria and Czechoslovakia, i.e., Jews living under the direct control or immediate threat of the Nazis, than to aid Jews of eastern European countries in which anti-Semitism was growing, like Poland or Rumania. The restriction of the Palestine mandatory rule decreased the emigration from Poland to Palestine drastically.

The Poles tried various ways to accelerate the Jewish exodus, a task to which the Polish Foreign Office lent a special hand. This activity had from a historical perspective one very characteristic aspect. The Poles had ambitions of becoming a world power, and so demanded colonies for themselves in the international arena; these colonialistic dreams fitted in with their plans to find a refuge for the Jews. The idea of a Jewish emigration to the island of Madagascar was especially popular. The Poles approached the French and suggested that they place the island at the disposal of the Jewish emigrants from Poland, and a special delegation including Jews set out to determine whether or not conditions were suitable for large-scale emigration.

Polish diplomacy backed the demands of the Zionist establishment to expand the immigration to Eretz Israel, and in Poland the *Irgun* and the *Hagana* (Jewish military underground organizations which operated in Palestine) held training courses under the auspices of the Polish government. A visible link was created between the revisionist disciples of Jabotinsky and the Polish ruling circles. The Land of Israel, however, was considered only one possible destination; incapable of solving the problem to the extent that Poland required many other variegated solutions had to be considered. In this matter talks were also held with the Nazi leaders and with the Third Reich authorities, with whom Poland maintained close relations. When Hitler, in a conversation held in September 1938 with the Polish ambassador to Berlin, J. Lipski, observed that after solving the Sudeten problem he would be free to deal with the question of the colonies, and that in this connection a way would also be found to solve *inter alia* the problem of Polish Jewry, the Polish diplomat did not claim that the question of Polish Jews was an internal Polish concern, but rather noted that if Hitler would find the desired solution, the Poles would erect a monument in his honor in the heart of Warsaw.[19]

In effect, the Jews were in a trap with no way out. On the one hand, the Polish state was urging them to leave, the extreme elements in this connection, using violence and not stopping even at violence, whereas, on the other hand, the world was closed before them. The economic situation and abject poverty of the Jews of Poland was sufficient to create in them a strong desire to leave, but, as we have said, this longing had no practical outlet. During the years 1931–1935, 51,300 Polish Jews emigrated to Palestine, and from 1936–1938 only 14,500. The decrease was of course the result of Arab riots and the restrictionist policy of the British Government. In all, around 400,000 Jews emigrated from Poland during the interwar period.

The place, time and energy devoted to the "Jewish problem" in

Poland, both in Government policy and in Parliament, in the opposition parties' public and political activity, in the press and in public opinion, turned the matter into a central social and political issue, often distracting attention from the real crises and dangers threatening Poland. Gleefully the Nazis took careful note of the anti-Semitic campaign in Poland, as can be seen from extensive descriptions devoted to the matter in reports relayed to Berlin by German diplomats in Warsaw. Neither are proofs lacking that the Nazis were active in stirring up this campaign, which helped in attaining their own political aims.

Certain groups of Pilsudski's followers did not wish to acquiesce with the policies of his heirs to power, their anti-Semitic policies and pro-Fascist leanings being among the main factors in their rejection. They abandoned the pro-Government camp and, together with liberal circles, founded the Democratic Club. The Polish Socialists were most consistent in their defense of the persecuted Jews, but in reaction to a pamphlet published by a Bund leader, Victor Alter, claiming that the mass emigration of Jews from Poland was no solution to Poland's real problem, there was published another pamphlet. Written by a Polish Socialist named Borski, it claimed, leaving no room for doubt, that even among the strata of Polish laborers the demand for Jewish emigration was widespread.[20]

During the final months before the outbreak of war, the attitude of Government circles and of most of the Poles toward the Jews underwent a change. The call for national unity in light of the concrete threat of war included the Jews and was aimed at them as well.

Jews joined in the patriotic effort with enthusiasm for two reasons. First, because of the change of attitude of the Poles and secondly, and primarily, because in the light of Hitler's threat, all their many accounts with Poland and the Poles faded into obscurity. However, the rapprochement between Jews and Poles, which developed in the course of digging trenches, collecting money and joining the army, and finally in a common blood sacrifice, did not present a fundamental long-range change. The sharp anti-Semitic attitudes and action of independent Poland between the wars was apparently in contradiction to the spirit of a long lasting Polish fight for liberation under the slogan "for your and our freedom." In the limits of our introductory remarks we could not deal with the profound reasons for the anti-Jewish stand during the period; we could only point to the most decisive trends and events of the time. In any case, the anti-Jewish wave which engulfed the two decades of the Polish independent Republic had a fateful influence on the developments of Polish-Jewish relations during the second World War.

Notes

1. Andrzej Chojnowski, *Koncepcja polityki narodowościowej rzadów polskich w latach 1921–1939*, Warszawa, 1979, pp. 18–26; Roman Wapinski, *Narodowa Demokracja 1893–1939*, Wroclaw, 1980, pp. 35–47, pp. 154–156. Andrzej Ajnenkiel, *Od rzadów ludowych do przewrotu majowego*, Zarys dziejów politycznych Polski, 1918–1926 (Warszawa. 1977), pp. 215–234.

2. The situation was bluntly described by Roman Dmowski, leader and theorist of the National Democrats (Endeks), in his book "Polish Policy and the Rebuilding of the State": "The fatalist policy of the Polish state in the centuries preceding partition, led to such widespread judaization of the country that the Jewish population (in Poland) exceeded that of the entire rest of the world. Poland thus virtually acquired the status of a Jewish European homeland and came to be regarded by the Jews as the new Land of Israel. They appointed for the Poles a fate similar to that of the Canaanite tribes, who formed the original population of the biblical Land of Israel. This aim could be easily achieved by causing Poland to enter a decline—surrendering Poland to a foreign government which could use Jewish aid in order to establish Poland's authority" . . .Roman Dmowski, *Polityka Polski i odbudowanie Państwa*, Warszawa, 1925, p. 36.

3. Stanislaw Mackiewicz (Cat), *O jedenastej—powiada aktor—sztuka jest skończona*, polityka Józefa Becka (London), p. 48.

4. On demographic and economic data with respect to the Jewish community in Poland between the wars, see: Refael Mahler, *Yehudei Polin Beyn Shtei Milhamot Olam, Historiyah Kalkalit Sotzialit le-Or ha-Statistikah* ("Polish Jewry between the World Wars, a socio-economic history in the light of statistical data"), Tel-Aviv, 1968; S. Bronsztejn, *Ludność żydowska w Polsce*

w okresie miedzywojennym, Warszawa, 1963.

5. Yitzhak Gruenbaum, article from "Milhamah li-Zhuyot Leumiyot" (The battle for national rights"), from *Milhemet Yehudei Polanyah* ("The battle of Polish Jewry"). 1920, p.78.

6. Benzion Dinur, *Dorot ve-Reshumot*, (Generations and records), Historical writings, volume four, Jerusalem, (1978), p. 201.

7. A noted Polish publicist wrote in his book on the League of Nations: "How was the idea of minority protection conceived? The history of the Peace Council gives a decisive answer. The minorities agreement was initiated solely by the Jewish delegations." Aleksander Bregman, *Liga Narodów, 1920–1930*, Warszawa, 1931, p. 93. Another Polish author stated that "the new system for the protection of minorities assumed a concrete form for the first time in the provisions of the agreement approved by the Super-Powers Conference of May 17, 1919. The initiator of this system was without doubt the Jewish delegation". Witold Sworakowski, *Miedzynarodowe zobowiazanie mniejszościowe Polski*, Warszawa, 1925, p. 50.

8. For details on the Pinsk pogrom, see Ezriel Shohat, "Parshat ha-Pogrom be-Pinsk ba-Hamishah be-April 1919" ("The Pinsk Pogrom of April 5, 1919"), in Gal-Ed, *On the History of the Jews in Poland*, Tel-Aviv, 1973, pp. 135–173.

9. A. Hartglas, "Milhemet Yehudei Polin al Zehuyoteihem ha-Ezrahiyot ve-ha-Leumiyot" ("The battle of Polish Jewry for their civil and national rights"), in *Bet Yisrael be-Polin* ("The House of Israel in Poland"), vol. I, Jerusalem, 1948, p.142. The estimation is of course exaggerate, but it expressed the feeling of discrimination and a great factual disproportion of taxation regarding the Jews.

10. See Jacob Lestschinsky's article, "Ha-Pauparizatziyah shel ha-Hamonim

ha-Yehudim" ("The pauperization of the Jewish masses") in the jubilee edition of the Yiddish newspaper "Haynt" printed in Warsaw. According to Leszczynski, Polish Jewry at the end of the 1930s could be divided into the following categories:

(1) Extremely poor (living solely on charity or supported by relatives)	400,000	12.4%
(2) Poor (in frequent need of support, but with a small income)	300,000	9.2%
(3) Poor (in need of support only during festivals)	600,000	18.4%
(4) Earners of a minimum living wage (not in need of support)	1,000,000	30.8%
(5) Earners of a sufficient income (to cover their needs)	600.000	18.4%
(6) Moderately well-to-do and prosperous	300,000	9.2%
(7) Wealthy and extremely wealthy	50,000	1.6%
	3,250,000	100%

"Haynt", *Yovel Bukh* (1908–1938), p. 150.

11. Wladyslaw Pobóg - Malinowski, *Najnowsza historia polityczna Polski*, v. II, 1914–1939, London, 1967, p. 806.

12. Tuwim Julian, "My Zydzi polscy...", Jerusalem, 1984 English version, p. 17

13. Yitzhak Gruenbaum, "Ha-Gorem ha-Antishemi" ("The anti-Semitic factor"). in *Entziklopediyah shel ha-Galuyot*, Varshah I, Jerusalem-Tel-

Aviv, 1953, p. 109.

14. Pobog-Malinowski, op. cit., v. II, the chapter 16, pp. 765–858.

15. A. Hlond, "Wielkopostny list pasterski", *Przewodnik Katolicki*, February 29, 1936.

16. E.D. Wynot Jr. "A Necessary Cruelty", in *Current History*, Nr. 48 (1938).

17. Yakov Leszczynski, "Ha-Praot be-Polin", in *Dappim le-Heker ha-Shoah ve-ha-Mered* (Pages for the study of the Catastrophe and the Revolt), 1952, p. 45.

18. On OZN, see Edward D. Wynot Jr., *Polish Politics in Transition, The Camp of National Unity and the Struggle for Power, 1935–1939*, Athens, 1974; about the policy of Camp of National Unity (OZN) toward the Jews: Emanuel Melzer, *Meawak Mediny be-Malkodet, Jehudey Polin 1935–1939* (Political strife in a blind alley, the Jews in Poland 1935–1939), Tel-Aviv, 1982.

19. J. Lipski, *Diplomat in Berlin, 1933–1939*, London, 1968, p. 411.

20. J.M. Borski, *Sprawa Zydowska a Socjalizm, polemika z Bundem*, Warszawa, 1937. The author writes in this pamphlet, "It is a well-known fact that rabid anti-Semitism is on the increase in Poland. Jews are not employed in agricultural work, and are barred from public institutions, monopolies, state-owned factories, municipal concerns and large privately-owned factories. Were the Jews to be 'reinstated' and the offensive and unjust restrictions abolished, it can easily be imagined what anti-Semitic agitation would ensue." (p. 14)

CHAPTER TWO

The Occupation

German troops attacked Poland, without a formal declaration of war, on September 1, 1939, at 4:45 a.m. The Germans overwhelmingly outnumbered the Polish armed forces, and, of even greater decisive import, enjoyed an enormous technical superiority. The factor of surprise also worked in their favor. On the very first day, the Polish army suffered horrendous defeats. Within several days the entire line of Polish resistance was broken. Suffering enormous losses, the Poles were forced to withdraw far into their hinterland. Vast numbers of their army units were completely smashed, while others were retreating in total disarray.

On September 3, England and France declared war on Germany. However, declaration was not followed by the initiation of any hostilities which alone could still salvage Poland. The condition of the Polish army thus remained precarious.

By September 8, the Germans had captured the major part of Western Poland, including a number of big cities, like Poznan, Katowice, Lodz, Czestochowa and Cracow. The same day the Germans reached the outskirts of Warsaw. The weeks-long siege of the Polish capital began. The single serious Polish counterattack in the entire campaign was launched mainly for the purpose of relieving Warsaw. It took place on September 9, in the region of Kutno (the so-called Bzura battle), but within days it faltered. By the middle of September, all western and central areas of Poland were already in German hands. The bulk of the Polish army collapsed.

On September 17, 1939 the eastern part of Poland was invaded by the Soviet army according to the secret clause of the German-Soviet agreement, the so called Ribbentrop-Molotov pact signed in August, 1939. The next day, the Polish president, Government, and army command crossed the frontier of Rumania, where they were all taken into custody. Within a few days all the eastern regions of Poland had been captured by the Red Army.

Between September 18 and October 5, several isolated pockets of Polish resistance were still active: in tightly surrounded

Warsaw, in the fortress of Modlin, and on Hel peninsula. The troops defending Warsaw surrendered on September 28. The fortress of Modlin surrendered the next day. The units commanded by General Kleeberg which fought the Germans in the last battle of the campaign in the region of Kock surrendered on October 2.

Germany and the Soviet Union partitioned the entire Polish terrritory. The new border between the countries, fixed by the Ribbentrop-Molotov pact on the line of rivers Pisa, Narew, Wisla and San, was in the end shifted east of the line, along the line of the river Bug.

Further changes took place in the political and administrative status of conquered Polish territories. Western and north-western areas of Poland were incorporated into the Third Reich. The Germans established new administrative units: Reichsgau Danzig-Westpreussen and Reichsgau Wartheland, Regierungsbezirk Zichenau (Ciechanow) as a part of East Prussia, and Ost-Oberschlesien as a part of German Silesia.

The districts of Bialystok, Wilno (except for the city of Wilno and its suburbs), Nowogrodek and Polesie were incorporated by the Russians into the Byelorussian Soviet Republic. The districts of Volhynia, Podolia, Stanislawow and Lwow were incorporated into the Ukrainian Soviet Republic. The city of Wilno together with a small area around it were handed over to Lithuania, to eventually become part of the Lithuanian Soviet Republic after the whole of Lithuania fell to the Soviet Union the following year.

The defeat of the Polish army and the occupation of the country thoroughly transformed the configuration of relationships between the Poles and the Jews. The relationship between the two populations became very different from that which existed either prior to September 1939 or in the days of the struggle against the German invader.

Essentially, the transformation was a direct outcome of the sharply different conditions to which the Jewish and the Polish population were exposed from the moment of the appearance of German troops. During the fighting, the Poles and the Jews shared the status of compatriots defending their homeland against the German conqueror. Once the German occupation began, the change was sudden and drastic. Although both the Jews and the Poles found themselves under the yoke of the common Nazi enemy, that enemy behaved towards each of the two populations quite differently. Terror, unprecedented in its scope and methods, was from the very onset of the Nazi rule applied against both. But as dreadful as Nazi terror against the Poles truly was, yet it was incommensurable with the terror which struck the Jews. The Poles became a conquered people, who by the notions of the Nazi ideology were an inferior Slavic race. Still, they were considered Aryans, and as such, much superior to the Jews, viewed by Nazi ideology as its chief target.

Terror against the Jews and the Poles differed not only in intensity, but also in quality. Anti-Polish terror was selective, aiming chiefly at the intelligentsia and at the inhabitants of the western territories incorporated into the Third Reich. In central Poland (i.e., in the so-called Government General, formed in the territories not annexed to the Reich) the urban population was much less affected by that terror and the rural population, at least at the initial stages of occupation, very little. In the territories incorporated by the Third Reich, a considerable number of Poles were defined as potentially Germanizable. The rules applying to them were different from those for other Poles.

Anti-Jewish terror was total, encompassing all segments of the Jewish population without exception. All the Jews were defined as the chief enemies of the Third Reich and of the German nation. The reprisals were universal in the sense of aiming at the totality of Jewry. They were also unique in their character.

Some policies of the Nazi terror were aimed against Pole and Jew alike. Their implementation, however, was marked by differential intensities. Terror directed against both the Jews and the Poles began with the activities of the operational groups of the SIPO and SD which bore the name of Einsatzgruppen. These units, about 2,700-strong, were formed for the special tasks of the war campaign in Poland. During the campaign of September 1939, the Einsatzgruppen units carried out arrests and executions in conquered areas. Their wave of terror which had the cover name Unternehmen Tannenberg, claimed many thousands of victims, both Jewish and Polish.

The bulk of the Polish victims were from the intelligentsia, especially from the elites of the Polish nation. Among the Jewish victims, by contrast, all population strata were represented evenly. Also, the Jewish population was more painfully hit by the wave of the Einsatzgruppen terror. Polish historian Czeslaw Madajczyk writes that while the number of Jewish victims exceeded the Polish losses in the districts of Cracow, Warsaw and Rzeszow, in the remaining districts the reverse was the case.[1] Once, however, we see these comparisons against the background of the 1:10 ratio between the respective population figures of the Jews and the Poles, we realize that roughly equal numerical losses meant a much higher intensity of terror against the former.

Mass deportations amounting to tens of thousands of Jews and Poles began already in the first month of the occupation. But here, again, the scope of the undertaking was different depending on who was the target. Nearly all of the many thousands of Polish deportees were residents of territories annexed to the Reich, to be resettled in Government General. As to the Jews, in addition to thousands from the territories annexed to the Reich, they included masses of residents of other areas. Thus, for example, over 20,000 Jews were in late September and in early October of 1939 expelled from the eastern part of the district of Rzeszow: including the entire Jewish population of the city of Jaroslaw and about 4,000 Jewish residents of Tarnobrzeg. Likewise, thousands of Jews were expelled from the eastern counties of the Warsaw district.[2]

From the first days of the occupation, the Germans undertook the systematic pillage of both Jewish and Polish property. But here again, the scale and the intensity of the destruction differed for the two groups. Polish property was pillaged selectively, affecting mainly some segments of the intelligentsia and the families resettled from western areas to Government General. The pillage of Jewish property was much more sustained, and it extended to all strata of the population and all regions of occupied Poland.

The initial wave of Nazi terror and intimidation included widespread burning and destruction of synagogues. Many synagogues were already set on fire in the first day of the occupation, quite often jointly with Jewish houses adjacent to them. Within a short time, several hundred synagogues in conquered Poland were either dynamited or burned.[3]

From the very first days of the occupation the Jewish population was also exposed to the ordeal of roundups intended to yield manpower for the performance of various odd jobs. Usually, the Jews caught in the roundups were subject to all possible kinds of harassment, and occasionally even murder.

The inhuman laws applied universally to the occupied territories caused great suffering also to the Poles. But the Jews were additionally subject to separate legal restrictions which aggravated their plight even beyond that of the Poles. A number of such restrictions made the conditions under which the Jews lived unbearable. The most important of them were:

On September 8, 1939, the new appointed chief of civilian administration attached to the German army command, Hans Frank, issued an order to be enforced the very next day, to the effect that all Jewish enterprises (shops, workshops, cafes, restaurants, etc., without exception) had to bear mandatory, distinct markings. The confidential telex (*Schnellbrief*) of September 21, 1939, from Reinhard Heydrich to all the *Einsatzgruppen* active in occupied Poland was the first document of importance stating the rules for discriminatory treatment of Jews in occupied territories. The telex contained the outline of policies specifically aimed at the Jewish population. The outline implied concentration of Jews in the cities and their removal from territories intended for annexation to the Third Reich. It recommended the formation of the Jewish Councils (*Judenrat*), subjection of the Jews to forced labor and to the duty of bearing distinct markings, and their removal from the country's economy.[4]

Before the end of 1939, numerous other detailed anti-Jewish measures had already been enacted. The most important of them dealt with compulsory marking, forced labor, restrictions on the right to use public transportation, the prohibition of ritual slaughter, and the imposition of high taxes levied upon nearly all Jewish communities.

Towards the end of 1939 a proclamation appeared, ordering the formation of the first Jewish ghetto in Piotrkow Trybunalski. This was the beginning of the intensive process of concentrating the Jewish population into ghettos, which involved mass resettlements of the majority of that population, as well as the accelerated plunder of Jewish property. As a result of the formation of the ghettos, the difference in the conditions of the Jews and of the Poles under German occupation became even more pronounced.

A report of the Delegate of the Polish Government-in-Exile which bears the title "Activities of the occupying authorities in the territory of the Republic from the period of September 1 to November 1, 1939" describes the Nazi policies intended specifically to hurt the Jews:

> The fate of the Jews since the first days of September can be described as an uninterrupted chain of suffering, humiliation and expropriation. This is the effect of both the network of discriminatory laws imposed by the authorities, and of the arbitrary and uncontrolled activities of the army, the Gestapo, the administration, and the German populace. Jewish property, their personal dignity, their freedom of movement, supplies, schooling, residential rights, religion, professional performance, social benefits all depend upon the whims of the administration, and even of particular officials or Volksdeutsche who gained an unlimited opportunity to revel in harassing the Jews.[5]

Different attitudes of the German occupier towards the Jews and the Poles, and the consequent manifest difference in the severity of their deprivations, had a far-reaching effect upon the recognition of their joint interests in the struggle against the common enemy. Discriminatory measures against the Jews were by an overwhelming majority of the Poles deemed to be the former's own problem, not affecting the interests of the latter.

From the very first months of the occupation, the Germans attempted to involve a part of the Polish society in anti-Jewish actions. Almost from the onset of occupation, the Polish population was exposed to rampant anti-Semitic propaganda.

The quoted report of the Delegate of the Polish Government-in-Exile defines some of the primary objectives of the German occupying authorities as:

> . . . harassment of the Jews, suppression of their political, economic and cultural role, accompanied by sustained although unsuccessful attempts to secure the participation of the Polish masses, and to convince the latter that the struggle against Jewry serves their interests.[6]

Indeed, a considerable German propaganda effort was made for the sake of enlisting the Poles in anti-Jewish actions. But contrary to what the report claims, this effort was by no means ineffectual. At least upon a segment of the Polish population it had a definite effect.

Soon after the arrival of German troops, in many localities of the occupied territories the Jewish population encountered anti-Semitic acts on the part of some of their Polish neighbors. There were instances of Polish participation in anti-Jewish violence organized by the Germans. The situation in Warsaw, just before and after the surrender of the Polish capital, was recorded by Emmanuel Ringelblum:

> Even before Warsaw fell, the hydra of anti-Semitism had already managed to raise its head. During the air raids the Jews were often denied entry to shelters in houses inhabited exclusively by Poles. I made this observation while serving in an air raid defense unit in a house on Dluga Street. A commander responsible for our well equipped shelter was in principle refusing entry to Jewish passers-by. During the air raids I lived at 18, Leszno Street. Across the street from my house, under No. 13, there was a shelter owned by the wood-trading company 'Paged'. When the rear section of my house was hit by a bomb, its tenants moved to seek refuge in that shelter. For anti-Semitic reasons we were turned away, notwithstanding the fact that our house had no shelter. The same happened in many other houses inhabited mainly by Poles.
>
> Quarrels between Jews and Poles flared up in the endless lines at the bakeries or the few groceries which stayed open with few items remaining for sale.
>
> Anti-Semitism also cropped up in the long line along the Vistula Riv-

er, where water was distributed. At the demand of anti-Semitic scum, there were separate Jewish and Aryan lines. The access to water was alternately given to 50 Aryans and to 5 Jews. Jews carrying water back were knocked down, beaten, even clobbered, and their water spilled. A Jew could wait the whole day in line, and then return home beaten, livid, with no water. . . .

Once the Germans were in, anti-Semitism reasserted itself fully. Its manifestations could be observed in charity missions operated by the National-Socialist Welfare (Nazional-Sozialistische Volkswohlfart, or N.S.V.). There was a time when huge lorries of the NSV located at important crossroad points, supplied the starving population of Warsaw with free bread and free soup made out of the agricultural produce commandeered elsewhere in Poland. At the beginning, Jews were not denied these supplies, probably because the whole action was being filmed. But in Muranowski Square I witnessed the following scene. First the German soldiers had encouraged the Jews to stand in line in front of a lorry, letting them have their bread and soup in view of the cameras. Then, as soon as the cameras were off, they dispersed the line, beating the Jews mercilessly. The anti-Semitic mob was bent on spotting Jews standing in lines to the NSV lorries. Pointing their fingers, they determined who was a "Jude": the single German word which the scum learned at once. Soon the roundup began, intended to supply skilled manpower for the performance of various works carried out by various military formations. Since the Jews didn't yet bear any markings, the Germans in charge of roundups had difficulties in distinguishing them from non-Jews. In this, the anti-Semitic riff-raff was perfectly willing to help, by pinpointing the Jews in a most servile manner. The first ties between the Nazis and the Polish anti-Semites were thus established.[7]

From the accounts of survivors of World War II we can learn about similar phenomena which occurred in localities other than Warsaw. Here are the examples extracted from a number of selected accounts:

A group of Poles led by one Feliks Mazur made a pogrom of Jews on October 9-10, in Zakrzowek, Janow Lubelski county. The gang broke into the apartments, and plundered them, beating their victims mercilessly. They killed a Pole, Jan Barnaszkiewicz, who had come to assist the Jews. A priest in Zakrzowek called for account-settling with the Jews from the pulpit. Similar pogroms carried out by the local Polish population also took place in other villages of the same area: Zolkiewka, Wysokie, Turobin, Bilgoraj, Frampol and Krzeszow.[8]

In November 1939, at the initiative of the mayor of Zamosc, Michal Wazowski, a levy in the amount of 75,000 zlotys was imposed upon the Jewish population of the city. The aim of the levy was to assist Polish refugees returning from territories captured by the Soviet Union.[9]

In the town of Zelechow, Lublin district, groups of local Poles helped the Germans to identify Jewish houses and shops in the hope of obtaining their share in the ensuing pillage of the Jewish property.[10]

In the town of Zolkiewka, Lublin district, a pogrom was made just before the arrival of the Germans. The local peasants murdered several wealthy Jewish families and grabbed their properties.[11]

Jakub Herzig recounts the plunder of Jewish shops in the city of Jaslo, Cracow district, which occured right after the arrival of the Germans. In this case, groups of local Poles were acting hand-in-hand with the Germans.[12]

Yitzhak Kalfus of Mielec, Cracow district, recounts how the local Poles were identifying the Jewish-owned houses for the Germans. About 150 Jews, including the local rabbi, the circumciser, and the members of the consistory were dragged out from these houses as a result.[13]

In Tarnow, the instances of participation of the local Polish population in the pillage of Jewish houses occurred on November 9, 1939: the day the Germans set the local synagogue on fire.[14] Similar pillage was recorded in Daleszyce, Kielce district, right after the arrival of the Germans;[15] as well as in the village of Pajeczno, Radomsko county[16] and in Mszczonow near Warsaw.[17] Bronislawa Goldsztejn recounts a similar incident of the plundering of Jewish property by Poles, that took place in Radzymin near Warsaw.[18]

In Warsaw itself, in the winter of 1939–1940 there were several instances of outbreaks of anti-Jewish violence on the part of groups of the Polish population. The most notorious of these eruptions constituted a real pogrom, made in February of 1940 in Warsaw's Jewish quarter by a several-hundred-strong group of Poles acting under the command of German soldiers. The event is thus described by Emmanuel Ringelblum:

> Each gang of mostly juvenile anti-Semites was being led by a single German who covered their rear and who functioned as a sort of a patron. The gangs were equipped with sticks, canes, iron bars and the like. Their slogans were: "extirpate the Jews", "down with the Jews", "long live sovereign Poland without Jews", and the like. On their way, the gangs smashed the window panes of the shops marked with the Star of David, pulling iron bars from their shutters, breaking into the shops, robbing the Jewish passers-by, hitting them, knocking them over, beating them up to the point of unconsciousness. The plunder of the shops constituted the finale of the pogrom, its crowning accomplishment. All this lasted for several days, with no one interfering.[19]

But Poles who took part in acts of anti-Jewish violence —whether mentioned or unmentioned here —usually amounted to no more than an infinitesimal proportion of the local Polish population. This fact is stressed in Yehezkiel Keselbrener's account of the responses of the Polish population to anti-Jewish measures undertaken by the Germans shortly after their arrival in the village of Ryki, in the district of Lublin. Keselbrener writes:

> The majority of Christian Poles showed compassion for persecuted Jews. Active participation in anti-Jewish violence was confined to no more than a fraction of the local riff-raff.[20]

Calek Perechodnik recounts an incident in Otwock near Warsaw. A Jewish baker named Kirszenbaum was forcibly dragged out of his own bakery by a Pole named Kalinowski. According to Perechodnik, Kalinowski was denounced by all Otwock Poles.[21]

The fact that no more than a tiny fraction of Poles took part in the anti-Jewish violence of the first months of Nazi occupation is likewise stressed in numerous other accounts. Yet no matter how trivial the number of active Polish participants in anti-Jewish riots and pogroms might have been, the fact itself was resented by the Jews very bitterly. This was understandable, as anti-Jewish rioting occurred immediately after a period of fraternity between the Jews and the Poles in the struggle against their common enemy, and at the very beginning of an occupation which subjected both to persecution. The rioting had the effect of making the Jews feel abandoned by the Poles and aggrieved at them.

In the territories seized by the Soviet Union the situation unfolded altogether differently. The Soviet leadership annexed these territories to the Soviet Union, making them parts of Soviet Byelorussia and Soviet Ukraine. Wilno and its surroundings was handed over to Lithuania, to become a part of the Lithuanian Soviet Republic in the aftermath of the subsequent incorportion of all of Lithuania to the Soviet Union.

Soviet citizenship was granted summarily to all the inhabitants of incorporated territories, without regard to their nationality and without asking for their consent. Yet differences in attitudes of Soviet authorities towards different nationalities did exist. Distinctly, the Ukrainians and the Byelorussians enjoyed preferential treatment. The objective of the Soviet authorities was first and foremost to strip the incorporated areas of the last vestiges of Polish statehood. By its very nature, this policy hit with particular severity the white-collar strata which were numerically strong and which consisted almost exclusively of Poles. Moreover, this policy offended the national sentiments of the Poles who, although a minority, almost without exception refused to reconcile themselves to becoming residents of Ukraine or Byelorussia.

Mass deportations from the areas incorporated into the USSR began in 1940. The deportees were shipped to forced-labor camps, mostly in northern parts of the USSR. In the most painful manner, the deportations affected all segments of the population of the captured territories.

As a result of Soviet policies, the Poles saw no difference between their situation under the Nazis and under the Soviet occupation. The character of both occupations was in their eyes more or less the same. As occupiers, the Germans and the Russians were for them no different.

But both the objective conditions and the subjective responses of the Jews were altogether different. Certainly, the situation of the Jews in territories captured by the Soviet Union changed considerably for the worse in comparison to what they had experienced in independent Poland. The Soviets promptly proceeeded to enforce the total suppression of Jewish social, cultural and religious institutions. The Hebrew school system was liquidated; Jewish social institutions, sports clubs and libraries were closed. Jewish newspapers ceased to appear. A considerable fraction of the Jewish population became rapidly impoverished. Political oppression and the banning of all political organizations affected the Jews no less than the Poles.

Deportations to forced labor camps affected the Jewish population probably in even greater measure than the Poles. Thus, for instance, Wladyslaw Wielhorski in his pamphlet *Los Polakow w niewoli Sowieckiej* (The Fate of the Poles in Soviet Bondage, London, 1956) reports that among the deportees over 50 percent were Poles, about 30 percent Ukrainians and Byelorussians, and about 20 percent Jews.[22] And in the report of the Delegate of the Polish Government-in-Exile which bears the title "Deportations from eastern Polish territories in the years 1939–1941" one can find the following information:

> Deportations affected all four nationalities inhabiting these territories: the Poles, the Jews, the Ukrainians and the Byelorussians. The politically active segments from the ranks of all four nationalities were affected alike, because the yardstick applied to all four populations was the same: in all of them the main thrust being in practice directed against the left-wing organizations. But in the mass deportations there was a certain differentation. The modal group were the Poles who amounted to about 52 percent of the deportees. Next came the Jews whose share was about 30 percent. Finally, the Ukrainians and the Byelorussians constituted some 18-20 percent.[23]

The Polish sources therefore differ in their estimates of the proportion of Jews among the deportees, the range being between 20 and 30 percent. However, since in the territories in question the Jews were fewer in number than any of the ramaining three nationalities, even the lower of the two estimates would mean that the percentage of deportees was highest in the Jewish group. Considering this, and considering also the suppression of Jewish cultural institutions, the persecutions of the Jews and the curtailment of their political freedoms in the territories captured by the USSR can be safely described as no milder than those affecting the Poles.

There was, however, a certain compensation in that thousands of Jews obtained the chance of employment in state or municipal administration, in the judiciary, in the militia, and in other institutions. In prewar Poland this opportunity had hardly existed as a result of official discrimination against Jews in government employment. The new employment opportunities gave the Jews the sense of full equality in civil rights not enjoyed before. Among some segments of Jewry, this factor contributed to the growth of pro-Soviet feelings.

But the pro-Soviet mood of some Jews stemmed from other reasons as well. Under Soviet rule both secondary schools and universities became open to the poor, Jewish as well as non-Jewish. In prewar Poland, the attendance at educational institutions was too costly for the poor. Jewish youth, anxious to learn, were impressed by this change.

But the difference between Jewish and Polish attitudes towards the Soviet Union must be understood first and foremost in terms of the abysmally different conditions of Jewish life under the Nazi occupation and in the areas incorporated by the USSR. Under Nazi rule the Jews became isolated overnight as a target of aggravated terror, of discriminatory legislation, of daily incidents of violence and robbery, of roundups for performance of menial work, and of constant assaults upon their dignity. In the areas annexed by the Soviet Union, by contrast, the bulk of restrictions and the curtailment of civil rights affected the totality of the population alike. With the exception of the suppression of Jewish schools and cultural institutions there were no discriminatory policies applying specifically to the Jews.

No matter how badly the conditions of the Jews in the Soviet-captured territories might have deteriorated, they still retained no comparison with their conditions under German occupation. No wonder, therefore, that even those Jews who had no pro-Soviet inclinations whatsoever, were articulate in expressing their preference for Soviet over Nazi rule, and looked upon the Russians as saviors from the nightmares of Nazi occupation. This accounts for the crucial difference between Jewish and Polish responses to the two occupations. The Poles saw the Russians and the Germans as occupiers, one as bad as the other. For the Jews, the difference was enormous.

Favorable attitudes of some Jews of the eastern territories towards the Soviet authorities were denounced by the Poles as manifestations of Jewish disloyalty towards Polish statehood. One of the most critical evaluations of Jewish behavior can be found in a report of the Polish Foreign Ministry in Exile which bears the title "Soviet administration of Polish eastern territories under occupation in 1939." The Report describes the events in Bialystok in October and November of 1939:

> Jewish teachers usually manifested excessive zeal and enthusiasm in their utterances during the propaganda or declaratory assemblies. Still, the restrained behavior of several teachers and of many school principals from southern Poland is to be noted as an exception. They expressed their concern over the fact that the Jews commit themselves so conspicuously to the side of the new power. A school principal named Tilleman was even suddenly fired. But a former principal of a Jewish grammar school, Maczewski, became an active member of the Municipal Council and a deputy on the Presidium of the Narodnoye Sobraniye Zapadnoy Byelarusi (National Assembly of Western Byelorussia) . . .
>
> About 200,000 Jewish refugees from Warsaw and Lodz who had reached Bialystok, applied en masse for employment inside Russia. They signed the requisite contracts. Several transports of such workers reached Minsk, Moscow and Kiev where they were welcomed with music and meals. Once on the spot, they realized how bad were their pay, living facilities and supplies. After several months the mass flight of Jews back to Poland began. About 1,000 of such returning refugees got together in Minsk, protesting against the prohibition to cross the old Polish-Soviet border. They were finally allowed to reach Stolpce and Baranowicze and arrested there. Several dozens of them found themselves in a Bialystok prison . . .
>
> The ranks of workers, artisans, petty tradesmen, school children and adolescents, including the ones from well-off families, actively sided with the occupiers, assisting them in electoral propaganda, assuming positions in the workers, militia, and applying for employment inside Russia. Property holders, factory owners, well-off merchants, businessmen, house owners and professionals (especially from the south of Poland) showed restraint and hesitancy. There were, however, two exceptions: A physician by the name of Kerszman and a lawyer by the name of Tilleman actively cooperated with the occupiers.[25]

A similar evaluation of Jewish attitudes towards Soviet authorities can be found in the minutes of the cabinet meeting of January 9, 1940 of the Polish Government-in-Exile:

> The Prime Minister stressed that under the Nazi occupation, the anti-Semitic mood declined considerably under the impact of the inhuman persecutions of the Jews by the Germans. The Poles resent these persecutions. In the areas under Soviet occupation about 70 percent of the Jews behave with decency, while about 30 percent side with the Communists, often in a manner which for the Poles is provocative. We have to ignore such provocations, mindful that it is forbidden to do anything that might be detrimental to the future of Poland . . . [26]

But in his public speech in London on November 16, 1940, the Polish Prime Minister Sikorski gave a rather different evaluation:

> It is to be stressed that our people are profoundly impressed by the proofs of loyalty towards Poland on the part of its Slavic and Jewish minorities.[27]

In Polish writings, both historical research and personal memoirs, one encounters extreme bitterness over the Jewish support of the Soviet Union during the Second World War. The resentment against the Jews over this issue stands out in this literature in sharp relief. At the same time, this literature is notably devoid of any serious effort to understand the dilemma which the Jews then faced, which can be succinctly stated as follows:

1. The fate of the Jews under Nazi occupation prompted them to look upon the Soviet Union as a salutary alternative to Nazi bestiality, notwithstanding the fact that the Soviet authorities did undertake measures hurting the Jewish population no less than the Polish rulers.

2. Since in the former eastern territories of Poland the Poles were no more than a minority, the Jews faced a grave conflict between the retention of loyalty to Polish statehood and the recognition of the aspirations of the Ukrainian and Byelorussian majority to independence as a just cause.

3. It also should be remembered that neither the policies of the Polish authorities, nor the behavior of the overwhelming majority of Poles in those areas in the period between the wars contributed to the emergence of resolutely pro-Polish attitudes among the Jews.

Once the occupation of Poland began, an additional factor appeared which had an adverse effect upon the unfolding configuration of relationships between the Poles and the Jews during the Second World War. Jewish political centers were excluded from any participation in the formation of the Polish underground.

In a germinal form, the Polish underground was set in motion already on the eve of the surrender of Warsaw. The foundations of the future Polish clandestine endeavor were laid in the beleaguered capital, by the army command in charge of the city's defense. Two days before the arms were laid down, when the necessity of surrendering the city was already fully apparent, the commander in charge, General Juliusz Rommel, ordered a certain group of officers to assume false identities and to carry on clandestine work. The officers were supplied with funds. Some stores of weaponry and other military equipment were placed at their disposal, to serve the needs of the future underground organization. In this way, a clandestine armed force named Sluzba Zwyciestwu Polski (Service for the Polish Victory) had already been set up prior to the fall of Warsaw. General Michal Tokarzewski-Karasiewicz was appointed as the commander of the new organization.

General Rommel wanted the new clandestine organization to assume a cross-national character, so as to be in the position to enjoy wide political support from all segments of the nation. For this purpose, a conference was convened, with the representatives of all major Polish political parties invited. Yet no Jewish public figure was invited; nor any representative of a Jewish political party; this despite the fact that the conference took place in Warsaw, whose population was then one-third Jewish. It was a conspicuous proof of the intention to restrict the Jews from membership in the centers of Polish resistance under occupation. Unaltered, this policy was subsequently followed by the leadership of the underground, acting under the orders of the Polish Government-in-Exile.

The new Polish Government, residing in Angers near Paris, was formed right after the fall of Poland, already in the first days of October 1939. After the subsequent fall of France in June 1940, the Government moved its residence to London where it operated until the end of the Second World War. The establishment of the channels of command over the Service for the Polish Victory was one of the first items on that Government's agenda. (The organization was later renamed Zwiazek Walki Zbrojnej, i.e. the Union for Armed Struggle, to be eventually renamed again Armia Krajowa, i.e. the Home Army.)[28]

The Polish Government-in-Exile spared no effort in order to extend its authority over all the spontaneously emerging underground organizations. For this purpose the so-called integrative action was undertaken, aiming at the incorporation of all such independently created groups into the Union for Armed Struggle. The Union itself was directly subordinated to the newly established superior political agency known under the name of the Office of the Government's Delegate (Delegatura Rzadu na Kraj). The Home Army was subsequently structured along the same lines. The Delegate's Office which comprised the representatives of all major Polish political groupings, acted under the orders of the Government-in-Exile. The position of the Delegate was proclaimed to be equivalent to the position of a Deputy Prime Minister.

Symptomatically, the Jews continued to be excluded from the activities of the Government-controlled Polish underground. No representative of the Jewish population was invited to the Delegate's Office. In the course of the integrative action, no one approached any representative of a Jewish organization with the proposition of recognizing the Delegate's Office as their superordinate authority. In effect, those Jewish leaders who attempted to organize Jewish resistance to Nazi occupation, were not cognizant of what was being done by the Government-in-Exile and by its Delegate for the purpose of setting clandestine work in motion. While the Polish underground benefited from Government leadership and Government assistance, the Jewish underground was deprived of both.

In consequence, the Jewish and the Polish undergrounds in the territories under German occupation were being formed totally independently: each without connection with the other. The organizational effort and the activities of the Jewish underground were handicapped by adversities incomparable with those which the Polish underground faced. Anti-Jewish measures of the German occupier, such as restrictions on freedom of movement, frequent sorties into Jewish apartments for purposes of plunder, deportations much wider in scope than those which affected the Poles, and street roundups had the effect of severely restricting the very capability of Jewish engagement in clandestine work. Denial of governmental assistance and support added further to this effect. It cannot be doubted that both the Jewish population and Jewish resistance could only benefit if Jewish representatives had been allowed to join the Delegate's Office, and if at least some Jewish clandestine organizations had been subordinated to that office.

The formation of an underground in the Soviet-dominated territories was an altogether different issue. Conditions brought about by the Soviet authorities turned out to be much less favorable for clandestine work than those under German occupation. Attempts to set up the Polish underground in these territories collapsed promptly. A real underground did not develop there until the time when these areas were captured by Germany in the summer of 1941.

Jewish clandestine work in these territories encountered the same difficulties as the Polish one. Neither succeeded in pursuing any extended activities. The sole exceptions were the Zionist groups: but their activity was essentially confined to the search for routes to let the Jewish youth reach Israel. And in truth, such attempts were crowned with only minor success.

Cooperation between the Jewish and the Polish clandestine groups in the Soviet-dominated areas barely existed.

In summary, one might point to three fundamental factors which in the initial period of the occupation shaped a distinct configuration of Polish-Jewish relationships that was to last throughout the Second World War. The factors were:

1. Different policies of the German occupier towards the Jews and towards the Poles.
2. A difference in the attitudes of the Poles and of the Jews towards the Soviet Union as conditioned by the different treatment of the Jews by the Germans
3. Exclusion of the Jews from participation in the Polish underground resistance.

NOTES

1. Madajczyk, C., *Polityka Trzeciej Rzeszy w okupowanej Polsce* (Policies of the Third Reich in occupied Poland), Warsaw: PWN, 1970, vol. 1, p. 45.
2. Ibid., pp. 45–46.
3. Datner, S., *55 dni Wehrmachtu w Polsce* (55 days of the Wehrmacht in Poland), Warsaw: MON, 1967, p. 74.
4. Eisenbach, A., *Hitlerowska polityka zaglady Zydow* (Nazi policies of extermination of the Jews), Warsaw: Ksiazka i Wiedza, 1961, p. 141.
5. This report was sent to London and published in a limited circulation publication of the Interior Ministry of the Polish Government-in-Exile A copy in Yad Vashem Archives (Thereafter: YVA), M-2/187.
6. YVA, M-2/187.
7. Ringelblum, E., *Stosunki polsko-zydowskie w czasie drugiej wojny swiatowej* (Polish-Jewish relations during the Second World War), YVA, M-10/PH/13-1-11, pp. 16–17.

8. YVA, account M-1/E-1563, by Gedalia Erenburg.
9. Garfinkel, M., YVA, O-33/322.
10. Boruchowicz, M., account in Jasny, W., ed., *Yizkor bukh fun der Zhelekhover yidishe kehile* (Memorial book of the Jewish community of Zelechow), Chicago, 1953, p. 366.
11. Lichtman, I., YVA, O-3/2309.
12. Herzig, J., YVA, O-33/194.
13. Kalfus, I., YVA, M-1/E-284.
14. Israel, I., YVA, O-33/432.
15. Guterman, M., YVA, O-3/2973.
16. Weiss, J., YVA, O-3/2023.
17. Goldman, J., YVA, O-3/2157.
18. Goldsztejn, B., YVA, O-3/1329.
19. Ringelblum, op. cit., p. 22.
20. Keselbrener, Y., YVA, O-3/2089.
21. Perechodmik, C., YVA, O-33/426.
22. Quoted after Turlejska, M., *Prawdy i fikcje: Wrzesien 1939—Grudzien 1941* (Truth and fiction: September 1939–December 1941), second edition, Warsaw: Ksiazka i Wiedza, 1968, p. 309.

23. Archives of the General Sikorski Historical Institute, London (Thereafter: GSHI), A.11.73/11.
24. The figure is exaggerated.
25. GSHI, A.11.73/2.
26. GSHI, PRM-K.102.
27. GSHI, PRM.36/5.

28. Korbonski, S., *Polskie Panstwo Podziemne: Przewodnik po podziemiu z lat 1939–1945)* (The Polish Clandestine State: Guidebook to the underground in the years 1939–1945), Paris: Instytut Literacki, 1975, pp. 22–23.

CHAPTER THREE

Towards the Ghetto

Towards the end of 1939 the confinement of the Jewish population in separate city districts, known as ghettos, was already in progress. The first ghetto was set up by the Nazis in Piotrkow Trybunalski in November of that year. In December ghettos were established in Pulawy and Radomsko. On February 8, 1940, the formation of a ghetto was announced in Lodz, the second biggest concentration of Jews in occupied Poland. On April 30, that ghetto was already cordoned off. In the spring and summer of 1940 a number of other ghettos were set up in the Warthegau district. In August, more ghettos were set up in some counties of Radom and Warsaw districts. On October 2, 1940, the formation of a ghetto was proclaimed in Warsaw. It was cordoned off on November 15.

During the summer and fall of 1940 ghettos were established in the district of Lublin. The district of Cracow was last in line: the Nazi occupation authorities proceeded to the formation of the ghettos there no sooner than in the spring of 1941. In the city of Cracow where the capital of the Government General was located, the ghetto was established in March of 1941. In the wake of the German invasion of the Soviet Union, the same process was resumed in what was formerly eastern Poland, now captured by the German army. In August of 1941 a ghetto was set up in Bialystok, in September in Wilno, and in November in Lwow.[1]

The formation of the ghettos entailed not only the forced displacement of the Jews from the so-called "Aryan" side, but also the reverse displacement of those Poles (or Byelorussians and Ukranians in the Eastern territories) who happened to reside in places designated to become ghettos and who now had to move to the "Aryan" side. The Jews forced to resettle in the ghettos were dealt a terrible blow. But the Poles too, who were forced to abandon their previous places of residence or work, bore the brunt of very serious inconvenience. The dislocations stemming from the formation of the ghetto in Warsaw are summarily described by the report of the Research Bureau of the Polish Government-in-Exile which

bears the title *Activities of occupation authorities on the territory of
the Republic between September 1, 1939 and November 1, 1940:*

> The formation of nationally exclusive residential quarters causes
> enormous social and economic complications. It is enough to mention
> the tragedies of mixed marriages, the loss of clientele, the costs of reset-
> tlement and the destruction of property incurred in the course of resettle-
> ments, disturbances in supplies of rationed foodstuffs, confusion in the
> work of the police, church parishes, telephone services, gas and power
> stations, and so on. Waste, administrative malfunction and chaos appear
> everywhere. The populace suffers indescribably, especially since
> resources and human resilience have already been exhausted.[2]

By far the worst damage resulting from resettlements enforced
during the formation of the ghettos was, however, suffered by the
Jews. The German authorities always designated very restricted
spaces for the ghettos. As a result of this, the population density in
Jewish quarters was bound to grow enormously. In Warsaw, for instance, about 150,000 Jews who moved from the "Aryan" areas of
the city to the ghetto took over the places of about 100,000 Poles
who had to move from the area designated as the ghetto to the areas
outside.[3]

The concentration of the Jewish population in cordoned-off
ghettos radically changed the entire configuration of economic
relationships between the Jews and the Poles. By the very nature of
things the economic change had a considerable impact upon the
shaping of the social and political relationships between the two
populations.

Sizeable quantities of abandoned Jewish realty, shops, artisan
workshops and movable property passed into Polish hands. Jews
were totally removed from professions and services benefiting
Polish clients. The confinement of the Jews in the ghettos turned
out, therefore, to bring benefits primarily to Polish merchants and
artisans, and secondarily to small segments of the intelligentsia
and to those workers who turned to trade and handicrafts, either in
order to exploit wartime opportunities or in order to take over the
places previously filled by the Jews.

Soon after the formation of the ghettos, the real prospect of
starvation became the constant torment of the Jews confined there.
Foodstuffs rationed to the Jews in the ghettos were a tiny fraction of
the rations which the Poles received. In terms of their nutritional
value, the respective figures for Warsaw in 1941 were 213 and 760
calories.[4]

The isolation of the ghettos and the discrimination in rationing
had a natural consequence in the emergence of tremendous

differences in free market prices of foodstuffs in the ghetto and on the "Aryan" side. The Jewish residents of the ghettos sought to escape the disaster of starvation either by selling out whatever they owned at dirt-cheap prices, or by some ventures in cheap and unlawful production or services for the benefit of the "Aryan" side. Report No. 6 of the Social Department of the Polish Ministry of Interior published in London dated December 23, 1942, describes the situation as follows:

> The hardships which most Jews had to suffer in the ghettos were heavy in the extreme. Nonetheless, the Jews did somehow manage to survive. The Jewish community did not acquiesce impassively to the shock of isolation. Under the most difficult of imaginable circumstances, this community defended itself with resolve in the field of economic activity and particularly of supplies. The case could be a subject of an extraordinarily interesting study, for which there is no space on these pages. But one can conclude that the Jews managed to solve almost satisfactorily the practical problems which they confronted . . . .[5]

The last statement of the quoted passage is an obvious and crude exaggeration. Problems were not solved "almost satisfactorily." The real accomplishment of the economic self-defense referred to here was that it gave people confined in the ghettos a measure of relief and as a result, some reduction in their mortality rate. In dozens of cities and villages more or less extensive unlawful economic ties between the ghettos and the "Aryan" side were established. These unusual economic relationships, shaped by the conditions imposed by the occupier, brought considerable material benefits to segments of Polish society which had economic ties with the starving ghettos. The quoted report of the Polish Ministry of Interior comments on this as follows:

> Thousands of Poles lived off the trade with the ghettos: the trade which involved very high stakes, up to the point of occasional bloodshed. . . .[6]

Typically, unlawful economic undertakings in the ghettos could succeed only through bribing the officials of Nazi administration who performed some functions within the ghetto area. A considerable number of such officials were Polish: like those employed in revenue offices, in gas or electric services, or in the so-called Polish "navy-blue" auxiliary police. The bribes demanded by these men for not noticing what they were supposed to notice, were as a rule exorbitant; but owing to them, an artisan workshop, for example, could perform work commissioned from the "Aryan" side without suffering disruptions in its communications across the ghetto walls.[7] A great many of such officials were ruthlessly exploiting the ghetto residents who sought some relief from the prospect of starvation. Thus, for instance, the conduct of the Polish tax collectors employed in the Warsaw ghetto is thus described by the chronicler of events in that ghetto, Emmanuel Ringelblum:

> For the ghetto, the tax collectors were a sheer nightmare. In the most ruthless manner, they robbed whomever they could, by extorting taxes for burned, bombed or pillaged industrial or commercial property. They demanded retroactive payments, knowing very well that receipts could have been lost during the air raids. Whoever did not want or could not pay instantly, had his belongings confiscated on the spot, in addition to undergoing a personal search. Property seizures amounted to sheer robbery. The officials would search all the inhabitants of a given apartment, forcefuly assembled together in a single room, so as to be at the same time free to pick up from other rooms whatever they desired without being inhibited by the owners or any other witnesses. Fearing retaliation on the part of aggrieved Jews, they began to appear in Jewish houses with firearms. They behaved like the Germans, whipping everyone who stood in their way. In cases where they encountered some resistance, they would come back in German trucks to pick up everything they could find in a given apartment or store.
>
> The desk clerks in tax offices were conniving with these plunderers, by hindering the Jewish clients from making their payments on time. The day after the expiration of a deadline, the tax collectors would appear in a frustrated taxpayer's apartment to seize everything they could find. In some instances, tax collectors unauthorized to work in the ghetto, would equip themselves at exorbitant prices with fake authorizations, just to get an opportunity for uninhibited plunder.[8]

Another group of Poles who derived benefits from the existence of the ghettos, were the owners of some plants, who were in a position to exploit the ghetto's cheap manpower. In some cases raw materials were smuggled into ghettos for manufacture; and the products thus manufactured were smuggled back to the "Aryan" side. There emerged an entire substructure of go-betweens who earned their living (and occasionally wealth) by smuggling merchandise back and forth between the "Aryan" side and the ghetto. This substructure was comprised of both Jews and Poles. The scope of these operations varied from ghetto to ghetto, depending on the degree of a given ghetto's isolation and, consequently, on the prospects of maintaining the lines of communication across the walls. Thus, for example, in the Warsaw ghetto a tremendous amount of smuggling was going on, while in the hermetically sealed ghetto of Lodz there was none.

The variations in prices were abnormal, in that the prices of foodstuffs which the ghetto residents purchased were very high; while the prices of textiles and other commodities which they were selling out were very low. This turned out to benefit some segments of the rural population, especially in villages advantageously located at not too great a distance from a ghetto to which foodstuffs could be smuggled.

The existence of specific segments of the Polish population in the position to take advantage of forced resettlements and of seclusion of the Jews in the ghettos was conducive to the growth of anti-Semitism. These groups had neither contributed to nor had they been responsible for the formation of the ghettos. But once they learned to take advantage of the ghettos, they began to show interest in their maintenance. Inevitably, this factor had an effect upon political attitudes.

The overwhelming majority of the Polish society derived no material benefits whatsoever from the ghettos. On the other hand, with the sole exception of inconveniences incurred by resettlement from the areas designated as ghettos no economic interests of any Polish social group were affected adversely by the formation of the ghettos either. Hence, while some social forces were interested in the maintenance of the ghettos no segment of Polish society had a vital interest in opposing their existence.

The rise of an anti-Semitic mood among the Polish population in 1940–1941 is documented by numerous accounts and situation reports. Undoubtedly, the material interest of a fraction of the Polish society in the maintenance of the ghettos and of anti-Jewish restrictions was a major factor. Most significant in this respect is the account of engineer Jozef Podoski who in September 1940 left Warsaw and succeeded in reaching London. There, in the course of a conversation with Dr. I. Schwarzbart on December 7, 1940, Podoski said:

> A large number of Poles, from the intelligentsia, from the bourgeoisie, and even from the working class have taken over the economic functions which the Jews were forced to relinquish as a result of Nazi legislation or Nazi pressures. The Poles hate Nazism and the German invaders. But the Polish policy which was always aimed at the revitalization of the Polish bourgeoisie has in this way achieved its objective. If the Jews ever seek restoration of their lost positions, they will by the very nature of things invite a rivalry, a conflict. For within their inner recesses, those strata of Poles are satisfied with this turn of events. I am inclined to anticipate the aggravation of anti-Semitism. In view of this configuration of economic interests, even the left-wing parties will in my opinion have to lean towards some anti-Semitic standpoints in order to win support from their constituencies.[9]

The growth of anti-Semitism among a considerable part of the Polish nation did, of course, influence the attitudes of the Polish underground towards the ghettos and towards the Jewish question in general. But the Polish underground consisted of three major distinguishable factions: the primary group around the Delegate's Office, the left-wing opposition, also linked with that Office, and the right-wing opposition which challenged the authority of that Office. The Delegate's Office periodically reported to the Government in London. These reports contain much evidence concerning the conditions of the Jews in occupied Poland and concerning the attitudes of the Polish underground towards the Jews. Because of that, they are of a major importance as a documentary source.

Thus, the report of June 11, 1941, deals with a three days-long pogrom which the Germans organized a fortnight earlier in Siedlce. The deeds of the German soldiers are described there as follows:

> The witnessed scenes were horrendous. The children, being held by their legs, were swung against the wall so as to leave their heads smashed. Women and men were being tossed from the windows on the pavement. The bodies lying on the pavement were ripped open with bayonets.[10]

Another report dealing with the internal situation up to January 30, 1941, provides some information about terror exerted against the Jewish inmates of forced labor camps:

> In the forced labor camps, most of which were located in the proximity of the present Soviet border, the conditions are terrible. Barracks are not heated, food is bad, work is hard, beating and harassment go on ceaselessly. Inadequate clothing of the inmates and their lack of previous experience with menial work are the sources of particular hardship. Mortality is enormous: it reaches 10%, thereof 6% from illnesses and 4% by firing squads. Once particular military projects are terminated, the Jews who had been working on them are shot. The treatment of the Jews is no less harsh than in concentration camps. For example, in Debica camp near Cracow the Jews are tied as punishment with wet leather straps which, as they dry up, suffocate the victim to the point of unconsciousness.[11]

The report of August 12, 1941, contains detailed data concerning mortality in the Warsaw ghetto. We learn, for instance, that the mortality figures for May 1941 was 3,821, and for the first half of June of the same year, 2,165.[12] But often the information to be found in these reports is biased, the generalizations unwarranted, and the conclusions indicative of the extreme anti-Semitism of their authors. To give a characteristic example, let us choose the report dealing with the situation in the Government General between October 15 and November 20, 1940. The report contains some genuine information about the forced labor camps of the Lublin district:

Along the present border with the Soviet Union the occupiers have set up a number of camps in which all the inmates are Jewish. Their temperature is checked every day: and those with a temperature exceeding 38 degrees centigrade are shot, as a precaution against contamination. The bulk of the inmates are employed in drainage projects. They are treated and fed very badly which results in diseases and high mortality. Other Jews are assigned either to work battalions or to fortification projects. These assignments are the worst. Whole teams of Jews, especially those who happen to have been assigned to work of military importance, are shot to make sure that secrets will be kept . . .

Thus far, the report is rather matter-of-fact. But then is continues:

Many official regulations appear which look as if the Jews were to be treated as the lowliest of people. In practice, however, these regulations are not implemented. In effect, the Jews live under better conditions than the Poles . . .

The attitudes of the Jews towards the Poles are resolutely hostile. Jewish cooperation with the Gestapo is rather extensive, and it is aimed first and foremost against the Polish nation. The Jews are influenced by the Communist propaganda, which, needless to say, also aims at harming Polish interests. The organization of work battalions follows the instructions of the Communist party: the aim being their transformation, at a convenient moment, into a Communist militia. . . .[13]

The complete spuriousness of this passage is easily demonstrable. How could the inmates of forced labor camps, totally severed from the outside world, possibly cooperate with the Gestapo against the Polish nation? Furthermore, no Communist underground was yet active at that time in occupied Poland. All the talk about propaganda and the instructions of the then non-existent Communist party is therefore patent nonsense. It can be presumed that the misinformation was in this particular case deliberate.

Another report which covers the period from March to April 15, 1941, says:

The mood of the Jews is nevertheless optimistic, notwithstanding the common presupposition that the poorer and the weaker among them have no chance of surviving the war. As far as their attitudes are concerned, it is obvious that with the exception of a certain amount of profit-motivated Gestapo informers, the bulk of the Jews lean towards hatred of the Germans. But there are many followers of the Soviet Union and Communism in their ranks, up to the point of constituting a sizable majority. The pro-Soviet elements take an active part in propaganda work, and they actively cooperate with the Communists who train and organize cadres in the event of a possible revolt. All the work teams are Communist-dominated and destined for a future role as organized detachments. To be sure, some Jews profess Communist ideology without leaning toward the Soviet Union, but they are a mere handful. Finally, a rather tiny percentage of Jews opt for the reconstruction of Poland and engage in something that resembles work for the sake of Polish independence. All these organizations are, of course, in the overwhelming majority pro-British, beacuse they expect Britain to defeat the Nazis. But there are also some who expect Russia to deal the decisive blow. The prospect of the war in the East animates the Jews greatly. Extensive and fanciful rumors which circulate in the ghettos revolve around this subject.[14]

The reports of the Delegate's Office also contain some evidence of the intensification of the anti-Semitic mood in the Polish society. Thus, for instance, the report of the Delegate's Office Interior Department which covers the period from August 15 to November 15, 1941, declares:

> The tide of anti-Semitism which had previously risen under the influence of the news about the conduct of the Jews under Soviet occupation, declined recently in response to the grim ordeal suffered by that nation. But the potential anti-Semitism which still lingers in Polish society, is being exploited by German propaganda and by the underground press of various right-wing persuasions. The issue is exceptionally sensitive; possibly, it may even split the society into two parts, each with different political attitudes. The prevailing viewpoint is that the Jewish problem can be solved only through a massive, internationally coordinated emigration of Jews from Poland. Once Jewish supremacy in economic life is gone, mutual relationships must be guided in the future by a compromise on the basis of the total loyalty of Jews towards the Polish state.[15]

Evidence of the condition of the Jews under German occupation can also be found in the clandestine press published by the Delegate's Office and by the Home Army command. To be sure, that press carried no editorials defining its views on the formation of the ghettos and the confinement of the entire Jewish population in them. In spite of this, the position of the Delegate's Office (or at least of the major political groups within it) on the Jewish question during the period of the formation of the ghettos can be assessed with accuracy on the basis of the preserved documents of that Office. One of the most important documents is a memo elaborated in March of 1940 by the head of the Delegate's Office's Foreign Department, Roman Knoll. The necessity of forced emigration of Jews from Poland after its liberation is for Knoll a foregone conclusion. To achieve this goal, he proposes a definite solution. Poland should occupy parts of the Soviet territory around Odessa, in order to sponsor Jewish settlement there.

A memo of November 8, 1941, written by another official of the Delegate's Office, "Ryszard," and addressed to the Polish Minister of Interior residing in London is no different from Knoll's memo in its sentiments. It contains the following passage:

All human compassion for Jewish misery notwithstanding, there is hardly a person in Poland that wouldn't demand a definite policy in regard to the Jewish question, and in particular in regard to the takeover of Jewish positions in economic life by the Poles. Without at least a minimal program towards this objective, no government will be able to maintian itself in power.

It finally must be explicitly stated that Polish society is bound to oppose fervently any attempt to grant equal rights to national minorities like the Germans, the Ukrainians, and the Jews. This society is now being martyred by the Germans. It has suffered the experience of Ukrainian ambushes against the withdrawing Polish armies. It has seen the triumphal gates which the Jews erected to welcome the Bolsheviks, and it remembers how the Jews behaved towards the Polish population under Bolshevik rule. I am raising these points deliberately, because no picture of the political moods in Poland can be formed as long as these issues are ignored. The views Polish society holds on these subjects can be accurately described as unwavering. One must take them into consideration.[16]

Still another official of the Delegate's Office, Mersin, voices similar sentiments. His report of December 31, 1940, dealing with the situation in Warsaw and in the Government General says:

The boldest dreams of the staunchest anti-Semites have been already exceeded by what the occupiers managed to accomplish in the field of the anti-Jewish struggle. But the fine structure which they erected may easily collapse after the victory of the democratic states. Our reactionary anti-Semites are haunted by this prospect; it is the fear which disturbs their sweetest dreams. They realize that German policies lack characteristics of permanency. In private, many Poles express satisfaction when they see how in this city and in other cities the Jews are being removed from Polish suburbs, offices, professions, industry and commerce. But under no circumstances will they demonstrate their satisfaction in public. For they are repelled by the methods resorted to: by the fact that the measures undertaken result in so much human grief. For this reason, they even have some tacit compassion for the Jews, helping them whenever possible, and at the very least refraining from contributing to further exacerbation of Jewish misery. (The evidence of such behavior can best be spotted in Polish offices and in commerce.) At the same time, a fraction of Poles display favorable attitudes towards the Jews openly. . . .[17]

Anti-Semitic sentiments in their most extreme form can be found in a report originating with the Polish Catholic Church. The report covers the period from June 1 to July 15, 1941. It was conveyed to London by the Delegate's Office. The report states:

The need to solve the Jewish question is urgent. Nowhere else in the world has that question reached such a climax, because no fewer than 4 million of these highly noxious and by all standards dangerous element live in Poland, or to be more precise, off Poland. . . .

And the report goes on:

> As far as the Jewish question is concerned, it must be seen as a singular dispensation of Divine Providence that the Germans have already made a good start, quite irrespective of all the wrongs they have done and continue to do to our country. They have shown that the liberation of Polish society from the Jewish plague is possible. They have blazed the trail for us which now must be followed: with less cruelty and brutality, to be sure, but no flagging consistently. Clearly, one can see the hand of God in the contribution to the solution of this urgent question being made by the occupiers: because the Polish nation, soft-hearted and inconstant as it is, could never muster enough energy to undertake measures which in this case are indispensable. The urgency of the problem is clear from the fact that the Jews wreak incalculable damage on our entire religious and national life. Not only do they curtail the development of Polish commerce and hamper the flow of excessive rural population to commerce, but they are responsible for stripping our cities and villages of their Catholic character. They also are the source from which multi-faceted depravation spreads upon the entire society. They advance corruption and bribery, they distort our public life through their abstruse influence upon governmental and administrative agencies, they bear a major responsibility for houses of prostitution, for trafficking in white slaves, and for pornography. They make our people into inveterate drinkers. They corrupt our youth. They infiltrate immoral and un-Catholic ideas into our literature, arts and public opinion. Finally, they always associate themselves with anything that may damage, weaken, or debase the Church and Poland. Even today, through some odd and peculiar psychological response mechanism, they innately hate the Poles more than the Germans, notwithstanding all the ruthless persecution they have suffered from the hands of the latter. And it is against the Poles that they nourish dreams of retaliation for their wrongs and losses.
>
> According to the most authoritative persons in the country, the Jewish question must be resolved differently in the reborn Poland. The long-range goal towards which a sustained effort must be made (on the international forum as well) is the emigration of the Jews to some state of their own overseas. But as long as this cannot be achieved, a far-reaching isolation of the Jews from our society will be mandatory. Unconditionally, they will have to leave the villages and small towns. In the bigger cities they will have to have their own closed off zones of settlement. They must have their own denominational schools, primary and secondary, and at the universities they must be subject to strict enforcement of the *numerus clausus*. They must be barred from army service, from public offices and from teaching Catholic youth. Finally, methods have to be found to restrict their share in the legislative chambers, in rendering professional services to Christians, and in selected branches of commerce and industry. All this will be very difficult. Friction can be expected on this score between the Government-in-Exile, which is rather exposed to Free-mason and Jewish influence, and the people in the country who already today are organized themselves. But the health of our Fatherland, restored with God's help, depends to a very great extent on such measures.[18]

In some documents emanating from the Delegate's Office, Jews
are reproached for merely contemplating the idea of the repeal of
all anti-Jewish rulings enacted by the Nazis, and of the return to the
prewar legislation. This theme can be detected in a report which
deals with national affairs and which covers the month of May
1941:

> The views of Polish-Jewish organizations reflect their uncertainties
> about the future. The dominant orientation is to look forward to the
> rescue from German captivity as coming from the East. As far as the
> relationships with the Poles are concerned, the Bund, the most active
> of all these organizations, advocates the solidarity of the Polish and
> Jewish working masses in the struggle against the occupier. It must be
> stressed that although no one doubts that the war will be won, there is
> no single block of Jewish opinion that would understand the difficulty
> of returning to the prewar state of affairs and the necessity of turning to
> new solutions of the Jewish problem after the war. The discipline in
> moral and religious matters like observance of the Sabbath or of dietary
> laws has been quite lax, with the rabbis' approval. The prospect that at
> a turning point the ghettos may become the carriers of the Communist
> work cannot be ignored.[19]

Many reports of the Delegate's Office voice some anti-Semitic
sentiments. But the report of the situation in the Government
General between November 16 and December 31, 1940, in this
respect constitutes an exception. The author of this report views
the formation of the ghettos as portending danger also to the Poles:

> The entire German conduct proves that it aims at the total destruc-
> tion of the Polish intelligentsia. But the German actions are not targeted
> solely against this stratum. The Government General was designed so
> as to supply Germany with agricultural produce and unskilled, mainly
> agricultural, manpower. This scheme leaves room for the rural popula-
> tion, but it makes the urban population expendable if not totally super-
> fluous. This explains the continuing policies aiming at the destruction
> of urban life and at the disruption of the urban productive framework.
> The best case in point are the methods used for the purpose of setting
> up the restricted and cordoned off ghettos areas, in order to erect a
> barrier between two large and mutually interconnected groups of the
> urban population: the Christian and the Jewish.[20]

The right-wing opposition to the Delegate's Office was at the
same time giving vent to the most extreme forms of anti-Semitism.
The zeal of its press in anti-Jewish advocacy was extraordinary,
and the style no different in essence from that of the Nazi press. Yet
its readership was quite extensive. Here is a sample of quotations.

Szaniec ("The Rampart") of January 31, 1940, in an article bearing the title "Justly so!":

Today, the Jewish tight-fisted snake squirms under the grip of the Teutonic viper. And it turns to the world with desperate and grievous lamentations. But to these lamentations, the world ought to have one single answer: Justly so! This is what we in Poland—which pays the highest price for Judah's deeds—are particularly entitled to say.

Walka ("The Struggle") of November 29, 1940:

Poland has two enemies: Germany and the Soviet Union. The Jews have only one enemy: Germany. The Ukrainians also have only one enemy: The Soviet Union. Accordingly, the Jews ally themselves with the Soviet Union, and the Ukrainians ally themselves with Germany. Therefore both ally themselves with one of our enemies, and thus they enter alliances against Poland.

The only major political group in the Polish underground which advocated fully equal rights for the Jews in liberated Poland, and which unambiguously denounced the formation of the ghettos as well as other anti-Jewish measures of the Nazis, was the Polish Socialist Party, then acting under the name "Wolnosc-Rownosc-Niepodlegosc" (Liberty-Equality-Independence).

Toward the end of 1940, the Polish socialists disseminated a clandestine pamphlet: "To the working people of Warsaw." The pamphlet, also published on December 4, 1940, in the underground newspaper *Wolnosc* ("Liberty"), No. 78 thus condemned the establishment of the ghetto in Warsaw:

A new element appeared in the endless chain of crimes and atrocities perpetrated by the Nazi conqueror in our country. The living body of the Polish capital has been subdivided by heinous walls. A single administrative ruling deprived thousands of people of employment opportunities and destroyed the foundations of their subsistence. 400,000 men, women and children, defined as the lowliest slaves, were cordoned off in an area named the Jewish District, where they are doomed to eventual starvation and left to the tender mercies of SS goons. History does not record bestiality practiced on such a scale.

The same newspaper in the issue No. 79 of December 7, 1940, published an article "Anti-Jewish measures of the occupier," which says:

The recent anti-Jewish measures of the occupier are not dictated just by the wish to exterminate a nation in a planned and systematic fashion. They are dictated by sheer sadism, by unbounded degeneracy, by the confluence of everything that is inhuman in man. . . .
. . . Jewish workers! At the moment of your worst adversity, the Polish workers turn to you with a message of reassurance. United in the struggle for common ideals, they offer you a cordial handshake.

The organs of "Liberty-Equality-Independence" also denounced
Polish anti-Semites. The weekly *Informator* of March 8, 1940,
wrote:

> There already are professors adapting the Nazi ideology for Polish
> consumption. There already are activists, daydreaming about setting
> up a radical Nazi party. To add to this, many of the anti-Semitic agita-
> tors from the prewar era have gone straight to the Gestapo to report
> themselves, to work for it, and to make money by looting Jewish
> property. Such symptoms need to be implacably resisted. Thus far,
> such human debasement forms no more than an interstice. But once the
> occupiers succeed in widening that interstice, everything which in
> Poland still remains healthy will of necessity sink in the filthy tide. We
> have to bear in mind that it is the Germans who get rich from the
> plunder of Jewish property: that by these means they get access to
> Polish commerce, industry and handicrafts, that it enables them to
> erect their outposts of the economic conquest of Poland.
>
> The persecution of the Jews paves the way to a similar persecution of
> the Polish people. It reconciles public opinion to the atrocities of the
> occupation. The goal anti-Semitic propaganda is to drive out real
> political ideas, and to conceal from Polish society the widespread
> destruction and plunder that the Germans have wrought and continue
> to wreak.
>
> He who takes even the smallest part in such actions, becomes an ally
> of the occupiers, their helper in the process of destruction of Poland,
> and therefore an enemy who needs to be relentlessly destroyed.

Alone among all the clandestine newspaper, the chief organ of
the Polish Socialists "WRN" (Liberty-Equality-Independence) was
reporting on Jewish resistance activities during the initial period of
the existence of the ghettos. In the issue dated November 1–10,
1940, the paper published an article "The standpoint of Jewish
workers." Here is an excerpt:

> As we already reported, Jewish workers have been engaged in ex-
> tensive clandestine activities, and they publish their own clandestine
> press. From the documents which have reached us, we learn of a
> number of clandestine gatherings and conferences, which testify to the
> vitality of the Jewish workers' movement. The movement's ideological
> identity, as revealed by its press and by the resolutions of its con-
> ferences can be summarized by four points: (1) loyalty towards an in-
> dependent Poland; (2) enmity towards the German occupier; (3)
> enmity towards the Russian occupier; (4) the faith that social and
> political justice and equal rights for all nationalities will materialize in
> the reborn Poland of the future.

Of all political groups which operated within the Delegate's
Office, "Liberty-Equality-Independence" was in 1940 and 1941
the only one which maintained any contact with at least one Jewish
resistance group: the *Bund*. No other group linked with that Office

showed any interest in establishing and maintaining contacts with Jewish organizations. The leadership of the Delegate's Office ignored the Jewish resistance altogether. It did absolutely nothing to establish contacts with or to place any Jewish organization under its influence: even during the so-called integrative action when a strenuous effort was made to incorporate and to subordinate all the Polish underground organizations, no matter how tiny. Jewish underground organizations were therefore not represented in the Delegate's Office. Accordingly, the leaders of the Jewish resistance were incapable of employing any means of influencing the attitudes of the Polish underground towards the Jews.

NOTES

1. For a more detailed treatment of the formation of the ghettos in occupied Poland, see Eisenbach, A., *Hitlerowska polityka zaglady Zydow* (Nazi politicies of extermination of the Jews), pp. 213–235.

2. "Activities of occupation authorities on the territory of the Republic between September 1 and November 1, 1940". The report was drafted by the Research Bureau which worked for the Polish Government-in-Exile, and it was signed by minister Kot on February 4, 1941. A copy in Yad Vashem Archives (Thereafter: YVA), M-2/187, p. 188.

3. Eisenbach, *op. cit.*, p.221.

4. Berenstein, T., "Ceny produktow zywnosciowych w Warszawie i w getcie warszawskim w latach okupacji hitlerowskiej" (The prices of foodstuffs in Warsaw and in Warsaw Ghetto in the years of Nazi occupation), *Biuletyn Zydowskiego Instytutu Historycznego* (Bulletin of the Jewish Historical Institute), 70(1969), p. 17, table 7.

5. YVA, M-2/196, p.45.

6. *Ibid.*, p. 48.

7. It is described in E. Ringelblum's study "Polish - Jewish relationships during the Second World War", YVA, M-10/PH/13–1–11, p. 41.

8. *Ibid.*, p. 41–42.

9. YVA, M-2/746.

10. YVA, O–25/89–11.

11. Archives of the General Sikorski Historical Institute, London (Thereafter: GSHI), PRM-K.85.

12. YVA, O–25/89–11.

13. GSHI, PRM-K.85.

14. *Ibid.*

15. Archives of the Central Committee of the Polish United Worker's Party (Thereafter: AKCPZPR), 202/II-6, p. 105.

16. YVA, O–25/89–16.

17. GSHI, PRM-K.86.

18. YVA, O–25/89–12.

19. GSHI, PRM-K.85.

20. *Ibid.*

CHAPTER FOUR

Polish Government and Underground Attitudes

THE JEWISH QUESTION IN THE NATIONAL COUNCIL AND IN THE POLISH GOVERNMENT-IN-EXILE (JANUARY 1940–JUNE 1941)

For the Polish authorities in exile, i.e. for the Government and for the National Council, the Jewish question assumed a different form than for the Government Delegate's Office which operated in occupied Poland. Unlike the latter, the former were exposed to the atmosphere prevalent in the democratic countries of Western Europe and the United States. Inevitably, this factor could not avoid influencing the attitudes of Polish politicians towards the Jews as a national minority at least to some extent. From the onset, Polish Government circles understood that the Jewish population of Poland must be represented in the National Council. This stood in sharp contrast to the situation in the Delegate's Office to which no representation of the Jewish population or of any Jewish political organizations was ever admitted. The presence of a Jewish representative in the National Council created an opportunity for exercising political influence, an option which the Jews were denied in the Delegate's Office.

Within the National Council, political action on behalf of Jewish interests centered on the persons of Dr. Yitzhak (Ignacy) Schwarzbart and Shmuel Zygielbojm. In the period covered by the present chapter, their objective was not so much to obtain relief for the Jews in occupied Poland, as to guarantee equal rights for the Jewish minority in Poland after the liberation.

Schwarzbart's idea was to mobilize the active support of Jewish political centers for Polish political interests in the international arena. He was convinced that only in this way could the prevalence of anti-Semitism in Polish politics of the time be somewhat attenuated.

Until the middle of 1941, Schwarzbart's activity in the National Council focused on five issues. They were: (1) The struggle against the program of Jewish emigration from Poland as advocated by the majority of Polish political groups; (2) Attempts to restore Polish citizenship in cases in which anti-Semitic measures of the prewar government had resulted in its annulment; (3) Campaigning for a declaration in which the Government-in-Exile would guarantee the rights of the Jewish minority after the liberation of Poland; (4) Attempts to establish contact with the Jewish underground in Poland via the Polish government; and (5) The struggle against anti-Semitic argumentation in England by the Polish Nationalist Party. Each of these points requires brief elaboration.

1. *"Emigrationism."* Schwarzbart attempted to convince the representatives of various strains of Polish political factions to forgo the program of forcing the Jews to emigrate from Poland. His efforts toward this goal were strenuous, but essentially futile. The issue was discussed in a conversation which Schwarzbart had on February 20, 1941, with the leaders of the Peasant Party in exile: Mikolajczyk, Kot, Banaczyk and Jaworski.

Mikolajczyk dismissed Schwarzbart's presentation with the following statement:

> The 1935 program of the Peasant Party takes a position on the issue of emigrationism. It supports the idea. It would be rather difficult to change this position now, when we are in exile.

The anti-emigrationist campaign of Schwarzbart ended in failure. Most segments of Polish political opinion never renounced the program of forced emigration of Jews. Some of these groups continued to debate the schemes for expelling the Jews as late as 1943–1944, i.e., after the overwhelming majority of the Jews had already been murdered by the Nazis. We will return to this subject in more depth in later chapters.

2. *The citizenship issue.* In the spring of 1941, Schwarzbart initiated action for the sake of the restoration of Polish citizenship to those Jews whose citizenship had been annulled under the anti-Semitic legislation of the prewar Government. The problem became a subject of lengthy debates in the National Council. In the end, Schwarzbart achieved some measure of success.

The debate dragged on for several months, but ultimately Schwarzbart was rewarded with one of his rare successes in the National Council. On November, 28, 1941, a decree of the President of the Polish Republic was signed, repealing the Denial-of-Citizenship bill of March 31, 1938. The new decree was made public in the Official Gazette of the Republic No. 8 which appeared on December 20, 1941, in London.

3. *The Equal Rights declaration.* Schwarzbart was frustrated in his endeavors to make the Polish Government and the National Council declare equal rights for Jews in a Poland liberated from Nazism. All that he did achieve, after protracted efforts, was an announcement to the same effect by the Information Minister, Stanczyk, made on November 3, 1941. The form of an announcement by a single minister was preferred to a declaration by the Government as a whole, apparently in order to placate the rabidly anti-Semitic opposition, in which a leading role was played by the National Party, and which was certain to oppose the declaration. Convinced that the announcement by a minister, as a substitute for a declaration by the Government, was a palliative, falling far short of what he demanded, Schwarzbart took the initiative to obtain an equal rights declaration in the form of a resolution of the National Council.

The National Council debates on the equal rights declaration dragged on. Schwarzbart tried to enlist the support of selected groups represented in the National Council. This was the background of the conversation of February 20, 1941, with the leaders of the Peasant Party mentioned above.[2]

But Schwarzbart's initiatives concerning the declaration encountered resistance. It came from two sources: from the National Party and from some vocal groups active in occupied Poland. Instructive evidence of the latter resistance can be found in a report bearing the title "Letters from the country," which was sent to London by the Delegate's Office towards the end of 1940. The report discusses the prevalent attitudes of Poles living under Nazi occupation:

> The ghetto issue is part of the Jewish question in general. Of course, Polish society does not approve of the methods which the occupier applies against the Jews. But it would be a great mistake to suppose that Polish anti-Semitism belongs to the past. Anti-Semitism persists in all strata of the population, but it has assumed a different form. Although Polish public opinion disapproves of anti-Jewish violence, it would most emphatically refuse to tolerate the return of the Jews to their prewar positions and influence. The Jews have lost their economic supremacy: in particular in industry and in the wholesale trade. Polish society will never agree if they ever try to regain the footholds they lost. The Government shows poor comprehension of this attitude: the best proof being the last radio message of minister Stanczyk which contained commitments to the effect of granting equal rights to the Jews in liberated Poland. In Poland, the message made a very unfavorable impression. It was resented even by working-class elements belonging to the Polish Socialist Party.[3]

In the meantime, Schwarzbart's endeavors lost all their purpose, as in Poland new realities emerged which turned out to be much more horrifying than anyone could have foreseen.

4. *The contact with the Jewish underground.* In view of these realities, Schwarzbart's attempts to establish contacts with the Jewish underground in Poland turned out to be much more timely and vital than anything he had done about the declaration. But these attempts proved a total failure. There was only one way to establish such contacts: through the couriers of the Government-in-Exile who were periodically dispatched to occupied Poland. The Jewish leaders had no technical resources of their own to reach the Jewish underground in Poland. Accordingly, they had to rely on the communication lines of the Government-in-Exile and of the Delegate's Office.

Schwarzbart broached this problem during the conversation with Prime Minister Sikorski of November 12, 1940. In Schwarzbart's diary, the conversation is described as follows:

> Schwarzbart: I would like to keep in touch with what is being done in Poland for the sake of military preparedness for the appropriate moment. To be specific, I want the Jews in Poland to be included in such activities. This is why I would like to have direct contacts.
> Sikorski (with approval and contentment): All right. The matter is under the authority of general Sosnkowski and minister Kot. I am making a note to convey the matter to them.
> Schwarzbart: I have already talked about it with minister Kot. He promised to convey the matter to you.
> Sikorski: I've heard nothing from him.
> The Prime Minister did make a note for himself.[4]

Two days later Schwarzbart had a conversation with minister Kot. The November 14, 1940, entry in his diary reports its content:

> I raised the matter with Kot in the same way as with Sikorski. I demanded a contact in order to be in a position to influence Jewish youth to join military preparedness efforts. I stressed clearly that I desire Jewish participation in future military action in Poland. And that this is how I conceive of the fulfillment of the premises of the declaration which speaks of mutual understanding between the two societies as materializing through common sufferings and common sacrifices. I see my task as doing everything in my might to influence the matter. I don't insist on being admitted to membership in the Committee, if it consists of ministers only. All that I am interested in, is the contact.
> The minister answered with noticeable restraint: In this case, extraordinary precautions are required insofar as the selection of persons to be admitted is concerned. Understandably, we have been urged in Poland to discuss these matters within as narrow a circle of people as

possible. Your view is correct, and we will have to think how to establish this contact. But apart from the issue of steady contact, I advise you to see Tabaczynski who is in possession of the latest reports which contain extensive information about the Jews. Their situation recently deteriorated.[5]

After much urging and canvassing, Schwarzbart was, in February 1941, finally allowed to meet two men who were to be sent to Poland as couriers. The meeting with one of them is described in Schwarzbart's diary, in the entry of February 10, 1941, as follows:

> At 3 o'clock came Mr. Y., sent by minister Kot to talk about contacts with Poland. My impression is that he is honest but mediocre. He belonged to the Peasant Youth Organization ("Wici"), and he recalled how, as a student of Lwow Polytechnical School, he had had his neck injured by National-Radical cutthroats. I gave him appropriate instructions. He inquired about various problems; in particular, he wanted to know how to answer questions about the attitudes of Jews towards Poland.[6]

The next day, February 11, 1941, Schwarzbart met the second courier. Here is his note from this meeting:

> Right after my phone conversation with minister Kot, Mr. X. came to me at 3 o'clock. He is the second courier. A young man of twenty-two, sympathizer of the Polish Socialist Party, sophisticated, brilliant, and very well-adapted to his dangerous and responsible mission. Just as I did yesterday, I gave him all possible instructions. He asked many questions, in particular about the standpoint of both Polish and the world's Jews vis-a-vis the Poland cause. I gave him the appropriate addresses in Cracow and Warsaw to facilitate recruitment of Jewish youth to clandestine work to be carried out in common with the Poles. The young man exuded great optimism about Polish-Jewish relationships. He estimated that National-Radical influence upon the army is rather limited.[7]

But it was all in vain. Neither of these couriers attempted to contact the Jewish underground in Poland; and with the sole exception of the courier Jan Karski (Kozielewski), the same unfortunately was true of the couriers dispatched to Poland later, already in the period of mass extermination. Karski's case will be discussed below.

Schwarzbart was certainly not helped in his task by the embarrassing dispute with Zygielbojm in the forum of the National Council (sessions of May 18 and May 20, 1942). Zygielbojm demanded to be recognized by the National Council as the sole representative of the Jewish underground in Poland. He argued that apart from the Bund, no other Jewish underground in Poland existed. In this he was, of course, totally wrong.[8]

The problem of the establishment of contacts with the Jewish underground in Poland via Polish Government channels was also raised by Ben-Gurion in a conversation with minister Kot that took place in Jerusalem on December 3, 1942. Ben-Gurion asked whether or not the Polish Government would agree to the idea of dispatching several appointees of the Jewish Agency to Poland, whose task would be to establish underground contacts and to report back about the situation of the Jews through Polish Government channels. Kot's answer was both evasive and calculating. He did not reject Ben-Gurion's idea flatly. But he pointed out that reports of couriers dispatched to Poland reached their destination with great obstacles and much delay; and furthermore, that once dispatched, couriers are not in a position to return. The latter information was plainly untrue, because many couriers did travel with clandestine mail back and forth between London and Poland.[9]

5. *Advocacy of anti-Semitism on British territory.* Schwarzbart made a major effort to counteract the impact of anti-Semitic propaganda carried out by some Polish political forces on the territory of Great Britain. Among these forces, a major role was played by the National Party which zealously pursued its traditional advocacy of anti-Semitism. Its newspaper *Jestem Polakiem* ("I am a Pole") distinguished itself in this respect, by carrying one Jew-baiting feature after another.

Advocacy of anti-Semitism on British territory in general and in the National Council in particular, repelled not only the Jewish leaders in Britain but also some British politicians. The public rebuttal of that advocacy was therefore harsh. Because of its impact, the National Party discontinued the publication of *Jestem Polakiem*; but in its place it very soon founded the new Nationalist journal *Mysl Polska* ("Polish Thought"). In the entry dated January 28, 1941, Schwarzbart commented:

> In place of the liquidated *Jestem Polakiem*, there will soon appear a new nationalist journal *Mysl Polska*. It will pretend to be devoted to literature, and on that ground it will qualify for a Government subsidy. The struggle of the Government against the *Jestem Polakiem* will thus terminate by granting a subsidy to its substitute.[10]

The Prime Minister of the Polish Government-in-Exile, along with a number of other Polish politicians, viewed the anti-Semitic propaganda of the National Party as a rather trifling matter. At the same time, however, they were extremely indignant about Jewish rejoinders to Polish anti-Semitism, on the assumption that they were intended to hurt Poland. Definite steps were also undertaken in order to suppress evidence of anti-Semitism so as to prevent its spreading to Poland. In this respect, the letter of June 11, 1941, from Stronski (then the Minister of Information and Documentation) to the Polish consul in Jerusalem is most enlightening:

> Highly esteemed Mr. Consul General:
> The Commission for the Polish Jews, operating from Jerusalem, has been distributing stencilled testimonies of Jews who succeeded in escaping from Poland. The so-called Internal Instruction appended to these testimonies states that they are intended for use by the press, with the proviso that the source is to be cited.
> There is extensive interesting evidence in these testimonies. The realities in Poland under the two occupations are usually portrayed accurately. But sometimes information crops up, that is supposed to prove that Polish society manifests anti-Semitism. Publicity for such testimonies is detrimental to Polish interests. The claim in question is incorrect, because reports of isolated anti-Semitic incidents, even if true, distort the general picture. In one testimony (by Dr. B. W., call number 51/121/12/13, protocols from December 1940) three southeastern districts are referred to as Western Ukraine. In this way the Polish character of this segment of the Republic is suspect.
> The Ministry of Information and Documentation requests exact information concerning the work of the above-mentioned Commission for Polish Jews. It also requests "that the protocols of the testimonies which this Commission disseminates be closely overseen."[11]

Schwarzbart interpreted the reluctance to oppose anti-Semitism as stemming from anti-Semitic leanings present also among politicians who stood far from the National Party in the political spectrum. In support of this interpretation, he refers to his June 6, 1941, conversation with Sikorski.

> I hope that everything will now work out satisfactorily. I've received a report from Ambassador Ciechanowski, to the effect of a relaxation in Polish-Jewish relationships in the United States after my visit there. Only for God's sake, don't annoy me with petty concerns and don't be over-sensitive, lest I myself become an anti-Semite.

Schwarzbart added his own comment on this statement:

> I have heard it from Sikorski already for the third time. His protestations reveal his leanings. I know that as late as a few days ago he had a talk with one of the British ministers to whom he suggested looking for territory in which Polish Jews could be resettled.[12]

From the beginning of 1941, the representatives of the Bund joined Schwarzbart in his efforts to mount pressure upon the Polish Government in matters of Jewish concern. For this purpose the Bund leaders arranged a meeting with Mikolajczyk and conferred with him on May 28, 1941. A letter to Mikolajczyk signed by Szlama Mendelson, Emmanuel Scherer and Shmuel Zygielbojm —

all three from the Bund — thus summarizes what transpired at that conference:

> To our sorrow, we are forced to conclude that the Polish Government has failed to find a befitting response to the ruthless persecution of the Jewish masses in Poland and to their heroic struggle for their liberation. The Government's solemn reassurances concerning the existence of equal rights for the Jews have been too vague, inadequate and untranslated into a practice which all too often remains affected by the tenets or by the habits of anti-Semitism.

In the same letter the leaders of the Bund called for the Polish government to meet the following demands:

1. To announce without equivocation that equal rights imply the need to repeal all discriminatory measures and procedures of prewar legislation;

2. To repudiate the assumptions of emigrationism;

3. To forward assistance to Jewish refugees;

4. To renounce advocacy of anti-Semitism;

5. To announce that the same standards will apply to the confiscation of Jewish and Polish businesses and to the pillage of Jewish and Polish property;

6. To condemn all the anti-Jewish measures of the occupier.

The full list of demands also included a seventh point, about admitting a representative of the Bund to the National Council.[13]

And then, tragic news began to arrive from Poland, which made all such efforts totally purposeless. The representatives of Polish Jewry in London were now confronted with entirely new tasks.

NOTES

1. YVA, M-2/747
2. YVA, M-2/12.
3. GSHI, PRM-K. 85.
4. YVA, M-2/746.
5. *Ibid.*
6. YVA, M-2/747.
7. *Ibid.*
8. YVA, M-4, pp. 8–10.
9. YVA, Bernfes documents.
10. YVA, M-2/747.
11. GSHI, A.9.5.2.
12. YVA, M-2/745.
13. YVA, M-2/517.

POLISH POLITICAL CIRCLES AND THE EXTERMINATION OF JEWS (JUNE 1941–DECEMBER 1942)

The commencement of the extensive operations aiming at the total extermination of the Jewish population coincided with the outbreak of the German-Soviet war in June 1941. In the territories of former eastern Poland now captured by the Germans, mass slaughters of Jews had already taken place in the first days of the war. Simultaneously, the living conditions in the ghettos of Central Poland deteriorated rapidly. In some ghettos, hunger and infectious diseases resulted in disastrously high levels of mortality. In December 1941 the first mass extermination camp was set up in Chelmno (on the Ner river, i.e. west from Lodz.) The next three were Belzec, Sobibor and Treblinka, established between the spring and summer of 1942. The biggest extermination camp — Auschwitz-Birkenau — was under construction in late 1941. By the end of 1942 the overwhelming majority of Polish Jews were already dead.

Information about the situation of the Jews in general, and about the development of the mass extermination in particular, was flowing from the Polish underground to the Government in London without major disruptions. Two media were involved: brief reports broadcast by radio and extensive reports (the so-called *Pro Memoria* dealing with conditions in Poland) sent by couriers. But evidence concerning Jews which these reports contained was rather scanty and fragmentary, especially when compared with evidence concerning the Poles. To all appearances for both the authors and the receivers of these reports, the Jewish issue was a rather secondary concern. Nevertheless, these reports do give a reasonably clear-cut picture of what was really happening as the Nazi extermination campaign unfolded.

One of the earliest reports on the subject was a *Pro Memoria* of October 1941, dealing with mass slaughters of the Jews in the Wilno district, perpetuated by the Lithuanians:

> Repugnant and horrifying news of brutal slayings of Jews by the Lithuanians have reached us from the Wilno district and from Lithuania. In those areas, groups of Lithuanians comprised chiefly of the *Shaulises*, of Lithuanian militia and of university and high school students have already managed to slay nearly the entire local Jewish population amounting to 170,000. In Wilno alone, of 90,000 Jewish residents of the local ghetto, the Lithuanians have already slain 30,000.[1]

The summary report covering the period from February 16 to February 28, 1942, mentions murders in Wilno, Kosow, Luck and Kiev (i.e. Babi Yar.)[2] More detailed evidence of the liquidation of the ghettos in the Lublin district can be found in another report covering the period up to April 1, 1942. Thus, for example, the report describes deportations from the Lublin ghetto during the night of March 23 to 24, 1942. The figures given are 2,500 Jews killed on the spot, and 26,000 sent in sealed railway cars to mass extermination camps in Belzec and Trawniki. In the words of the report, "There are sufficient grounds to conjecture that in those camps people are murdered en masse by poison gas."[3] Another report contains excerpts from an account written by a fugitive from Treblinka, who had been deported there from the Warsaw ghetto on September 7, 1942.[4] Finally, there is a special report of July 10, 1942, describing the killings of the Jews in Belzec.

Extensive information on living conditions of the Jews in the Warsaw ghetto and on the deportations from that ghetto can be found in the reports of the Delegate's Office. Furthermore these reports contain detailed evidence related to extermination from every region, virtually from the entire territory of Poland within its 1938 borders.

In January 1943 a report was sent to London which recapitulates what had been previously reported about the situation of the Jews. It says:

> As of the first days of 1943, the situation can be described as follows: The still surviving remnant of the masses of Jewish people continue to undergo physical annihilation. The employment of Jews no longer exists as a rational issue. The policy to isolate the Semites is no longer carried out either. All that remains is the chasing and the slaying of the remnant of survivors, an extermination that is absolute and ultimate.[5]

Extensive extermination-related evidence can also be found in the Polish clandestine press. Data derived from this source were periodically summarized by the Delegate's Office's Press and Information Department, and conveyed to the Government-in-Exile in condensed form. For the situation in occupied Poland in general, and for the extermination of the Jews in particular, these condensations are an important if auxiliary source.

Some examples of the coverage of extermination by the Polish clandestine press deserve attention. Thus, the Socialist paper *Barykada Wolnosci* ("The Barricade of Freedom") of June 1, 1942, provides an extensive description of the extermination of Jews in those Polish territories which were annexed to the Third Reich. The Jewish residents of these territories were being deported to be slain in the Chelmno camp. Following a detailed description of the methods of mass killings practiced in that camp, *Barykada Wolnosci* comments:

> The likelihood is very high that all the Jews from the territories annexed to the Reich will meet the same fate. Considering what is already known about the mass executions in the Ukraine, Byelorussia and Lithuania (100,000 Jews in Wilno alone!), we can scarcely doubt that we are confronted with a case of planned and systematic extermination of the Jewish people. . . .

This was the aim of setting up the ghettos. In Warsaw, out of the total population of 450,000, 60,000 ghetto residents died during the last year alone. . . . The fate of the Lodz ghetto is totally unknown, since the local ghetto is severed from the outside world completely. . . . The mystery surrounding the murders of Chelmno cannot be without a cause. Of course, it is not the Jews or even the Poles that Hitler is afraid of. He is afraid of a retaliation by the entire free world.

The chief organ of the Home Army *Biuletyn Informacyjny* ("Information Bulletin") of July 9, 1942, thus describes the conditions reigning in the Warsaw ghetto shortly before the deportations, starting with July 22 of that year:

Lately, the Germans find it fashionable to slay the Jewish "bandits" outright upon the city streets and to leave their remains on the pavement. This is the method of dealing with Jews caught outside of the ghetto walls: they are led inside to be shot in public view. The victims include the renowned movie producer H. Szpiro who supported himself by smuggling foodstuffs from southern Poland, as well as some leading figures of political or social organizations, like the chairman of a section of the Union of War Invalids, Gorka. On June 8 the number of people thus shot to death totaled sixty-four, on June 9, thirty people suffered the same fate. Eventually, they were buried on the Skra playground, after being stripped naked, without any identification being permitted. The ghetto residents were tormented and captive witnesses to these street killings, but the ghetto itself experienced macabre sensations as well. A German film production team arrived there to make a movie portraying negative (and stereotyped) Jewish characteristics such as uncleanliness, pornography and ritual baths.

In the issue of August 20, 1942, the same paper describes the events accompanying the mass deportations from the Warsaw ghetto in Treblinka:

As of this moment, over 200,000 ghetto residents have already been deported. Seven revenue agencies which until now busied themselves with extracting from the Jews all kinds of taxes, have been ordered to close their accounts by July 15 and to vacate their offices. The looting of property abandoned by its deported owners goes on all the time: with the German Police, the Lithuanians, the Ukrainians and the Latvians all taking their turns. Scuffles over the distribution of loot break out often. In one incident, several men serving in auxiliary detachments were shot. We succeeded in finding out that the way to kill people in the Treblinka camp is the gas chamber. For twenty-four hours a day, a dredging machine, brought for that sole purpose, digs a deep ditch. The corpses of the victims are then simply tossed into that ditch.

On the basis of all such information—whether arriving by radio or through the couriers—the Interior Ministry in exile published periodic reports describing the living conditions in the occupied Polish territories. The Interior Ministry reports were distributed to all the National Council deputies and to State officials of upper ranks. The time lag between the date of a covered event and the publication of a corresponding report would necessarily be considerable: no fewer than several months. The cabinest ministers, however, received their information about the events in Poland quite promptly: the most essential facts by radio, after a few days, and more extensive information from the reports carried directly by the couriers after several weeks. The National Council deputies, including the Jewish ones, had no access to this information. They had to rely mainly on the dated reports of the Interior Ministry.

The reports sent to the London Government by the subordinate organs of the Polish underground prove beyond any reasonable doubt that the Delegate's Office and the Home Army command, due to their country-wide network of cells, were immediately and accurately cognizant of all the German measures applied in occupied Poland against the Jews. By contrast, the leadership of the Jewish underground, operating in the ghettos isolated both from the surrounding cities and from other ghettos, had no access to accurate information. This is why the Polish underground and the Polish society at large had much more intimate knowledge of extermination-related developments than the Jewish underground and the Jewish society at large could have had under the extreme conditions of confinement in hundreds of ghettos and camps.

How then did the Polish political circles behave while witnessing the extermination of the Jews by the Germans?

Undeniably, neither the Polish underground nor the entire Polish society could possibly do anything to prevent the extermination. The slaughter would have continued even if all the Poles were perfectly warm-hearted towards their Jewish co-citizens. But the attitude of the Polish underground directly and decisively affected the prospects of survival for tens of thousands of Jews who succeeded in escaping from the ghettos during the deportations or from the camps. The leadership of Polish clandestine organizations was in the position to mold the attitudes of Polish society towards the fugitives and towards those who sought an opportunity to escape form a ghetto or from a camp. Furthermore, the underground was in a position to influence the Government-in-Exile. The relationships between the Government-in-Exile, the various strains within the Polish underground, and the Polish society were marked by mutual interconnections and mutual interdependence. We will now deal in succession with the attitudes of the underground, of the Government, and of the society at large until the end of 1942, i.e. during the crucial phase of extermination which engulfed the majority of the Polish Jews. The attitudes of the Polish society towards the remnant of Jews who sought to survive among the Poles in 1943–1944 will be discussed in the next chapters.

The Polish underground in confrontation with the extermination of the Jews

Until the fall of 1942, the Delegate's Office did nothing beyond reporting to London the actual process of extermination in detail. At that time, no assistance to the victims of extermination was yet envisaged. Both the Delegate's Office and the Home Army viewed themselves as authorized to represent and to defend the ethnic Poles alone. No initiatives to help Polish citizens of Jewish stock were under consideration at least until late in the fall of 1942. This is why both the Delegate's Office and the Home Army's command for a rather lengthy period refrained from any official response to the ongoing extermination. To compound the situation, the bulk of the political groups belonging to that section of the Polish underground which was subordinated to the Government-in-Exile continued to call for the emigration of Jews from Poland even when the extermination was already in high gear.

The primary concern of the leaders of the Polish underground revolved around the precautionary measures to be applied in the event of a German decision to exterminate the Polish population in a way already tested on the Jews. Apprehensions concerning this possibility find their emphatic expression in the memo sent by the Delegate's Office to London towards the end of 1942. Significantly, the memo does not discuss the extermination of the Jews at all. It merely presents the ideas circulating in the Polish underground about what could possibly be done to forestall the threat of the extermination of the Poles:

> The apparatus of German administration and police is firmly established, and the Polish masses are rather inactive. These two factors are likely to encourage the occupier to intensify and to accelerate the reign of terror. Apart from political effects, the increased anxiety is certain to bring enormous pay-offs through social and political exploitation. . . .
>
> One can no longer doubt the authenticity of Himmler's secret orders from last March and July. Too much of their content has already been corroboratd by events. The orders anticipate the final solution of the Jewish question in Eastern Europe before the end of this year. But they also anticipate the pacification of the Poles by extirpating the leading stratum of the country's population. While the world keeps its silence, the Poles are witnessing the rapid and efficient extermination of

several million Jews. And they await their own turn.

Already in the coming months, special demolition detachments which received their training in action against the Jews, are going to be used for the purpose of crushing all the resistance centers of the Polish nation. This is to be done by extirpating the leading strata and by reducing the rest to the condition of a listless herd toiling for their German masters. Such threats have been heard for some time, and their credibility grows each day. The focus of power is shifting in favor of the police and the Nazi party circles. It means that in the Government General Frank's influence is declining, while Krueger's is expanding. Krueger is a superior commander of the SS and police, and the State Secretary in charge of security. His concept of security is to massively exterminate all who are hostile towards Germany.

Increasingly people wonder what purpose an Allied victory in the war will serve, if an overwhelming majority of the Polish nation becomes extinct beforehand.

In view of the threat of mass murders, the concern with the fate of the nation, and especially with the fate of the intelligentsia, is shared by people from all walks of life. Under these conditions, the rather impulsive demands of retaliation for the acts of German terror become a natural response.[7]

Similar themes can be found in the report bearing the title "Poland in the fourth year of the war." The report was sent to London in September, 1942, and published there in the Interior Ministry pamphlet No. 6/421 on the situation in Poland:

The public lives in constant uncertainty over what will happen today or tomorrow. Anyone can be at a moment's notice caught in a roundup and deported to the Reich as a laborer, or evicted overnight from his apartment, or have his workshop or personal property confiscated, or otherwise fall prey to any one or more of the huge number of anti-Polish administrative measures of the Germans. Nothing can be known in advance. The mood of dejection reaches unprecedented intensities when one witnesses the dreadful and horrifying spectacles of the mass murders of Jews, perpetrated by the Germans and by their Latvian, Lithuanian and Ukrainian mercenaries; and when one hears rumors that the units trained in the soon to be concluded "liquidation" of the Jews will be next used by the Germans for launching aggravated terror against the Poles.[8]

Similar concerns can also be noticed in the resolution of the Democratic Party adopted at a special session of July 16, 1942. The resolution deals with the plans to extirpate the Polish population, and anticipates the necessity of moving from passive to active forms of resistance. Significantly, the resolution does not mention in a single word the extermination of the Jews then in progress.[9]

Concern over the prospect of exterminating the Poles in the same way as the Jews found its dramatic expression in a memorandum of the Peasant Union of Women to the Prime Minister of the Polish

Government-in-Exile, General Sikorski. The memorandum was published in the clandestine monthly organ of that Union *Zywia* ("The Ones Who Nourish") of August 1942:

> For several weeks we have been witnessing mass execution. Day after day, week after week, month after month people are being murdered. Whole families, whole groups. Women separately, men separately, children separately.
>
> It goes on in Warsaw, Lwow, Cracow, Lublin, Przemysl, Przeworsk. In hundreds of small towns. In hundreds of villages. It is being called the liquidation of the Jewish element. But we call it the murder of human beings.
>
> Every day thousands of people are being deported from Warsaw. Their destination is Belzec, Sobibor, Treblinka and Pelkiny.[10]
>
> Every day, masses of people are being poisoned by gas or by fumes of slaked lime in tightly locked freight cars, or machine-gunned, or buried while still half-alive, or chemically processed in underground factories.
>
> Every day, entire families commit suicide. Every day, mothers jump with their babies from upper floor windows to die on the pavement. Every day, children are driven to insanity. Or they try to flee; but then German, Latvian, Lithuanian and Ukrainian soldiery shoot them on ghetto streets like wild game. . . .
>
> Not many Jews are still left to be killed. But the unbridled beast is already prospecting for new victims.
>
> There have already been roundups of old beggars in south-central Poland of men and women alike.
>
> A mass execution of beggars has taken place near Lancut. Polish bread is precious. By eating it, an elderly Pole diminishes the ration of a German soldier. Therefore, the elderly Pole must die according to German logic.
>
> It is already rumored that orders will be given to kill the elderly right in their homes; no longer only on the streets.
>
> Tomorrow we will quiver over the lives of our fathers and mothers, in the way in which we are quivering today over the lives of our children.
>
> In Deblin, countless trains are being stopped, with all passengers driven away to unknown destinations.
>
> We watch it all the time, day after day.
>
> We await answers from you but none arrive.
>
> All that we hear is silence. We cannot believe that there are no bombs: Polish, British, American. Why, then, do you keep quiet?
>
> Our hearts are hardened and we become automatons. We can no longer feel anything. We can no longer cry. The tears are no more; and if blood still flows in our veins, it is only for the greater glory and integrity of the Polish soil, onto which it is going to gush.
>
> But we are still alive! We know how to die for Poland but we want to live for her! Tomorrow, we want to contribute to her recreation! This is why today we cry out and make demands.
>
> In retaliation for every bloody massacre in Poland, we demand air raids against German civilians.

In retaliation for every Polish orphanage or home for the elderly vacated by German murderers we demand one German city reduced to rubble.

In retaliation for every dozen of hanged or executed Poles, we demand dozens upon dozens of executed Germans.

This is what we want to hear by radio. Every day we pray to the Lord to make the German mothers wail in despair. We want our prayer fulfilled; we want to see the German women wailing; not laughing scornfully as we see them now all the time; laughing on the streets, laughing in streetcars, laughing even behind the walls of neighboring apartments.

Stop offering us token expressions of appreciation. Stop extolling our sacrifices. Stop imploring us to persevere because we have developed the art of persevering to perfection. But instead convince the Allied governments to give you free rein and the requisite resources to strike immediately with retaliatory raids. Hasn't our air force grown stronger now than before the war? Why, then, shouldn't the Allies agree to its deployment? Then, strike with formidable power so as to make the explosions in German houses resound. We wish to hear these explosions too, so that our hearts will be bolstered by the recognition of our strength. Perhaps we can summon a breath of fresh air to our lungs in the realization that we are not descending alone into the abyss.

There surely must be avengers to come forward in our defense.

This is how our military report reads today, General. The report submitted to you on the occasion of the Soldier's Day, on the occasion of the Day of the Peasant Deed. Pay attention to this report, General!

Polish anxieties of that time are also reported in German documents. Thus for instance the governor of the Warsaw district describes in the following terms the situation in his district during the months of June and July, 1942 in a report dated August 15 of that year and sent to the Government General authorities:

In the period covered by the present report the attitudes of the Polish population have remained basically the same as before. One can still describe these attitudes as passive. . . .

The Polish public is perfectly cognizant of the resettlement of the Jewish residential district in Warsaw. But the feelings are rather mixed. There is little recognition of the fact that the resettlement was intended to serve Polish interests. Instead, the response was a welter of most fantastic rumors. Fed by the propaganda of the resistance movement, many Poles have come to believe that after the deportations of the Jewish population, their turn will come. Among the citizens of Warsaw, apprehensions to this effect are rampant.[12]

The Delegate's Office finally did find it opportune to come forward with an official statement on the extermination of Jews. But the statement was drafted after the overwhelming majority of Polish Jews had already been murdered by the Nazis. It assumed the rather modest form of a protest resolution of the Leadership of

Civilian Struggle, published in the Home Army's clandestine organ
Biuletyn Informacyjny ("Information Bulletin") of September 17,
1942; i.e. 5 days after the termination of the nearly two months-long
deportations of Warsaw ghetto Jews to Treblinka, and nine months
after the establishment of the first extermination camp in Chelmno.
The resolution states:

> The Polish society is being decimated by the enemy. But alongside of
> that tragedy, another unfolds. For almost an entire year, Jews are being
> systematically slain in our country by dreadful methods. This mass
> murder has no precedent in the history of the world. All historically
> recorded atrocities pale by comparison. Infants, children, youth, adults,
> the elderly, the infirm, the sick, the healthy, male, female, the con-
> verted and unconverted alike are ruthlessly murdered, poisoned by
> gas, buried alive or pushed from windows to the pavement. Before
> dying, they all undergo the torment of slow agony, the inferno of being
> pursued while having no home, the cynical and unbridled harassment
> by their executioners. The number of victims killed by such methods
> already exceeds one million, and it grows day by day.
>
> The Leadership of Civilian Struggle has no way of stopping the
> crimes perpetrated upon the Jews. But it denounces these crimes
> vigorously, in the name of the entire Polish society. All Polish political
> and social organizations join us in this condemnation.
>
> The executioners and their accomplices will be made personally
> responsible for these crimes, in the same way as for the crime
> perpetrated against the Polish victims.

The resolution of the Leadership of Civilian Struggle therefore
took the form of a protest, on the assumption that the Polish underground had no choice but to remain inactive while the extermination of the Jews in Polish territory was in progress. This assumption
was echoed in the order No. 71 of the Home Army commander-in-
chief, General Rowecki, dated November 10, 1942. The order anticipates a counteraction only if Nazi exterminatory measures fall
upon a population of ethnic Poles.

> 1. Polish society is apprehensive that in the aftermath of the current
> extermination of the Jews, the Germans may proceed in the application
> of similar methods of extermination against the Poles. I call for restraint
> and for counter-balancing the apprehensions with reassuring persu-
> asions. The chief German objective in regard to us can be described as
> the absorption of our nation. Attempts to exterminate the resistant
> segments of our nation by methods applied against the Jews cannot,
> however, be ruled out.
>
> 2. In the event the Germans indeed undertake such attempts, they
> will encounter our resistance. Irrespective of the scheduled timing of
> our uprising, the units under my command shall proceed to armed
> struggle in defense of the life of the nation. In the course of the struggle,
> we shall switch from defense to attack, with the aim of undercutting the
> entire network of enemy lines to the Eastern front. This decision of

mine shall be communicated to all ranks of the clandestine armed forces.

3. In order to prevent possible enemy provocations, I assign to myself the exclusive authority to make decisions concerning the timing and the location of hostilities.

4. I order the area and district commanders:

  a. to report to me without delay all confirmed instances of application against the Poles of the methods of mass extermination which the Germans currently apply against the Jews;

  b. to brace ourselves for rapid and efficient initiation of hostilities in a designated area, depending upon my orders:

  c. to comply with points (a) and (b) so as to rule out any disruption or any exposure of preparations for the uprising.[13]

No sooner than towards the end of 1942, when almost all the ghettos in Poland were already vacated, and not without insistent pressures on the part of Jewish spokesmen, was set up the Council for Aiding Jews. Resources allocated to the Council were rather meager, as compared to what the Delegate's Office was in the position to mobilize for the purpose. The activities of the Council for Aiding Jews were therefore circumscribed. Nonetheless, the Council did contribute to saving the lives of several thousands of Jews hiding on the Aryan side, mainly in Warsaw, and of somewhat fewer numbers also in Cracow, Lwow, and several other towns. The circumstances of the formation of the Council for Aiding Jews and its activities will be described in considerable detail in a separate chapter.

By way of recapitulation, it can therefore be stated that from the middle of 1941 till the end of 1942, when the masses of Polish Jewry were already undergoing extermination, the leadership of the Polish underground acting under the orders of the Polish Government-in-Exile, assumed an official position implying total inaction vis-a-vis the Jews. At the same time, however, the prospect of extending the exterminatory measures to the ethnically Polish population was recognized as calling for active counter-measures on the part of the underground. The limited initiative of the Polish underground to proffer aid to the Jews begins no earlier than towards the end of 1942. At exactly the same time, however, a section of the Polish underground volunteered to lend their hand to actions against the Jews. The aid proffered to the Jews and the active participation in anti-Jewish undertakings can be described as the two opposite poles of the Polish underground's behavior. Both will receive a more extensive treatment in the next chapter. In this chapter, we will confine ourselves to the analysis of the reasons for inactivity of the Delegate's Office and the Home Army command until the end of 1942, i.e. throughout the time the bulk of Polish Jewry was already undergoing extermination.

The Polish historian Jerzy Janusz Terej, who investigated the history of the National Party during the Nazi occupation, thus describes the attitude of that party towards the Jews in the period of their extermination.

> The leadership of the party did reject the genocidal practices of the extermination of the Jews as contrary to the principles of Christian ethics. But it never revised its anti-Semitic program. Confronted with the tragedy which befell millions of their Polish compatriots, the Party leadership found it opportune to emphasize in its press and propaganda the Party's reservations about the London Government's Jewish policies. (In instructions and memos intended for internal circulation, those reservations were presented with much greater vituperation.) Even more importantly, the Party throughout this period continued to call for "restraint" in manifesting compassion for the Jewish victims of extermination. This attitude found its emphatic expression in the article bearing the title "The triangle of our enemies bursts"[14] which was simultaneously published in a number of the Party organs in September 1942, i.e. at a time when the unprecedented large scale deportations from the Warsaw ghetto had already lasted for more than a month, and when the systematic biological extinction of the Jewish population by the Nazis had reached all corners of the country."[15]

One can learn from Terej's study that the National Party under Nazi occupation disseminated the Protocols of the Elders of Zion. In the milieu of sympathizers of the Party, the Protocols won quite a wide readership.[16]

In January 1943 the so-called All-Polish Congress of the National Party convened in Warsaw. According to Terej:

> The Congress proclaimed itself to be the supreme authority of the Party in wartime, on the ground that the elected authorities of the Party had held no single session since June 25, 1939, when the Central Council of the National Party convened for the last time. The attendance at the Congress amounted to about 100 delegates. . . . Under the conditions of clandestinity, it was a genuine organizational accomplishment.[17]

The Congress passed a number of resolutions on constitutional matters, on economy, on national minorities. Here are the excerpts which contain references to the Jews:

> In the cities, the functions performed to date by the Germans and by the Jews will now have to be performed by the Polish farmers.[18]
>
> A premature uprising is contrary to the interests of our nation. It would serve the interests of Communism and of Jewry.[19]

In a separate resolution dealing with agriculture, the Congress did call for redistribution of land ownership. But priority was assigned to the partitioning of "lands owned by foreigners, Jewish and German."[20] Likewise, according to section two of the resolution on rural economic development, "Jews and Germans shall be barred from ownership of real estate."[21] On the basis of these resolutions, the so-called National Party's Legal Expert Teams were to proceed to study the problem defined as "The take-over of Jewish and German immobile property."[22]

All this talk portended worse to come: the pursuit and murder of Jews in hiding, and the attacks on Jewish partisans. In this respect, the activities of the National Party became quite extensive in scale.

In addition, the press of the Peasant Party was by no means free from anti-Semitic overtones. Thus, for instance, in issue No. 11 of the organ of the party *Ku zwyciestwu* ("Toward the Victory") of April 30, 1942, the following statements can be found:

> The Jewish question is an international question. The growth of the Jewish mass in Poland to its present size is an outcome of persecutions and expulsions of Jews from other countries. This gives us the innate right to demand from the entire world a concern with and participation in our efforts to devise solutions to the Jewish question.
>
> The Polish Government ought to raise the Jewish question in the international forum. Its speedy and effective solution must be guaranteed by peace treaties.

Another organ of the Peasant Party, *Orka* ("Plowing") in its issue No. 8 (16) of December 25, 1942, published an article under the title "Are we racists?" The article demands legislation against "cross-hybridization of races." Here is an excerpt:

> For our ignorance of these problems and for our inability to apply the rules of social hygiene, history will yet appraise our era as barbarian. In recognition of this, we now declare that we will demand that the marriage laws of future Poland include measures protecting the nation from degeneracy.

But it was a group which opposed the Government-in-Exile and its Delegate's Office, viz. the National-Radical Camp, which excelled in advocacy of anti-Semitism in its crudest and most blatant forms. The anti-Jewish abuse reached its zenith in the National-Radical organ *Szaniec* ("Rampart"). Here is a sample:

From the issue of January 31, 1942:

> The Jews were, are, and will be our enemies always and everywhere.... Hence the question must be posed, how shall we treat them?... To this question we have but one answer: as enemies. And certainly no fewer than 90% of the Poles agree with us on that score.... The two last Polish constitutions guaranteed equal rights for

all the residents of the state, therefore also for national minorities. It was a fundamental mistake. There is only one correct solution, devoid of diffidence and false shame: to grant political rights to Poles alone.

From the issue of April 15, 1942, an excerpt from a long article under the title "A problem of confinement for health reasons":

> There are decaying and unhealthy peoples which must be placed under tutelage lest they become peril and a disaster for civilization. The outstanding examples of such nations are the Jews, the Germans, and the Russians.

> . . .

The same article, further on states:

> We haven't put up a fight with either the Jews or the Russians. But now, the Germans are exterminating both of them more thoroughly and efficiently than anyone, including ourselves, would be capable of. . . .

And additionally:

> There is no point in long deliberations on the subject of the Jews. We know them all too well. Eventually, they may yet prove capable of joining the community of peace-loving nations; but no sooner than when their taste for revolutions is stamped out without a trace, and no sooner than when the ashes of their professional revolutionaries fertilize the sterile fallows of the Jewish soul.[23]

> . . .

Issue No. 13 of October 21, 1942 comes up with full approval of Nazi extermination:

> The German-made pogroms of Jews in Poland follow all the rules of modern technology. The job is well done. The outstanding Jewish writer Shalom Asch would invent nothing better to murder the Poles.

Another organ of the National-Radical Camp, *Placowka* ("Outpost"). Issue No. 44 of October 21, 1942:

> Now is the time to resolve that no Jews shall live in Poland any more. This can be done by legislation prohibiting Jewish settlement. The prohibition will hurt no one. It will imply no more than an exercise of the right of the host who permits no one else but decent visitors to cross the threshold of his home. All the Jews who survive the current pogroms will under this law have to leave Poland. And along with them, all the mixed-bloods who in vain try to conceal their hatred of the Poles, who remain strangers amongst us, and who are of no use to us, will have to leave Poland as well.

On November 26, 1942, an article appeared in *Szaniec*, bearing the title "Beware of the promises." The article criticized the statement made by the Polish Prime Minister, General Sikorski at a rally in London organized in protest against the Nazi mass murders of the Jews. Sikorski said:

As a head of the Polish Government I declare that the Jewish citizens of Poland will after the war be entitled to an equal share in all the benefits and in all the achievements, on the same terms as other Polish citizens. As a soldier I warn Hitler that all acts of violence and harrassment committed against the citizens of Poland will in due time be avenged.

Quoting this statement, *Szaniec* retorted:

General Sikorski's softness on the point of the Jews is well known. Something else, however, is not known the extent to which his softness is being reciprocated, and will continue to be reciprocated in the future. We would voice no objection, had General Sikorski taken part in a Jewish rally as a private person. But he made it explicit that he spoke in the capacity of the Prime Minister of the Polish Government and Commander-in-Chief of the Polish Army. The point is that statesmen are supposed to be capable of controlling their emotions; or at the very least to avoid placing themselves in situations which cause their emotions to take an upper hand. . . .

But what about the rights of the Jews, and about avenging and rewarding them for their sufferings? In the first place, their present plight has nothing to do with their status as Polish citizens. In the second place, it needs to be determined to which Jews the references apply: those who are being murdered under the German occupation, or those who were murdering the Poles under Soviet occupation. Both were Polish citizens. . . .

In any event, decisions in those matters cannot be made by a Prime Minister, in London or even in Warsaw. Such decisions will be made by millions of genuine Polish citizens who, for the privilege of being Polish citizens, have paid and continue to pay to the Germans and to the Jews the price in blood and property.

Finally, *Szaniec* of January 1, 1943, greeted the New Year in the following fashion:

To Poland and to all the Poles we wish Divine protection from hunger, fire, plague and democracy. For only then, will we be able to protect ourselves from the Germans from the West, from the Russians from the East and from the Jews in our midst.[24]

But there existed organizations which denounced Polish anti-Semitism in the sharpest of terms. One of these was the Catholic Front Odrodzenia Polski (Front of Polish Rebirth). Thus, for instance, in the issue No. 2 of its organ *Prawda* ("Truth") of May 1942 there appeared an article under the title "Prophecies are being fulfilled." Here is an excerpt:

The slaughter of innocent Jews is capable of reducing us to the point of utter corruption and savagery. It is not only the *Shaulises*, the *Volksdeutsche* or the Ukrainians who serve as accomplices in the most horrendous executions. In many localities it was the local populace who volunteered to take part in the massacres. The disgrace must be eradicated by whatever means are available: by persuasions, by condemnations in the clandestine press, by surrounding the executioners with social ostracism, by reminding the murderers of the harshest of penalties that are going to be meted out by the courts of the free Republic.

The Polish Worker's Party which stood in left-wing opposition to the Delegate's Office, responded to the extermination of Jews in a different way than was usual for parties represented in that Office. The Party, which before 1942 did not even exist, was during that year still a newcomer to clandestine operations. Its following in Polish society was in that period still quite small. Accordingly, its capability to influence the attitudes of Polish society towards the exterminated Jews was at that time highly problematic.

The political program of the Polish Worker's Party was for the first time laid down in March 1942 in the clandestine pamphlet "What is to be done." Like the Polish Socialist Party, the program called for fully equal rights for the Jews.

Information about the developments during the 1942 liquidation of the ghettos is quite scarce in the Polish Worker's Party's press. Also, the crystallization of the exact viewpoint on this issue was rather late in coming. The first document defining the position of the Party on extermination is the article under the title "The Pogrom of Jews in Warsaw" which appeared in its chief organ *Trybuna Wolnosci* ("Tribune of Freedom") of August 1, 1942. Here is an excerpt:

> The occupier knows of no mercy and no compromise. To defend their lives, the Jews must match him in their intransigence. They must be courageous, heroic, totally indifferent towards death. Waiting for the moment of slaughter in resignation won't help. Only active and stubborn resistance in any contingency is capable of saving thousands and perhaps tens of thousands, at whatever cost in casualties. Let the heroic resistance of the Jews in Nowogrodek and other towns be an example to follow. In Nowogrodek, the heroism of a few individuals brought rescue to thousands already led to their death. What needs to be done is to force one's way out of the ghetto and out of Warsaw—to the forests where the enemy can be fought more effectively. The police must be resisted. Every house must become a fortress. The convoy escort must be overpowered. One must flee to partisan detachments. All this is very difficult to do, but possible. Nothing else can guarantee survival.[25]

The article appeared when the mass deportation had already been under way in the Warsaw ghetto. Of course, it failed to reach the Jewish underground, let alone the Jewish population at large. Contentwise, the article conformed to the general political line of the Polish Worker's Party which called for the Polish society to proceed immediately to broad-scale armed struggles against Nazi occupiers. At that point in time, however, such appeals were altogether out of touch with reality. Polish society was as yet entirely unprepared for any armed resistance, no matter how limited in scale. As for the Jews, there was absolutely no way in which their heroism, no matter how great or how common, could succeed in saving the masses. The cited example of Nowogrodek was total fiction. Still, the article concluded with an appeal to the Poles to lend the Jews a helping hand:

All Poles have the duty to help persecuted Jews. Those who rejoice at these persecutions or support them in any way, are either vicious or ignorant, for they don't realize that after the Jews, the "resettlement" of the Poles "to the East" will begin. The Poles must unite with the Jews in active efforts to frustrate the horrendous schemes of the brown-shirted executioners of both nations.[26]

These words were not backed by deeds. In the wake of this appeal, no concrete steps were undertaken by the Polish Worker's Party to deliver the called-for aid. No organizational forms were established for that purpose. All that was done, were the scattered acts of helping individual fugitives from ghettos and camps, and the likewise scattered acts of support for some Jewish partisan detachments. The latter will be discussed in the next chapter.

Trybuna Wolnosci of August 15, 1942, came out with a second article on the subject of extermination. This article (its title was "The planned extermination of the Jewish people") makes it even clearer that the Polish Worker's Party's propagandistic notions about the extermination of the Jews served the purpose of the advocacy of the immediate transition to direct armed struggles. But this article, too, calls for offering aid to Jews:

The pogrom of Jews in Poland has the quality of a preliminary probing operation, intended to test the behavior of conquered nations. The pogroms help the police apparatus to become more efficient, and to intimidate the populace to the point of paralysis. The gangs of *Shaulises* and Latvian fascists, well-trained in beastly murders, are preparing and are desirous for a succession of new assignments. The crimes against the Jews are therefore to be looked upon as a poignant warning for all the conquered nations. . . .

The aim of the Germans is to divide the nations living under their yoke. Our aim is to unite them for the common struggle. This is why the pogrom against the Jews in the ghettos is a defeat for the Polish nation. The Jews must be morally and materially assisted in all possible forms. They must be encouraged to flee the ghettos. The fugitives must be sheltered. The struggle "for our freedom and yours" must be intensified.

The crimes against the Jews must therefore be seen by the Polish nation as a warning. Conclusions must be drawn and the tasks in the struggle defined. The nation's capacity to survive depends on its attitude. During the impending assault of the occupier upon the entire nation, scattered acts of desperation will not save us. Our struggle must be collective and effective, prudently planned and well-organized. The only path to survival and freedom is through the unity of the nation in an active and immediate armed struggle.[27]

Several articles published in the clandestine press of the Polish Worker's Party excoriated the pervasive anti-Semitism of part of the Polish underground. In the Party's theoretical organ *Przelom*("Breakthrough") of October-November 1942 an article authored by Wladyslaw Bienkowski appeared under the title "Conclusions to be drawn," we read:

A fraction of the Polish society watches the murders of Jews as if there were no need to be concerned. Another fraction rejoices that "an alien element is being extricated from the Polish body." Some go as far as to cooperate actively with the murderers. Long years of efforts of native reactionaries, long centuries of the cumulative impact of retrograde and noxious social forces have succeeded in producing this insensitivity with which the Polish society now responds to a preponderance of the Nazi crimes.

And on December 15, 1942, *Trybuna Wolnosci* rebuked the entire leadership of the Polish underground connected with the Government-in-Exile for confining its response to the extermination to verbal protests, like the resolution of the Leadership of the Civilian Struggle of September 17, 1942 noted above:

When Jews were being murdered, the Leadership of Civilian Struggle kept silence. It issued nothing more than a meager verbal protest when it was already all over.

The Polish Government-in-Exile
in confrontation with the extermination of the Jews.

Owing to the reports arriving from the underground in Poland, the members of the Government-in-Exile had access to detailed and updated information about German mass murders of Jews, first on newly-occupied Eastern territories, and then in mass extermination camps. However anti-Semitic programs espoused by many of these leaders were hardly revised despite the impact of this news. The Jewish question continued to play its unsavory role in the in-fighting between the political parties represented in the Government and in the National Council. Anti-Semitic pronouncements in the National Council and in speeches and writings authored by

Polish politicians continued to be widespread. Various schemes of anti-Semitic legislation, like the forced emigration of Jews or their removal from positions of economic influence, or even the retention of the ghettos continued to be designed for implementation in future Poland when freed of its subjugation by Germans. Elaboration of such schemes did not cease even when there was hardly a ghetto remaining in Poland.

The National Party continued to function as a moving force behind anti-Semitic advocacy and behind schemes of anti-Semitic legislation in the National Council and the Government. In October 1941 the leaders of Polish political parties were engaged in negotiations intended to bring the National Party back into the Government coalition. The former National Party cabinet minister, Seyda, was in favor of returning to the Government. But another leader of the party, Bielecki, was opposed; and he ultimately prevailed. Negotiations were broken off. From a leader of the Labor Party, minister Popiel, Schwarzbart received a briefing on why the negotiations failed. This is what Popiel said to Schwarzbart:

> At the present moment negotiations have broken off. The reason is Bielecki's principled opposition on three points. First, against the very commitment to democracy. Second, against the motion of the three remaining parties concerning the voting regulations. And third, against the passage in the draft of the proposed agreement, which dealt with the protection of national minorities, especially the Jewish minority. Bielecki forced Seyda to resign because Seyda had voted in favor of granting equal rights to the Jews.[28]

The National Party politicians were not alone in seeking to remove the Jews from liberated Poland, or to prejudice their citizenship rights in as many ways as possible. Politicians belonging to other parties also busied themselves with such projects. To make matters worse, some official agencies of the Government-in-Exile also contributed their efforts to designing measures of this nature.

Instructive in this respect is the conversation Schwarzbart had with Stanislaw Grabski on October 21, 1941, soon after the latter arrived in London from prison in the Soviet Union. Schwarzbart made a shorthand record of this conversation. Here is an excerpt from this record:

> I submitted to the Government a memo dealing with our current policies. In the constitutional project, we included a separate ruling aiming at elimination of hatreds between social classes, religious denominations and nationalities. On the other hand, the Jewish question calls for a solution which must be achieved in the spirit of good will and civility.

If economic realities are different, if there is enough bread for all, there will be bread for the Jews too. But if economic realities are harsh, and if they can be improved by emigration, how can you expect me to advocate the emigration of Poles—of Polish peasants, for example—rather than Jews? It would be impossible.[29]

On December 10, 1941, Schwarzbart met Katelbach, an Information Minister official in charge of the area of Central Europe. The problematics of Polish Jews lay within the field of this man's formal experience. As Schwarzbart notes in his diary, Katelbach "does not envisage that a solution of the Jewish question in Poland might be reached by mutual consent. He is utterly worried that the state of affairs which reigned in prewar Poland may reappear in the Poland of the future. He thinks the Nazis may have possibly succeeded in leaving an indelible imprint upon the young generation of Poles."[30]

Katelbach authored a plan of resettling a considerable number of Polish Jews in an area of Eastern Germany that would be expressly designated for this purpose. The territory would be under international control, but Poland would exercise special authority there.[31]

On December 11, 1941, Schwarzbart met Kraczkiewicz, an official of the Polish Foreign Ministry in charge of Jewish affairs. In that capacity, Kraczkiewicz busied himself with designing schemes for Jewish emigration independently of the ones designated by Katelbach: the difference being that the former acted on behalf of the Foreign Ministry, while the latter functioned on behalf of the Information Ministry. The meeting with Kraczkiewicz is recorded in Schwarzbart's diary as follows:

> In the morning I received the Foreign Ministry official in charge of Jewish affairs, Mr. Kraczkiewicz. He remained in conference with me for nearly two hours. We discussed the Jewish question and all of its implications. Kraczkiewicz clearly defined the Jewish question as a matter of population size. It was easy to see his motive. His problem is how to prevail upon the Jewish circles to come to a voluntary agreement with Poland on the subject of the emigration of masses of Jews to Palestine or anywhere else. Kraczkiewicz reassured me, of course, that he was unequivocally for equal rights. He also fully agreed with my views of economic matters; specifically with my suggestion, that whatever is ultimately decided upon restratification of the Jews, all their lost property must first be returned to them, without exceptions. He welcomed my suggestions on restratification. But then he expressed an apprehension that was quite revealing. He said that much as one may resent Nazism, one has to take into consideration its possible influence upon Polish attitudes towards the Jews.[32]

Schwarzbart was bent on going from one Polish politician to another in order to probe their positions on the Jewish question. Next after Kraczkiewicz, he met the chief army chaplain Kaczynski, a priest with the rank of colonel. Kaczynski formulated his views on the Jewish question as follows:

I envisage no solution of the Jewish question other than the outflow of one million to one million-and-a-half Jews from future Poland. There have been plans to designate some stretches of Polish land for Jewish settlement. I consider all such plans quite illusory. For me, the best solution is to settle the Polish Jews in Bessarabia. Mind you, there are about 200,000 Poles in Bukovina. A part of Bukovina where they live would be annexed to Poland, with the local Jews being permitted to reside. The remainder of Bukovina could be incorporated into Bessarabia.

There are hardly any Rumanians there. So Bessarabia would be incorporated into Russia, and Russia's agreement to Jewish settlement there can be counted upon as certain. I've been to Palestine. I was even quite cordially received in Tel Aviv, but I toured the country and I don't think any mass colonization could succeed there. One would need to nibble the soil bare from its crust. It would last for generations and take enormous sums of money. Since we need to settle the problem fast, I propose Bessarabia. For the Jews it would be a blessing, because Bessarabia has some of the most fertile land in Europe.[33]

Kaczynski presented his plans of Jewish colonization to the ambassador of the Soviet Union in Washington, Litvinov, and to Rumanian representatives in London. He relayed the content of his conversation with Litvinov to Schwarzbart during the second meeting on June 2, 1942. Kaczynski then told Schwarzbart (version as recorded in Schwarzbart's diary):

I presented to Litvinov my plans of settling the Polish Jews in Bessarabia. Litvinov was taken by surprise, but he made notes and promised to convey the matter to his government. While presenting my ideas, I stressed that Bessarabia, although a part of Russia, would be administered by Poland and Russia jointly for the benefit of the colonization of those Jews who would opt for settlement there. Litvinov, surprised, pointed out that my proposal of joint administration of a territory belonging to the Soviet Union implied an expansion of Polish influence at Soviet expense. He asked what grounds I have for nourishing such hopes.[34]

On June 2, 1942, Kaczynski went to present his plan of the solution of the Jewish question to the National Council. In his presentation there, he stressed his belief in the unfeasibility of the establishment of a Jewish state in Palestine.[35]

Schwarzbart: But do you anticipate that Russia will cede Bessarabia to Poland, Father?

Kaczynski: Nothing is impossible. We should act in concert. One thing that I know is that the Jews are attached to Poland. I've seen this attachment everywhere. No wonder the Jews would like to remain in Poland. But as a realistic politician, I take realities into account.[36]

The ambivalence of the Polish Government-in-Exile on Jewish issues can be accounted for by two conflicting considerations. On the one hand, the Government feared that public opinion in Poland, crudely anti-Semitic as it basically was, might blame it for being too good for the Jews. On the other hand, it badly wanted to appear as committed to democracy and to equal rights for national minorities in the eyes of Western public opinion.[37]

The conflict between these considerations is characteristically revealed by two successive briefs of Prime Minister Sikorski to the Government's Delegate in Poland. In his Brief No. 5 of September 15, 1942, Sikorski wrote:

> It reached my attention that the followers of Pilsudski acting in concert with the National Radicals are apparently intensifying their activities in Poland. As an outcome of this, totally baseless rumors are apparently being spread concerning the subject of my policies towards the Soviet Union. It is sheer demagoguery, falsehood from beginning to end. The Government is also being reproached for its exuberantly pro-Jewish stand. . . .[38]

And in his Brief No. 6 of October 14, 1942, Sikorski wrote:

> The Polish Government recently firmly denounced the measures taken against the Polish Jews in unoccupied France. Through its diplomatic outposts, the Government has extended its protection over those people since they are Polish citizens. Laval's Government is condemned by a consensus of French opinion for its servility towards the Germans. Anti-Semitism has no support in France even among the right-wingers. The leading Catholic circles also oppose anti-Semitism.
>
> I request an intensification of the advocacy of democratic ideals in Poland to the maximum extent possible. After all, this is our aim in fighting this war.[39]

In the meantime increasingly ghastly reports of the progress in the extermination of Jews continued to arrive from occupied Poland. The Polish Government-in-Exile, however, continued to apply different standards to reports of terror against ethnic Poles and to reports of the extermination of the Jews. The former were conveyed to public attention with rapidity and with all possible details. The dissemination of the latter, however, was stalled at first for a considerable period of time, to become next deliberately delayed; and contentwise the reports were rather vague, and biased in the sense of the consistent underestimation of the extent of the disaster. Interestingly, the clandestine organ of the Polish Socialist Party *Robotnik* ("The Worker") spelled out the principles governing the dissemination of atrocity reports as early as May 1, 1943:

We recall that events of a hundred-fold less importance were known in London promptly and broadcast to all corners of the world. But about the recent extermination of the Jews which claimed one and a half million casualties, the world only learned after it was all over. The travesty of the aid of the so-called Government bodies, which was administered by the members of the National Party, arrived like the proverbial mustard after the meal had already been consumed.[40]

An example is a case of underestimating the scope of extermination. It occurred in the National Council speech of July 7, 1942, by Mikolajczyk, then the Interior Minister. Following a lengthy and detailed presentation of German atrocities against the Poles, Mikolajczyk said:

> The conditions of the Jews are even worse. Everybody knows about the ghetto of Warsaw. The pictures which we have received are extremely revealing. Disease, hunger and death decimate the Jewish population steadily and systematically. During the night of March 23/24 the entire Jewish population of Lublin was driven to one site. The sick and the infirm were killed on the spot. 108 children from a local orphanage, ranging in age from two to nine were driven to the outskirts of the city and murdered there, together with the nurses. The total number of casualties of that night amounts to 2,500; the remaining 26,000 were deported to the camps in Belzec and Trawniki. In Izbica Kujawska 8,000 persons were deported to an unknown destination. The murders in Belzec and Trawniki were apparently perpetrated by means of a poison gas. Mass murders also occurred in Rawa Ruska and in Bilgoraj. In both localities the Jewish communities exist no more. In Wawolnica, near Kazimierz, on March 22 SS men shot 120 persons on the main square, while an unknown number were murdered after being driven outside the town. On March 30, the Jews were forced to march from Opole to Naleczow, 350 were killed on the road; while the remainder were put in sealed box cars and deported. In Mielec on March 9, 1,300 persons were killed. In Mir there were 2,000 Jews murdered, in Nowogrodek 2,500, in Wolozyn 1,800, in Kajdanow 4,000. 30,000 Jews from Hamburg arrived in Minsk: all were shot. The number of Jews murdered in Lwow is estimated at 30,000, in Wilno 60,000, in Stanislawow 15,000, in Tarnopol 5,000, in Zloczow 2,000, and in Brzezany 4,000. Mass murders are also reported from Tarnow, Radom, Zborow, Kolomyja, Sambor, Stryj, Drohobycz, Zbaraz, Brody, Przemysl, Kolo, and Dabie. . . .
>
> The estimate of known casualties among the Poles who perished or who were murdered or tormented to death exceeds 200,000 today. The figure for murdered Jews can be reliably estimated as also close to 200,000.[41]

The account gives some conception of the ghastly methods of Nazi genocide. But the sum total of 200,000 murdered Jews is a vast understatement. By that time Mikolajczyk could not fail to realize that the actual figure was already several times as high. But not only on this occasion did he underreport the already known casualty figures, while obscuring the realities by resorting to imprecise descriptions. He did the same at the press conference convened in London on July 9, 1942, by the Polish Information Ministry. During tht conference, Mikolajczyk said:

> You will certainly be shocked by the figure of Polish citizens who have been shot, or murdered in other ways, which numbers over 400,000. It is almost certain that the figure is in reality still higher, but I restrict myself to those cases which are documented. One year ago the figure was 80,000, later it was 100,000 and then 140,000, and then in the last two months it has risen to 400,000 murdered Poles and Jews. There were two reasons for this increase: first, the tremendous increase in the terror applied to the Poles, and secondarily, the beginning of the wholesale extermination of the Jews. . . .[42]

The term "wholesale extermination" corresponded perfectly to realities and proved Mikolajczyk to be well aware of Nazi intentions. Yet the figures he cited were grossly underrated, and they could not fail to misrepresent badly the actual horror of the situation. And yet, despite the underestimation of the number of victims, it was the Polish Government-in-Exile which transferred to the free world the first information of the mass extermination of the Jews.

In the middle of October 1942 the Polish diplomatic representatives in Istanbul reported to the Foreign Ministry in London that the Jewish leaders had already received reliable information on mass deportations from the Warsaw and other ghettos to extermination camps. On October 15, 1942, the report was immediately conveyed by the Foreign Ministry to the President, the Prime Minister and the Deputy Prime Minister.[43]

The Polish authorities in exile made up their minds to confirm the reports. This was the origin of the public protest demonstration that took place in Albert Hall in London on October 29, 1942, with the participation of Polish politicians, Jewish leaders, and representatives of British opinion. The demonstration was presided over by the Archbishop of Canterbury, and the main speaker was Prime Minister Sikorski. Sikorski informed the assembled public of the mass extermination of Jews in Poland, warned the Nazis that they would pay for the consequences of their crimes, and announced that the Jews would be granted the same rights as other citizens.

Even on that occasion there were prevarications. The integral text of Sikorski's speech appeared in British press alone. In the official Polish version which appeared in *Dziennik Polski* of October 30, 1942, the passages dealing with equal rights for the Jews were expunged. It amounted to the Government's outright surrender to anti-Semites: both from Poland and from exile. This distortion of the text of Sikorski's speech prompted Schwarzbart to come out with a sharply-worded motion at the National Council session of November 25, 1942.[44]

Even at the Albert Hall demonstration, the Polish Government still refrained from revealing everything it knew about the actual scope of the deportations of Jews to mass extermination camps. Thereafter, as well, the published news was being systematically understated. Accordingly, recognition of the state of affairs in Poland by Jewish leaders in the West continued to be somewhat vague. Even Schwarzbart, who as a member of the Polish National Council had close links with the Polish Government in-Exile, continued to perceive the situation in a way that was far from accurate.

It was from a report of the Jewish Agency, rather than from any Polish document, that Schwarzbart finally learned the truth about the actual scope of the disaster. Immediately after acquainting himself with this report, Schwarzbart asked for appointments with the Interior Minister Mikolajczyk and with the Interior Ministry official in charge of contacts with Poland, Siudak. Both meetings took place on November 16, 1942. First, the conversation with Siudak as noted down by Schwarzbart:

> Before conferring with Interior Minister Mikolajczyk, I paid a visit to the official in charge of contacts in Poland, Mr. Siudak, in order to obtain some prior briefing on the situation in Poland, in connection with information that reached me through the Jewish Agency. But there was an even more direct reason for urgency in requesting that appointment. It was the terrifying news which I received from Mieczyslaw Szerer who referred to director Nagorski as his source. According to this information which came directly from Poland, but which remained confidential, only 140,000 Jews still are sequestered in the Warsaw ghetto, while the remainder have already all been deported and murdered. Only 100,000 continue to receive food rations. I immediately phone Nagorski who acknowledged his cognizance of these figures. But he refused to cite his source: for that, he said, he needed prior authorization.
>
> That was why I went to Siudak. Siudak confirmed the accuracy of the information, surmised that I learned it from Szerer, and told me that it was sent by the Delegate's Office in early September. The message is at present being decoded and the pertinent passages can be handed to me in two days' time. Siudak described the evidence to be found in this document as a veritable nightmare, and said that it surpasses in horror everything that has happened to date. He told me that Mikolajczyk ordered a study of the state of affairs in Warsaw and in other ghettos.

But he requested that in the meantime I refrain from passing the information on to the public.[45]

Directly from the conversation with Siudak, Schwarzbart went to confer with Mikolajczyk. Here are his notes:

Mikolajczyk confirmed Siudak's information, and promised further details in a few days' time. He also confirmed that he demanded an updated report to be sent to him from Poland.[46] I read the document handed to me by Mikolajczyk. Its content transcends all the ghastliness and all the agony ever known. It proves that man can be reduced to the depths of depravity. The ultimate meaning of the evidence is that by the middle of September two million Jews had disappeared from Poland. Incidentally, the behavior of both Mikolajczyk and Siudak was revealing in that neither showed the slightest emotion. Perhaps I am over-sensitive, but I feel that in essence they are rather satisfied having circumvented problems with the Jewish question.[47]

Schwarzbart could not conceal his bitterness about Mikolajczyk's delays in revealing the evidence of the extermination. In the entry of October 24, 1944, he noted:

I will never forgive Mikolajczyk that from late July until September 1942 he concealed the evidence of Jewish extermination. Also, I will never forgive him that he duped me with stories about relief money that was being sent in 1941-1942 to Poland for the Jews.[48]

The embitterment over the delays in publicizing evidence of extermination reappears in Schwarzbart's letter of June 3, 1958, to Dr. Wajsblum, a scholar who spent years researching the Polish-Jewish relationships during World War II:

One of the innumerable questions that interests me is why the reports from the Polish Underground Movement had been handed over to us, that is, to the Jewish representatives in the National Council, with such delay? Who is guilty, the Polish Government or London? The delay is inexplicable.[49]

Schwarzbart was not alone in his initial confusion about the actual dimensions of the disaster which descended upon Polish Jewry. Until November 1942, other Jewish leaders in the free world were no less badly confused. On the basis of evidence reaching them mainly via the Polish Government and its entourage, they leaned towards the theory that a wave of pogroms of an unprecedented scope was sweeping Poland. They didn't yet quite comprehend that the Jewish people was being annihilated methodically, and to the last man. This initial failure to comprehend the entire truth is documented in a report of the Representation of Polish Jews:

We did not realize the whole horrifying truth until the arrival of the first group of Palestinian citizens exchanged for German citizens in accordance with the Anglo-German agreement. The Jewish part of the group was comprised of nine men, thirty-four women, and twenty-six children. They arrived in Palestine on November 16, 1942, but were detained for a few days in Athlit. Due to their detention, their detailed testimonies about the real state of affairs in Poland could be heard no sooner than on November 25, 1942. On that day, Mr. Jakub Hersz Kurc from Piotrkow told the plenary session of the Delegation about what he eye-witnessed. The sheer horror of his narrative virtually benumbed the members of the Delegation in the audience. These were no longer press reports, nor statistical figures subject to conflicting interpretations, and therefore potentially suspect of serving some propaganda purpose. Here was a flesh-and-blood human being, a Jew, who owing to a fortunate coincidence succeeded in escaping from the inferno. And what this man told us surpassed all the boundaries of a humanly conceivable reality. It is no wonder that we all felt transfixed.[50]

It was as late as November 1942, therefore, that the Jewish leaders in the free world finally learned the whole truth about the disaster to which the Jews under Nazi occupation fell prey. They immediately realized that the Polish Government could have undertaken some practical initiatives instead of confining its response to the disaster to the Albert Hall protest. Accordingly, Schwarzbart and Zygielbojm, who until that time devoted their best efforts to the guarantees of equal rights for the Jews in the liberated Poland of the future, from then on began to press the Government for affirmative action. Their first step was to demand that an appropriate resolution be passed by the National Council in Exile.[51]

It was Schwarzbart who moved to convene the plenary session of the National Council of November 27, 1942, which finally voted the resolution condemning the extermination of Jews in Poland. But the voting on the resolution was preceded by a lengthy debate, whose main feature was a speech by Mikolajczyk. He then said:

With an overriding sense of heavy responsibility, the Polish Government has done everything in its power to stop German terror, without neglecting at the same time to inform the entire world about mass murders and other German atrocities in Poland. The German aim is to extirpate the Polish nation and to obliterate all traces of its very existence. We are well aware that there is no way of repulsing the enemy aims except by quickly defeating him. Only in this way can the period of struggles and sufferings of the Polish citizens be soon terminated.

This is why the Polish Government finds it imperative to support the demands of the people in Poland for the opening of the second front and for the acceleration of the conduct of hostilities in general. The developments of recent weeks on the war fronts, which prove that the Allied forces are able to regain offensive initiatives and to win victo-

ries, have been received with great relief and authentic joy. People of
Poland responded instantly to events in Africa, by offering con-
gratulations to President Roosevelt and Prime Minister Churchill.

A separate chapter in Polish martyrology is the persecution of the
Jewish minority in Poland. Hitler's orders that at least one half of the
Polish Jewry are to be extirpated by 1942, are being executed with a
ruthlessness and barbarity without precedent in the entire history of
humanity. I don't need to reiterate the specifics, because you know
them anyway, Gentlemen. The figures are most revealing. Out of
400,000 residents of the Warsaw ghetto, over 260,000 have been exterminated within less than three months, beginning July 17. Mass
murders go on throughout the entire territory of Poland, and their
victims are the Polish Jews alongside of the Jews brought to Poland
from other countries. . . .

This forces us, the Polish Catholics, to speak up. We do not wish to
behave like Pontius Pilate. *We are powerless, we can save no one, we
can do nothing to stop the German killings.* (Emphasis added) But we
protest from the depth of our compassionate, indignant and horror-
stricken hearts. This protest of ours is commanded by God who forbade
killing. This protest is commanded by our Christian conscience. Every
being that is called human has the right to be loved by others. The blood
of defenseless victims calls for a vengeance of the heavens. He, who
refuses to join us in this protest, is Catholic no longer.

But at the same time we protest as Poles. We do not believe that
German atrocities can in any possible way serve Polish interests. The
contrary is the case. We detect hostile intentions in the persistent
silence of international Jewry as well as in the efforts of German propaganda which already strives to place the opprobrium for the slaughter
of the Jews on the Lithuanians and . . . the Poles. Today, the Poles are
forced to participate as onlookers in the bloody spectacle that unfolds
on their soil. Watching the crime is indeed capable of sowing the seeds
of poison: of breeding insensitivity to grief, of grooming sadism, and,
above all of spreading the ugly belief that a fellow human being may be
murdered with impunity. He who does not understand it, he who dares
to profess proudly his commitment to the free Poland of the future
while niggardly rejoicing in the misfortune of his fellow human being
at present—is neither a Catholic nor a Pole. . . .

And Mikolajczyk continued:

At the moment at which the Poles and the Jews are victims of the
same murders, we have the right to demand from those few Jews who
live in the world beyond the Nazi reach, that they refrain from spreading stories which are not true and which do irreparable damage to
Poland. For the enemy is determined to exterminate both nations: only
the Jews, being fewer in number, are being exterminated faster.

May this protest of the Government and of the National Council
which represents all segments of the Polish nation shake the conscience of the world! May it reach every place where decisions are
being made, so as to contribute to the acceleration of hostilities, and to
more strenuous efforts to rescue people who are still alive. May it also
lead to the resolve of all the Allies to punish these crimes so as to warn

their perpetrators that, their deeds being closely watched and their names recorded, they have not the slightest chance of escaping the harshest and most chastening justice which they so richly deserve.[52]

The main points of Mikolajczyk's speech merit close attention. The Jewish casualty figures which he presented to the National Council are strikingly low as compared to what he could know from the Delegate's Office reports which he was regularly receiving. At the same time he stated without any equivocation that the Polish Government is "powerless, can save no one, can do nothing to stop the German killings." This amounted to saying that the Polish Government had no alternative but to confine itself to verbal protest. Yet the Polish Government was then still in control of quite considerable sums of money. It was in a position to allocate a fraction of this money for a rescue effort; in the first place for making it easier for the fugitives from the camps and the ghettos to survive in hiding. Yet by late November 1942, when the vast majority of Polish Jews had already been murdered, the Interior Minister responsible for contacts with Poland still did not even contemplate any relief action for the remnant of Jewish survivors. At the same time, his speech proves him to be very concerned about criticisms of Polish attitudes as voiced by the Jewish opinion centers: up to the point of making it apparent that this might well have been his top-priority concern.

One of the speakers in the debate was Zygielbojm:

> In the earlier reports there were detailed data on the scope and the manner of slaughters of the Jews in dozens of large and smaller cities of central and south-eastern Poland. On the joint basis of these reports and of the approximate but detailed estimates of a more recent date, it is possible to compute the following tragic sum-totals: Out of approximately three-and-a-half million Jews who lived in the Republic, some half-a-million were deported by the Soviet authorities inland to Russia during the 1940 deportations. Of the remaining three millions, several hundred thousand perished in the ghettos either from starvation, or as a result of the Nazis' deliberate denial to provide the Jews with even basic sanitary and hygienic facilities. The subsequent mass slaughter absorbed about one million and a half. It follows that between one million and 1,250,000 Jews remained alive.
>
> But it means that between one million and 1,250,000 Jews remained alive by August 31, which is the date of the last report. It was nearly three months ago. From there, they write us that they understand our difficulties well. At this moment I don't even want to read the massive and detailed evidence of what happened in one city or another. The time for extensive documentation hasn't yet come. Right now, something else becomes the most urgent, the most burning and the highest priority issue. It is the issue of rescuing from certain death the last remaining million or million and a half of surviving Jews. This remnant

is scattered through towns and villages, and exposed at every time of day and night to operations of the exterminating machinery. The deceased, the murdered, those tortured to death cannot be resuscitated. One must rescue the living. This is our first priority, dictated to us both by those who still can be rescued, and by the memory of the one-and-a-half million of Jewish victims of Nazism who rest in their mass graves. Decisions and resolutions to punish the Nazi murderers after the war are devoid of meaning and will be devoid of effects, for before the war ends, the entire surviving remnant of Jewish society will perish without a trace, including those whom the German army still finds productive and useful for its purposes. All that will remain, will be one giant graveyard in which the former several million-strong community of Jews will be buried. What we need, are deeds, immediate and effective deeds. . . .

And further on:

I have no doubt, Gentlemen, that after the war the criminals will be duly punished and their victims avenged. And that the retaliation to come will not be just Jewish, contrary to what Goering said in his speech while trying to frighten the Germans by what awaits them in the event of their defeat. The ghosts of millions of innocently slaughtered victims will continue to haunt the criminals forever. In this way they will be punished and their victims avenged. The crimes against the Jewish population in Poland are the crimes against the entire population of Poland. It is the entire population of Poland which will punish the murderers and take its revenge. But no postwar punishment will revive the dead. At this moment we don't yet know how many Jews are still alive. But in order to save those who have thus far succeeded in escaping from the hands of their executioners, there are measures which must be undertaken immediately.

This is why, in accordance with an instruction which I received from Poland, I hereby submit the following motions:

1. The National Council calls on the Government of the Polish Republic to turn immediately to the Governments of the United States, of Great Britain and of other Allied countries to unite in the preparation of a plan of retaliatory measures capable of forcing Germany to stop the mass murders of civilians and the extermination of everyone who is of Jewish nationality.

2. The National Council calls on the Government of the Polish Republic to undertake the necessary steps for the sake of convening, as soon as possible, the inter-Allied conference on the subject of the historically unprecedented act of extermination of the entire Jewish population of Poland. The conference is to be convened in order to come forward, in the name of all the nations fighting for freedom and democracy, with a fiery protest and a stern warning directed to the German nation and the German Government.

3. The National Council calls on the Governmant of the Polish Republic to see to it that leaflets in the German language, describing in minute detail the horrifying crimes perpetrated in the German nation's name by the occupation authorities in Poland are dropped from Allied aircraft over German territory and inundate the populace; and that the

same information is broadcast in German by radio.

The instruction which I received also contains a fourth demand which, I believe, can and will be met without a separate resolution of the National Council. The demand is that the Government shall without any further delay assign extraordinary allotments of money for relief of the Polish Jews who have remained alive. This is why I refrain from submitting a separate motion, leaving the matter for discussions with the Deputy Prime Minister or with the Minister of Labor and Welfare. I reiterate that I don't think that this matter requires a separate resolution of the National Council.[53]

The National Council declined to support Zygielbojm's motions, voting instead a resolution drafted in the spirit of Mikolajczyk's speech. The resolution, published in *Dziennik Polski* of November 30, 1942, was in fact limited to verbal protest and condemnation of Nazi crimes. But for some Polish politicians, primarily the ones affiliated with the National Party, even this was too placatory to Jewish demands. Their goal was to avoid any special emphasis on the Nazi crimes against the Jews, without a concurrent or even stronger emphasis on the Nazi crimes against the Poles. Towards this goal they mounted pressures upon the Government. And they succeeded: for indeed, in the Government broadcasts to Poland of that time, there was a noticeable tendency to avoid any pro-Jewish accents. Schwarzbart spotted this tendency, as proven by the entry of December 7, 1942, in his diary:

In the morning a letter to Raczynski in haste. I expressed my indignation over last Saturday's broadcast by the Polish Radio, with a report of the conversation between Raczynski and Eden. Nothing was said in this broadcast, beyond the statement that the German terror in Poland has become more intense.[54]

As a result of the pressures of the National Party leaders, the National Council voted on January 7, 1943, a modified resolution concerning Nazi crimes in Poland, in which the extermination of the Jews was perfunctorily mentioned in barely one sentence; whereas the whole emphasis stressed the sufferings of the ethnic Poles. Here is the text of this resolution in its entirety:

On the basis of the documents received by the Government of the Polish Republic in the last days of the month of December 1942, the National Council of the Polish Republic contends that all strata of the Polish society are already subject to Nazi exterminatory measures to the extent of affecting the very biological existence of the nation.

All the nations of the world should be acquainted with the methods used by the Germans against the Polish residents of the areas designated for extermination. Children up to six are forcibly separated from their parents and deported to Germany with the intention of raising them as Germans. Parents who defend their children are murdered.

The elderly, the infirm and the physically weak are deported to "unknown destinations" which means that they are killed in special "death camps." Persons believed to be local leaders are sent to Auschwitz, while the remainder, if assessed as able-bodied, are dispatched to labor camps in Germany or in Poland. Fifty-four villages of the Lublin district were in this way destroyed in December 1942 alone. The residents of some villages designated for destruction are retaliating with armed resistance. Thus the entire male population of the village of Kitow fell in combat. At the same time, the slaughter of the entire Jewish population goes on without regard for sex or age.

The National Council of the Polish Republic asserts that since 1939 the Polish nation has been engaged in a continuous armed struggle with Germany, that it has refused any collaboration, that it has produced no Quisling and that it formed a new Polish army which has fought beyond the borders of Poland.

The National Council of the Polish Republic submits that it was the unbending oppositon of the Polish nation against the idea of the common Polish-German invasion of Russia which in 1939 saved the USSR from war. The National Council of the Polish Republic also submits that all the present-day Allies gained time for the preparation of resistance against Germany at the expense of millions of Polish lives.

The unique contribution of the Polish nation to the conduct of the war entitles the National Council of the Polish Republic to solemnly proclaim that Allied aid to Poland ought to be immediately increased as an integral part of the overall plan of the conduct of hostilities.

Evidence again shows the horrifying character of German methods of subjugation. It also shows the inadequacy of the measures undertaken thus far against the planned extermination of entire nations of the occupied countries. All the protests and all the warnings to prosecute the perpetrators of the crimes after the war remain without effects.

Sharing with the entire Polish resistance the responsibility for the preservation of the threat to the very existence of the Nation, the National Council of the Polish Republic thinks that only through extraordinary measures can the Governments of the Allied nations succeed in stopping the planned extermination of the peoples of the occupied countries.

The National Council of the Polish Republic shares the viewpoint of the Government that the acceleration of a counter-offensive is the only way to subvert German barbarities. Accordingly, it supports the Government's efforts towards achieving that goal.

In total solidarity with the Government of the Polish Republic, the National Council of the Polish Republic views the countermeasures against German violence as the most urgent and the most important of all its tasks. Accordingly, it gives its total and unconditional support to the Government's efforts to design and to implement jointly with other Allied governments the retaliatory measures intended to force the Germans immediately to cease their mass exterminations of entire nations in the countries under their occupation.[55]

In this way, the National Council in London clearly refused to recognize the crime of genocide committed against the Jewish nation as *sui generis*. Everything was done to obscure the glaring difference between the admittedly extraordinarily atrocious German terror against other nations of occupied Europe, and the total extermination applied against the Jewish nation alone. Consequently, no steps suited to the extraordinary situation of the Jews were allowed to be undertaken. All action for the Jews was limited to verbal protests and announcements of penalties to be meted out to the criminals after the war would be terminated. These policy assumptions of the Polish authorities were actually reasserted in the letter of December 3, 1942, by the Foreign Minister Raczynski to the then President of the World Zionist Federation, Chaim Weizman:

> The Polish Government receives almost daily reports on the untold atrocities perpetrated by the Germans against the people in Poland. From these sources they have recently obtained the confirmation of the monstrous slaughters undertaken by the Germans upon the Jews in Poland. These terrible crimes afflict both the Polish Jews and the large numbers of Jews from other countries whom the Germans have deported to Poland in order to exterminate them. The Polish Government and the Polish nation have condemned with horrified indignation these mass murders committed on the soil of Poland by the German authorities of occupation.
>
> Profoundly affected by these horrible reports, I hasten to convey to you, the most eminent representative of the Jewish national idea, the expression of my heartfelt compassion with the martyrdom which the German barbarians have inflicted upon the Jewish nation. I can assure you that the Polish Government is determined that the dehumanized perpetrators of these dreadful crimes shall receive a punishment commensurate with their guilt.

There was a marked difference in the way the Polish Government reacted to reports on the extermination of the Jews and to reports on atrocities against the ethnic Poles. This difference was brought into sharp relief when the Polish Government learned of the deportations of the Polish rural population from the Zamosc region. The deportations began in late December 1942. People in Poland watched these developments apprehensively, as the likely beginning of the extermination of the Poles to be modeled after the extermination of the Jews. But in this case, the reaction of the Polish political centers was rapid. The double standard was glaring: On the one hand, delays in passing the evidence of the extermination of Jews to public notice, on the other hand, instant publicity given to the evidence of terror and deportations against the Poles. On the one hand, the underestimation of the scope of the ongoing genocide against the Jews, on the other hand, a strong emphasis on German measures against the Poles.

The attempts to use the Vatican as the intermediary for the purpose of restraining the Germans show exactly how this double standard worked. On January 2, 1943, President Raczkiewicz drafted the appeal to the Pope concerning the developments of the previous month in the Zamosc region. Raczkiewicz wrote:

> Dreadful events took place in the last weeks of the past year. Terror which for four years victimized all strata and all segments of the Polish society, has now assumed new forms, marked not only by the intentional cruelty of methods, but also by the extensiveness of its scope. Extermination of the Jews which included many Christians of the Semitic race, turned out to be merely an attempt at pre-testing the methods of the scientifically designed and systematically implemented mass murder. At present the same methods of mass extermination are applied against the native Polish population of the entire counties of Zamosc and Hrubieszow, and of parts of the counties of Tomaszow, Pulawy and Lublin. In the county of Zamosc alone fifty-four villages have been depopulated and over 10,000 farms expropriated. The children, in particular those under the age of six, were deported to Germany. Mothers who stood in defense of their children were murdered. The elderly and the infirm were relocated to "unknown destinations": a phrase which is known to stand for death. The leading farmers were interned in the Auschwitz concentration camp; whereas the remainder of the adult rural population were escorted under guard to forced labor sites. When resistance was encountered in the village of Kitow, 170 peasants were killed in retaliation.[56]

The Government-in-Exile decided to turn to the Vatican concerning the extermination of the Jews no sooner than in December 1942, i.e. a year and a half after the extermination began. The intervention assumed the form of a note handed on December 21, 1942, by the Polish ambassador in the Vatican, K. Papée to the Secretary of the Congregation for Extraordinary Affairs and the First Deputy of the Cardinal of State, Monsignor Tardini. On the occasion of the delivery of the note, a conversation ensued, during which Papée, according to his own report to the Polish authorities "expressed the opinion that the Holy See will clearly and distinctly condemn these as well as the other German crimes which in terms of their scope have no precedent in the history of the world." To this, Monsignor Tardini answered that the Soviet crimes against the same Polish nation deserve condemnation as well. "In my reply"—reports Ambassador Papée—"I made it clear, that personally I have no objections whatsoever when the matter is stated in this way."[57]

Papée's intervention in the Vatican was therefore another example of the Polish Government's refusal to view the extermination of the Jews as *sui generis*. The extermination of the Jews always tended to be discussed jointly with the persecutions of the Poles; and the emphasis, if any, was that the latter was more important, for the fear that the evidence of the Jewish extermination might overshadow the evidence of Polish sufferings.

NOTES

1. AKC PZPR, Party, 202/I, 29, p. 43.
2. YVA, O-25/90.
3. *Ibid.*
4. *Ibid.*
5. YVA, O-25/91.
6. YVA, M-2/193.
7. YVA, O-25/90.
8. YVA, M-2/196.
9. GSHC, A.9.III.2a/4.
10. Error in the original. There was no death camp in Pelkiny.
11. The document was published in the Monthly *Zywia* ("The ones who nourish") of August 1942. The source of the quotation is "Materialy zrodlowe do historii polskiego ruchu ludowego" (Source materials to the history of the Polish Peasant movement), vol. 4, pp. 69–73.
12. YVA, microfilm JM/3431. Original in German.
13. Caban and Mankowski, *ZWZ i AK okregu lubelskim* ("The Union for the Armed Struggle and the Home Army in the Lublin district"), part 2, pp. 60–65.
14. The article was also published in the National Party's organ *Wielka Polska* ("Great Poland") of November 27, 1942.
15. Terej, J.J. *Rzeczywistosc i polityka: Ze studiow nad dziejami najnowszymi Narodowej Demokraeji* (Reality and politics: selected studies in the recent history of the National-Democratic movement"), Warsaw, 1971, p. 240.
16. *Op. cit.*, p. 196.
17. *Op. cit.*, p. 279.
18. *Op. cit.*, p. 281.
19. *Op. cit.*, p. 283.
20. *Op. cit.*, p. 355.
21. *Op. cit.*, p. 356.
22. *Op. cit.*, p. 191.
23. Penzik, A. (Ed.) *W przededniu* (On the eve). New York, 1944, pp. 81–83.

24. *Op. cit.*, p. 80.
25. *Publicystyka konspiracyjna PPR* ("Clandestine journalism of the Polish Workers' Party"), vol. 1, p. 62.
26. *Op. cit.*, pp. 62–63.
27. *Op. cit.*, pp. 70–72.
28. YVA., M-2/752.
29. YVA., M-2/749.
30. *Ibid.*
31. *Ibid.*
32. *Ibid.*
33. *Ibid.*
34. YVA., M-2/750.
35. YVA., M-2/751.
36. *Ibid.*
37. YVA., M-2/750.
38. Polish Underground Study Trust, Interior Ministry, K., folder 10, item 162.
39. *Ibid.*, folder 10, item 173.
40. YVA., M-2/4.
41. *Ibid.*
42. GSHI, A, 10.9/3. Original in English.
43. YVA, the Bernfes collection.
44. YVA, M-2/7.
45. YVA, M-2/751.
46. *Ibid.*
47. *Ibid.*
48. YVA, M-2/755.
49. YVA, Archive Frisner, the Wajsblum folder. Original in English, with the exception of the phrases "to mimic the Jew-folk" which is in Polish.
50. Report of the Representation of Polish Jews, p. 46.
51. *Op. cit.*, p. 53.
52. YVA, M-2/20.
53. *Ibid.*
54. YVA, M-2/751.
55. GSHI, A.10.9/7. Original in English.
56. GSHI, A.44.122/30.
57. GSHI, A.44.122/28.

THE POLISH UNDERGROUND AND
THE JEWS IN 1943–1944

As a mass-scale undertaking, the deportations from the ghettos to the extermination camps had practically been completed by the fall of 1942. By the end of that year the Germans already managed to slaughter the vast majority of Polish Jews. Nearly all the ghettos of occupied Poland were by then entirely liquidated. The few which still existed were considerably reduced in size. Together with the forced-labor camps and the concentration camps they totaled no more than several hundred thousand Jews. A report of March 23, 1943, sent by the Government's Delegate in Poland to his authorities in London describes the situation of the Jews at that point in the following words:

> Insofar as it can be ascertained, the fate of the Jews has undergone a further deterioration, as compared to the conditions of the others. Considering that barely several hundred thousand Jews have remained out of 3,500,000 one has a fair insight concerning the scale of atrocities that have been perpetrated.[1]

Broken down by regions of the country, the approximate numbers of Jews still alive at the beginning of 1943 can be estimated as follows:

Following the mass deportations from the Warsaw ghetto which took place between July 22 and September 13, 1942 some 60,000 remained, approximately one half clandestinely. All other Jewish concentrations of the Warsaw district were liquidated in the same period of time. The only exceptions were two small forced-labor camps in Siedlce and in Wegrow which operated for a while, until their liquidation in May 1943.[2]

In the Radom district there still existed the single pared down ghetto of Czestochowa, with about 4,000 residents, and eight small forced-labor camps (Blizyn, Starachowice, Pionki, Radom, Skarzysko-Kamienna, Ostrowiec Swietokrzyski, Kielce and Sandomierz) whose joint population did not exceed several thousand Jewish inmates.[3]

In the Lublin district there were 6 small secondary ghettos (in Wlodawa, Hrubieszow, Izbica, Belzyce, Piaski and Miedzyrzec Podlaski, all pared down in size). A certain number of Jews were still alive in five forced-labor camps (Biala Podlaska, Budzyn, Krasnik, Leczna and Deblin), in the camp for the Jewish POWs of the Polish army in Lublin, and in the Majdanek concentration camp.

In the Cracow district mass deportations took place between June and November 1942 claiming about 100,000 Jewish lives. In their wake six ghettos remained, all of them radically pared down in size: in Cracow with about 10,000, in Debica with about 2,000, in Bochnia with about 3,500, in Przemysl with about 5,500, in Rzeszow with about 3,000 and in Tarnow with about 12,000. Five forced-labor camps operated in Mielec near Rzeszow, in Pustkow, in Stalowa Wola, in Zaslaw and in Szebnia. In Plaszow near Cracow there was a concentration camp.[5]

The deportations and mass executions in the district of Galicja claimed about 300,000 Jewish lives in the period between March and December 1942 alone. At the beginning of 1943 there still existed the pared down ghetto of Lwow with about 20,000 residents, of whom 8,000 lived there clandestinely, as well as a number of secondary ghettos and forced-labor camps. Out of twenty-two secondary ghettos, seven (in Buczacz, Zloczow, Tarnopol, Zbaraz, Trembowla, Skalat and Zborow) were liquidated in April 1943, five (in Sokal, Kopyczynka, Luste, Brody and Przemyslany) in May 1943, and the remaining 10 (in Borszczow, Czortkow, Stryj, Sambor, Boryslaw, Drohobycz, Brzezany, Kozowa, Podhajce and Rohatyn) in June 1943; so that by June 23, 1943, there was no single secondary ghetto in the Galicja district left. Also the ghetto of Lwow was ultimately liquidated in June 1943, the only remaining Jewish concentration in that city being the large camp of Janowska Street. Other camps of the Galicja district were located in Buczacz, Jaryczow Nowy, Mosty Wielkie, Winniki, Bolechow, Skole, Tarnopol, Jezierna, Podwoloczyska, Kamionka, Sasow, Przemyslany, Olesko, Brody, and Zloczow. Every one of these camps was liquidated during the summer of 1943.[6]

Among the territories incorporated into the Reich there existed the large ghetto of Lodz, which even after a number of deportations in 1941 and 1942 still had about 80,000 residents, as well as the smaller concentrations in Bedzin and Sosnowiec.[7]

Most Jews of the Bialystok region had already been murdered in the first days of November 1942, when nearly all the ghettos of the region were liquidated. Two minor ghettos of Jasionowka and Pruzana, however, were at that time not affected. Moreover, in Krynki, Sokolka, Grodno and Bialystok itself the remnants of the former ghettos still remained in existence after November 1942, jointly accounting for some 80,000 residents. Of that figure, about 25,000 Jews from Grodno, Jesionowka, Krynki and Sokolka were murdered in January 1943, and an additional 15,000 from Bialystok and Grodno in February 1943. The Bialystok ghetto which in July 1943 still numbered some 35,000 to 40,000 was ultimately liquidated in August 1943. After that date, there was no single ghetto left in the region.[8]

In the Wilno region the last major ghetto in Wilno itself survived until September 1943.

In the regions of Nowogrodek, Polesie and Volhynia all Jewish concentrations were liquidated without exception during 1942.

During the peak of deportations in the summer and fall of 1942 two new phenomena emerged:

1. Mass escapes to the forests, in search of opportunities for hiding from Nazi pursuit. On a somewhat lesser scale, escapes to villages and over to the "Aryan sides" of some cities, in search of opportunities for hiding in the midst of the local population, whether Polish, or Byelorussian in the East, or to a lesser extent even Ukrainian.

2. The rise of Jewish armed resistance, which expressed itself in the formation of a considerable number of partisan groups or detachments, or in organizing for purposes of resistance in those ghettos and camps which were not yet totally liquidated.

In the period of deportations to extermination camps mass escapes of Jews occurred on the entire territory of the Government General, and in the regions of Bialystok, Wilno, Nowogrodek, Polesie and Volhynia. In Silesia, however, relatively few Jews managed to escape; and in the Poznan region (i.e. the Warthegau) almost none.

After the liquidation of the ghettos, large numbers of Jews still succeeded in escaping from various forced-labor camps. Nonetheless, escapes from the ghettos, whether prior to or during the deportations, from the transports to the camps or from the camps themselves were a venture bristling with difficulty and risk. The prospects of achieving success were very low. The fugitives had to travel through the networks of police guardposts or to sneak out from closely guarded convoys. They risked crippling injuries while jumping from a speeding train, or, even worse, unspeakable tortures if caught by the executioners. There exist numerous accounts written by Polish eyewitnesses, who describe the tragic plight of the fugitives and the unbelievable obstacles they had to overcome. For example, a Polish teacher named S. Zeminski thus describes what he saw on November 8, 1942, in Lukow in the district of Lublin:

> In the marketplace I saw a crowd of Jews huddled together in a small area surrounded by Ukrainians. Time and again the latter would shoot, as if to prove that they can do their job well. The day was cold, windy, foggy. They were kept in this square for the entire day. At twilight they

were escorted to the railway station. Their route happened to pass through the neighborhood of my house. I was just digging in my garden when I heard screams interspersed by recurrent shooting. I went out into the street to see a giant procession of some 2,000 to 3,000 tightly jammed people: men, women and children of all ages, including the babies in the arms of their parents. A compact escort of armed Ukrainians, each ready to open fire, marched on both sides of the column. Any Jew who attempted to stray from the column was killed on the spot.[9]

Another Polish eyewitness, Stanislaw Szefler, happened to live at that time in Malkinia, a small town located on the railway line to Treblinka. In his diary, he noted:

The transports to Treblinka keep moving without interruption. Some prisoners are trying to escape. The corpses along the railway tracks and around our neighborhood show how many of them failed.[10]

Likewise, Zygmunt Klukowski, a renowned chronicler of the Nazi occupation wrote in his diary in the entry of May 28, 1943:

For a long period of time nothing could be heard about the Jews in our region. Now, long trains packed with Jews again keep crossing the Szczebrzeszyn station in the direction of Chelm. They are transported entirely naked, in decrepit freight cars. On the way some jump out, but those who do are immediately shot at by the gendarmes, and usually either killed or at least wounded. Along the railway track naked Jewish corpses can be seen scattered about. A few days ago a young Jewess with a seven year old child jumped from a speeding train in the close vicinity of the "Alwa" factory. She was killed on the spot by a gendarme's bullet, but the child was merely injured while falling down. The workers from "Alwa" fed him, and then notified the gendarmerie post in Szcebrzeszyn. Scarcely several hours passed before the gendarmes appeared. They killed the child in front of all the workers, who were then ordered to bury the body.[11]

The odds were overwhelming for those who attempted escape. The Jews knew that the prospects of survival after even a successful escape were almost nil. Nevertheless the escapes assumed a mass scale. The total number of Jewish fugitives in the forests and villages is difficult to estimate. It certainly exceeded 100,000 without counting those who sought to hide themselves on the "Aryan side" of cities, particularly in Warsaw.

The mass character of escapes is attested by the Government Delegate's cable of December 1, 1943:

A considerable number of Jews have hidden themselves in the forests and in the fields. It can be estimated that about 40,000 Jews have survived and are at present in hiding.[12]

It must be understood that the quoted report is dated a year after the deportations to death camps had reached their peak. Throughout that year, the vast majority of the fugitives had already been caught in one or another of the incessant raids, carried out by German police forces, usually assisted either by German army units, or by Polish, Ukrainian or Byelorussian auxiliary police, or by the so-called "Ostlegion" units, or simply by the local rural populace.

The testimony of the scope which the Jewish escapes from the ghettos and from the camps assumed, is provided by the hundreds of scattered gravesites, discovered after the war in the woods, in the fields, in the swamps, and in roadside ditches. The number of such gravesites in the territory of post-1945 Poland as well as the approximate numbers of Jews buried in them are known from questionnaires distributed shortly after the war to all county and village councils by the Main Commission for the Investigation of Nazi Crimes in Poland.[13]

In this way, 400 collective gravesites with no fewer than 8,500 buried Jewish fugitives were located in the districts of Cracow and Rzeszow alone.[14] Almost 1,000 corpses were found in a single county of the Warsaw district, that of Wegrow. These were the Jews who escaped either during the deportations or from the transports destined for Treblinka and were caught.[15] In the same district, in Zelechow and its immediate vicinity, 800 Jews were shot either during escape attempts, or after being caught in their hiding places, whether in the forest or in villages. In the nearby locality of Irena, over 1,600 Jews were shot, out of 5,000 who had lived there. The number of Jews shot in Lukow county is estimated as over 2,000.[16]

For the district of Lublin, the number of Jewish fugitives who were caught and shot is estimated at about 20,000. Mass gravesites discovered after the war in the counties of Parczew and Wlodawa produce the following estimates regarding the Jews shot during the raids on their hiding places in forests, fields and villages: 1,020 in the graves near Leczna, 750 near Parczew, 550 near Adampol, 400 near Wlodawa, 270 near Slawatycze, 240 near Cycow, 205 near Polod, 100 near Luta, 100 near Kodeniec, and more in mass graves located elsewhere. Over 4,000 were thus shot in the two named counties alone; all of them either in 1942 or 1943.[17]

Escapes were even more common in the southern part of the Lublin district. No fewer than 200 gravesites were discovered after the war in the counties of Janow, Bilgoraj, Krasnystaw, Zamosc and Hrubieszow; all of them containing the corpses of Jews caught and shot during the raids on their hiding places. In most of these graves the number of disinterred corpses ranged between ten and one hundred. Graves with hundreds or even thousands of victims of the largest raids were also discovered. Thus, in Hrubieszow county about 3,000 executed Jews were buried on the former artillery range of the Polish army and in the adjoining cemetery. In the Bilgoraj county, about 2,000 Jewish corpses were found buried in a single site near the village of Jozefow. Likewise, about 2,500 Jewish corpses were found buried together near the village of Komarow, in the Tomaszow Lubelski county. Major gravesites containing the bodies of Jews who were caught and shot were also found near Tarnogrod (about 1,000 corpses), near Tyszowce in Tomaszow Lubelski county (also about 1,000), near Krzeszow in Bilgoraj county (about 600), near Krasnicz in the Zamosc county (about 150), in Zaklikow in the Krasnik county (about 120), and near Krasnik (about 100 corpses).[18]

In the Kielce district, the number of Jews who escaped but were caught and shot can be estimated at 15,000. Thus, for instance, out of 3,200 Jewish residents of Zarki 1,600 escaped; out of 4,000 Jewish residents of Wodzislaw 1,000 escaped; out of about 1,000 Jewish residents of Gomulice, 500 escaped. About 2,000 escaped from Ostrowiec, several hundred from Jedrzejow. Nearly one half of the 8,000-strong ghetto of Opatow succeeded in fleeing to the forests. 300 fled from nearby Iwaniska. During the deportations in Pilica on September 5, 1942 over 1,000 succeeded in escaping out of the total of 2,500. After the ghettos were already liquidated many still succeeded in escaping in 1943 and 1944 from the forced-labor camps in the Kielce district.[19]

The total number of Jews buried in collective graves of the Bialystok district can be estimated on the basis of the questionnaires of the Main Commission for the Investigation of Nazi Crimes in Poland as ranging between 25,000 and 35,000.[20]

The Jews who succeeded in getting out to the forest formed dozens of partisan units for the twofold purpose of commencing armed resistance against the Nazis and of providing the Jewish fugitives in hiding with armed protection from raids. The following Jewish partisan units won a measure of renown:

— of Fainsztat, Gewircman, Haberman, Finkler, and Ajzenman-Kaniewski in the Kielce district;

— of Drenger, Amsterdam, and Birman in the Cracow district;

— of Mlynowski, Oszlak, and the one named after Anielewicz in the Warsaw district;

— of Grynszpan, Jegier, Cymerman, Forst and Braun in the Lublin district;

— of Lewinger, Birenbaum, Cukier, Gerszowski, and Frydland in Eastern Galicja;

— of Bobrow, Segal, Abugow, Gildenman, and Horowicz in Volhynia and Polesie;

— of Brojde, and the one known under the name of "Forward" in the Bialystok region;

— of Kaplinski, Atlas, Bielski, Zorin, Dworecki, Fiodorowicz, and Zalmanowicz in the Nowogrodek region;

— of Pinczow, Wolach, Ariowicz, "Revenge," "Death to Fascism," "Avenger," "Struggle," and "Towards Victory" in the Wilno region.

The Jews who survived the 1942 deportations in the pared down or secondary ghettos and in forced-labor or concentration camps established armed organizations there also. The purpose was either to prepare armed resistance in the event of the liquidation of a given ghetto or camp, or to organize a forced breakout from a given ghetto or camp, with the intention of joining or forming the partisan units in a given region's forests.

Serious armed resistance organizations were set up in five major ghettos: in Warsaw, Wilno, Bialystok, Cracow, and Czestochowa; as well as in 45 other ghettos: Braslaw, Swieciany, Lida, Mir, Stolpce, Zdzieciol, Grodno, Nieswiez, Molczadz, Kleck, Baranowicze, Slonim, Dereczyn, Krynki, Lachwa, Kobryn, Brzesc, Kamien Koszyrski, Poborsk, Tuczyn, Luck, Zdolbunow, Krzemieniec, Brody, Lwow, Jaworow, Brzezany, Buczacz, Borszczow, Horodenka, Rohatyn, Miedzyrzec Podlaski, Radzyn, Zelechow, Rzeszow, Tarnow, Bochnia, Dzialoszyce, Sandomierz, Radom, Pilica, Bedzin, Sosnowiec, Opatow and Wlodawa. Likewise, armed organizations of some note appeared in the extermination camps of Sobibor, Treblinka and Auschwitz, in the concentration camps of Plaszow and Lwow-Janowska, in the Jewish P.O.W. camp in Lublin and in 18 forced-labor camps: Kielce, Skarzysko-Kamienna, Ostrowiec Swietokrzyski, Kruszyna, Minsk Mazowiecki, Budzyn, Krasnik, Sasow, Stryj, Kamionka, Hancewicze, Koldyczewo, Dworzec, Swiezna, Iwie, Wilejka, Kureniec and Biala-Waka.

In the ethnically Polish areas west of the Bug River, the survival chances of the fugitives hidden in the woods or in the villages depended exclusively upon the attitudes manifested towards them by Polish political organizations and by the common Polish populace, especially in the countryside. In the areas located east of the river Bug, the crucial factors were the attitudes of the Ukrainians and Byelorussians. The good will of the Polish minority residing there was also essential, but not as absolutely decisive.

Polish clandestine organizations differed enormously in their attitudes towards the Jews, in 1943–1944 no less so than in the preceding period. The nature of these attitudes depended essentially on the political and ideological preconceptions of a given group. These varying preconceptions are described in a confidential document issued towards the end of 1943 by the Bureau for Information and Propaganda of the Chief Command of the Home Army. The documents, which bears the number 171/43 and which was never intended for publication, contains elaborate characteristics of all the major groups active in the Polish underground. In summary, it reveals the following range of opinions on the Jewish question within the major political groups attached to the Delegate's Office:

1. The National Party: *emigration of the Jews*
2. The Confederacy of the Nation: *extermination of the Jews.*
3. The (Christian) Labor Party: *getting rid of the Jews.*
4. The Camp of the Fighting Poland (a splinter group of Pilsudski followers): *emigration of the Jews.*
5. The Convention of Organizations for Independent Statehood (another splinter group of Pilsudski followers): *fully equal rights for the Jews.*
6. The Peasant Party: *emigration of the Jews.*
7. The Democratic Party: *equal rights for the Jews.*
8. The Syndicalists: *equal rights for the Jews.*
9. Freedom-Equality-Independence (the main body of the former Polish Socialist Party): *equal rights for the Jews.*
10. Minor organizations like the Raclawice, the Union for the Reconstruction of the Republic, the Polish Union for Liberty, the Sovereign-Poland: *emigration of the Jews.*

These were the positions advocated in 1943, i.e. at the time when the vast majority of the Polish Jews had already been murdered. Even then, nine out of the thirteen listed political groups affiliated with the Delegate's Office advanced anti-Semitic programs of either forced emigration or extermination of the surviving remnant of the Jewish people. Only four groups adopted the democratic tenet of granting to the Jews equal rights after the defeat of the Nazis and the liberation of Poland from slavery.

Insofar as the political groups unaffiliated with the Delegate's Office are concerned, an anti-Semitic program of elimination of the Jews from Poland was advocated by the Camp of Great Poland (a splinter group from the National Party). On the other hand, the

(Communist) Polish Workers' Party and the Polish Socialist Workers' Party (a splinter group from the former Polish Socialist Party) stood for equal rights for the Jews.[21]

Let us examine more closely the political preconceptions under-lying these various programs. They are spelled out in the press organs which each of the listed organizations published clandes-tinely. The opinions extracted from the clandestine press will then be compared with the actual conduct of respective organizations, so as to gauge the extent to which their political practice corresponded with their political theory. Let us begin with the groups represented in the Delegate's Office.

The Delegate's Office had access to very reliable information concerning the conditions of the Jews in particular regions of Poland. It accurately perceived the aims of the Nazi extermination policies in regard to the surviving remnant of the Jews. This can be seen from the third volume (for the years 1942–1943) of its Situation Reports, especially from the chapter bearing the title "The condition of Poland at the turn of 1942/1943." Here is an excerpt:

> The extermination of Jews in Poland is dictated by the general politi-cal aims of the Germans. Regardless of the outcome of the war, the Germans intend to create as many *faits accomplis* as possible. The total extermination of European Jewry is on the list of the essential tasks the Germans are determined to perform. The extermination of Jews is therefore, not restricted to Poland, but extends to all of occupied Europe. Indeed, apart from the mass murders of Polish Jews, the Germans are transporting Jews from western Europe to Poland in order to gradually exterminate them here. This is being done on the territory of Poland because the machinery of mass murder has been perfected here to the utmost throughout the long years of the war in order to prepare it for the extermination of the whole Polish nation of thirty-five million. In the meantime, this machinery is being deployed in the ex-termination of the Polish Jews from all over Europe.[22]

Similar insights can be found in the Delegate Office's Report on Jewish affairs for the month of January 1943:

> As of the first days of 1943, the situation can be described as follows: The still surviving remnant of the masses of Jewish people continue to undergo unceasing physical annihilation. The employment of Jews no longer exists as a rational issue. The policy to isolate the Semites is no longer carried out either. The only remaining activity is capturing and slaying the remnant of survivors: an extermination that is absolute and ultimate.[23]

Towards the end of 1942 after the most feverish stage of deporta-tions to death camps had already been completed, and after the vast majority of Polish Jews had already been slain, the Delegate's

Office responded with two perfectly well intentioned initiatives. It set up the Council for Aiding Jews (code named Zegota), and it established agreements and some forms of cooperation with the Jewish underground in the ghetto of Warsaw.

Both these steps were nevertheless limited: in scope, in space, and in scale of undertaking. The present chapter is confined to the analysis of what the Delegate's Office and the Home Army did in 1943 and 1944 relative to Jews beyond Warsaw.

The attitude of the Delegate's Office towards the Jews can be described as a synthesis of the attitudes of groups comprised by that Office. This is why an analysis of the aims and of the deeds of the Delegate's Office must begin with an analysis of the aims and of the deeds of its constituent parts. As far as the aims are concerned, the clandestine press is a reliable source, capable of shedding much light upon the problems under present discussion. A good beginning, therefore, should include a brief review of the editorials which the press of diverse political groups published in 1943 and 1944 on the subject of the Jews.

The *National Party.* In terms of sheer quantity, no political party published nearly as much on the subject of the Jews as this one. With the exception of a few articles (to be dealt with in another chaper) concerning the Warsaw ghetto uprising, the tone of these publications was rabidly anti-Semitic, and their contents not very different from what was appearing in the Nazi press. The clandestine press of the National Party continued its anti-Semitic agitation throughout 1943 and 1944. Here is a sample:

The organ of the National Party, *Warszawski Dziennik Narodowy* ("Warsaw National Daily"), in No. 14 of April 3, 1943, in an article "A grist for whose mill?":

> The Jews spread the seeds of dissent and disunity, and they stupefy minds. In this way they can wreck the inner cohesiveness of a society by relying on proxies who are uncritical but hungry for power and honors. Yet there is no reason why Jewish and Freemason influence should succeed in undermining the innate patriotism and their love for their Fatherland. Shall we continue to let the Jews and Freemasons lead us on a string, to the detriment of the clear interests of our Fatherland? Or shall we shake the hypnosis off ourselves, put our petty bickering aside, and join hands in accord like brothers, in order to march together under the banner on which the supreme commandment is written in huge letters: the commandment that our country has a single goal and that there is but one single way to reach that goal.

The same *Warsaw National Daily* in its No. 16 of April 17, 1943 published an article under the title "National Economy." The article deals with foreign loans which are viewed as a capital resource enabling the future Polish economy to stand on its own feet. The author believes that no danger of strengthening the Jewish influence exists when money is loaned by the state. The danger does exist, however, when:

> ... foreign capital penetrates the country through private hands. Despite their defeat, world Jewry have not given up their plans to repossess their property in Poland. They will keep developing their own national economy to the detriment of Polish national interest. To achieve this goal, they will use all political and economic means at their disposal, in particular the relief funds dispensed to their coreligionists in Poland. The strictest fiscal precautions against the infiltration of capital from this source cannot be effectual enough. Reconstruction and stabilization of Jewish economy must be prevented by other, legal and political means. As long as the Jews enjoy equal rights, any economic or fiscal policies aiming at stopping the growth of Jewish economy are bound to be fruitless.

Another organ of the National Party, *Walka* ("The Struggle") of July 28, 1943, came out with an article bearing the title "The danger of spurious solutions".

> Slowly we already begin to become oblivious about the Jewish question which tormented Poland in the period between the wars. Occasionally, the ruins of the burned ghetto of Warsaw keep reminding us of the "wars of the Jews," with its brotherhood-in-arms of the SS with the Jewish militia on the one hand, and of the Jews with the "Polish" Workers' Party and the "Polish" Socialists on the other. . . . Occasionally, these ruins still remind us of the existence in hiding of a remnant of a once all-powerful minority, who, as heirs to our prewar traditions, "must be provided with all the relief available," We emphatically condemn the bestialities of the Nazi gangsters, but we refuse to give up our economic and political struggle against the Jewry. We refuse to be moved by the crocodile tears of Jewish financial moguls and Jewish politicians who already brace themselves to reestablish their power.[24]

Again *The Struggle* in the issue for the month of August 1943:

> The armed Bolshevik gangs which already prowl throughout the Lublin district with impunity grow in strength. They are joined by fugitive Soviet POWs, by local criminals, and by Jews who managed to remain outside of the ghettos. Obviously, this Bolshevik-Jewish company is not in the least concerned with the loss of either human life or the property of entire villages.[25]

The young generation of Nationalists had their own organ *Mloda Polska* ("Young Poland"). In the issue No. 18 (32) of October 13, 1943, there is a very significant statement:

> Some may shed a tear over the burned ghetto, but the programs of all

Polish political groups concur in respect to the need to eliminate Jewish influence. The victory has been won.

Another organ of the National Party, *Polak* ("The Pole") of November 3, 1943, came out with the following proclamation:

> Poles of all walks of life and all persuasions! Unite in the life-and-death struggle against the Nazi-commune and the Judeo-commune! Brace yourselves!

In 1944 when no more than a tiny remnant of Jews was still left anywhere in Poland, the anti-Semitic agitation in the National Party press continued. Thus, *Wielka Polska* ("Great Poland") of April 27, 1944, published an article bearing the title "The curse of tolerance". It is a programmatic statement against granting equal rights to national minorities after the liberation from the German occupation:

> We've been the most tolerant nation of the world. And our tolerance has become a curse, more so than for any other nation. This is why we today declare:
> 1. The Polish nation is to be the sole master of Poland. The interests of the Polish nation are to be the predominate interests. All nationalities residing in the Polish State will have to serve those interests.
> 2. The interests of non-Polish nationalities may be recognized by the Polish nation only when they do not conflict with Polish national interests.
> 3. Only the Poles can enjoy full political rights in Poland. Such rights will have to be denied in particular to the Jews, the Germans, and the Ukrainians.

Warszawski Glos Narodowy ("Warsaw National Voice") of May 27, 1944, published an article "Mikolajczyk on Polish tolerance." It is a critique of a speech which the then Prime Minister of the Polish Government-in-Exile made in the Polish Foyer in London, in honor of the Archbishop of Canterbury. Mikolajczyk is quoted to have then said:

> While looking into the future, I can assure you that the Government of this Republic, in accord with its constitution and with its programmatic declaration of February 24, 1942, stands unbendingly by the principle of the rights and freedoms of all loyal citizens of the Republic, without regard for their ethnicity, religion or race.

Commenting on this statement, *Warsaw National Voice* writes:

> Unfortunately, Mr. Mikolajczyk neglected to say that as a result of their tolerance towards the Jews, the Germans and other non-Catholics, the Poles had to shed later seas of blood in self-defense and to suffer mass poverty. He unfortunately also neglected to say that the

"minorities" and other religious denominations he was referring to, have very frequently been either betraying the Polish cause, or deliberately acting as a fifth column.

Narodowa Agencja Prasowa ("National Press Agency"), issue No. 6, June 28, 1944:

> We call upon all who love the free and happy Fatherland, and who refuse to become Jewish slaves, to rally together to resist the Jewish offensive supported by the Left which is comprised of Freemasonry, the Polish Socialist Party and the small group which constitutes the present leadership of the Peasant Party. The rule to be enforced is that the Polish nation is to be the sole master of the Polish state.

Freedom-Equality-Independence, i.e. the continuation of the prewar Polish Socialist Party. Alone among the four major parties comprising the Delegate's Office, it was firmly committed to equal rights for the Jews, and it opposed the anti-Semitism of the mainstream parties tenaciously. Thus, its newspaper *W.R.N.* ("Freedom-Equality-Independence"), in the issue No. 1 of January 8, 1943, came out with a harsh criticism of the nationalist tenets in regard to the Jewish question:

> While surveying our political scene, it is impossible to escape the realization of how ill-qualified our nation is in meeting the emergencies of the current situation. We are supposed to be fighting for a democracy; yet the ghosts of our native fascism loom clear. They worship violence while openly deriding democracy, and while seeking to destroy it. We are supposed to become a confederacy of nations; yet zoological nationalism and chauvinism still haunt some Polish heads, posing the threat to all the ideals of international amity which hatred and oppression may well eviscerate. In spite of the grim tragedy which occurred right before our eyes, some circles of our society continue to serve as the breeding ground for anti-Semitism.

Minor political groups. The clandestine press of minor groups represented in the Delegate's Office did not speak on the Jewish question with one voice. An exceptionally articulate lengthy appeal for unconditional solidarity with and for supplies of relief to the persecuted Jews, appeared in *Glos Demokracji* ("The Voice of Democracy") which represented the Democratic Party in the issue of September 4, 1943. The title of the article is "For an active humanitarianism."

> The murders of the Jewish people have revealed the German barbarity in one of its most flagrant forms. We helplessly watch outright crimes. . . . We have no power to defend ourselves, let alone to stop the executioners in their disgraceful slaughter of the Jewish population.

But is has been and continues to be our duty to provide the fugitives who escaped the hands of their executioners with shelter and other forms of relief. The vast majority of the Polish society has in this respect lived up to the task. It has been proven by countless heroic and sacrificial deeds, involving a heavy and always well understood risk to one's own life. The heroic and sacrificial acts of helping the Jews will add to the record of glory of the Polish underground in no lesser measure than the acts of similar quality committed in performance of other underground tasks.

The bestial murder of the Jews which we are witnessing, as well as pillage of Jewish property which follows the patterns once tested in Germany, amount to more than plain anti-Semitism. Through such means, totalitarian nationalism aims at breaking all cultural and moral inhibitions, so as to release savage instincts dormant in human nature; and then to use this released blind and brutal force for its own political ends. This aspect of the tragedy which goes on before our eyes is too little noticed and too little spoken of.

Little is being done to protect the society, in particular its young generation, from moral gangrene, ensuing from the callous reaction to the crimes perpetrated around us.

This is why helping the victims of persecution, quite apart from its material meaning for the recipients, has a paramount moral meaning for the entire Polish society. Our interventions to provide the victims of violence with support are for us the only rational and effective means of self-defense against deliberately spread corruption. This is why public opinion must pillory not only the rabble (fortunately there are not too many of them) who collaborate with the Germans by either informing on the Jews or blackmailing them, but also those who tell us to remain aloof, and who thus impede whatever relief can be secured to save the Jews from death.

Unfortunately the manifestations of callousness in the face of the Jewish agony are quite common. To make matters worse, the supposedly "national" organizations call upon us to remain callous. Their advocacy has the character of a well-planned and well-organized campaign. There have been instances in which persons hiding the Jews would receive letters reprimanding them for acting against the "national interest"! There have been hints, obscure and yet intelligible, that the recipients of the letters may be reported to the Nazi authorities! The very fact that such things happen proves that German propaganda does have its corrupting impact; that it does affect feebler minds and meaner hearts; that to counteract it, public opinion must be vigilant. What is at stake are not the views on the Jewish question. Every citizen is entitled to his own view on this subject. In free Poland, the Polish society will in due time find an opportunity to solve that question. But we all have to recognize that what we face today, is not a solution of the Jewish question, but the most heinous mass crime. This is why there is but one humane and honest attitude: contempt and revulsion for the criminals and commiseration for the tormented victims. He who cannot muster such feelings, doesn't deserve to be called a human being, and ought to be ostracized from the human community.

A critique of anti-Semitism was also voiced by the [Catholic] Front of the Polish Rebirth. In the March 1943, issue of its newspaper *Prawda* ("Truth"), there appeared an article "In the name of the Republic," which reported the imposition of death penalty on two traitors and the execution of that penalty by underground squads. *Truth* commented on this as follows:

> There is no need for hypocritical talk. No prestige considerations, in particular vis-a-vis the foreigners, shall make us keep quiet about the existence of native Polish canaille who prey upon human grief and misery. The hosts of informers and blackmailers have grown, to reach incredible, terrifying numbers. The blackmailers make life intolerable for the ever growing number of victims of Nazi persecutions. They trail their victims relentlessly. No wonder they feel like hunted wild animals.
>
> Yes, we are concerned about the Jews. They are the chief target of the blackmailers. In the past, we have made our attitude towards the Jews clear. Today we wish to emphasize that we are witnessing the most disgraceful conduct conceivable on the part of those who prey on their misfortune. In no way can this conduct be justified. No ideological anti-Semitism can excuse the utter depravity of the blackmailer.

But the clandestine press of a number of minor Catholic-nationalist groups continued to come out with Jew-baiting statements. Thus, for instance, *Prawda Mlodych* ("Young People's Truth:..") for the month of May 1943 wrote:

> The Jews have been parasites living off the bodies of European nations. This is why they have been universally loathed and detested. They have been fighting everybody, but always by subterfuge, never openly, with weapons in hand. Of all the wars fought by the European nations, at least three fourths are attributable to their machinations. But they have managed carefully to obliterate the traces of their powerful influence. On the surface, they have always behaved with complete innocence. Jewish cowardice has become proverbial. They have lost all human dignity.

Slowa Prawdy ("Words of Truth") of October 30, 1943, in an article, bearing the title "Jewish minority" wrote:

> Everyone should know what the Jews have done in the past, what they are still doing at present, and what they may yet do in the future. The Jews have beset us, like a plague. Poland was their breeding ground, a place for incubation. Out of fourteen million Jews in the world, a fourth lived amongst us, getting fattened off our Polish misery. . . . .

And the article continues:

> About 2,275,000 Jews have been murdered. About 550,000 remain in the ghettos, in the camps, and in hiding. About 525,000 have

emigrated, primarily to the Soviet Union. It means that one million Jews, mostly the young ones, will leave their ghettos and their places of hiding in the woods, or will return as Soviet soldiers when the Soviet army advances towards our borders. In a critical moment the Jews will resurface, trying to exact retribution and to deny us the fruits of victory. All their influence and their connections in both the West and Russia will be used for that purpose.

No less anti-Semitic was the Camp of Fighting Poland. In January 1943 its organ *Polska* ("Poland") wrote:

> In Poland the Jews had optimal conditions for development. Yet they have always worked to the detriment of our country. They have always loathed Poland and the Poles. After the present war, we will have to treat them differently, no matter how reduced their numbers. Land will have to be off limits for the Jews. So will industry. And all the media: the press, the movie industry, the book trade. They may be permitted to enter the professions and to take part in commerce, but in strictly controlled numbers. If they don't like it, they will be free to go to Palestine. Only without the right to take Polish currency with them.

The persistent advocacy of anti-Semitism by a vocal segment of the clandestine press impelled the leaders of the Jewish underground to ultimately futile interventions. Possibly the first such intervention was the letter of February 2, 1942, by the Central Committee of the Bund to the Government Delegate. A passage of the letter reads:

> We understand that you have no authority to interfere with what the fraction of the underground press referred to is doing, no matter how harmful these actions may be. However, we deplore the fact that the press representing the Government's point of view has done virtually nothing to oppose anti-Semitic agitation.[26]

Indeed, open anti-Semitism was absent from the clandestine press appearing under direct auspices of the Delegate's Office or the Chief Command of the Home Army. But there was no critique of anti-Semitism either, no matter how extensive its advocacy by vocal groups active in the underground. Two exceptions are, however, to be noted: the article "Hyenas" in the *Information Bulletin* (i.e. the organ of the Chief Command of the Home Army) of March 18, 1943; and the article "Preying on the terrible tragedy," published in the issue No.8 (59) of the *Polish Republic* (i.e. the organ of the Delegate's Office) of May 6, 1943. The former conveyed to public attention the announcement of the Leadership of the Civilian Struggle forewarning that blackmailers preying on Jewish fugitives from the ghettos are liable for clandestine prosecution. The latter made the following points:

The past year has produced another variety of war-time hyenas: the ones who exploit the tragedy of the hiding and pursued Jews for the sake of extortion and blackmail. The core of the Polish society influenced by the Christian teachings have remained morally sane. They are repelled by the crimes of the German executioners against the Jews, and they approach the victims of these crimes in the spirit of deep and genuine compassion. Unfortunately, there are depraved individuals, often clad in police uniforms, who have no qualms about taking advantage of the tragedy of harried and tormented Jews in order to extort exorbitant ransoms through blackmail.

The thinking of the Delegate's Office on the subject of the Jews could not avoid being seriously influenced by the anti-Semitic beliefs and programs of the vocal groups which were constituent parts of that Office. The anti-Semitic mood of the functionaries of that Office can be easily detected in its statements and reports dispatched to the Polish Government in London. It can be seen that anti-Semitic beliefs were not just a peculiarity of a particular individual who happened to author a given report; but that they constituted a dominant mode of thinking in the leadership ranks of the Delegate's Office.

Consider, for instance, the following report of deportations from the Warsaw ghetto, which was subsequently published in London in the issue No. 5 (43) of the "Reports of the Social Department of the Interior Ministry" of August 31, 1943:

Untold bestialities are rumored to have been committed during the fusillades which resulted in slaying the populations of whole towns and villages. But there is a difference between what is known second-hand and what is experienced with one's own eyes. This is why at least some of us, while appalled by the dreadfulness of the methods, and while revolted by the disgrace of murdering women and children, wonder about the meaning of the reported developments in terms of the prospects they portend for domestic relations in future Poland. They ask themselves if the prospects are not favorable. For, really, the numbers of Jews exceeded all proportions! And they were entirely and for ever alien to our culture, our traditions, and our statehood. . . .

And further on, by the same author:

. . . there probably is no other human collectivity that would be so repulsive, that would abound with individual characteristics as distinct and as offensive as those which the Jews share.[27]

The "Report on Communist activities in Poland for the period from November 1942–1943" which was also sent to London, explains the matters as follows:

Elimination of the Jews weakens the impact of Communist ideology. On the other hand, the relentless struggle of the Nazis with Polishness, with our national dignity, and with our political, cultural, and moral heritage enhances national sentiment. It arouses and strengthens national identity even among those who in the past tended to put class-based grievances as their foremost concern.[28]

The "Situation Report" No. 9 for the months May and June 1943 makes similar points:

> The organizational structure of Communist centers has recently been adversely affected by the total destruction of the ghettos. Given the leading role of Jewish elements in Communist operations, the blow dealt to Communism by the nearly total extirpation of Jewry in Polish towns and villages can only be seen as lethal. It applies particularly to Warsaw. At one stroke, Communists lost their shelters (e.g. printing presses, weaponry stores, etc.), their human resources and their financial resources.[29]

In its propaganda inside Poland, the Delegate's Office and the Home Army Command were invariably making quite unambiguous hints to the effect of the restriction of their concern to the affairs and interests of the ethnic Poles. The affairs of Jewish nationals of Poland were as a rule treated by these agencies as lying beyond the scope of their interests. This concept found its clear expression in the leaflet disseminated by the Home Army in Warsaw in the summer of 1943. The leaflet opens as follows:

> Poles!
> Again dreadful events have occurred. Again, a satanically repulsive German bestiality has been brought to light. Again, a mass murder has been committed.
> THE LARGEST MASS MURDER IN THE CAPITAL! (Emphasis original.)
> In several installments, the Gestapo gangsters recently murdered almost one thousand political prisoners, some of them female. For several days before the murders, the ill-fated victims were beaten, humiliated, pitilessly tormented.
> The corridors of the Pawiak prison are flooded with blood! . . .

In its sequel the leaflet reveals the details of the grisly murder of almost 1,000 political prisoners.[30] The details are authentic: it was by all means one of the worst atrocities perpetrated by the Nazis in Warsaw. What is peculiar, however, is that the leaflet chose to describe the event as the largest mass murder ever committed in Warsaw, shortly after not 1,000 but 400,000 people were slaughtered during the liquidation of the Warsaw ghetto.

A particularly reliable account of the position of the Delegate's Office on the Jewish question can be found in one of the successive memos written by Roman Knoll, already mentioned above, who held the post of the Foreign Department director there. The memo in question was written and sent to London in the summer of 1943. It defines with precision the opinions held in the Delegate's Office on foreign policies and the policies in regard to national minorities. The memo has eleven typewritten pages. The passage dealing with the Jews is on pp. 8–9. It reads:

> One of our national problems is the Jewish problem. On the surface, the problem might be thought of as domestic. In reality, it has always been connected with international problems, and it has always affected our international position. It can be anticipated that this problem will be expanded after the present war, for the simple reason that international Jewry has a formally recognized standing within one of the belligerent camps. The German mass murders of the Polish Jews will reduce the scale of the problem, but they cannot eliminate it entirely. In all certainty, a considerable number of Jews will survive. Others, who are now abroad, will reenter Poland. This is why the postwar Jewish population is to be estimated as ranging between one and two million. In response to dreadful persecutions which have befallen the Jews of Europe, world public opinion will be even more sensitive about their fate, and it will supervise their interests accordingly. In Poland the dominant mood at this moment is Christian compassion towards the tormented Jews: but in the eastern parts of Poland very intense grievances against them remain from the time of the Bolshevik occupation. *Yet regardless of such psychological aspects, the state of affairs in the entire country precludes the very possibility of even a very limited return of the Jews to their previously held positions.* (Emphasis added.) Throughout towns and villages, these positions have already been taken over by the non-Jewish population. In this respect a cardinal and irrevocable change occurred, at least over major areas of Polish territory.
>
> If the mass of the Jews ever return, our population will not recognize their restitution claims, but will treat them instead as invaders, resisting them by violent means if need be. For our politics, it would be a tragic outcome, if in moments of settling our national boundaries, of obtaining foreign credits, or of entering alliances or federations, Poland is pilloried by world opinion as a country of violent anti-Semitism. All our enemies would take advantage of our ill-repute to harass us and to deny us the fruits of our so very dearly purchased victory. The Government is right in reassuring world opinion that there will be no anti-Semitism in Poland. The point is, however, that the absence of anti-Semitism will be conditional upon the abstention of the Jewish survivors of the pogroms from returning *en masse* to Polish towns and villages. The dilemma is difficult, and there exists in our opinion only one solution. The Government will be well-advised to come out in advance, as soon as possible, with invitations to provide the East-European Jews with a national home. Endeavors towards this goal should be launched jointly with the Zionist-leaning Jewish politicians. But they should aim at setting up a future Jewish state somewhere in Eastern Europe itself. This location is preferable to Palestine which is too small, too exotic and triggers too much conflict with the Arab world; and also preferable to any colonial territory in the tropics which

will repel Jews from desiring to settle there. It may still be too early to decide which territory can serve the purpose. Our position on this issue must be pro-Jewish, not anti-Jewish. It must be based on the recognition of the Jews as a nation which has the right to its own territory and to a stratificational differentiation on this territory. Diaspora has been for the Jews a curse. For all the dreadful persecutions of the present time the Jewry deserves to be recompensed. And the nations which have hosted the Jews for centuries should be the first to show concern for recompensing them, as well as the first to follow the amicable parting with them by economic assistance and by joint military action in defense of the new order in the world. We do not know how easy or difficult it may be to achieve this goal. But we suppose the task may be easier at the time of the world-wide revision of state boundaries and of the formation of new state organisms, than it would have been at a time of stable peace. Whatever the situation, we deem it imperative to advance toward this goal strenuously, both through diplomatic channels and by means of propaganda.[31]

After it reached London, the memo was brought to the attention of the Cabinet ministers, and eventually also of the National Council members. Schwarzbart became acquainted with its contents no earlier than in December 1943. At the National Council session of December 23, 1943, he criticized the memo pungently, but to no avail. Undeterred Schwarzbart tried to fight the memo by other methods, but these again turned out to be futile. Prompted by the absence of any critical response to the memo on the part of the Polish politicians, Schwarzbart turned to the Foreign Minister with a formal parliamentary interpellation. The interpellation consisted of two questions:

> 1. Are you willing to defend the avowed policy principles of the Government in regard to national minorities in general, and the Jewish minority in particular, by taking a public stand against the views enunciated by the director of the Foreign Affairs' Commission of the Delegate's Office in Poland?
> 2. Is the author of this memo still performing the function of the Foreign Affairs' Commission director? If he is, does the Government (or you personally) intend to discharge him from his responsibilities, so that the vital interests of the Republic and of its Government may be protected by the refusal to take responsibility for the views of this man and for possible developments which his views may spur?[32]

Independently of Schwarzbart, the Representation of Polish Jews, and a number of other Jewish leaders protested on their own. The protests had some resonance in British political circles. This was the background of the July 11, 1944, meeting between the counselor of the British Embassy accredited to the Polish Government-in-Exile, Frank Savery, with Professor Olgierd Gorka, Chief of the Interior Ministry's Nationalities Department. Obviously following the instructions of the Polish authorities, Gorka adopted the tactics of denying the Knoll report's existence. Right after the conversation with Savery, he reported its contents to the Interior Minister as follows:

> In conformity with our denial, I told him that neither you, nor the Social Department, nor the Nationalities' Department ever received such a document. I also told him that the Government Delegate never authored such a document either. At the same time I was willing to give him confidential clarifications not contained in our statement of denial. I acknowledged that a document with such contents had indeed been elaborated by a group acting on the fringes of the National and National-Radical parties, and then sent abroad without the Delegate's knowledge, and through channels other than the Government's. I added that it was sent through Church channels to Rome, and that it was delivered to London from there. While already in London, it reached Schwarzbart through a leak. . . .

But the topic of the conversation shifted when Savery referred to ongoing debates raging both in Poland and in exile on the subject of the need to restore confiscated Jewish property to its rightful owners after the war. Gorka reports the sequel of his conversation with Savery as follows:

> Since the conversation shifted to the substantive issue of the future disposition of confiscated Jewish property in Poland, I said that obstacles can here be expected from the Jewish side rather than from the Polish one. Referring to the pronouncements of Prime Minister Mikolajczyk in the United States, I assured Mr. Savery that as long as the policies of the present Government have force, there are no valid grounds for apprehensions that the issue of Jewish property might not be settled justly and satisfactorily for the Jewish individuals affected. But I also raised a point which was new to Mr. Savery. I told him of an idea, broached recently in America, to transfer all former Jewish property in Poland for which no heirs will be found to the Jewry or the Jewish nation as a whole. I disqualified this idea as unfeasible, because a nation cannot be a party to a contract. And I pointed to another pitfall. The World Zionist Organization which authored the idea equates the "Jewish nation as a whole" with themselves. This, I explained, is bound to be opposed by the Bund, which represents a sizeable part of Polish Jewry and which will never consent to defining the totality of Polish Jews as Zionists.[33]

ATTITUDES TOWARDS JEWISH PARTISANS

Political programs of various organizations attached to the Delegate's Office and popular ideas on the Jewish question had their immediate reflection in practical measures adopted by the respective organizations in regard to Jewish fugitives from the ghettos and the camps: both in regard to those who sought to form partisan detachments, and to those who merely sought opportunities for hiding amongst the Poles.

Concomitantly with the peak period of deportations, Jewish partisan detachments began to crop up in the Polish forests by the middle of 1942. The attitude of the leadership of the Polish underground towards this new phenomenon can well be gauged from the reports of the Delegate's Office and from those clandestine press organs which were published directly either by that Office or by the Chief Command of the Home Army. Most revealing is their vocabulary. Jewish partisan detachments are emphatically referred to as "gangs," a term routinely applied by the Nazis to any guerrilla formations, including the Polish ones. To be sure, in the Home Army documents, the same term is also applied to the Soviet partisans, and to the detachments formed by the Polish Workers' Party which comprised the Communists and the Left-wing Socialists. In the documents of the Delegate's Office, the Jewish partisans are accused of provoking Nazi reprisals against Polish villages, of collaborating with the Soviet partisans, of pro-Communist leanings, and of robberies of Polish peasant households. As can be seen from the following examples, the reports to the Polish Government-in-Exile which made such claims were usually quite distinctly anti-Semitic.

The Delegate's Office Situation Report of October 25, 1942, describes the state of affairs in the Lublin region thus:

> The parachuted Soviet agents and the common brigands came in largest numbers in July. . . . Since September the growth of the Jewish element can be observed. This is a result of anticipations that the Jews might be exterminated. The numbers of Jews continue to grow.[34]

The Report for the month of October, 1942 thus describes the situation in the Cracow region:

> An ever growing number of Jews find places of hiding in the countryside and in the forests. They are forming gangs for purposes of holdups. Some gangs have been found to be exclusively Jewish; but for the most part the Jews join either the diversionary Bolshevik or the Polish brigand gangs.[35]

The Situation Report of January 20, 1943, states:

> Nearly all the Jews of the Lublin district have been murdered. But a few are hiding in the woods and organizing themselves to make holdups.[36]

The Report for the first quarter of 1943, subsequently published by the Polish Interior Ministry in London in vol. 4 (for 1942–1943) of the Situation Reports from Poland, says this:

> Apart from the guerrilla regulars, the murders of Poles and the wreckage of their property are perpetrated by joint gangs of Jews and POWs. Such gangs are interspersed throughout the entire area, but their size usually ranges from fifteen to thirty members. They are too small to be capable of fighting the Germans or the local police. Therefore they limit all their activity to assaults on the manors. The gangs which are exclusively Jewish are notable for their atrocities. One such gang, led by a Jewess from Smorgon, operated for a long time in Oszmiana county. In respect to the savagery with which it perpetrated the murders, including the murders of women, it by far exceeded the Bolsheviks. The landowners and the farming population bear the gruelling burden of such operations.[37]

The same report thus describes the situation in the Bialystok region:

> As an outcome of the liquidation of the ghettos, the numbers of Jews who have joined the diversionary squads have grown considerably.

The report of April 13, 1943, dealing with Grojec county states:

> The number of robbery assaults in the county has grown. Jews have been observed as members of the gangs. The joint Polish-Jewish gangs act very aggressively. The behavior of purely Polish gangs is by comparison much milder.[38]

The situation report for the month of May, 1943 states:

> Communist-Jewish gangs operate in the Kielce county. One of them, about 200-strong, is prowling in the vicinity of Bodzentyn and Nowa Slupia. It is comprised of Polish Communists, Jews, and of parachuted Bolshevik agents. It claims to be a Polish partisan detachment. Its Jewish commander is a veritable animal.[39]

The report devoted to Soviet political and diversionary activity in the month of May, 1943 states:

> The activity of Communist elements in Siedlce county has in recent months grown immensely. These elements are being reinforced by the Jews from Warsaw, and by the parachutists from the Soviet Union.[40]

The report from the region of Opatow and Ilza for the month of January, 1944 states:

> On January 21 the combined detachments of German gendarmerie from Ostrowiec, Starachowice, Skarzysko and Kielce massively raided the forests behind the Kamienna River. The purpose of the raid was to capture the Jewish-Communist gangs. But in the end, no more than ten Jews were caught. They were shot on the spot.[41]

On March 17, 1944, the then Interior Minister of the Polish

Government-in-Exile, Banaczyk, handed to Prime Minister Mikolajczyk the report dealing with the so-called Communist activities in Poland, which was compiled on the basis of various source documents arriving from occupied Poland. This is how Banaczyk's report describes the situation in the Lublin district:

> Intense Communist activity can of late be observed in a number of counties. Members of the Polish Workers' Party, acting in concert with the Jews, engage in increasingly extensive work of destruction. In the countryside they act flagrantly in the open. In the villages, they impose "commanders" who prove to be quite up to their tasks. The Polish Workers' Party gangs, with their 50% Jewish membership, attack and rob farms, intimidate, disseminate "The Partisan" leaflets which call for acts of sabotage and diversion, and even assemble the local population for open rallies. They have broadcasting and receiving equipment, and presses, with Jewish students in charge of publications. Their units are well-organized. The populace demand counteraction by the Home Army. It is rumored that on March 1 the Communist authorities instructed their units to murder all the officers and all the leaders of the independent underground. The Home Army is a particular target.
>
> P.P.R. membership is recruited from the dregs of Jewish nationality and Bolsheviks of Russian nationality. It is reported that recently they began contemplating the systematic liquidation of the leading elite of the Polish society. In the northern part of Zegrzyna county, a Bolshevik aircraft recently provided P.P.R. members with weapons and ammunition.[42]

A decisive negative turn in the attitudes of the Home Army towards the Jews came in the summer of 1943. To a certain extent it is attributable to the appointment of Tadeusz Bor-Komorowski to the post of the Chief Commander of the Home Army. Ideologically, Komorowski was close to the National Party.[43] This appointment coincided with the rise of nationalist influence within the Home Army, with the admission of the rabidly anti-Semitic National Armed Forces (NSZ) to Home Army ranks, and with a modicum of consolidation of the first forest-based detachments of the Home Army. It was the latter which turned in force against the Jewish partisans.

The assaults of the Home Army against the Jewish partisans had official sanction in General Bor-Komorowski's order No. 116 of September 15, 1943. In this order, the newly appointed Chief Commander of the Home Army wrote:

> Heavily armed gangs are continuously prowling the towns and villages, assaulting the manors, banks, commercial and industrial enterprises, houses, apartments, and larger farms. Robbery assaults, often accompanied by murders, are being perpetrated either by forest-based Soviet partisan detachments or by ordinary gangs of robbers.

> Among the perpetrators there are not only men, but also women, in particular Jewish women. . . . I have instructed the regional and district commanders to resist the elements responsible for pillage, banditry or subversion, by force if need be.[44]

The reference to Jewish women served under the circumstances as a veiled indication that Jewish partisan units were also to be met by force. In these units, unlike all other armed groups, the proportion of women was indeed quite high. It is a proven fact, that in many units of the Home Army the order quoted was understood to define the Jewish partisans as outlaws. Anyway, the order did equate the Jewish partisan units with ordinary robber gangs which at that time were indeed quite common; and it did this without paying any heed to the fact that the armed Jews fought against Nazism for their own survival, and for the survival of other Jews hiding under their protection. It was very different from ordinary brigandage. The clandestine press dealt often with the real gangs, and knew how different they were from fighting or hiding groups of Jews. One of the best informed is the article "The sources of evil" which appeared in the organ of the Peasant Battalions "Regional Press Agency-Podlasie" of April 3, 1944. The article deserves to be quoted:

> A tide of banditry floods the entire country. Peaceful people live under the terror of assailants who appear during the night. Their terror is no less dreadful, no less ruthless and no less grievous than the terror of daytime bandits from the Gestapo and gendarmerie. But it goes much farther than ordinary robbery: for it involves a truly terrifying threat to our ability to live together. The phenomenon in question needs to be identified concisely, carefully, and emphatically: *the most depraved behavior assumes the form of banditry, drunkenness, wanton license, the absence of any restraints, and of sheer savagery, such elements spread in the ranks of underground organizations supposed to fight for national independence.* (Emphasis original.)

And further on:

> The assailants are usually residents of neighboring villages. They frequently appear hooded. The incidence of assaults is so high, that no one even bothers to report them to the police. Besides, people refrain from reporting in order not to expose themselves to subsequent retribution. For the assailants are protected by their organizational affiliations. . . . The people of the Podlasie region know well of the pacification and total destruction of the village of Osolinki. The tragedy of this village leans heavily on the conscience of the Home Army command of the Biala-Podlaska county which billeted there a squad comprised exclusively of former convicts of prewar days. Of course, this squad had no regard for the population nor its security. All they cared about was how to terrorize and plunder; and in this they gradually succeeded.

Throughout all this time—in fact, until this very day—these men formally constitute an underground unit. No one ever monitored their activities, no one stopped them in time.[45]

Neither the armed Jewish units nor the individual Jews hiding or fighting in the forests had anything in common with such ordinary criminals. Of course, there was a problem of food supplies, identical with that of any other partisans in a forest. Certainly the Jews who operated in the forests seldom had money or commodities which would enable then to obtain foodstuffs from the peasants through purchase or barter. There was no way, therefore, of avoiding being a burden on the rural populace. Yet the Delegate's Office as the underground government *de facto* with widely recognized authority, surely could solve easily the problem of feeding several Jewish partisan groups or detachments.

The rural population could be justifiably wary of retaliations for the acts of partisan units. This is the subject of a testimony by Waclaw Gryta "Michalowka, Lubartow county" which was published in the book *Bread and Blood: My Village Under Occupation* :

> The Jewish detachment totaling fourteen persons, led by Dworecki[46] visited our village frequently. They were no better armed than we in the Peasant Battalions. The village knew them well, because each time they came, they set up their quarters in a different house. Each time they courteously asked the farmer who happened to be their host for bread. Getting potatoes and salt was no problem; while bacon, often fresh with bristles, was theirs. They would eat, sleep overnight protected from the cold, and in the morning they would leave for the forest. In the winter of 1944 they ambushed the policeman Kowalski who at twilight was crossing the village of Michalowka in a sledge. The Jews killed him with two shots and took his rifle.
>
> On that night only the most daring made up their minds to remain, not only in Michalowka, but also, in neighboring Stanislawow. All the rest sought refuge in neighboring villages out of fear of German reprisals.
>
> At sunrise, a dozen "navy blue" police officers appeared in the village of Stanislawow Maly. It is difficult to say what would have happened had the village not been empty. Perhaps they would have merely tried to catch Kowalski's killers, perhaps they would have retaliated against the entire village, as the Nazis used to do. I witnessed them raiding the village; I observed them from my hiding place.[47]

Such events have to be seen in the context of the unwillingness of the Delegate's Office and of the Home Army Command to place the Jewish partisan units under their authority, in contrast to their attempts to extend their authority over any partisan units comprised of ethnic Poles. Had their policy been different, not only could the food supplies problem have been easily solved, but also the choice of sites for action could have been coordinated, with the aim of avoiding giving pretexts to the Nazis for retaliation against villages which happened to be located in the same area. Remarkably, a Home Army officer, Colonel Henryk Wolinski did submit to his authorities a proposal to incorporate the Jewish units: but the Chief Command rejected the idea. (The subject will be dealt with below.) Numerous Jewish initatives towards the same goal were also thwarted. The Chief Command chose otherwise; and as a consequence of this decision the Jewish partisan units were doomed to gradual extermination.

In the wake of Bor-Komorowski's order, the assaults of the Home Army detachments upon Jewish partisans began to increase in frequency. But their frequency varied from one region of Poland to another. In many cases, the treatment of Jewish partisans depended not so much on the instructions of the Chief Command, as on the attitude of the local Home Army commander. The murder of Jewish partisans by the units of the Home Army are documented by the numerous accounts of former Jewish partisans, as well as by many Polish sources. Some of these documents are worth quoting.

The account of Eliahu Liberman concerns the assaults of the Home Army unit upon the Jewish detachment commanded by Jechiel Grynszpan which operated in Parczew forests:

> Some Home Army units were also stationed in the village of Makoszka in the Parczew forest's region. Whenever they came upon a lone Jew, they would kill him. But they avoided fights whenever they met a group or a whole detachment of us, whether in the woods, or in the village during an action or during requisition of foodstuffs from peasants. They were afraid to start, because they knew that whenever they had tried, we shot back. But many from our ranks perished by their hands. [48]

The fact of the Home Army assaults on Jews, Soviet Partisans and (Communist) People's Guard partisans in the Parczew forest has been confirmed by the Lublin district commander of the People's Guard, Mieczyslaw Moczar. In his report of June 1943 to the People's Guard command Moczar wrote:

> Our units must now fight on two fronts. The leadership of the clandestine struggle [i.e. the Home Army Command] is organizing its units for the task of "liquidating the Communist, POW and Jewish gangs." They acknowledge this objective openly, and they issue orders accordingly. They are very well armed, and they operate more or less in the open. The Germans do not pursue them, nor do they assault the Germans.[49]

In the summer and fall of 1943 assaults on Jewish partisans in the Parczew forests were made by a Home Army detachment led by Lieutenant Konstanty Witwicki (Miller).[50] Nearby, in the counties of Pulawy and Lubartow, it was the Home Army outposts in Boguczyn and Tomaszowice which bore a major responsibility for such assaults.[51] The first serious clash between Jewish partisans and a local Home Army unit in this area took place as early as February 1943. Two Jewish partisans, Yitzhak Morel and a fugitive from Garbow whose name has not been identified, were reconnoitering the village of Lugow where they stayed with a Pole who pretended to be friendly. There they were ambushed by the local Home Army men and killed. In response, the commander of the Jewish detachment, Samuel Jegier, dispatched his men who succeeded in capturing the perpetrators and in locating the corpses of their comrades. The leader of the group which ambushed and killed the two Jews was executed as punishment, and two houses owned by Home Army members were burned. The Polish auxiliary police were alerted, and its patrol arrived on the spot where it was fired upon by the Jews. This successful retaliation had a deterrent effect. For a time, the assaults by local Home Army groups on Jewish partisans ceased.[52]

But in the summer of 1943 the tension between the Jews and the Home Army of Pulawy and Lubartow counties exacerbated, leading to renewed skirmishes. This time, the conflict stemmed from the dispute over the apportionment of foodstuffs from manors which were local Home Army strongholds. The Jewish partisans wanted the local landowners to cede them a portion of foodstuffs. However, the landowners refused, feeling protected by the local Home Army units.[53]

In the southern area of the Lublin district, the Home Army assaults on the Jewish partisans assumed much more serious forms. Particularly hostile towards the local Jewish partisans led by Jakub Met was a Home Army detachment quartered in the village of Kosznia, located midway between Frampol and Turobin.[54]

In the region of Annopol, Janow county, the local Home Army units made recurrent attacks upon the Jewish partisan unit led by Ruwen Pintel. Pintel, his deputy Israel Lichtenstein, and other partisans from this unit were murdered by the Home Army.[55]

In the vicinity of the village Majdan Tyszowski, Tomaszow Lubelski county, a Jewish partisan unit, commanded by a young Jew from Lublin named Cadok established contact with the local unit of the Home Army. There ensued a number of joint operations against the Germans, the most important being the assault on Zabia Wola manor which was under German administration. Two weeks after this joint and successful operation, the Home Army unit invited the Jewish combatants for a feast. Caught unawares, the Jews were first served poisoned vodka, and then fired upon. No one survived.[56]

In the autumn of 1943 detachments of the Home Army murdered a number of survivors of the Sobibor uprising. Two such survivors, Yitzhak Lichtman and Yehezkel Menche, described the fate of eight of their less fortunate comrades who succeeded in escaping from Sobibor, only to be murdered by the Home Army.[57]

In September 1943 a Home Army unit under the command of Szymbierski (Eagle) took a group of Jewish partisans, who were members of the Jewish Combat Organization from the ghetto of Czestochowa by surprise. What made the surprise possible, was the fact that the Jews did not suspect hostile intentions on the part of a haphazardly encountered detachment of men in Polish Army uniforms. The Home Army men took seven prisoners: four Jews, one Russian and two Poles who were with the Jewish unit. One Jew succeeded in escaping. The three remaining Jews and the Russian were shot on the spot. The two Poles were interrogated and shot after they divulged information about the unit and the location of its headquarters in the vicinity of the village Starzyna. Curiously, the crime is well-documented by a preserved diary of one of the accomplices in the murder, a member of Szymbierski's unit. The entry, dated the night of September 10/11, 1943, tells the story:

> A large group under the command of Lieutenant Eagle advances towards the village of Starzyna to search for bandits and Communists. Before we enter the village, our reconnoiterers tell us that someone is there, because there are guardposts. We prepare for a fight. We disarm the first entry, and a short while later, three others. Our soldiers continue to search the village and find three more. All seven are by then in our hands; five Jews and two Poles. They came to plunder, and they have already killed a bull owned by the village agronomist. They are flabbergasted by the surprise encounter. We kill five Jews at once, and we take the other two to our headquarters for interrogation. . . . All this happened at a minimal cost indeed, without a single shot. And we recovered four rifles, four pistols and one hand grenade. No wonder that in the morning we are all mightily pleased. The gang has been liquidated. We keep reminiscing the events of the previous night.

And the same diary, under the entry of September 11:

> In the morning we eat breakfast and we sleep until 2 p.m. Then, we interrogated our captives with the help of the "shoes of justice." They

betrayed everything: their accomplices and the site of their bunker. In the evening, we intend to liquidate them too.[58]

Only one day before this crime, the same unit committed another. It murdered a Jewish girl, Dora Rozenberg, seventeen, hiding in the same area.[59]

During the night of September 12 Szymbierski's unit indeed went towards the bunker of the Jewish Combat Organization partisans, whose site was revealed to them by the two terrorized Poles. (Their names were Morawski and Kulawiak.) But the Jews succeeded in leaving their bunker in time. They did survive; but the bunker in the construction of which they had invested so much effort was wrecked, and the foodstuffs which they had stored for wintertime were seized by Szymbierski's men. Those Jews were helped by a young Polish Communist, Stanislaw Hanyz. Upon learning this, Szymbierski's men broke into his home. He was fortunate enough to be absent at that particular time. But his parents were badly beaten and their house burned down.

Another group of members of the Jewish Combat Organization from Czestochowa operated in the region of Zloty Potok, and was betrayed there by the Home Army unit commanded by "Thunderbolt." The Jewish partisans were invited to Zeleslawice manor, where, as they were told, they would receive foodstuffs, before moving to Czarna Kepa for the purpose of reinforcing a Polish partisan unit which operated in this village. An alleged order to this effect from higher authorities of the Home Army was referred to for the purpose of allaying their suspicions. When they approached Zeleslawice, they found themselves ambushed by German police, densely entrenched throughout the entire area. Two Jews, Jurek Chajutin and Ehrlich, still believing that Home Army representatives were expecting them in the manor, reached the place, and were caught and killed. The remainder waited for their return while exposed to rapid German fire. No more than three Jews survived. Having nowhere else to go, they entered the nearby Hasag camp where some of their comrades from Czestochowa managed to engage in some clandestine work.[60]

On February 9, 1943, in the region of Ostrowiec Swietokrzyski fifteen Jews were murdered by a unit of Zwiazek Odwetu (Revenge Union), an organization which acted under Home Army orders. The fifteen were former members of the clandestine organization in the Ostrowiec labor camp, who succeeded in escaping from that camp, and who intended to turn to the Home Army for help in forming a partisan detachment. The sequence of events unfolded as follows: First, brothers Moses and Kopel Stein, who led the clandestine organization in the Ostrowiec camp, established contact with Jozef Mularski, Edward Perzynski and Leon Nowak who commanded the Revenge Union. Owing to the latter's assistance, a group of 17 Jews escaped from the camp to a bunker prepared for them in advance, in a nearby forest. After a short while, the Revenge Union staged a swearing ceremony under the white-red banners of Poland. The oath was supposed to precede joint combat actions. The real intention was to kill them during the ceremony, when they were all assembled together. Of the seventeen, only two succeeded in escaping the scene.[61]

In the Cracow district, the Jewish partisan unit commanded by Szymon Draenger was attacked by local units of the Home Army, mainly by a group commanded by Mikulski, which had its headquarters in the village of Tymowa.[62]

Jewish partisan units which operated in the region of Zelechow, and which were commanded by Shmuel Oszlak, Mendel Gerecht and Yaakov Rochman suffered major casualties during assaults by Home Army units on them. The first such assault took place on July 26, 1943, in the vicinity of the village Felikszyn. Five Jews were then killed: Yehoshua Feinsilber, Yitzhak Behagen, Listman, a girl from Garwolin, and a boy from Baranow. (The names of the last two have not been determined.)[63]

The next Home Army assault on the same cluster of Jewish units took place in September 1943, when the latter stayed in the estate of Teodorow. Suddenly, they were surrounded and assailed by large forces of the Home Army. The skirmish lasted two hours, and three Jewish partisans fell. But the Jews succeeded in repelling the attack and in breaking out of the encirclement.[64]

The attacks of Home Army units upon the Jews intensified in early 1944. Oftentimes the members of local Home Army units provided the German with leads to forest bunkers occupied by Jewish partisans. Whenever the identity of the informers was revealed, the Jewish partisans attempted to capture and to punish them. But local Home Army commanders protected the informers and resisted Jewish punitive expeditions. This was the background of many bloody clashes. The most serious of such clashes was the surprise assault of an overwhelming and well-armed force of the Home Army upon the Jews under the command of Yaakov Rochman. It took place in the locality Krystyna, near Kleczow. The Jews were killed to the last man.[65]

Home Army units also decimated a Jewish detachment which operated in Wyszkow forests. The detachment had been set up by fugitive members of the Jewish Fighting Organization after the Warsaw ghetto uprising.[66]

Towards the end of 1943, a Jewish unit commanded by Abraham Amsterdam which operated in Dolcza forest in the Cracow district was attacked by local units of the Home Army. The commander's brother, Mendel Amsterdam, was among the casualties of this attack.[67]

The Jewish unit commanded by Yosef Brojde, which operated in the Bransk forests in the Bransk Podlaski region also suffered many casualties in clashes with the Home Army.[68]

Nearly all the Jewish partisan units of Wilno and Nowogrodek districts were at one time or another the targets of Home Army attacks. Tadeusz Konwicki, a former member of a Home Army unit commanded by Orzeszko, which operated in the Wilno district, thus describes in his recollections the passage of the unit through the Rudniki forests, after the area had already been liberated by the Soviet Army:

> For a day we stopped in old Jewish bunkers. About one thousand Jews had survived German raids there. The bunkers were shoddy. But the Jews had apparently been helped by the Soviet partisans, because from us they could expect one thing only, a bullet in the neck.[69]

There is an account of the attacks of the Home Army on Jewish partisans in the Rudniki forests, by a survivor of these clashes, Ewa Haubenstock.[70]

Two other accounts, by Abraham Lipkonski and by Yaakov Golst deal with the attacks of the Home Army upon Jewish partisans in the Narocz forest. Among the fallen in the clashes with the Home Army they mention Leyb Kac, Hillel Margolis, Moshe Paczter and Avigdor Barg; among the wounded Yitzhak Manski and Abraham Asner.[71]

Considerable casualties are also reported in the account of Rivka Glezer[72] dealing with Home Army attacks upon the Jewish partisans in the Nacka forests, and in the account of Shmuel Geler[73] dealing with similar attacks against a Jewish detachment in the Naliboki forest.[74] Chaim Berkowicz recounts murders perpetrated by the Home Army against Jewish partisans operating in the vicinity of Radun.[75] And there are many other accounts which show the hostile attitude of the Home Army towards the Jewish partisans throughout the entire area of Western Byelorussia and the Wilno district.

Instances are known of individual Jews joining the Home Army as Poles, to be murdered by their comrades-in-arms, either when their real ethnicity was revealed, or when they were no longer needed. Revealing in this respect is an incident cited in the recollections of Cyprian Sadowski who served as a physician in the Home Army group "Kampinos":

> One of the medics, still a student, was Jewish. He was badly afflicted by asthma. His recurrent attacks incapacitated him. Normally he was too exhausted to participate in cavalry actions. For this reason, he was constantly under suspicion of cowardice and faking. This is why he came to our commission. We cleared him as incapable of army service. With this document, I went to our commander for a signature of authorization. He signed, and then summoned an adjutant, to whom he issued the order: "To escort him away to the forest and to take off his uniform." "What does it mean to take off his uniform?" I asked. "He first needs a civilian suit. Only then can he be escorted away and released." But I was answered: "No, he won't need any civilian clothes."
>
> I understood instantly. Hurriedly, I returned to our tiny hospital. "You won't go anywhere," I told the boy. "You won't be discharged. Go now to bed, and don't ever dare to move beyond the premises of the hospital."
>
> He also understood. Years later I met him in Warsaw. He thanked me for saving his life.[76]

Still, the Home Army attacks on Jewish partisans were not the rule. Some units of the Home Army behaved loyally and sometimes even quite friendly towards the Jewish units operating in the same surroundings. This holds particularly true for the units of the Peasant Battalions and of the Socialist Combat Organization, both integral parts of the Home Army. There were even instances in which the maintenance of friendly relations involved the countermanding of explicit orders of the Home Army command. Thus, Tuvia Miller who commanded a Jewish partisan detachment in the region of Minsk Mazowiecki, reveals how his unit managed for a long time to survive under exceptionally unfavorable circumstances, owing to the friendly attitude of the local Home Army commander, Wozniak:

> Once an unknown man came to us and said: "Boys, you are going to be raided. And the raid will be big. I don't know when; perhaps tomorrow, perhaps the day after tomorrow, but surely this week. You've got to disappear." It later turned out that he was a Home Army commander, Wozniak from Stodzew. Whenever he received orders from his command to destroy us, he would come to notify us and to make a deal: we disappear, he comes with a raiding force, searches, reports back that no one was found, and goes away. It happened over and over. The deal with him made us secure in the forest.[77]

The only area of prewar Poland in which quite close cooperation between Home Army units and the Jewish partisans was the rule was the district of Volhynia, but this exception from the prevalent pattern of the Home Army's enmity occurred for a special reason. The dominant force in Volhynia were the Ukrainian nationalists who frequently assailed the Polish minority, slaughtering entire villages in the most atrocious manner. Under those circumstances the task of the Home Army was to defend the Polish villages against the Ukrainians. No wonder, then, that the outnumbered Home Army outposts which were stationed in vulnerable villages looked on the Jewish partisans as most desirable reinforcements. Accordingly, the Jewish partisans could there rely on the support of the Polish villagers. The enemy of the Polish villagers and of the Jews was the same: the Ukrainians were murdering both.

An excellent case in point is the behavior of the Home Army outpost under the command of Sergeant Kazimierz Wojtowicz (Brier) which was stationed in the village of Hanaczow, and of the two Home Army detachments commanded respectively by Captain Fryderyk Staub (Gunpowder) and by Lieutenant "Arrow," which operated in the nearby forests. The Polish populace of Hanaczow supplied the Jewish partisans with foodstuffs free of charge; and whenever possible, the villagers permitted the Jews to set up quarters in the village itself. On their part, the Jewish partisans fought in defense of the village during two major Ukrainian assaults, during the night of February 2–3, 1944 and the night of April 9–10 of the same year.[78] Cooperation between the Jewish partisans and the Home Army outpost stationed in the village of Panska Dolina developed along more or less the same lines.[79]

* * *

We need to generalize in such a way as to cover both the political program and the actual practice of the Delegate's Office and of the Chief Command of the Home Army in regard to the Jews in 1943 and 1944 in all regions of Poland. Within this frame, one can tentatively offer the following generalization: Although certain political groups subordinated to the Delegate's Office, like the Socialists, the Democrats, the Syndicalists and some Catholics stood by the principle of fully equal rights for the surviving remnant of the Jews, the majority of forces comprised by the Delegate's Office were anti-Semitic. This anti-Semitic majority prevailed, to the point of shaping an anti-Semitic political program typified by the Knoll memo and by various anti-Semitic statements of the clandestine press. This program had a counterpart in the practice of fighting the

Jewish partisan units, and, as the next chapter will show, participating in the murders of Jewish fugitives in hiding.

THE RIGHT-WING OPPOSITION

The Right-wing opposition to the Delegate's Office manifested an overt and unambiguous hostility towards the Jews. It essentially consisted of three splinter groups from the National-Radical Camp respectively known under the names of *Falanga* ("Phalanx"), Szaniec ("Rampart"), and the "Confederacy of the Nation." The attitudes and behavior of all three groups towards the Jews remained unchanged: even in 1943 and 1944 they differed little from the Nazi behavior. Their following was in those years steadily expanding. Their influence upon the Polish Government and the National Council in exile remained negligible. But in the Polish underground, they in the end became a force to be reckoned with. This fact is stressed by Polish scholar, Jerzy Janusz Terej, who says of these groups:

> Unlike the weak satellite groups around the National Party in exile, these were powerful, dynamic and influential political forces. In principle they recognized the leading role of the National Party, but in practice this recognition was conditional and qualified.[80]

The growth in influence and popularity of the "Rampart" splinter is asserted on p. 17 of the updated report of the Interior Department of the Delegate's Office (sent to London towards the end of 1942), which bears the title "Reports on clandestine organizations":

> Beyond any doubt, the "Rampart" group is expanding. Their press has a high circulation, and it reaches all regions of the Government General and annexed territories. Their activities in the countryside undergo a noticeable intensification. Most recently, they proceeded to the publication of a newspaper for the workers. Its name is *Zaloga* ("The Crew"). They have considerable backing in the working class populace of the Lodz, Kielce, and Silesia districts.[81]

The advocacy of rabid anti-Semitism was pursued throughout 1943 and 1944 in the clandestine press organs of all three movements. Thus, the very first issue of *Zaloga*, of January 1, 1943, commented on a news report that some Jews in London had assembled for a prayer for Poland in the following way. (The title of the quoted article is "Poland—the homeland of the Jews"):

> We will chase the Jew away with the last breath in our chests and to the limits of brawn in our fists. Let him live wherever he wishes to

settle, let him do whatever he pleases, let him trade, profiteer, cheat. Only, God forbid, not in our midst. If a rabbi chants in London, everything is satisfactory. But if he ever tries to chant in Poland, the sound will soon turn into a lament, for he will feel thoroughly defeated.

Praca i walka ("Work and struggle") in the issue No. 6, of March 27, 1944:

> The accursed Jewish incubus has left so much poison in the blood of civilized nations, produced so much evil and so many calamities, that the time has finally come to mete out a well-deserved punishment, capable of deterring the Jews once and forever from their subversive plotting.

Such words were consistent with the deeds. Towards the end of 1942 the Commander of the newly formed National Armed Forces (NSZ), Colonel Czeslaw Oziewicz, issued orders for the so-called Special Task No. 1:

> Our partisan groups can and must immediately proceed to the cleansing of the terrain from subversive and criminal gangs and from minority formations which are hostile to us. We shall also undertake self-defensive counteractions against the punitive expeditions of the occupier in cases when German repression is glaringly unjustified.[83]

A Polish historian of the anti-Nazi underground, Bogdan Hillebrandt, explains the meaning of the concept "minority formations":

> The units of the National Armed Forces assigned top priority to internecine warfare against the partisan units of the People's Guard which they called "subversive gangs," and against groups comprised of Jewish fugitives from the ghettos which they called "minority formations."[83]

Acting in conformity with this program, the units of the National Armed Forces from the moment of their formation proceeded to attack Jewish partisan units and detachments, and to murder in their places of hiding the unarmed Jewish fugitives from the ghettos and the camps. A particular zeal in the performance of these tasks was displayed by the units of the National Armed Forces which operated in the southern part of the Lublin district. Their commanders were Aleksander Zdanowicz (Tooth), a parachutist who had arrived shortly before from England, and Leon Cybulski (Torch), a former policeman.[84] In the Kielce district the units of the National Armed Forces pursued the Jews in close collaboration with the Nazis.[85]

THE LEFT-WING OPPOSITION: THE POLISH WORKERS' PARTY

The program of the Polish Workers' Party stood for completely equal citizenship rights for the Jews. This point was reiterated in a number of programmatic declarations, e.g. in the first proclamation of the PWP of January 1942, and in the programmatic declaration "What are we fighting for?" published in November 1943. To be sure, there was nothing in these declarations beyond generalities about equal rights for all citizens, including the Jews; in particular nothing about concrete day-to-day survival problems of the Jewish population living under the threat of total extermination. But the clear and unequivocal espousal of the principle of equal rights for the Jews was sufficient to account for the definite rise in PWP's popularity among the surviving remnant of Polish Jewry.

The overriding objective of the Polish Workers' Party's propaganda was the mobilization of the civilian masses of the Polish society for the immediate launching of armed resistance against the Germans. In the advocacy of this goal, it was expedient for the PWP to resort to the argument that the Jews had been victims of their own alleged inaction. Such a presentation of the causes of the Jewish tragedy, in addition to being devoid of all validity, had the unintended effect of fortifying popular resentment against the Jews. The nature of this propaganda can be seen from the quotes that follow.

Glos Lodzi ("The voice of Lodz"), issue No. 3 of January 13, 1943, in the article "The struggle of the nations of Europe":

> The Polish nation already realizes that inaction does not appease the beast, but makes it even more offensive than before. Inaction only makes it easier to perpetrate mass murders of Poles in the concentration camps. In the Treblinka death camp alone, over two million Jews were murdered in the most atrocious manner possible.[86]

Trybuna Wolnosci ("The Tribune of Liberty") in its issue No. 24 of January 15, 1943, published an article "Now they again call for keeping calm." The intention of the article was to rebut the standpoint of the Home Army which warned against premature attempts at armed resistance:

> The comparison with the murders of Jews is striking. Until the very end, the Jewish Councils had an authoritative role. Even when the occupier's intention to kill everyone was already common knowledge, the council officials continued to entreat people to avoid "provocations." Through this comparison we can see today how the futile appeals to keep calm can help the occupier.[87]

The paper of the Lublin district's People's Guard *Powstanie*

("Uprising") of March 1943 wrote in the article "He who waits
commits a crime":

> Some say that the time is not yet ripe. Let us then ask the advocates of
> inaction, when does the time become ripe? When we are already
> driven into the ovens of Treblinka, like the Jews? When most of us
> already fall prey to Nazi despotism and the remainder of the nation is
> too incapacitated to defend themselves.[88]

A proclamation of August 10, 1943, issued by the Krasnik county
committee of the Polish Workers' Party reads:

> To the soldiers of the People's Army, to the peasants, to the workers,
> to working intelligentsia!
> Poles!
> Four years of Hitler's reign have resulted in six million Polish deaths
> from the executioner's axe. The best of the nation continue to perish,
> day after day. Before the war's end, many peasants and workers will
> fall from the bullets of the Nazi executioners. Yet you know how pre-
> cious is the life of every single Pole who fights for Free and In-
> dependent Poland.
> In order to thwart Hitler's design to exterminate the Polish nation,
> the People's Guard has formed partisan units in the forests. Those units
> will defend themselves against the Germans. They will not go to death
> without resistance, as the Jews have done and as the Nationalists want
> us to do.[89]

Trybuna Ludu ("Tribune of the People"), issue No. 8 of
November 15, 1943, in the article "Long live the general strike":

> An uprising, even if limited in scope, would be under present
> circumstances a calamity for the Germans. The prospect of an uprising
> terrifies them. Fright prompts them to apply precautions; that is why
> they commit horrible atrocities. Today, they want nothing so much as
> that we keep quiet; in the same way as they wanted the Jews to keep
> quiet when they were about to liquidate them. But then, they were able
> to achieve their objective through artful tricks and subterfuge.[90]

Tribune of Liberty, issue No. 55 of May 1, 1944, in the article
"The defense of the Warsaw ghetto" commemorating the first
anniversary of the Warsaw ghetto uprising:

> The campaign of April 1943 ended in the Jewish defeat. The Jews
> were defeated because they fought under conditions of total isolation
> and because they faced the technological might of the Nazi war
> machinery all alone. But also because earlier—in the summer of
> 1942—when the aims of the Nazi criminals could still be thwarted
> through determined resistance, the Jews' hope had been dashed both
> morally and politically.[91]

But apart from a number of articles or publications dealing with
the Warsaw ghetto uprising, the clandestine press of the PWP

published next to nothing about the ways in which the Jews were surviving or the circumstances under which they were hiding, about the resistance of Jewish partisans, or about the continuing exterminatory operations of the Germans. One of the very few exceptions was an article bearing the title "To condemn and to punish the reactionary criminals" which appeared in issue No. 51 of *Tribune of Liberty* of March 2, 1944. The article describes murders of Left-wing politicians and of fugitive Soviet POWs committed by the Home Army, and it mentions that:

> The same forces pursue the hiding Jews, and either murder them or deliver them to the Gestapo.[92]

The PPR did not extend its sponsorship to any relief action for the benefit of the Jews, such as the Delegate's Office-sponsored Council for Aiding Jews (*Zegota*).[93]

Yet the emergence of the Polish Workers' Party and the formation of its People's Guard did have consequences advantageous for the Jewish partisans. The program of recruiting anyone at hand for the purpose of the immediate initiation of armed resistance against the Nazi occupier led to extending the PWP's aid and support to numerous Jewish partisan detachments formed in 1942 or 1943. In many regions, the People's Guard was the only allied force the Jewish partisans could rely upon. Without that alliance, some Jewish partisan units would have been forced to discontinue their operations.

In sum total, nine Jewish partisan units joined the People's Guard: (1) the unit commanded by Julian Ajzenman-Kaniewski which operated in the Opoczno region of Kielce district; (2) the unit of Lejb Birman operating in the vicinity of Rzeszow; (3) Abraham Braun in the Janow forests; (4) Jechiel Grynszpan in the Parczew forests; (5) Szmuel Gruber in the Lubartow region of the Lublin district; (6) Szmuel Jegier in the same area; (7) Michael Majtek in the Pinczow region; (8) Zalman Fajnsztat in the same region; and (9) Edward Forst in the Krasnik region in the southern part of the Lublin district. The Jewish detachment named after Mordechaj Anielewicz, which was comprised of members of the Jewish Fighting Organization, and which operated in the Wyszkow forests was also formally a part of the People's Guard, and can therefore be counted as the tenth on the list.

In addition to this, the People's Guard had thirteen ethnically mixed partisan units (Polish-Jewish, Jewish-Russian, or Polish-Jewish-Russian), with Jews—at least in the initial period of the units' combat activity—accounting for no less than a third of their total membership. They were known under the names of (1) Janowski, (2) Wanda Wasilewska, (3)Hawk, (4) Stefan Kola, (5) Wolf, (6) Hunchback, (7) Bartosz Glowacki, (8) Kielce Land, (9) Kosciuszko, and (10) The Special Unit of the Lublin District. Three units without special names were commanded by (11) Rajewski, (12) Mastelarz, and (13) Kowalow.

In the districts of Volhynia and Polesie the Polish Communists organized several partisan units which were subsequently integrated within large Soviet partisan concentrations. There were four major units of this type, commanded respectively by Satanowski, Klim, Sobiesiak, and Major Bronislaw Dabrowski; the latter better known as the "Wanda Wasilewska Brigade." The guiding principles and the practical conduct of these units in regard to the armed and hidden groups of Jews were fundamentally the same as on ethnically Polish territories. All four units included Jewish partisans, and there were also a number of Jewish fugitives from the ghettos, in hiding, whom these units protected. The first of the aforementioned unit commanders, Moshe (Robert) Satanowski was a Jewish partisan himself. The "Wanda Wasilewska Brigade" included about twenty Jews, some of them paratroopers, officers and soldiers of the regular Polish Army parachuted to Polesie with the task of organizing guerrilla activities there. In January 1944 a Jewish detachment of about thirty partisans joined this unit, making a total of about fifty Jews.[94]

A number of PWP activists extended their help to Jews in hiding as individuals, out of humanitarian or ideological considerations. Since most such cases occurred in Warsaw, they are dealt with in the chapter devoted to the developments in that city.

NOTES

1. YVA, 0-25/91-4.

2. Brustin-Berenstein, T. "Deportacja i zaglada skupisk zydowskich w dystrykcie warszawskim" (Deportations and extermination of Jewish concentrations in the Warsaw district), *Biuletyn Zydowskiego Instytutu Historycznego* (Bulletin of the Jewish Historical Institute; henceforth BZIH), 3, 1952, pp. 83–125.

3. Rutkowski, A. "Martyrologia, walka i zaglada ludnosci zydowskiej w dystrykcie radomskim podczas okupacji hitlerowskiej" (Martyrdom, struggle, and extermination of the Jewish population of the Radom district during the Nazi occupation), BZIH, 15–16, 1955, pp. 75–182; Rutkowski, A. "Hitlerowskie obozy pracy dla Zydow w dystrykcie radomskim" (Nazi labor camps for the Jews in the Radom district), BZIH, 17–18, 1956, pp. 106–128.

4. Berenstein, T. "Martyrologia, opor i zaglada ludnosci zydowskiej w dystrykcie lubelskim" (Martyrdom, resistance and extermination of the Jewish population of the Lublin district), BZIH, 21, 1957, pp. 21–92.

5. Podhorizer-Sandel, E. "O zagladzie Zydow w dystrykcie krakowskim" (On

the extermination of the Jews in the Cracow district), BZIH, 30, 1959, pp. 87–109.

6. Berenstein, T. "Eksterminacja ludnosci zydowskiej w dystrykcie Galicja 1941–1943" (Extermination of the Jewish population in the Galicja district 1941–1943), BZIH, 61, 1967, pp. 3–58.

7. Dabrowska, D. "Zaglada skupisk zydowskich w Kraju Warty w okresie okupacji hitlerowskiej" (Extermination of the Jewish concentrations in Warthegau during the Nazi occupation), BZIH, 13–14, 1955, pp. 122–184; Szternfinkel, N. "Zaglada Zydow Sosnowca" (Extermination of Sosnowiec Jews)

8. Datner, S. "Eksterminacja ludnosci zydowskiej w okregu bialostockim" (Extermination of the Jewish population in the Bialystok region), BZIH, 30, 1966, pp. 3–50.

9. Zeminski, S. "Kartki z dziennika nauczyciela w Lukowie z okresu okupacji hitlerowskiej" (Pages from the diary of a Lukow teacher from the period of Nazi occupation), BZIH, 27, 1958, p. 109.

10. Szefler, S. Okupacyjne drogi (The ways of occupation), Warsaw, 1967, pp. 207–208.

11. Klukowski, Z. Dziennik z lat okupacji Zamojszczyzny (Diary from the years of occupation of the Zamosc region), Lublin, 1959, p. 336.

12. YVA, 0–25/93–16.

13. These materials have been investigated by a researcher of the Central Commission for the Study of the Nazi Crimes in Poland, Kazimierz Leszczynski, and published in issues 8 and 9 of that Commission's bulletin hencefully referred to as BGKBZHP).

14. BGKBZHP, 9, 1957, pp. 113–169.

15. BGKBZHP, 11, 1960.

16. BGKBZHP, 10, 1960, pp. 239–248; BGKBZHP, 9, 1957, pp. 209–214.

17. BGKBZHP, 9, 1957, pp. 170–225.

18. Ibid.

19. Rutkowski, A. "Martyrologia, walka i zaglada ludnosci zydowskiej w dystrykcie radomskim podczas okupacji hitlerowskiej" (Martyrdom, struggle and extermination of the Jewish population of the Radom district during the Nazi occupation), BZIH, 15–16, p. 182; Grodecki, Z., account in YVA, 0–3/1252;

Rusinek, E., account in the Archive of the Jewish Historical Institute in Warsaw, 520; Bleter far geshihte, 7, 1969, p. 136.

20. BGKBZHP, Vol. VIII, pp. 123–143.

21. The document is published in full in the journal Wojskowy Przeglad Historyczny (Military History Review), 4, 1971, pp. 145–153.

22. YVA, O–25/83–3.

23. YVA, O–25/91–1.

24. Quoted according to Terej, J.J., op. cit., p. 242.

25. Quoted according to Terej, op. cit., pp. 330–331.

26. Archive of the Central Committee of the Polish Unified Workers' Party (henceforth referred to as AZHP), 202–XV–2, p. 31.

27. YVA, M–2/205.

28. YVA, M–2/204.

29. YVA, M–2/209.

30. A photostat of the leaflet is published in Landau, L., op cit. vol. 3, between p. 96–97.

31. YVA, M–2/334.

32. YVA, M–2/334.

33. GSHI, PRM–142.

34. AZHP, 202/II–11, p. 219.

35. AZHP, 202/III–28, p. 312.

36. AZHP, 202/II–11, p. 255.

37. YVA, 0/25/84–1.

38. AZHP, 202/II–11, p. 26.

39. AZHP, 202/III–136, p. 254.

40. YVA, 0–25/91–9.

41. AZHP, 202/III–21, p. 2.

42. GSHI, PRM–L3.

43. Bor-Komorowski's affiliations with the National Party are described by Rzepecki, J., "Organizacja i dzialanie Biura Informacji i Propagandy KG AK" (Organization and activities of the Bureau for Information and Propaganda of the Home Army's Chief Command), Wojskowy Przeglad Historyczny ("Military History Review"), 2, 1971, p. 151. Rzepecki was an officer (of the rank of colonel) of the Home Army's Chief Command, and after the war a renowned military historian.

44. Polskie sily zbrojne w drugiej wojnie swiatowej ("Polish armed forces in the Second World War"), vol. 3, p. 431.

45. Hirsz, Z. J., Lubelska prasa konspiracyjna 1939–1944), Lublin, 1968, pp. 473–474.

46. *The detachment in question, commanded by Marek Dworecki, was a part of a larger Jewish partisan unit, commanded by Shmuel Jegier.*

47. See Gryta, W., *"Michalowka, powait Lubartow" (Michalowka, Lubartow county), in the collection Chleb i krew; moja wies w czasie okupacji* (Bread and blood: my village during the occupation), p. 183.

48. Liberman, E., account in YVA, 0–3/1824.

49. *Zrodla i materialy do dziejow ruchu oporu na Lubelszczyznie* (Sources and materials to the history of the resistance in the Lublin region), vol. 1, Lublin, 1960, pp. 71–72.

50. Sulewski, W., *Lasy Parczewskie* (The Parczew forests), pp. 155, 268; Gronczewski, *op cit.*, p. 245; Sidor, *op cit.*, p. 245.

51. *Hurbanah v'gvuratah shel haayarah Markuszew* (Extermination and heroism of the village Markuszew), p. 376.

52. Gothelf, D., account in *Hurbanah v'gvuratah...*, pp. 159–194.

53. *Hurbanah v'gvuratah...*, p. 376.

54. Ben Moshe, A., account in *Sefer Frampol* (The Book of Frampol), p. 100.

55. Fiszman, A., account in YVA, M–1/E–714.

56. *Dos buch fun Lublin* (The Book of Lublin), p. 550; Brener, H., account in the Archive of the Jewish Historical Institute, 275.

57. Lichtman, I., account in YVA, 0/3/2309 Menche, J., account in YVA, M–1/E–651.

58. The file of the District Court in Kielce, vol. 1, III/K–15/52. Quoted after Nazarewicz, R., *Nad gorna Warta i Pilica* (Near upper Warta and Pilica Rivers), pp. 178–179.

59. Brener, L., "Ruch podziemny czestochowskiego ghetta" (Resistance movement in the ghetto of Czestochowa), BZIH, 45–46, 1963, p. 173.

60. Jakobson, I., "W zydowskim oddziale partyzanckim" (In a Jewish partisan unit), *Tygodnik Powszechny*, 24(90) of June 18, 1967. See also the list of the fallen in *Sefer Czestochowa* (The Book of Czestochowa).

61. Three leaders of the Revenge Union in Ostrowiec—Jozef Mulewski, Edward Perzynski and Leon Nowak— were tried for this murder in Sandomierz on September 13, 1949. See Ruthkowski, A., "Martyrologia walka i zaglada ludnosci zydowskiej w dystrykcie radomskim podczas okupacji hitlerowskiej" (Martyrdom, struggle, and extermination of the Jewish population of the Radom district during the Nazi occupation), BZIH, 15–16, 1955, p. 133, footnote 164. See also *Sefer Ostrowiec* (The Book of Ostrowiec), p. 438.

62. Bauminger, A., Bosak, M. and Gerber, N. M. *Sefer Kraka: Ir v'am, be-Israel* (The Book of Cracow: The City and Its People in Israel), Jerusalem, 1959, pp. 425–428. See also Kalfus, J., account in YVA, 0–3/1391.

63. Laksman, account in *Sefer Zelechow* (The Book of Zelechow), p. 246.

64. Gerecht, account *ibid.*, p. 276.

65. Laksman, *ibid.*, p. 249.

66. Miedzyrzecka, Wladka (Vladka Meed. *On Both Sides of the Wall* pp. 187, 233. Also the report No. 6 of September 5, 1943 as published in BZIH, 5, p. 31. Also Jaworski, B., account in the Archive of the Jewish Historical Institute, 5016.

67. Pinkus, M., YVA, 0–33/894; Amsterdam, J., account in *Sefer Radomysl* (The Book of Radomysl).

68. Broide, J., *Beyaaroth Bransk: zikhronoth shel partizan yehudi* (In the forests of Bransk: recollections of a Jewish partisan), Tel Aviv, 1974. Also Brener, I., account in YVA, 0–33/151.

69. Konwicki, T., *Rojstry*, Warsaw, 1959, p. 128.

70. Haubenstock, E., account in YVA, 0–3/1286.

71. Lipkonski, A., YVA, 0–33/588; Golst, J., account in YVA, 0–33/568.

72. Glezer-Kaplan, R., account in YVA, M–1/E–1782.

73. Geler, Sh., YVA, 0–3/2103.

74. *Ayarateinu Naliboki* (Our village of Naliboki), p. 139.

75. Berkowicz, Ch., YVA, M–1/E–1613.

76. Recollections of C. Sadowski in *Pamietniki lekarzy* (Diaries of physicians), p. 617.

77. Miller, T., YVA, 0–3/2078.

78. A letter by W. Bialoszewicz, F. Staub and D. Wegierski to *Wojskowy Przeglad Historyczny* (Military History Review), 1, 1974, pp. 446–447. Also Ende, S., account in YVA, M–1/E–574; Sztatfeld, S., "Partizan yehudi beyaar

Hanaczow" (A Jewish partisan in the forest of Hanaczow), *Yalkut Moreshet* (The Store of Heritage), April 1977, pp. 25–38.

79. *Sefer Trubicz* (The Book of Trubicz), p. 349; *Sefer Mlynow* (The Book of Klynow), pp. 305–306.

80. Terej, J. J., *op. cit.*, p. 221.

81. AZHP, 202/II–22, p. 80.

82. Hillebrandt, B., *Partyzantka na Kielecczyznie* (Partisan warfare in the Kielce region), pp. 220–221.

83. *Ibid.*

84. Sulewski, W., *Partyzanckie sciezki* (Partisan paths), p.15. Szymanski., T., *My ze spalonych wsi* (We from the burned villages), p. 199.

85. Described by Hillebrandt, *op. cit.*

86. Quoted after *Publicystyka konspiracyjna* PPR (Clandetine journalism of the PWP), vol. 2, p. 26.

87. *Ibid.*, vol. 2. p. 34.

88. Hirsz, Z. J., *op. cit.*, pp. 279–280.

89. Szymanski, *op. cit.*, p. 260.

90. *Publicystyka konspiracyjna PPR,* p. 434.

91. *Ibid.*, vol. 3, p. 190.

92. *Ibid.*, p.106.

93. YVA, M–2/209.

94. The History of these units has been extensively dealt with by Shmuel Krakowski, *The war of the doomed: Jewish armed resistance in Poland 1942-1944*; Holmes and Meyer, New York, 1984.

CHAPTER FIVE

In Warsaw

RESISTANCE

The Polish underground organization—consisting of the Delegate's Office and its agencies, and of resistance units affiliated with the AK—appeared both within the country and to the outside world as the Polish government's official representative in occupied Poland. The institutions and agencies operating on behalf of these bodies were subordinate to the Polish Government-in-Exile, which was recognized by the Western Allies as the legitimate government of independent Poland within the established frontiers of the interwar period, and claimed to represent the entire population, inclusive of ethnic minorities, residing within those boundaries. Thus the Polish Government-in-Exile and its civilian and military underground organizations had in effect assumed responsibility for the well-being of all Polish citizens, Jews as well as Christians, and committed itself to defending their lives and safety against the German occupation regime.

Clearly, the Government-in-Exile did not officially confine itself to representing ethnic Poles only; moreover, its claims to being the legitimate government of Poland were founded in its constitution and its decisions with respect to all minorities and all of the areas in which it was active. Therefore, we should have every reason to expect that the Delegate's Office and the forces of armed resistance in occupied Poland (i.e., the ZWZ or *Zwiazek Walki Zbrojnej*, and, later the AK or *Armia Krajowa*) would have sought to unify the entire citizenry of the country and, accordingly, bring the nation's populace as a whole, including the Jews, within the scope of their operations. What we discover instead is a contradiction, indeed a conflict, between the Polish Government-in-Exile's proclaimed policy and often its actions, on the one hand—and the statements and conduct of the civil and military underground in occupied Poland, on the other.

In a report written late In May 1944 expressly for the Polish head

of state, Witold Bienkowski, chief of the Jewish section in the
Delegate's office, claimed that from the point of view of the Poles no
problem of Jews existed until the end of 1941, "in either a political
or emotional sense."[1] And Iranek-Osmecki, in his strongly
apologetic book, argued: "From 1939 until the autumn of 1942 the
Jews maintained a passive attitude. They did not envision an
armed rising nor did they prepare for it. The Home Army [AK] also
had no reason to take an interest in the paramilitary training of
Jews. The situation changed only when Jews decided to defend
themselves and when they formed the Jewish Fighting Organization"[2] In his memorandum Bienkowski did not explain why the
extensive suffering of the Jews, both as human beings and as Polish
citizens, failed to inspire any political commitment or emotional
sympathy. That the Delegate's Office and its agencies did not
regard it their duty to come to the aid of Jews incarcerated in the
ghettos is inexplicable. Assistance in the form of food and money
might have saved tens of thousands from death by starvation in the
Warsaw Ghetto and the ghettos of other cities in Poland. However,
while the Jewish community was being slowly decimated by
famine and disease, we hear of no initiative being undertaken by
elements in the Polish underground to come to its rescue, nor even
of any proposal to appeal to the Government-in-Exile, and through
it to the organizations and leadership of the world Jewish community, for aid to be sent to the Jews in Poland.

This inaction and utter callousness concerning Jewish suffering
on the part of those who had been entrusted with responsibility for
the welfare of Polish citizens under the occupation is beyond
comprehension. It is impossible to discern the slightest legitimate
basis for such an attitude.

We shall shortly turn to a detailed account of the supposed
"passivity" of Jews which—as Polish sources suggest—released the
AK from its responsibilities to the Jewish community and the need
to take action in its behalf. But even if such were the case, we
should be justified in asking if the AK did anything positive to
rouse the Jews from their passivity. Did it encourage them to participate in the anti-Nazi resistance movement, or give them the
opportunity to take part in the national struggle against the invader? The regrettable truth is that the AK neither recruited Jews
individually nor attempted to organize resistance cells within the
Jewish community. It offered the Jews no money, arms, guidance,
intelligence or liaison facilities with the outside world—in fact
none of the essentials that would have encouraged a will to resist or
made possible the establishment of an operational armed force. We

therefore turn in vain to Polish sources for an explanation of this neglect.

Polish emigre circles in London have published an exhaustive study of the Polish armed forces in the Second World War and their contributions to the war effort both at home and abroad. The third volume of this work covers the activities of the AK.[3] It traces the history of the AK in great detail, and gives an account of the conflicts and tensions between the military and civil branches of the underground over seniority, and of the difficulties experienced in consolidating the various political movements that had been active in Poland before the war into a single unified force; most importantly, it furnishes us with a record of orders and directives originating in London that were of major significance to the formation of the underground resistance movement in Poland. The volume does not confine itself only to a description of the national anti-Nazi struggle and the military operations of the underground; it also gives extensive coverage to the political considerations involved in the struggle and to the periodic communications sent by the AK to London containing detailed reports and analyses of events at home.

The volume mentioned contains a minor subchapter which treats ethnic minorities and other nationalities. In a series of brief passages the editors dispose of each of the ethnic minorities and the "Polish underground state's" policy toward them. The discussion of the Jews is perfunctorily sandwiched between the passages concerning the Germans and Lithuanians. Of the Germans it is maintained quite accurately that "Polish citizens of German nationality, with few exceptions, went over to the invader, and not only did they fail to show loyalty to the Polish state but joined the ranks of the most brutal murderers among the occupation forces." Concerning the Lithuanians the observation is made that "the Russian invader used the Lithuanians as an anti-Polish element. The German invader did the same, although with much greater success."[5] The passage concerning the Jews opens with the assertion: "The Jews began by taking a conditional attitude, making their conduct dependent on the treatment they would receive from the invaders." We should note that by referring to "invaders" in the plural, the editors imply that the German occupation and Soviet annexation were comparable in all respects. The text then continues:

> "Within the area of German occupation [and] isolated by ghetto walls from the outside world, they turned to organized self-defense only when the horror of the occupation took on ever increasingly brutal forms. Faced with total annihilation, the Jews set about creating within

the ghettos the underground Jewish Fighting Organization. But it never achieved the status of a mass movement of the Warsaw Ghetto in April 1943; only a small segment of the population was involved in the armed struggle. The AK established a liaison with the ZOB and assisted it during the armed operation in Warsaw by supplying the ghetto with certain quantities of arms and ammunition. A unit of the AK also tried to breach the ring of walls encircling the ghetto on the outside in order to facilitate the efforts of the Jews to break out. Despite the frightful situation of the Jews, general conditions in the country made it impossible to undertake a timely military operation in their defense."[7]

The inclusion of the Jews in the same context with the German, Lithuanian and Ukrainian minorities cannot be allowed to pass unchallenged. After all, the non-Jewish ethnic minorities in Poland possessed clearly defined national identities; they were connected with peoples and countries bordering on Poland and were concentrated, for the most part, in specific geographical regions. Morevoer, all of these groups were irredentist, never having come to terms with their status as minorities within the Polish state. Many among them, probably even the majority, thought of the Poles as foreign conquerors—just as the Poles regarded the Germans and Russians during the Second World War.

From almost no logical point of view can a parallel be legitimately drawn between Polish Jews and the other ethnic minorities, all of whom had national and territorial claims against Poland. Jews, by contrast, had been settled in Poland for centuries, and for a substantial number of them Poland was their only homeland and, at least in a political sense, their only national affiliation; even the Zionists, for all of their commitment to the establishment of a Jewish political entity and their insistence that Jews were a distinct nationality, were in no political conflict with the Polish state. For the Jews, German occupation meant being racially oppressed, despoiled of their property, decimated by degrees and, in the end, totally annihilated.

The grouping together of the Jews with ethnic minorities seeking political independence from Poland is an indication of the extent to which Poles regarded Jews to be an alien element. In modern times, as the forces of anti-Semitism came increasingly to dominate Polish life, tolerance for the Jewish presence waned—especially during the period between the wars—and there was a growing demand by Poles for Jews to be removed from their midst. And although there were differences of opinion concerning just how this was to be managed, Poles mostly agreed that the Jews had to be removed. This was the dominant attitude even among those who were in the resistance—at the time of the German invasion and during the occupation; and it persisted without change until the end of 1942, when the campaign of total liquidation of the Jews began. Even subsequently, no substantial change of attitude took place, apart from some Poles manifesting a readiness to help Jews either on humanitarian grounds or because of practical political considerations. The belief that Jews were essentially an alien presence in Poland determined the approach to the Jewish problem by the underground, by most of the Polish political parties and by the armed forces of the resistance. In Poland both the civil and military branches of the underground regarded Jews to be an alien presence on Polish soil for which they felt no responsibility. This attitude was the source of considerable embarrassment to the Polish Government-in-Exile. On the one hand most of the political factions in the government coalition were wholly in sympathy with the attitude of the underground toward Jews. On the other hand, it was in the government's interest as mentioned to appear as the spokesman of the entire population of Poland, including the country's ethnic minorities; moreover, as a member of the democratic anti-Nazi alliance it had to stand by democratic principles, or at least make a pretense of doing so, even though these had not been very much in evidence in Poland between the wars nor among Polish resistance organizations during the occupation.

We now turn to the alleged passivity of Polish Jews during the war. The fact is that a Jewish political underground was formed immediately after German occupation in Polish territories, including those that had been annexed by the Soviet Union, and it was constantly active throughout all of the phases of the German occupation both in the ghettos and the camps. Very soon thereafter a body was established which coordinated the activity of the Jewish political parties in the underground, the youth movements and the organs of the self-help organization. By no stretch of the imagination could the Jews interned in the ghettos of Poland be described as passive. For a period of over two years, during which the occupation authorities issued endless decrees and prohibitions that degraded and segregated Jews, robbed them of their possessions and deprived them of the very essentials of survival, Jews put on a tenacious fight for their lives, struggling in secret both as individuals and in organized groups. Writing in his diary in October 1940, Chaim Aaron Kaplan observed, "We are forbidden everything, but we do everything."[8] And the focus of Jewish resistance were the very prohibitions that threatened Jewish physical survival. Underground manufacture, the smuggling of food and illicit trade required the daring and resourcefulness of a great many ghetto inmates. At a time when Nazi authorities had condemned the entire Jewish community to death by starvation and disease, breaching the ghetto walls and creating an underground economy became a necessary and palpable expression of Jewish resistance, and the achievements of the Jews in these areas were nothing short of spectacular.

The struggle for survival in the ghettos, which unified the entire Jewish populace, involved all sectors in the community. It involved not only the Jewish community at large but a political underground as well, which operated in the ghettos and had its main center in the Warsaw Ghetto, and for which the Jewish political parties and youth movements were principally responsible.

The political underground controlled an extensive illegal press, maintained a clandestine educational network and organized secret cells in which political and ideological issues were discussed. The Jewish community as a whole, too, was active in the field of education; thus despite the official ban on schools in the Warsaw Ghetto, a number of elementary schools and high schools operated clandestinely. For a while religious services had also been forbidden, but great numbers of Jews nevertheless continued to meet for communal prayers. Still, it was the political underground that dedicated itself to the human aspect of the struggle, and in doing so created the germ that was later to evolve into an organized armed resistance.

We know of no contacts between the Jewish organized underground and any of the headquarters of the Polish underground during the early phases of the occupation and in the period immediately following the establishment of the ghettos. Whatever contacts did take place were sporadic, and occurred between individuals and groups sharing social or political ties that had been established before the war. Thus members of the socialist Bund were in touch with Polish socialist factions; members of the *Hashomer Hatzair* kept up their close association with a number of the activists in the Gentile Scout movement; and there were veteran Revisionist Zionists who managed to communicate with former Polish army officers who seem to have been active in the Polish underground. However, as we have noted, these contacts were based on narrow personal friendship or political association in the past, and were not the result of the initiative underground leadership.

The Jewish underground could pursue its activities in the economic, political and informational fields without obtaining the help of the Polish underground. But it could neither organize nor undertake armed resistance without substantial help from the outside. In occupied Poland only the Poles could have offered such assistance. The idea of actually engaging the enemy in battle therefore came rather late to Jews, and only after it was becoming evident that the Nazis were aiming at the destruction of the Jewish people as a whole. When the leadership of the political underground finally concluded that the end was at hand it realized that there was no longer any point to its desperate efforts to preserve the spark of life among the people by unarmed action.

The armed struggle of young Jews in the ghettos, and especially in the Warsaw Ghetto, was very different from the military and political resistance of other peoples in occupied Europe. Poles and Frenchmen built up their military underground forces in order to take part in the Allied war effort, and in the hope of playing a role in the defeat of Nazism and enjoying the fruits of victory. The case of Jewish resistance in the ghetto was in no way comparable. Their struggle was without hope of victory, its timing dictated wholly by the operations of Nazi extermination units, and its inevitable result the death of all Jews, both civilians and armed fighters. The choice to take up arms with no practical political gain in mind, and in the absence of any chance of winning or of even surviving, is rarely made and only a minority would be ready to engage in such desperate warfare. One would have thought that those who succeeded in escaping from the ghettos and joined partisan units might have undertaken rescue operations in connection with their war on the enemy. But the Jewish partisans in the forests were dependent, too, on arms and backing from the Polish underground; if anything they were even more dependent on the good will and assisstance of the Polish underground than were the ghetto fighters.

Jewish fighters were in desperate need of arms and ammunition, of which they had practically none. On the other hand, the Polish underground had succeeded in salvaging and hiding quantities of weapons after the fighting in 1939, and had received deliveries of arms from the Allies. Small arms, such as pistols and revolvers were available for purchase outside the ghetto from soldiers who were serving in units of the Axis powers that were passing through Warsaw on their way to and from the front, and who were venal enough not to be put off by any qualms about selling firearms to hostile elements. But such transactions could only be carried out on the "Aryan side" of the city, and required connections and financial resources which only the Polish underground possessed.

Moreover, the Jews had need of intelligence concerning Nazi plans, channels of communication with the free world and guidance and help in forming a battle strategy of their own; these forms of assistance, too, could only have been given by the Polish underground. So that when, at last, the Jewish underground decided on making a last-ditch stand, they had of necessity to turn to the Polish resistance organizations for help.

Therefore, when the first Jewish fighting group was formed in Vilna in 1942, its leaders appealed to the Poles for assistance. The results of the appeal are described in the postwar testimonies of survivors from the Vilna group:

> "The principal underground organization was that of the Polish Nationalists, who had issued a call to prepare for the decisive moment, after the victory of the Soviet Union over Germany, so as to be able to fight the Soviets for an independent and greater Poland that would include Vilna. Until then they preferred to remain idle, their arms at their feet. . . . To the appeal for assistance in arms (of which they had great quantities) made by the FPO [Fareynikte Partizaner Organizatsie, or "United Partisans Organization"] they replied, after various delays and pretexts, that according to orders received from the Polish government in London it was forbidden to give arms to Jews residing in border regions adjoining the Soviet Union. There was fear, they argued, that when the time came the Jews would turn these arms against Poles who were fighting the Soviets."[9]

There exists no documentary evidence of the Polish government ever having studied any such request for arms, nor of its having responded in the manner described. In all probability the matter was never referred to London and never taken up for discussion by the Polish government or any of its offices. The decision must have been made by local resistance headquarters, which needed to go no higher for advice than the district underground authorities. In any case the request was turned down. But what is interesting from the point of view of the historian is that the Jewish underground fighters leveled almost the identical accusations against the Poles as the latter had against the Jews. In the eyes of Jews it was the Poles who were being passive and avoiding battle with the invader; it was they who were concerned only with their own narrow interests, without a thought for the Allied war effort, and certainly none for the fate of the Jews.

Another request for assistance addressed to Polish military authorities is preserved in a copy of a letter sent on April 2, 1943, to the "Civilian War Leadership of the Bialystok District" by the chief of the Jewish Fighting Organization in Bialystok, Mordecai Tenenbaum-Tamarof. Tenenbaum did not survive the war, but his letter was found among the papers he and his comrades had left behind in Bialystok. In it we read that in response to a request for "assistance in arming and transferring our people for the purpose of directly engaging the invader," official Polish underground agencies replied:

> "in approximately the following words: It is most unpleasant for us to inform you that the quantity of arms in our possession is trifling in the extreme. We have more than enough volunteers. It is patently clear to us that so far as the Germans are concerned your position is as resolute as ours. . . ."[10]

In Warsaw the establishment of a Jewish armed defense organization was first mooted when news arrived of the mass murder of Jews by *Einsatzgruppen*, and of the liquidation of substantial sections of the Jewish communities in Wilna and Kovno, in the regions annexed by the Soviet Union and Russia proper, during the latter half of 1941. It was some time before the Jewish underground fully grasped the significance of events in the East. When the massacres were first reported it was generally believed that they were acts of reprisal against Jews suspected of being Communists, or that they had been committed in the course of anti-Jewish riots in areas where no civilian occupation government had yet been established. Many thought they were isolated episodes of violence and did not regard them as evidence that the Nazis were embarking on a campaign of total annihilation of the Jewish people.

On January 1, 1942, one of the earliest Jewish resistance groups in Poland was to be formed in Vilna, issued a manifesto, written by Abba Kovner, in which it warned: "Hitler aims to destroy all the Jews of Europe. The Jews of Lithuania are fated to be the first in line."[11] The warning was taken seriously only within the youth movements active in the underground. Veteran members of the political parties were skeptical, however, regarding the prediction as exaggerated in the extreme and initiated by the shock of experiencing Nazi atrocities at first hand in areas that had been hardest hit by the violence. Then, early in 1942, news was received concerning the mass murder of Jews in Chelmno, near Lodz—this time in the western part of Poland, within the territory that had been annexed into the Third Reich. Soon after, news began to spread of deportations from Lublin and the establishment of extermination camps in the region of the Government General. The intelligence was now distressing enough to move some sections of the Jewish underground, and particularly the Zionist youth movements, to an attempt to form an armed resistance organization. But there were no illusions relating to the likely outcome of an armed struggle. Thus, Tenenbaum wrote:

> "We knew: defense was impossible. The force of the invader, which has crushed entire countries, would be able to easily overwhelm us, a mere handful of young people. It was an act of desperation, of determination. We had only one goal: to do our best that our lives should be exchanged for the highest possible price."[12]

At this time the Jewish youth movements made the first urgent attempts to relate to the Polish military underground and establish ties of cooperation. All their efforts were in vain. At the first general meeting of the representatives of all the political parties in the Warsaw Jewish underground, in March 1942, the delegates were unable to reach a consensus of opinion or to agree to a common course of action. The representatives of the *Bund* were opposed to the formation of a separate Jewish resistance organization, and argued that activities should be coordinated with the Polish socialists. We also learn from remarks made by delegates of the Zionist pioneer youth movements that they were interested in collaborating with the *Bund*, through whom they hoped to make contact with the commands of the Polish underground and receive assistance from them.[13]

Since the *Bund* had for the time being rejected the formation of a separate Jewish organization, alternative strategies were sought. This is where the Communists interceded. The Communist (PPR) Party had recently renewed its activities in the underground and was seeking to strengthen its position among Poles on the "Aryan side" and within the Jewish community. For the purpose an "Anti-Fascist Bloc" was established in the Warsaw ghetto which included not only pro-Soviet groups but also other groups who had joined in the hope that with Communist, or rather Soviet support, a Jewish resistance organization could be set up in the ghetto and armed. Tenenbaum explains the reasons for turning to the Communists in a letter intended for friends in the free world:

> "Why did we make contact with the Communists? The official circles of the Polish movement—under the control of Sikorski—regarded propaganda, education, and the civilian struggle mainly in the area of economics to be their chief task. Any action involving the direct waging of war against occupation authorities they regarded as a provocation. The time had not yet come. Reserves had to be husbanded for the day when the Polish government issued the order for weapons to be drawn. . . ."[14]

Among the Poles the Communists were pushing for prompt military action; they hoped that an immediate strike at the Germans launched from within Poland would pin down German troops in sufficient numbers to blunt the Wehrmacht's fighting capacities on the Russian front. Hence there was a unanimity of interests between the Polish Communists, who were anxious to strike at the Germans immediately, and the Jews, who were facing the imminent threat of annihilation. But much as the Communists may have treated the Jews with sympathy and goodwill, it soon became evident that they were powerless to translate their brave words and promises into action. The Communists inside Poland could maintain no routine or direct communications with the Soviet Union, nor did they possess the resources and materiel for a military undertaking. Indeed, they were themselves in need of assistance locally; and although they were seeking help from the Jews in the ghetto, they had almost nothing to give in return. Shortly thereafter, however, the Anti-Fascist Block collapsed and ceased to exist altogether. Nevertheless, despite its failure, the Anti-Fascist Bloc had chalked up at least one achievement to its credit: It represented the first alliance of different political groups for the purpose of engaging the enemy in actual combat.[15]

In desperation the Jews once again turned for help to the leadership of the Polish underground forces loyal to the Government-in-Exile. Finally. toward the end of September 1942 a regular liaison was established. This was rather late in the day: the mass deportation of Jews from Warsaw had already taken place, and the ghetto was emptied of 300,000 or approximately 85% of its population. Hence, as in the case of Polish efforts to rescue Jews from the ghetto, Polish military assistance to Jews came only after the mass deportation had been all but completed, and only remnants of the Jews, anticipating their end to come at any moment, were still within the ghetto precinct.

Again, two versions concerning Polish attitudes toward the Jews during the deportation and the establishment of a liaison between the AK and the Jewish resistance organization have come down to us. The Jewish Fighting Organization, or Zydowska Organizacja Bojowa (ZOB), in its initial and more limited scope, was formed on July 28, 1942, one week after the mass deportation from Warsaw had begun. One of its first decisions was to appoint a delegation, under the leadership of Aryeh Wilner ("Jurek"), to make contact with Polish resistance forces on the "Aryan side" of the city in order to appeal for their assistance in organizing the ghetto fight. A Polish version of events is contained in General Tadeusz Bor-Komorowski's book *The Secret Army.* Bor-Komorowski was deputy commander of the AK, and later, after the arrest of General Rowecki, became CG of the AK and commander of the August 1944

Polish uprising in Warsaw. In his book Bor-Komorowski relates:

> As early as July 29th (1942) we learned from the reports of railroad
> workers that the transports were being sent to the concentration camp
> at Treblinka and that there the Jews disappeared without a trace. There
> could be no further doubt this time that the deportations were but a
> prelude to extermination.
>
> General Rowecki, swift in his decisions as always, made up his mind
> that we could not remain passive, and that at all costs we must help
> Jews so far as it lay in our power. He called a conference, at which,
> however, some doubts were expressed. The argument ran:
>
> If America and Great Britain, with powerful armies and air forces
> behind them and equipped with all the means of modern warfare, are
> not able to stop this crime and have to look on impotently while the
> Germans perpetrate every kind of horror in the occupied countries,
> how can we hope to stop them?
>
> Rowecki's opinion was that failure to demonstrate active resistance
> would only encourage the Germans to further exterminations.
>
> We had a department in our organization which arranged protection
> and help for escaped Jews and the distribution of money to them which
> had been sent to us from London for the purpose. A certain "Waclaw"
> was chief of the department, and he was now instructed by Rowecki to
> get through to the Ghetto and establish contact with the Jews leaders.
> He was to tell them that the Home Army was ready to come to the
> assistance of the Jews with supplies of arms and ammunition and to
> co-ordinate their attacks outside with Jewish resistance from within.
>
> The Jewish leaders, however, rejected the offer, arguing that if they
> behaved quietly the Germans might deport and murder 20,000 or
> 30,000 and perhaps even 60,000 of them, but it was inconceivable that
> they should exterminate everyone; while if they resisted, the Germans
> would certainly do so. When Waclaw reported this to Rowecki, the
> General decided to intensify the sabotaging of German lines of commu-
> nication in such a way as to hamper and delay the deportations.[16]

The story told by Bor-Komorowski, a man of very high authority
in the Polish underground movement, who for years stood at the
head of the armed forces of the official Polish resistance, is fiction
from beginning to end. It is difficult to understand the motives in
fabricating such a tale—unless it was the fact that, writing after the
war, he felt obliged to say something about the fate of the Jews in
Poland and, having chosen an apologetic tack, he found it expedient to manufacture this piece of pernicious fiction. Not only
does his story misrepresent Polish behavior, but it libels Polish
Jewish leadership and places the onus of responsibility on the
dead, who are unable to defend themselves. It is to the credit of
Iranek-Osmecki, Wladyslaw Bartoszewski and Czeslaw Madajczyk, who published their books after Bor-Komorowski, that they
chose to pass over his account in silence, making no use of it at all.[17]

About the only truth contained in Bor-Komorowski's account is his naming of "Waclaw" (*nom de guerre* of Henryk Wolinski, who had been a lawyer in civilian life) as the officer in charge of the Jewish section of the AK. As for the rest—the elaborate tale of the meeting, decision, contact with Jewish leaders, the gallant offer of arms and military collaboration, and, finally, of the AK's undertaking on its own to sabotage German lines of communication during the deportations, even after the Jews had rejected Polish offers of help—the whole of it is the product of Bor-Komorowski's self-serving imagination. The only person mentioned other than Rowecki in the account is Henryk Wolinski-"Waclaw," whose report of December 1944 on the activities of the Jewish department of the AK survives[18]. In it he wrote:

> "The department was established on February 1, 1942. Its function during the early period of its operations was limited to informational service only.... In addition to the routine informational service, which encompassed the period of the liquidation of the Warsaw Ghetto (June-September 1942), a collective report was prepared on the situation of the Jews in Poland, as well as the 'First Black Book.' "

Clearly, then, Wolinski's department had only one function during the period under discussion: coordinating and transmitting to London intelligence that had been gathered concerning the Jews. Bor-Komorowski's claims about the department's rendering assistance and distributing money to escaping Jews are therefore completely untrue, at least for the time period covered in his account.

Henryk Wolinski-"Waclaw" then goes on to state in his report:

> ... toward the end of the liquidation of the Warsaw Ghetto, the first official contact was established between the ghetto and the army [i.e., the AK] (end of August 1942). The "Bund" representative, Mikolaj [Leon Feiner], contacted the department wishing to send a telegram to Member of the Central National Committee [in London], Zygelbojm. The telegram, which described the situation in a few words and requested financial assistance, was sent. In October, 5,000 dollars arrived for Mikolaj. In October 1942 there arrived at the department's administrative office, with the help of guides from our Scout Movement, representatives of the Jewish youth movement,"Hehalutz." The contact was made with Jurek [Aryeh Wilner], who represented the "Jewish National Committee." ... During the first conversation Jurek related that this was their second attempt to make contact with the Polish army in the country [the AK]. The attempt, made in August, during the concentrated operation to liquidate the Warsaw Ghetto, to get help for organizing armed resistance against the Germans met with an unfavorable response from army authorities [the AK]. An investigation into the matter undertaken by High Command—as a result of my report—revealed the veracity of Jurek's claim, as it did the private nature of the refusal to make any attempt to contact the proper quarters.

Thus according to Waclaw it was the Jews rather than the Poles who made the first liaison attempt; and after Wilner had finally managed to communicate with members of the AK, it was the Poles who bear the responsibility for frustrating the attempt. Wolinski implies that Wilner was unsuccessful because he had contacted persons who were unauthorized to undertake negotiations. Bartoszewski, who was also connected with the AK and one of the founding members of *Zegota*, makes much the same point in a version of events that differs only slightly from that of Wolinski:

> Aryeh Wilner ("Jurek), an activist in Hashomer Hatzair, was the official liaison officer between the Jewish Fighting Organization and the Polish underground. As early as September 1942, he made the first attempt to make contact with a representative of the Underground Army in order to obtain aid for the armed resistance movement in the ghetto. But he got through to cells in the AK that were not authorized to make decisions of this nature. Word of "Jurek's" mission did not reach the proper quarters in the AK Higher Command at the time.[19]

Both accounts substantially agree, except that Bartoszewski dates Aryeh Wilner's first attempt to contact the AK as having occurred in September rather than August 1942. Neither, however, offers us any clue concerning the identity of motives or the "unauthorized persons" who rejected Wilner's request for help without transmitting word of this mission to the proper quarters; nor is there any clarification from postwar revelations and testimonies. In any event, Wolinski's and Bartoszewski's reports show beyond any doubt that the truth was the reverse of what Bor-Komorowski claimed. There had been no Polish initiative, allegedly rejected by the Jews, to organize a Jewish resistance at the time of the mass deportation from Warsaw; rather, it was the Jews who initiated contact for that purpose and the Poles who turned it down for reasons that still remain obscure.

During October and November 1942 the groups that had founded the ZOB were joined by all of the other political movements in the Jewish underground in Warsaw Ghetto, with the exception of the Revisionists, who formed their own independent resistance organization known by the initials ZZW (*Zydowski Zwiazek Wojskowy*-Jewish Military Union). In addition to the fighting units of the ZOB, a civil body (Jewish National Committee and Coordination Committee) was created in order to provide the resistance movement with wide authority and backing.

The changes which brought about the expansion of the ZOB and strengthened its public base took place not only within the underground movement but throughout the Jewish community that remained in Warsaw after the mass deportation. As we have noted, after the deportation only about 60,000 Jews of the original 350,000 occupants remained in the ghetto. So long as the deportation went on, the overriding concern of everyone was to elude the roundups; so absorbed were individuals in their efforts to save themselves and their families that no energy was left among the ghetto populace for attending to the situation as it affected the community as a whole. It was only after the deportation had been carried out that the scope and the significance of the calamity was fully grasped. Only then did those who escaped the roundups realize that all of their ingenuity and resourcefulness in evading deportation had gained them merely a temporary reprieve; another deportation campaign was destined to follow, and this time no one in the ghetto would survive. Thoughts now turned to retribution, and many regretted not having resisted while the deportation was going on. The change of mood among the survivors created an atmosphere in the ghetto community receptive to the idea of organizing an armed resistance.

At the same time a change was taking place in Polish attitudes. On a popular level the great majority of Poles still remained indifferent to the fate of the Jews, while a minority wavered between pity at the suffering of Jews and malicious pleasure at their downfall. However, here and there individual Poles were sufficiently moved by the unprecedented horror of the atrocities being committed against the Jews to take action on their behalf, despite the hazards they faced in doing so. Such were the motives of the men and women who founded *Zegota* (see chapter on *Zegota*); the same impulse now drove some members of the AK to work for the establishment of a Jewish armed resistance force. Additionally, reports were coming in at the time from London revealing the shock with which news of the mass extermination of Jews was being received in the free world. As a consequence both the Government-in-Exile in London and the underground leadership in Poland were beginning to realize they would have to take affirmative action of some sort to assist the Jews.

These were the two principal factors underlying the change in Polish policy, the effects of which began to make themselves felt after the mass deportation. And, more than likely, this was the background of the sympathetic response met with by Aryeh Wilner during his second attempt at linking up with the AK, in which he was probably aided by Aleksander Kaminski, a member of the

Polish Scout Movement friendly to *Hehalutz* and the editor of *Biuletyn Informacyjny* ("Information Bulletin"), the official organ of the AK.

As a result of Wilner's contact with Wolinski and the subsequent official Polish approval of the establishment of the liaison, the Jews decided to draft a declaration in two copies, one of which was addressed to civilian underground authorities (in the person of the Delegate, or the chief of the civil underground organization, who was then Professor Jan Piekalkiewicz of the Polish Peasants' Party), and the other to the AK, then under the command of Stefan Rowecki. The statement was signed by "Mikolaj" (Leon Feiner) and "Jurek" (Aryeh Wilner), in the name of the interparty Coordination Committee (*Komisja Koordynacyjna*) and of the ZOB; in it the Jewish representatives affirmed that they represented the Jewish underground, inclusive of its various political factions, and declared in the name of the Jewish organization their readiness to prepare for an armed struggle.

According to Wolinski, the reply of the Supreme Commander of the AK, General Rowecki, came in the order drafted by him on November 11, 1942. In it Rowecki expressed his appreciation of Jewish readiness to fight, and advised that the ZOB organize its fighting force into five-man combat squads. The ZOB responded to Rowecki's order by transmitting a copy of its regulations to the Polish military underground. The document opens with an account of the organizational structure of the ZOB. Listed first among the functions of the Coordinating Committee is "the organizing of the defense of the ghetto in case the operation of evacuation continues." Most of the document is taken up by a description of the structure of the Jewish Fighting Organization, its problems in procuring arms, the planning of its military operations, and its military targets. The document is accompanied by a memorandum written by Wolinski in which he stresses the fact that the feeling among Jews was that they should be armed *without delay*, "since they have no doubt whatever that the liquidation campaign in Warsaw had not ended, and it was likely to be renewed at any moment."[20]

In his report Wolinski noted:

> In the military domain Jewish requests aimed at obtaining arms and professional assistance for the last and final battle of the Warsaw Ghetto. The "Jewish Fighting Organization" has taken the resolute stand that the fate of the Warsaw Ghetto, as the fate of all other centers of Jewish concentration, has been decided; that it is doomed to annihilation, sooner or later. Accordingly, their wish is to die with honor, that

is—with weapons in their hands. After making vigorous requests, the "Jewish Fighting Organization" was sent, by order of Supreme Command, ten pistols and a small quantity of ammunition. These weapons were in very bad condition and only a fraction of them were fit for use.[21]

The supply of arms became a major subject for grievance against the Poles by the Jewish Fighting Organization. The Jews felt that the A.K. had no serious intention of arming them effectively, and only wished to make a symbolic gesture. Wolinski asserts that the Poles had delivered altogether 20 pistols, which were partly in very bad conditions. According to Jewish sources the organization received till January 18, 10 pistols only.[22] That the Jews were correct in their assumption that the Polish underground command had no wish to create a significant Jewish fighting force, but sought to fulfill its obligation by halfway measures, is apparent from the telegram sent to London by General Rowecki on January 2, 1943: " . . . Jews from a variety of groups, among them Communists, have appealed to us at a late date asking for arms, as if our own arsenals were full. As a trial I offered them a few pistols. I have no confidence that they will make use of any of these arms at all. I will give no additional arms, because, as you know, we ourselves do not have any."[23] Not only does the telegram reveal Rowecki's aloofness, or—more precisely—his estrangement from the Jews, but it expresses the widespread prejudice in the Polish army that Jews were incapable of fighting and could not be relied on militarily.

According to *Polskie Sily Zbrojne* (Vol. 3, p. 234) the AK possessed in the Warsaw region only the following stocks of arms since 1939: 135 heavy machine guns 16,800 rounds of ammunition; 190 light machine guns with 54,000 rounds; 6,045 rifles with 794,000 rounds; 1,070 pistols and revolvers with 8,708 rounds; 7,561 grenades; seven small anti-tank guns with 2,147 rounds. This did not include 200 containers of arms and ammunition dropped from Britain in the period August 1, 1942 to April 30, 1943. Each of the containers included 10 to 18 STEN guns and 20 to 40 Mills bombs, in addition to grenades, explosives and ammunition. It also doesn't include local purchases.

Nevertheless, Rowecki did not keep to his decision to supply no more arms to the ZOB. Rowecki and his comrades' change of heart came about because of the events that took place during the second mass deportation from the Warsaw Ghetto between January 18 and 22, 1943. Following their experience of the first deportation, the Jews prepared to make the next German attempt at deportation the last. And when the January deportation—or, "the second Aktion" as it is referred to in Jewish sources—came, the reaction in the ghetto was very different from what it had been during the first deportation. When the SS ordered Jews to report for selection, most of the ghetto population went into hiding rather than obey, and a number of groups belonging to the Jewish Fighting Organization swung into action with what meager arms they possessed. The most important clash took place on the first day of the deportation roundups, when a group of Jewish fighters under the command of Mordecai Anielewicz joined a line of Jews being marched away to a transport and, at a signal, opened fire on the German guards. During the fighting that ensued in the street almost all of the Jewish fighters were killed. Anielewicz managed to escape after overcoming one of the German troopers. Armed groups also attacked German soldiers who attempted to enter buildings that served as bases for Jewish fighters. The attacks by armed groups and mass efforts to elude deportation had a deterrent effect on the German operation. German troops avoided entering the basements and attics that served as hiding places and were forced to proceed with great caution. The result was that only about 5,000 Jews, or 10 percent of the ghetto population, were deported or killed on the spot.

The AK's *Biuletyn Informacyjny* ("Information Bulletin") wrote in its January 28 issue that "the courageous resistance of the Jews, who during the most anguished moments of the Jewish experience never lost their sense of honor, arouses admiration and is a luminous chapter in the history of Polish Jewry." One activist in the Polish underground observed that "there is a growing opinion that the only form of self-defense likely to bring results is armed resistance and reprisal. The attempt to renew the transports to the gas chambers of Treblinka was met by the Jews—and this for the first time—with gunfire. After three days the Germans halted the operation and withdrew police contingents from the ghetto."[24] In a "review of the situation" sent to London by the Delegate's Office we read, "The attempt to liquidate the remains of the population in the Warsaw Ghetto on January 18, 1943, has had the strongest repercussions. This attempt was met by resistance. It may be that the resistance aroused anxieties lest the resistance psychosis take hold of Poles too, or that the goals of the liquidation were limited, but public opinion in any case has linked the fact of resistance with the supposed total halt to the liquidation. . . ."[25]

The conjecture in Polish underground circles was that the Germans had broken off their attempt out of fear that the example of resistance in the ghetto would inspire Poles to take up arms as well. The January deportation affected the relations of the Polish military underground with the Jewish fighters in the ghetto. The deep impression that the Jewish resistance made on the Polish populace was impossible to ignore. Events had, after all, refuted General Rowecki's opinion that the Jews would never use the arms they had been given. It seems not unlikely, therefore, that the attitude of the Polish military, which was quite capable of appreciating the military initiative shown by the Jewish resistance, should have undergone at least a temporary change. One of the leading figures among the ghetto fighters observed at the time: "The entire Polish underground is full of admiration for us."[26]

The Jews now received more substantial assistance in arms and ammunition from the Poles. According to Wolinski the AK sent: "fifty pistols, a large quantity of bullets, about eighty kgs of material for the manufacture of 'bottles' and a quantity of defensive grenades." General Tadeusz Pelczynski in London during the 1960s gave the following estimates of Polish aid: "At the end of 1942 and in the first quarter of 1943 the AK delivered to the ZOB from its relatively small stock the following arms and munitions: At least seventy pistols, ten rifles, two machine guns, a light machine gun—all these together with magazines and ammunition. In addition, 600 incendiary hand grenades, thirty kgs of 'plastic' type explosive received by the AK from parachuted consignments, 120 kgs of cheddite, homemade explosive material, 400 detonators for bombs and grenades, thirty kgs of postash for the manufacture of incendiary bottles, a highly important weapon in street fighting, and large quantities of saltpeter required for the manufacture of black explosive material."[27] Pelczynski's relations with the Jews were unquestionably sincere, and by specifying the types and quantities of arms and war supplies furnished by the AK to the ZOB he wished to establish both the existence of an alliance between the two organizations in the war against the Nazis and the sympathy felt by Poles toward the struggle of the Jews. Nevertheless, the fact that the AK had sent obsolete pistols—and some of them defective at that—testifies to the AK's appalling failure to appreciate the nature of the fighting the ZOB would have to face. There is every reason to believe that the experienced professional officers who made up the AK command knew perfectly well that pistols would be useless in street combat, and that what the ZOB needed were rifles, grenades and machine guns. The Jews for their part, having had no combat experience, had no way of knowing that short-barrelled weapons, such as pistols, were of insufficient range to be useful in street fighting.

The importance of the change in the AK's policy toward the ZOB cannot be underestimated, but it must be seen in proper perspective. The recognition granted the ZOB had given the Jewish Fighting Organization the status of a group recognized as the Jewish armed resistance organization operating in the ghetto. It is doubtful, however, that the deliveries of military supplies was prompted by any genuine concern for the Jewish Fighting Organization.

Immediately prior to the Warsaw Ghetto uprising in April 1943, the ZOB had no more than five hundred fighting men at its disposal. Shortage of arms was the principal factor that prevented the organization from increasing its manpower. In fact, there were not enough arms to go around. Even if we accept the figures cited by Pelczynski as accurate, we find that the ghetto fighters had available to them only one pistol for every seven men, one rifle for every fifty men, and one machine gun for more than every hundred and fifty men. The AK's claim about the inadequacy of its own store of arms can be considered from a variety of points of view. The types and quantities of weapons and ammunition available to the AK were certainly inadequate for it to confront the German army in the field. But the claim that the few scores of pistols handed over to the ZOB represented a significant sacrifice on the part of the Polish military underground cannot be taken seriously, when we consider that the AK possessed tens of thousands of rifles and approximately one thousand light machine guns. In any event, the unsuitability of the arms made available to the ZOB was patently revealed to the Jews by the time of the ghetto rebellion. So we find Mordecai Anielewicz, commander of the Warsaw Ghetto uprising, writing to Yitzhak Zuckerman, the ZOB representative to the Poles, on April 23, 1943: ". . . and you should know that pistols are absolutely useless, we've almost not used them at all. What we need is: grenades, rifles, machine guns and explosives."

The heads of the Jewish Fighting Organizaition seem to have been aware of the AK leadership's reservations, even hostility, as expressed by their failure to arm the ZOB adequately during the initial phases of its formations and preparations for battle. In March 1943, as units of the ZOB clashed with the Germans in the ghetto, a letter attributed to Anielewicz was sent to the Jewish underground representative to the Poles. The letter included the following statement: "Please inform the authorities in our name that if massive assistance does not arrive at once, it will look as if the representation and the authorities are indifferent to the fate of the Jews of Warsaw. The allocation of weapons without ammunition seems like a bitter joke and a confirmation of the suspicion that the poison of anti-Semitism still permeates the ruling circles of Poland in full force, despite the tragic and brutal experience of the past three years. We are not about to prove to anyone our readiness and ability to fight. Since January 18 the Jewish community in Warsaw has existed in a state of war with the invader and his noxious henchmen. Whoever denies or doubts this is merely an anti-Semite out of spite."[28]

Most of the weapons the ZOB fought with had to be purchased. The Polish Communists were more magnanimous than the AK in helping the Jewish Fighting Organization; but their resources were so limited as to render their assistance nearly worthless.

The second resistance group, ZZW, which went into operation in the ghetto at a later stage, received no official recognition from Polish underground authorities and was forced to obtain its arms from private sources, and through the assistance of either private individuals or of groups in the AK that were acting neither in the AK's name nor upon its orders.

The members of ZZW managed to secure support from two groups affiliated with AK KB and PLAN but which has no independent status and no competence to negotiate on behalf of AK. According to testimonies of Major Iwanski he, his family and a few of his subordinates and an associate were strongly involved in the action of supplying weapons and cooperation with ZZW and they took an active part in the uprising of the ghetto. This claim is not confirmed by Jewish or first-hand sources, but know that the ZZW was equipped with more heavy arms that the ZOB, and that ZZW managed to established contacts with cells of the Polish underground. On the other hand another Polish officer involved in the connection with ZZW testified that he was interested in profit rather than other motives, and in this case it was a business deal than an act of help motivated only by humanitarian or ideological principles. On the other hand, Iwanski's approach and a group of Polish undeground activits seems to be an expression of personal deep involvement and a desire to help the Jews in their struggle.

The last theme in our discussions of the relations between the AK and the ZOB in Warsaw involves events immediately preceding the Warsaw Ghetto uprising and the fighting during April and May of 1943, deserve special consideration. Early in March Aryeh Wilner ("Jurek"), the Jewish Fighting Organization's liaison agent to the Polish underground, was arrested. A quantity of arms purchased for the ghetto was seized in his apartment on the "Aryan side" of Warsaw. Wilner's arrest and the seizure of the arms cache became a source of tension between the leadership of the Polish and Jewish underground. The Poles feared that the capture of a key figure in the Jewish underground could be disastrous for them; Wilner knew the names and addresses of a great many Poles in the underground. But the Poles were furious when they learned that Wilner had been storing arms in his apartment—this in defiance of Wolinski's warning to him that he should desist from becoming personally involved in the purchase of weapons and stay clear of those trafficking in arms. Accordng to Wolinski, Wilner replied that the repeated refusals of AK command to assist the Jews with arms had left him no alternative but to support any transaction by which weapons might be obtained.

Aryeh Wilner's arrest led to a temporary break in contacts between the AK and the ZOB. During his interrogation he underwent painful and protracted tortures, but the Germans failed to extract from him either his own identity or the names of his associates. Finally, with the help of a member of the Polish Scout Movement, Henryk Grabowski, he managed to escape from detention. Battered in body but unbroken in spirit, "Jurek" made it back to the ghetto, where he was joyfully received by his comrades.

About Wilner's activity before his detention by the Gestapo, Yitzhak Zuckerman relates:

> Before his arrest Aryeh Wilner began to work out two plans with the Poles for helping the ghetto. One plan with the AK and another with the AL. According to the plans members of the AK would attack at the start of the uprising from the direction of the *Umschlagplatz*. Members of the AL would be required to attack from the direction of Leszno Street.[29]

The AL (Armia Ludowa-People's Army) was the fighting arm of the Polish Communist Party. It should be noted, however, that the AK and the AL were uncompromisingly hostile to one another, and that there existed neither contacts nor mutual recognition between the two groups. AK command had therefore to be kept in the dark by the Jewish underground about its connections and collaboration with the Communists. For their part the Communists, being aware of their inability to render adequate military assistance to the Jews on the their own, agreed to the Jewish Fighting Organization's working in concert with the AK. Some members of the Polish underground, among them Wolinski, may have known of Jewish contacts with the Communists and condoned them, because they realized that the plight of the Jews was so desperate that they had no choice but to turn to anyone willing to help them. At all events, the two plans were worked out independently and without any coordination between the AK and the AL.

Wolinski reported that the arrest of Wilner "put a restraint on the work being done in the domain of cooperation between the 'Jewish Fighting Organization' and 'Drapacz' [code name of the AK in the Warsaw district]. In fact ten days following the arrest I had a talk with Konar [General Antoni Chrusciel, commander of the AK in the Warsaw district]. The subject of the conversation concerned the definition of the aim of the cooperation of our units with the besieged ghetto. The aim was supposed to be the removal from the Warsaw area of the greatest possible number of Jews and providing them with shelter, something which I could have done at any time. This plan was not carried out. No unit set out for the area assigned to it. The 'Jewish Fighting Organization' insisted that it would be out of the question for its people to break out to a distance of hundreds of kilometers [in the direction of Lublin and Volhynia]."[30]

It is evident from Wolinski's report that the AK had devised plans of its own, involving not military assistance to the ghetto but the total removal of Jewish fighters from the ghetto. The point of the plan was clearly to prevent military action from taking place within the ghetto area.

How, then, are we to explain the contradiction between the plans described by Wolinski and Zuckerman? It seems doubtful that the contrast was the result of a change in plan arising out of Wilner's arrest and the subsequent crisis in the relations between the AK and the ZOB. Certainly Wolinski does not suggest that this was the case. A more likely explanation is that Polish underground authorities had at some point concluded that armed resistance in the ghetto was not in the best Polish interests; indeed, that it conflicted with fundamental Polish strategy, which was to avoid armed confrontation with the Germans until the time was ripe for a decisive military engagement. A ghetto uprising could only disrupt Polish plans and had, therefore, to be prevented—regardless of conditions that prevailed among the Polish population or the turn that Nazi oppression took.

This attitude was by no means universal among Poles. There were fears among large sections of the Polish populace that once the Germans had completed their massacre of the Jews they would undertake the mass extermination of Poles by the same methods. The Communists repeatedly warned that this would be the case, arguing that prevention of the massacre of the Jews and assisting the Jews to resist the Germans could only serve Polish interests.

In the same section of Yitzhak Zuckerman's memoirs from which we have quoted,[31] he relates that, between the time of Wilner's escape from detention and the Jewish uprising, a message was received from outside the city by telephone saying: "If you do not want the salt to arrive after the meal, contact immediately."[32] In response, it was decided to send a ZOB representative in the person of Zuckerman to the Polish underground. Zuckerman, who was on the staff of ZOB headquarters and went under the code name of "Antek," left the ghetto for the "Aryan side" about two or three weeks before the uprising in the Warsaw ghetto on April 19, 1943. "Immediatley on leaving," Zuckerman writes, "I met with the AK representative, Waclaw, for a talk which greatly disappointed me. An upright and sincere man, incidentally; I wouldn't be wrong in calling him pro-Jewish. He was following orders . . . . They, that is the Poles, were asking us not to begin the ghetto uprising; they were ready to get our fighters out and into the forests. I protested: 'But the whole time, during the second half of 1942, you kept complaining to us that we weren't fighting. When we fought in January, you claimed you were pleased. Now you know that we are preparing for an uprising. The fact is that you, too, gave us arms, and we didn't only buy them.' He answered that command headquarters would do everything to find fighting bases in the forests for us, and that it was still to early to fight in Warsaw. My answer was: The battle will be in Warsaw."[32]

And, as Zuckerman promised, the battle did take place in Warsaw. The Warsaw Ghetto uprising became the first general rebellion of an urban community against the invader. As hundreds fought the Germans with guns, tens of thousands of others resisted deportation stubbornly, albeit passively by barricading themselves in bunkers. The Germans were literally forced to fight their way through the ghetto building by building, then to set fire to the wreckage and blow up cellars and bunkers. The Warsaw Ghetto held out against the German army for longer than had many countries in Europe during the war; and the uprising taught the world that a population, though practically unarmed and unaided, could light the fires of rebellion if it was unified in its will to resist, even to the point of death.

What were the attitudes of the AK toward the resistance in the ghetto and what actions did the AK take on its behalf once the Warsaw Ghetto rebellion had begun? Wolinski makes no mention of aid in any form being offered by the Polish underground during the uprising itself. However, Adolf Berman, who was active in the Polish quarter of Warsaw on behalf of the Jewish National Committee, testifies:

The director of the Department of Jewish Affairs in the Organization of Armed Struggle (AK), Waclaw, proved to be warmly sympathetic toward the ghetto fighters during those tragic days. He tried to help the Jewish Fighting Organization, and forwarded all of the dispatches and requests of the Jewish underground movement to his superiors; he himself sent an urgent message of his own, but the position of the commander of the ZWZ (AK) was unquestionably negative. Waclaw related that the commander of the ZWZ (AK) in Warsaw had already promised a number of times to carry out diversionary operations against the Germans attacking the ghetto, but these operations were never undertaken. The ghetto received neither arms nor ammunition. Encouraging words were all that arrived.[33]

In this connection it would be appropriate for us to quote in full a letter wirtten to Wolinski ("Waclaw") by "Konar" (General Chrusciel), the AK commander in the Warsaw district, a few days after the beginning of the Warsaw Ghetto uprising, April 24, 1943:

Mr. Waclaw, all of your urgent letters reach me without delay. Please do not become alarmed and explain to Antek [Zuckerman] that at this time of emergency personal contacts are out of the question; now is the time to act. Our contacts with Jurek were productive. This is now apparent to us. The Warsaw Army feels confident in the Jews, congratulates them on their spirit of rebellion and wants to assist them. We have been active since 19 April, 19:12. As a result of our operation in Bonifraterska Street we had many killed and wounded. We continue to fight from the outside. Our common aim is to bring about the disintegration of the invader's forces besieging the ghetto. We cannot offer assistance in money or food, because these are not to be had. By lightning assaults we are destroying squads of encircling police. Thus far our attempt to blow up the walls has failed because the German besieging force has established itself inside buildings within the ghetto. *We have been ready for action and kept watch* along the whole northern side!! Break out through the breaches in the wall on the Powazki Cemetery side; after that it will be easier. The world is beginning to learn of the ghetto's gallant struggle. We congratulate the Jews and call for a continuation of the resistance against the enemy by the citizens of Poland. The date of 4/23 must be the focal day of the struggle for us and for them.[34]

An unsuccessful attempt at breaching the wall of the ghetto is mentioned in AK sources and by General Chrusciel in another of his letters. Captain Jozef Pszenny tells of an assault on April 19 for the purpose of breaching the wall during which the AK lost two of its men.[35] Nowhere, however, is mention made of any operation taking place on April 24, the date which General Chrusciel speaks of as the decisive one in the battle of the ghetto. It is difficult, moreover, to conceive of how the AK, even had it successfully breached the ghetto wall, could have made contact with the Jewish fighters and those hiding in bunkers in the ghetto, unless there had been careful coordination beforehand between Jewish and Polish forces on the nature, timing and strategy of the operation. In fact, no such coordination took place either before April 19 nor while the Warsaw Ghetto was uprising in progress.

Some years later a Jewish version of events was given by Yitzhak Zuckerman: "Using my own means I sent a letter to Grot (Grot-Rowecki), the Supreme Commander of the AK. A day later I received a letter of reply for Konar, commander of the AK in Warsaw. The letter begins:

> "The Polish Army salutes the Jewish fighters. We have had friendly relations with Jurek for a long time. The time is not appropriate for a meeting now. We must act.' How could he have acted without the ghetto? He honors us . . . . And the last meeting with them concerned the withdrawal of fighters through the sewage conduits. On this I got an answer that they had no maps. They didn't know how. I asked for hiding places, until we could transfer the fighters. They had no hideouts, no places to spend the night and no transfer routes. There the matter ended."[36]

During the uprising the bulletin issued on the "Aryan side" of Warsaw by the Jewish National Committee proclaimed:

> "The battle being waged by the Jewish Fighting Organization for the past nine days, which began as warfare from emplacements and is now a partisan war against the German army, had inevitably to make an impression on the Polish population of Warsaw; a legend of 'Ghettograd' has spread throughout the whole world and will certainly have a decisive effect in arousing the desire to repay terror with terror."[37]

On May 5 the head of the Polish Government-in-Exile, General Sikorski, addressed himself to the nation:

> "The greatest slaughter in the history of mankind is now being perpetrated. We know that you are helping the afflicted Jewish people to the best of your ability. I thank you, my people, in my own and the government's name. I ask you to help them in every way, and that at the same time you put a stop to these brutal deeds."[38]

This time the Polish head of government was calling for action, and making it unmistakably clear that this was his personal will and that he expected it to be fulfilled.

Adam Ciolkosz, a Polish Socialist who spent the war in London and was known to be sympathetic with the Jews, has argued that the delay in Sikorski's appeal to the nation to come to the defense of the Jews was caused by the Polish leader's preoccupation with the

Katyn Forest massacre and the crisis in relations with the Soviet Union. That these were of overwhelming concern to Polish statesmen at the time is beyond dispute. However, Ciolkosz does confirm in retrospect that, as always, Polish leadership felt no special urgency about dealing with the problems of the Jews even now, when tens of thousands of the Jewish remnant in Warsaw were being murdered and Jews were demonstrating an unparalleled resistance against the soldiers of Nazi Germany.

The last of the Jewish fighters, a few score survivors of the battle, withdrew from the ghetto by way of the sewers. They were helped to escape by some Polish Communists who were close to the Jewish underground, and a group of liaison agents and other activists of the Jewish Fighting Organization who had been operating on the "Aryan side" of the city. Only a very few of these exceptional people survived the war. Although they were intent on continuing their struggle, the AK did nothing to help them to carry on; to make matters even worse—it refused to provide them with adequate protection, as we learn from the orders of the AK's Supreme Commander contained in a dispatch sent to the military underground's Jewish department:

> Concerning the matter of Jewish participation in the partisan struggle, I am hereby transmitting to you the following decision of the Commander: "Execution of the Supreme Commander's order of November 10, 1942, and later orders [concerning active collaboration with Jewish fighters] has encountered insurmountable difficulties. The general mood with regard to armed Jews is so hostile that we are unable, in view of the limited possibilities that exist under the conditions of underground operations, to assume responsibility for the security of armed Jewish units in the area."[39]

Polish attitudes and conduct with respect to the Jewish resistance in Warsaw was not as unrelievedly unsympathetic as a dry account of the events makes them appear. There were some Poles who did everything that was in their power to advance the interests of Jewish armed resistance. But the official representatives of the "military authorities in the underground"—the commanders and upper political echelons—tended on the whole to regard the catastrophe of the Jews and Jewish appeals for assistance as something remote from their immediate concerns. Only when long-range Polish interests became involved, or when the appeals of men and women of conscience became too insistent to be ignored, were they moved to act, though only hesitantly, on a small scope and without conviction.

NOTES

1. See Yisrael Gutman, "Din ve-Heshbon shel Ish ha-Mahteret ha-Polanit al ha-Yahasim bein ha-Polanim ve-ha-ye hudim be-Polin ha-Kvushah" ("Report by a Member of the Polish Underground on Relations between Poles and Jews in Occupied Poland"), in *Michael VI*, Tel Aviv University, 1980, pp. 102–114.

2. Kazimierz Iranek-Osmecki, *"He Who Saves One Life"*, New York, p. 151.

3. *Polskie Sity Zbrojne w Drugiej Wojne Swiatowej*, Amia Krajowa, T. 3, London, 1950.

5. *Polskie Sily Zbrojne*, p. 47.

6. *Ibid.*, p. 48.

7. *Ibid.*, p. 47.

8. See C. A. Kaplan, (The Scroll of Agony), diary of the Warsaw ghetto, 1939–4.8. 1942, New York, 1962, p. 350, entry of October 2, 1940, eve of Rosh Hashanah, 1941.

9. *Sefer ha-Partizanim ha-Yehudim* ("Book of Jewish Partisans"), Merhavia, 1959, vol. 1, p. 26.

10. Mordechai Tenenbaum-Tamarof, *Dapim min ha-Dleykah* ("Pages from the Conflagration"), 1948, p. 119.

11. See the proclamation in full in: *Documents on the Holocaust*, Selected Sources on the Destruction of the Jews of Germany and Austria, Poland, and the Soviet Union, edited by Y. Arad, I. Gutman, A. Margaliot, Jerusalem, 1981, p. 431.

12. *Dapim min ha-Dleykah*, p. 126.

13. On the meeting in March 1942, and the attitudes of the various sides, see: Yisrael Gutman. *Jews of Warsaw 1939–1943, Ghetto, Underground, Revolt*, Indiana, 1982, pp. 168–170.

14. *Dapim min ha-Dleykah. .op. cit.*, see letter, pp. 129–130

15. See: Y. Gutman *Jews of Warsaw*, op. cit, pp. 170-175.

16. Tadeusz Bor-Komorowski, *The Secret Army*, New York, 1951, pp. 99–100

17. See: Kazimierz Iranek-Osmecki, Wladyslaw Bartoszewski and Zofia Lewin, Madajczyk *op. cit:*

18. The report of Wolinski appeared in the book: B. Mark, *Powstanie w getcie Warszawskim, Nowe uzupelni-* *one Wydanie Zbiór dokumentów*, Warsaw 1963, 342–51.

19. See Bartoszewski's introduction to *Righteous Among Nations.*

20. The documents in question—the code of regulations and Wolinski's memorandum—are in the book by B. Mark, *op. cit.*, pp. 195–200.

21. See Wolinski's report, Mark op. cit., pp. 342–315.

22. The letter sent by Yitzhak Zuckerman, the last liaison between the Z.O.B. and the AK, to the AK Commander in November 1943, i.e. after the end of the revold, states, *inter alia:* "Following our request for arms in November 1942, we received ten pistols in December of that year, and upon renewed appeals in January 1943, forty-nine pistols, fifty hand-grenades and explosives, for which we thank you once again." It is inconceivable that Zuckerman would have made inaccurate statements in a letter written to the source from which the arms were received. See Zuckerman's letter in: *Resistance and Revolt in the Warsaw Ghetto*, A Documentary History, Eds. N. Blumental, J. Kermish, Jerusalem, 1965, pp. 141–143.

23. See original text of the telegram in the AK Archive in London, copy in Yad Vashem Archive, and an inaccurate copy in Mark's book, *op. cit.*, and the documentary collection by Blumental and Kermish.

24. Waclaw Zagorski, Wolnosc w Niewoli, London, 1971, p. 340.

25. Yad Vashem Archives, copy of a report on the situation in Poland by the "Delegates Office" from January 1, 1943, to February 15, 1943.

26. See: Mark Edelman, *Getto Walczy*, Warszawa, 1946, p. 48

27. Gen. Brygady T. Pelczynski, "Opor Zbrojny n Ghetcie warszawskim", przedruk z "Bellony", ron XLV, 1–2, 1963 pp. 4–5.

28. See text of the letter in collection by documents by Mark, *op. cit.*, pp. 221–223.

29. See text of Yitzhak Zuckerman's (Antek) words in *Yalkut Moreshet*, No. 32, 1981.

30. See report by Wolinski Mark, *op. cit,* pp. 342–351.

31. See *Yalkut Moreshet,* No 32.

32. *Ibid.* See also Zuckerman's aricle, "Mered ha-Yehudim" ("Revolt of the Jews") in *Mibifnim,* vol. 12, No. 3, June 1947.

33. See. Avraham-Adolf Berman. *Mimei ha-Mahteret,* Tel Aviv, 1971, p. 112.

34. See letter by Chrusciel in *Ha-Meri ve-ha-Mered,* (documents) *op. cit.,* p. 404.

35. Report by Captain Jozef Pszenny, *Ha-Meri ve-he-Mered,* pp. 404–406.

36. See *Yalkut Moreshet,* No 32, 1981

37. *Berman, op. cit.* p. 113.

38. *Ha-Meri ve-ha-Mered* (documents), *op. cit.,* pp. 392–393.

39. A. Berman, *ha-Yehudim be-tzad ha-Ari,* (The Jews on the Aryen side of the city) in *Encyclopaedia of the Jewish Diaspora,* Jerusalem, Tel-Aviv, 1953, p. 714

FUGITIVES

The relations that developed between Jews and Poles in Warsaw and the political directives that were issued by underground groups in the city were of great significance in determining the fate of Jews both locally and in other areas of the country. The political-geographical division of Poland into separate regions of occupation and, what is much more important, the confinement of Jews to urban internment centers that were wholly cut off from one another led to the creation of unique social and economic conditions and to the development, in Warsaw, of a special system of relations between Jews and Poles. Warsaw's position of prime importance in this derived from the size and political significance of its Jewish population, and from the fact that it had previously been the captial of independent Poland. It was in Warsaw that the largest concentration of Polish Jews lived. During the war, when the city's Jewish population was at a peak, Warsaw's Jewish community numbered about 450 thousand, and at times constituted as much as one quarter of all Jews residing in the area of the Government General. The centers of the Jewish political underground, the principal Jewish welfare institutions and, later, the Jewish fighting organizations were all founded in Warsaw, and it was out of Warsaw that all of them operated. Although the Germans had chosen Cracow to be the captial of the Government General, for Poles Warsaw remained the center of national life and became the nation's "underground capital."

At this point in our discussion a short general survey of the history of the Polish capital during the war would be useful. The defense of Warsaw lasted until as late as September 28, 1939, that is until after almost all Polish armed forces had been routed. Warsaw's stubborn defense was carried out by units of the Polish army that had entrenched themselves in the city and were supported by Warsaw's population and energetic mayor, Stefan Starzynski. The city paid dearly for its continuing resistance to the invader. For a period of four weeks the city was continuously bombed from the air and shelled by artillery, with the result that about a quarter of Warsaw's buildings were either damaged or destroyed and about fifty thousand of its inhabitants wounded or killed.[1]

It was not until November 1940—more than a year after the German occupation of Poland had begun—that a ghetto was established in Warsaw. During the interim Jews in Warsaw experienced almost no limitations on their contacts with the Polish population of the city. But once the ghetto was established in Warsaw, it became the most tightly sealed in the entire Government General and severely restricted and contacts between the city's Jews and Poles. However, as we have seen, relations between the two ethnic groups were not entirely severed. For the Warsaw Ghetto had been set up not in some remote outlying suburb but in the densely populated Jewish quarter in the city's northern district, and was surrounded by Polish neighborhoods. So that everything that took place there, including the deportations and the ghetto revolt, occured within full view of the non-Jewish residents of the city.

For a while it was mainly Poles who suffered from the policies instituted by the Germans for security reasons, although there were many cases of Jews, too, being victimized by the political reprisals. However, the punitive economic measures—consisting chiefly of dismissal from work, reduction of rationing allotments, humiliation, prevention of the free movement of provisions and cracking down on smuggling—hit Jews much harder than it did the Poles.

The liquidation of the Warsaw Ghetto began in the second half of 1942. In the summer of that year about 275 thousand Jews of the Ghetto, or seventy-five percent of those interned, were deported to death camps or killed. During the later phases of deportation, the Jews of the Ghetto prepared for resistance and took up arms in January and April 1943. Finally, during the great Warsaw Ghetto uprising in April-May 1943, the Ghetto was destroyed completely, its building were blown up and the entire ghetto area was reduced to rubble.

In August 1944 Polish armed resistance organizations launched a general uprising in Warsaw at the initiative of the Home Army (Armia Krajowa-AK.) The rebellion in Warsaw was a nationwide revolt that would lead to the liberation of the country by the Polish people themselves. But as it turned out, the Poles has miscalculated. The Germans were still sufficiently strong to put down a military rebellion undertaken without benefit of advanced heavy armament. The Soviets, for their part, being well aware of the Poles' intention of turning the liberation of their capital city into a symbol of Polish independence, decided to grant their troops an extended rest on the east bank of the Vistula. From this vantage point they were able to watch the carnage and destruction taking place at their leisure.

The rebellion ended in a blood bath in which more than 150 thousand Poles lost their lives, and in the mass expulsion of the population of Warsaw and the city's total physical ruin. Warsaw became a ghost town. So great indeed was the destruction that when the war came to an end the Poles themselves debated the question of whether to undertake the restoration of the city or simply to abandon it and move the nation's capital elsewhere. The issue was finally determined by the city's role in the war. For Poles, Warsaw had been the "Hero City," and the rebuilding of the city came to be regarded as a major national enterprise by both the regime and the people as a whole.

We should now consider the relations and contacts between Jews and Poles in Warsaw during the period of the war. The history of the relations breaks down chronologically into six major periods: (1) The brief period of Polish-German belligerency ending on September 27, 1939, during which the Poles engaged the Germans in full-scale military action; (2) The period of German occupation until the establishment of the Warsaw Ghetto, that is from the end of September 1939 to November 15, 1940; (3) The period of the "big ghetto" up to the beginning of deportations on July 22, 1942; (4) The period of deportations and armed struggle ending in the utter annihilation of the Warsaw Ghetto in May 1943; (5) The period up to August 1944, during which some Jewish survivors from the Ghetto lived hiding on the "Aryan side" of the city; (6) The period of the Polish rebellion in August-September 1944.

THE PERIOD OF POLISH-GERMAN BELLIGERENCE

Before the actual outbreak of the war there had been a brief interval during which a thaw in Polish-Jewish relations took place, to the extent that one might even speak of a reconciliation between the two groups. In retrospect, however, these few short months of rapprochement between Poles and Jews represented neither a profound nor permanent change in the relations between them, but rather a convergence of feeling at a moment of common peril. Faced by the German threat, Poles were no longer preoccupied with the "burning Jewish question," which had for a number of years dominated the mind of the public in Poland. With a real threat of survival hanging over the nation, all secondary and imaginary internal conflicts were set aside. Even the opposition, on both the political left and right, declared themselves to have joined the struggle against the common enemy. It was in this spirit that the leftist poet Wladyslaw Broniewski wrote a poem that was a call to arms, saying: "When they come to set fire to the house—the home in which you live—Poland," then "settling accounts with the injustices of the homeland" must be set aside, and for "the hand which is raised against the homeland—a bullet in the head!"

For Jews the expected outbreak of hostilities had a particular significance, apart from the anxieties they were experiencing at the time. There was no doubt in the minds of Polish Jews about where their loyalties lay in the approaching conflict. In most of the wars that had been fought in modern European history up until that time there were no basic Jewish interests involved, and Jews faced one another at the front as soldiers in the armies of whatever nation they happened to be citizens. Not so this time: there were no Jews serving in the German army, and the country and the regime with which Poland was about to go to war represented the most dangerous enemy Jews had faced in their entire history.

It was only natural, therefore, that the combined stimulus of political crisis and the coming peril should have given rise to understanding and cooperation between the two segments of the population of Poland. Jews were scrupulous in reporting for military conscription, and Jewish civilians worked beside Poles in digging trenches at the entrances to Warsaw.

THE FIRST PERIOD OF GERMAN OCCUPATION: SEPTEMBER 28, 1939–NOVEMBER 15, 1940

Poland's defeat was swift and sudden, and contrasted starkly to the illusions fostered among the Polish people by the government's vain boasts concerning the country's ability to hold its own in a military confrontation with the Third Reich. The public's embarrassment and frustration grew even greater when no sooner had the first battles been fought than the Polish government, military command and the whole of Polish senior officialdom fled the country, leaving behind no parting word of instruction, not even a token staff to guide the nation. For awhile the bitterness and disappointment silenced the entire leadership of the country's political parties. And as for ordinary Poles, many took perverse consolation from the fact that military defeat had brought worse suffering upon the Jews than it had on the rest of the population. Still, in the early weeks of the occupation, no hostile acts against Jews were committed by Poles. Hartglas even considered that "in the Warsaw district relations had improved." Nevertheless, the first signs of alienation appeared already during the battle. On September 20 an emergency Civilian Committe consisting of 27 members was established in besieged Warsaw; not a single Jew was coopted into its ranks.[1]

One of the guiding principles of German occupation policy in what had formerly been the Polish state was the segregation of the region's ethnic groups and widening the differences and conflicts among them. Thus in a memorandum issued in May 1940 Himmler asserted: "We are most interested not in the unity of the population in the East but in the opposite, in its splitting up into parts and countless fragments."[3] This aim was given special priority with respect to Jews. From the moment the Nazis took power in Germany they perceived the spread of anti-Semitism to be an effective instrument of policy and propaganda. But it was also obvious to Nazi leadership that a doctrine which denied sovereignty to other peoples on the basis of their racial origin and granted it exclusively to Germans would not be acceptable to ethnic minorities, especially those who stood to lose by it. They were careful to stress, therefore, that they had no intention of exporting National Socialism but only anti-Semitism. In September 1938, in the course of political talks with the Polish ambassador, Hitler stated that he wished to help the Poles achieve "a solution to the Jewish problem in their country," and despite the fact that the offer smacked strongly of interference in the internal affairs of Poland, Josef Lipski, the Polish ambassador to Berlin, received the German proposal with considerable enthusiasm.[4] German authorities in the Government General were aware that anti-German sentiment ran strong among the Polish people, and that the occupation itself as well as the occupation regime's policies toward the Poles were fanning popular opposition to German rule. Only on anti-Semitism and anti-Jewish policy could the Germans hope to get approval and support from a significant part of the populace. One observer at the time noted that while the German-language newspapers put out for Germans in occupied Poland took a very strong anti-Polish line, the Polish language publications supported by the occupation government agitated strongly against the Jews.

The Poles were aware of German aims, and the progressive elements in the underground called the public's attention to the subtle use the Germans were making of anti-Semitism in order to undermine Polish national solidarity. In March 2, 1940 the organ of the moderate Socialist faction in Poland, Informator published the following commentary on the subject:

> A wall has been created between the occupier and the Polish public, a fact which testifies to the health of our body politic. But there are also cracks in this wall through which human corruption has been seeping. One such minor crack is the association of certain Polish men and women for the purpose of collaborating in the conduct of dubious business deals and ventures. Corruption of this kind can only inspire revul-

sion. And one crack which has been growing ever wider was introduced into the consciousness of the Polish public even before the war by the propaganda of Polish Hitlerism. Not only are many Poles unmoved by the barbarous anti-Semitism which has been instigated by the occupier against Jewish citizens of Poland, but now and then we encounter the desire to revive the anti-Semitic movement under the German aegis and out of German loyalty. There are already professors working out a Nazi ideology for Polish use. "Political activists" have already appeared who dream about the establishment of a radical Nazi party. We should add that many anti-Semitic public personalities of this type from before the war have simply reported for duty at the Gestapo, work for them and profit from the theft of Jewish property. An uncompromising struggle must be undertaken against such manifestations . . .[5]

Anti-Semitic agitation among Poles served an additional German aim. The Nazis introduced a practice in Warsaw similar to the one they subsequently put into operation in other major cities in the East. At the beginning of the occupation anti-Jewish violence was made to appear to have been initiated and carried out by the local population. Such incidents served to justify Nazi policy and violence against Jews, which could be presented to both the German people and the world as merely a response to the will of the populations in the countries of German occupation. There were repeated incidents of street violence against Jews in occupied Poland; and the Germans missed no opportunity to photograph the local pogroms. Occasionally the Germans would even trot out the argument that the ghetto had only been established in order to protect Jews from violence arising from Polish indignation against them.[6]

Nevertheless, there exists no homogeneity of attitude among the different sectors of Polish society on the occupation regime's exclusion of Jews from the economic life of the country or on the spate of ordinances issued by the Germans for the purpose of humiliating Jews. Thus, for example, the Warsaw Lawyers' Council refused to give in to German demands that Jews be eliminated from its list of attorneys; this despite the fact that the organization's head was Leon Nowodworski, a member of the National Party which had in the past tried to prevent Jews from entering the legal profession. The Lawyers' Council rejected the German demand on the grounds that it ran counter to the spirit of the Polish constitution; in other words, German dictates were unacceptable, even on matters concerning the Jews. Among Polish citizens who stood firm in resisting Nazi policy, even when punitive measures were taken against them, were many on the staff of the Lawyers' Council.

Another episode exemplifies a somewhat different response of prominent Poles to the Jewish issue. Early in September 1939 the

Polish government established a welfare agency in Warsaw in anticipation of the emergency during the approaching hostilities. The agency was put under the management of a committee of respectable public figures (*Stoleczny Komitet Samopomocy Spolecznej*), and a generous budget, drawn from the Polish treasury, was apportioned to it. Immediately after the establishment of the agency, which incorporated various welfare organizations active in the Polish community, Jewish welfare groups decided to join it as well. But the committee's operations within an organizational framework that included Jews lasted for only a brief time. Shortly after the Germans had taken control, the Polish leadership on the committee announced that they were severing their connection with the Jewish welfare organizations and would no longer place welfare funds at their disposal. According to the Polish committee's representatives their actions were the result of German orders. From the documentary sources available to us it is impossible to determine whether or not this was entirely a case of submission to German will under duress, or whether Polish initiative was in some way involved as well. But there are hints contained in Jewish sources of the existence of suspicions at the time that the cessation of Polish-Jewish cooperation in the field of welfare had come about because of Polish initiative in the matter.[7] In any event when a general welfare agency was established a little later throughout the Government General, it was the Germans who, for reasons of their own, favored the inclusion of Jews in the agency's activities both while it was being organized and during its operation. But whatever the case may be, it is evident that the Poles made no attempt to resist German instructions. Nor, for that matter, did the Jews receive a fair portion from the funds the committee had received from the Polish government, and so were denied full partnerhsip in the organization despite their status as Polish citizens and taxpayers.

The two cases seem to illuminate a tendency characteristic of two important groups in Polish society as a whole and in the Polish underground movement. Neither group wished to become directly involved in the anti-Jewish actions of the Nazis or be a party to the implementation of anti-Semitic policies. At the same time they were also reluctant to work together with Jews or cooperate with the organization of the Jewish community, and took advantage of the situation created by the occupation in order to break off whatever friendly relations did exist up to that time.

The responses of individual Poles to the German anti-Jewish campaign varied as well. In his report after leaving occupied Poland Apolinary Hartglas wrote: "The Jewish badge was attached to clothing so the German could easily identify Jews and seize them on the street for labor, and also in order to incite the Polish masses against the Jews." Concerning the response of ordinary Poles we read the following account in the recorded testimony of one witness: "In the beginning Poles often showed sympathy for Jews wearing the armbands, but as time passed this attitude toward Jews cooled, and Poles seemed to avoid meeting in public with Jewish friends wearing armbands." And further on, we read: There were cases on city streetcars, when Jews were required to wear badges, and when Jewish women wearing the badges would get on the streetcars, Polish men would rise to give them their seats. And there was one case where a German got on a streetcar and ordered: "Jews out!" And a Pole, a dignified old man, got up and said: "If the Jews get off, I'll get off too." And he stood up and got off, and all the rest of the Poles got off with him. . . . There were also cases of Polish youngsters chasing Jews off streetcars.[8]

In his book *Accursed Years* (Zaklete Lata), the Polish author Wladyslaw Smólski writes: "First the Jews were ordered to wear armbands with stars. The Germans would often seize passers-by wearing armbands for labor, and at the same time beat and maltreat them . . . . In addition they were assaulted by Polish riff-raff who had been instigated by the Germans."[9]

But the development that most undermined the trust between Jews and Poles in Warsaw during the early period of the occupation had nothing to do with the attitudes and conduct of individuals or of groups and sectors in Polish society. The events that exerted the most profound effect at the time were the repeated incidents of Polish street violence against Jews. These assaults on Jews took place over a considerable span of time, and at their height assumed the dimensions of a pogrom. Anti-Jewish riots broke out in public places and in full view of crowds of passers-by. They left behind a residue of bitter feeling and heightened anxiety among the Jewish residents.

The riots are described in detail in diaries and journals of Jews who had witnessed the violence. Thus, Ch. A. Kaplan, a teacher who had sworn an oath to keep a daily records of events for the duration of the war, made the following entry in his diary on February 1, 1940:

> ". . . no nation lacks for hooligan groups. And for such as these the occupier has found an outlet, has gone and let them understand that Jews are beyond the pale of the law; that the authorities would not be overly strict with them if Jews were their victims. And for hooligans a wink is as good as a nod. Recently there has been no letup in attacks on Jews perpetrated in broad daylight and on public thoroughfares."[10]

Adam Czerniakow, chairman of the *Judenrat* in Warsaw, is terse and to the point in his diary entry for January 27: "On Marszalkowska and Poznanska Streets Jews beaten all day and night."[11] And in his entry for the next day he records: "At 2 o'clock in the afternoon a gang of young hoodlums who have been beating up Jews for several days now rushed past the Jewish community and smashed windows in front of them."[12] The historian Ringelblum, gives us the following account of events: "Yesterday (January 28) Polish gangs ran wild . . . Today, the 30th of the month, I had a difficult time of it. While walking through the Saxon Park with my armband on, I was spotted by a gang of thugs, aged approximately fourteen. I barely escaped from them with my life."[13]

An eyewitness who managed to escape from Warsaw early in the Spring of 1940 and reached Palestine told about the severe attacks in March 1940:

> The pogrom commited against the Jews of Warsaw during the Passover holiday lasted for about eight days. It broke out suddenly, and ended just as suddenly. It was perpetrated by a bunch of hoodlums, about 1000 of them, who spontaneously appeared on the streets of Warsaw. They hadn't been seen before and haven't been seen since. They were probably reckless and irresponsible youths who had come together for this purpose from all over the city. . . For the most part the hoodlums acted on their own, but there were also instances in which German soldiers joined in on their assaults.[14]

From the evidence it would appear that the Polish public remained indifferent, for the most part, to the violence being perpetrated against Jews. Though there were cases of opposition by Poles to the riots and even intervention on behalf of Jews, these were rare and hardly in evidence throughout the period of mass violence. Almost all of our witnesses agree that it was only members of the Polish intelligentsia who condemned the violence or attempted to defend the Jews from the rioters. Nowhere do we find even the mention of any attempt to intervene, either in word or deed, by the organized underground resistance in Poland.

The riots stopped quite suddenly never to be resumed, at least not in the form of street violence. Julian Kulski, the wartime mayor of Warsaw, claims in his memoirs that he had appealed to the German authorities toward the end of March to restore order and prevent further outbursts of violence. According to Kulski the Germans responded by promising to put an end to the riots and allow no further attacks to take place in the city streets.[15] On the other hand, Jewish sources indicate that the attacks ended when Dr. F. Arlt, chief of the German Section for the Population and

Welfare in the administration of the Government General, interceded. In March 1940 Arlt was busy setting up the general welfare agency in which Jews were to be included. When he met with Jewish representatives, including Czerniakow, in Cracow, he was told that there was no point in even discussing welfare so long as Polish hooligans were committing outrages against Jews with impunity. Dr. Arlt temporized at first, but finally agreed to contact Warsaw by telephone: one well-placed call by him was all that was needed to put an end to the anti-Jewish violence.[16]

THE GHETTO PERIOD: JEWS INSIDE THE GHETTO

The ghetto period isolated the Jewish community from the outside world and brought an end to routine contacts between Jews and Poles. The wall divided the city's population into two distinct areas. The only Jews allowed through the gates of the Ghetto were the few with special passes and those who left in labor columns that were rushed out of the Ghetto at the first light of dawn and rushed back in again at the end of a long and weary day's work. A number of Poles had permission to enter the Ghetto, but they too had to show special passes in order to get in and were only allowed inside to carry out specific tasks.

The Warsaw Ghetto, which had been sealed from the moment it was established on November 15, 1940, was officially represented as one of three ethnic districts in the city—the other two being the German and Polish districts. The Germans made certain that it should always be referred to by its official designation as the "Jewish Residential Quarter in the City of Warsaw." Obviously there was a difference between the "Jewish Quarter" in Warsaw and the city's other ethnic residential districts. Only the Jewish neighborhood was sealed off, with its entire population—excepting those who were taken out for work—kept in virtual quarantine. Under the conditions that prevailed in the Ghetto—the body-wasting famine, terrible crowding and filth, and the absence of greenery—infectious diseases ran wild, with the result that tens of thousands of its residents were quite literally gradually dying from a combination of adverse factors.

It was the Germans who came up with the epithet "death boxes" for the ghettos. We have no way of knowing for certain if the Germans actually intended to bring about the extinction of all Jews in the ghettos by denying them food and other essential requirements for survival. However, a document does exist in which the German governor of the Government General, Hans

Frank, states that if existing conditions in the ghettos do not bring about the mass extinction of Jews it would be necessary to employ other means.[17] However, according to other evidence on hand, one of the German senior police officials in the Government General, Streckenbach, is recorded to have remarked during a high-level consultation on Jews that "it would not be possible to starve them [the Jews] to death."[18] But even if there were no clearly conceived plans to bring about the mass liquidation of Jews by means of the ghetto, indifference to the fate of Jews and to the conditions in which they lived in the ghettos amounted to the same thing in practice. In the Warsaw Ghetto alone a total of 100 thousand of its residents died, mostly of starvation and infectious diseases by the time of its liquidation in April-May 1943—or one out of every four ghetto inmates.

Before considering the form and nature of the contacts between Jews and Poles that developed during the ghetto period, we ought first to examine Polish attitudes to the ghetto plan in the period immediately prior to its implementation.

Again, the attitude of the public in Warsaw was not homogeneous. Undoubtedly the plan of sealing Jews off in a ghetto was exclusively a German initiative. The Polish representatives of the Warsaw municipality, the heads of the central welfare organization, RGO, and the press of the underground resistance all opposed the project. The Poles in the municipal government even let the Germans know of their opposition. Waldemar Schoen—the German appointed to the task of planning the ghetto project—when speaking to a group of German officials described the response of Poles in the municipality when the plan was aired:

> "Opposition was voiced from various quarters, and especially from the municipal administration. They argued that the creation of the ghetto would cause significant disruptions in industry and the economy as a whole. It was stated that about 80% of skilled workers were Jews and that they could not be withdrawn because they were essential. Finally, the argument was raised that it would be impossible to feed Jews concentrated in a sealed-off neighborhood."[19]

As the ghetto project was getting under way, the AK's *Information Bulletin* commented, "The ghetto in Warsaw is assuming the dimensions of a monumental crime," and went on to describe the Warsaw Ghetto's establishment as an "insane German plan to intern 410,000 human beings in a tiny sealed-off area containing absolutely no open spaces and greenery." Apparently, however, there were also Poles who did support the establishment of a Jewish ghetto in the city. Thus Czerniakow recorded in his diary on

October 23, 1940, that "important Polish political figures support the ghetto."[20]

Julian Kulski, who was mayor of Warsaw during the occupation and in touch with Polish resistance, describes the opposition he and his colleagues took on the ghetto dilemma in a book of recollections of his wartime activity published after the war. A report was submitted containing, as it were, a statistical character: estimates determining the size of the area in respect of the numerical relationship between one section of the population and the other.[21]

Kulski's claims are not supported in any of the sources contemporary with the events. Thus one of the resistance newspapers, *Polish News*, observed shortly before the establishment of the Warsaw Ghetto:

> Many delegations of Poles set out for Cracow in order to obtain a change in the boundaries, or at least to have the date of the ghetto's establishment put off until the spring. On Friday, October 19, when the evacuation had been almost completed, the population was informed about changes in the ghetto boundaries and their reduction by about thirty percent.[22]

And we find Ludwik Landau, a Polish economist of Jewish origin, writing in his wartime journal on October 15, 1940:

> . . . various efforts on behalf of the population are also being made by the city administration, which in its guise as directorate often regards itself to be in effect the representative of the Gentile sector of the population, and because of this is engaged in a conflict with the Jewish community leadership representing the Jewish population.[23]

Ringelblum noted in October 1940:

> "A Jewish-Polish consultation took place yesterday with Baron Ronikier. The latter spoke in opposition to the current practice among some Poles of grabbing as many of the streets in the ghetto as possible. It is his view that a common struggle should be waged against the ghetto rather than a war between the two peoples."[24]

The effect of these efforts was to reduce the ghetto precinct by degrees, increasing the congestion to a point where there remained "no free corner, no empty cranny; not a hole that wasn't occupied."[25]

At one stage the municipality and the Jewish community leadership established a housing exchange bureau for Poles and Jews, a step that helped reduce some of the pressure on those who had to change neighborhoods. But relatively few exchange deals actually took place. The reason, we are told, was that "the Aryans who until now resided in the Jewish area were mostly from the poorer strata of society. Their apartments were below average and were low in price. Not so the other party. Jews who until now had lived in the Aryan quarter were mostly from the affluent strata of society, and their apartments were attractive, comfortable and expensive."[26] Then there were the thousands of Jews who lived in the Praga suburb of Warsaw, on the east bank of the Vistula; they had expected to be allowed to remain in their homes and were caught unprepared when the time came to evacuate the neighborhood. There were many Jews as well who had neither the opportunity nor the means to find living quarters in the ghetto area.

Although the Poles bore no responsibility in the plan of establishing the Warsaw Ghetto and had even tried to prevent its formation, by their sometimes selfish behavior when the ghetto decree was finally implemented they had to a certain extent acted to reduce the living space of Jews.

A special problem concerned people of Jewish extraction who regarded themselves as Poles and maintained no connection with the Jewish community or Judaism. They too were defined as Jews under German racial ordinances and required by law to move into the ghetto.

A number of converted and assimilated Jews tried to obtain exemptions from the decree. One of them was Professor Ludwik Hirszfeld, whose research in the field of blood types had gained him an international reputation. Hirszfeld had converted in his youth and severed all ties with Jews and Judaism. He tells of how he and a number of others in the same position had asked Polish welfare officials to intervene on their behalf for an exemption from the requirement. Hirszfeld relates that the German authorities promised to consider the requests and asked for a list of the names and addresses of the applicants. The Germans ultimately rejected the applicants' requests to be granted the status of persons "eligible for the rights of the Polish nation," but made sinister use of the list. According to Hirszfeld, when the time came to implement the ghetto decree all those whose names had appeared on the list were personally ordered to move into the ghetto.[27] Arnold Szyfman, the founder and manager of the prestigious Polish Theater in Warsaw, was a Jew by origin but Polish in every other respect and with no ties whatever with the Jewish community or Jewish culture. Before the establishment of the ghetto he was arrested twice by the Gestapo and warned about his failure to wear a Jewish armband.[28]

The situation that Christians of Jewish origin and assimilated Jews suddenly had to face when the ghetto was established is described in *Occupation Chronicle*, one of the newspapers of the Polish underground: "The Jewish intelligentsia and [intelligentsia] of Jewish origin, which is entirely rooted in Polish culture, has had imposed on it a totally alien existence and been cut off from everything the members of the group have cherished."[29] The November-December 1940 edition of the same paper reported that the RGO had succeeded in obtaining exemptions from the ghetto decree of ten Christians of Jewish origin, and that additional requests for exemptions would be considered individually on their own merits. We have found no evidence confirming that such releases had actually been obtained. The position of extreme anti-Semites in Poland was expressed by the Newspaper *Miecz i Plug* ("The Sword and the Plow,") which regarded the confinement of Jews to the ghetto as a welcome development while speaking scornfully of Ronikier and Archbishop Sapieha as "friends of the neophytes" because of their efforts to release converts from having to live in the ghetto. This paper, which was published under the auspices of the extreme rightist faction, also advised "Aryan" partners in mixed marriages to obtain a divorce.

There were Christians of Jewish extraction—as well as a small number of unconverted Jews— who did not obey the ghetto decree and continued living outside the ghetto in the Polish district. The number of such persons residing in Warsaw is unknown. They lived a precarious existence, exposed as they constantly were to betrayal by people who had known them in the past. Those who had been privileged and famous before the occupation had an especially hard time of it. Arnold Szyfman belonged to the latter category of Jews living outside the ghetto, and has left us with an account of his ordeal:

> Spring augured unrest for Warsaw. The mechanical division of the city into three districts (German, Polish and Jewish) created a multitude of complex problems that poisoned people's existence, which even prior to this had been far from sweet . . . . Around November 15 we moved to Mokotow, a Polish neighborhood far enough away from town, but all the same I did not feel secure even there. Too many people knew me, the gutters overflowed with evil, so that I was hemmed in by danger on every side. Therefore I decided to leave Warsaw; out there it was quieter, at least for the time being.[30]

According to the figures recorded by the statistical section of the *Judenrat* in the Warsaw Ghetto in 1941, the population of the ghetto then included 1540 Catholics, 148 Protestants, thirty Orthodox Christians, and forty-three members of other non-Jewish religious denominations. Three churches had remained within the ghetto precinct, and these were placed at the disposal of Christians of Jewish extraction residing in the ghetto. According to one source, "these churches were filled with worshippers on Sundays. The central church on Leszno Street served not only as a place of worship but as a social center for Catholics in the ghetto and as a school and play area for children."[31]

In his work about Jewish-Polish relations during the war, Ringelblum describes the days immediately following November 15, during which Poles were still permitted to enter the area of the ghetto. He writes "At that time the streets were filled with masses of Poles who had come to say farewell to their Jewish friends for the last time, bringing food with them.[31] He makes a special point of describing the scenes of emotional leave-taking between Jewish and Polish friends that took place at the gates of the ghetto as the shocked ghetto gendarmerie looked on in disbelief. According to the testimony of a suburban Praga rabbi, Rabbi Silberstein, which was recorded by Rabbi Shimon Huberband, a member of the archival staff of the ghetto underground, "The attitude of Poles [at the time of the deportation of the Jews of Praga to the Warsaw Ghetto] was generally one of indifference. There were also many cases of Poles expressing sympathy. There were no cases of hostility."[32]

As we have observed, the establishment of the ghetto artificially severed Jews from the Polish community. Jewish stores in the Polish district of Warsaw were closed and confiscated. Jewish craftsmen whose customers had been Poles lost their livelihood. Jews who had worked outside the ghetto precinct were deprived of their jobs. These economic deprivations were added to the list of those already in force. The Jews had been excised from the economic system; their assets and businesses were appropriated and the only economic role that was left to them was to work as forced labor for the Germans.

In addition to the great many Jewish houses there were about 1,700 Jewish grocery shops and 2,500 Jewish business establishments of all sorts located in the Gentile neighborhoods of Warsaw. In some cases Jews transferred their places of businesses and stocks of merchandise to Polish acquaintances. Occasionally Jews even had their businesses registered in the names of Poles, so that although the Germans regarded all Jewish property to be their spoils, a considerable quantity of this property was transferred into Polish hands.

With the exclusion of Jews from the economic life of the country, one would have expected anti-Semitism to recede if not disappear altogether in Poland. Polish anti-Semites had maintained all along that anti-Jewish sentiment in the country was entirely due to the fact that Jews were competing economically with Poles and had taken over sources of livelihood that rightfully belonged to them.

There were even Jews who took a similar view, regarding Polish anti-Semitism to be economically motivated, in essence, and its continued existence a result of the persistence of the economic contradictions that gave it birth. Nevertheless, the elimination of Jews from the Polish economy was not followed by a decrease in Polish anti-Semitism. If anything it even increased, and the elimination of Jews from the nation's economic life was, paradoxically, one of the major causes for growing Polish hostility to Jews during the war. The reasons were twofold: fear that when the war ended Jews would return to reclaim their property and their prior status in the country's economy; and bad conscience on the part of Poles who had taken advantage of the opportunities created during the occupation to enrich themselves at the expense of Jews, and now sought to exculpate themselves by maligning the character and conduct of those whom they had robbed. The Jewish historian Prof. Ben-Zion Dinur has pointed out that anti-Jewish libels were less a pretext for pogroms than their by-product, because those who committed the outrages sought to assuage their own guilt by proclaiming the extensive sins of their victims.

Anxieties over the prospect of Jews returning to their former status was not confined to Poles who had taken over Jewish property and jobs; echoes of it can be discerned in the political considerations of key elements in the Polish underground. Roman Knoll, who was for a time foreign minister in the prewar Polish government and now held the post of political adviser in the organization of the civilian underground, went so far as to warn the Government-in-Exile in London against restoring Jewish property and jobs now held by Poles, because such a policy would meet with strong, perhaps even violent, public opposition in Poland.[33]

During the war, the Polish literary scholar, Prof. Kazimierz Wyka, wrote a penetrating essay on Polish economy under the occupation. In the section entitled "Jews and Polish Commerce," he describes Jewish trade as a form of commerce that is alien "to the moral fabric of existence with in a state." But having said this, he then goes on to assert:

> The more important issue is that the forms in which *the expulsion*[of Jews] *took place and the way in which our public wished, and still wishes, it to be carried out* were unacceptable both from the moral and the practical point of view. Therefore, even if I must stand alone in what I say and find no one to back me, I will go on repeating—No, a thousand times No. Such methods and such expectations are shameful, wicked and base, because in essence the moral-economic attitude of the average Pole toward the Jewish tragedy is this: In destroying the Jews the Germans are carrying out acts of murder. We would never have done that. For that crime the Germans will pay the penalty; they have soiled their conscience. But we Poles only reap the benfits

without disturbing our conscience or staining our hands with
blood . . . ." [Emphasis in the original].[34]

Traffic in contraband food was the one area of ongoing contact
between the ghetto and the Polish district of Warsaw. Smuggling
was the principal means by which food made its way into the
ghetto, and throughout all of the changes in German policy on
smuggling, the movement of contraband food and commodities
between the ghetto and the city did not cease for a single day from
the moment of the Warsaw Ghetto's establishment to the time of its
liquidation.[35]

The Germans introduced a policy of official food-rationing
whereby each of the three ethnic sectors of the population was
allotted amounts calculated in calories; Germans received 2,613
calories; Poles, 669; Jews, 184 calories a day. Thus the Jewish food
ration was only 15% of the minimum amount of food required to
stay alive, and anyone depending solely on his ghetto ration for his
nourishment had no mathematical chance of surviving. Poles, too,
had need of adding to their rations.[36] The persistence of the
smuggling was a subject of black humor among ghetto wags, a
relevant example of which is quoted by Ringelblum: "There are
three unconquerable things; the German army, the British Isles and
Jewish smuggling.

Although the Germans were unable to stop the smuggling, their
attempts to control it, and the attendant increase in confiscations,
inflated prices in direct ratio to the increasing risks and losses of
the smugglers and middlemen. Kaplan and other diarists record
that food could be bought in the ghetto, but cost twenty-five percent
more than outside—the difference being accounted for by smuggling
costs. Of course prices rose when times became difficult. So, during the period of deportations, the price of food rose severalfold
above a level which was already prohibitive. There were relatively
few wage earners in the ghetto, and most of them earned very much
less than what was needed for bare subsistence. Most had to live
from savings or by selling off personal effects. The cost of food was
a matter of life and death in the ghetto—and as the price of food
inexorably rose, the number of ghetto paupers grew and increasing
numbers of people died of starvation.

We possess little detailed knowledge about the smuggler bands
operation in the Polish district of Warsaw. Polish smugglers either
purchased their goods in the city or brought them in from the
countryside, and delivered the consignments at appointed times to
locations agreed upon. They were also involved in smuggling
goods into the ghetto—and out of it. The traffic was not all one way.

A variety of items, including clothing, household furniture and even pianos made their way from the ghetto into the Polish district. Smuggling was a dangerour game for Poles, too—although German guards were less likely to gun down Poles than Jews.

Wholesale smuggling accounted for most of the contraband entering the ghetto. A reasonable estimate of its fraction of the illicit trade would be eighty-five percent. If we consider that the population of the ghetto reached almost half a million at its height, and that smuggling supplied most of the commodities and food that the residents of the ghetto consumed, we get a fair idea of the enormous scale of the enterprise.

After the war some Polish writers argued that smuggling was one of the forms taken by Polish assistance to Jews during the occupation. A similar argument was advocated at a scholars conference held in Poland. The claim is without foundation. Our own research has revealed no motive in the smuggling activities other than profit. While food prices were rising tenfold during the war the movable property with which Jews paid for their food accumulated on the "Aryan side." It would be no exaggeration to say, therefore, that the Jews paid for the bread that came from the Polish district with possessions that had been collected over many generations of hard work and struggle for existence.

Yet, the press of the Polish underground approved of and encouraged smuggling, which it regarded as an expression of resistance to the Nazis and valued for disrupting the occupier's plans. The smuggling of produce from the countryside to the city deprived Germans of quantities of food that would have been requisitioned for the German war effort. Thus Ringelblum wrote in his diary: "Everything considered, Polish-Jewish cooperation in the field of smuggling is one of the better pages in the history of the relations between the two peoples during the war."

The other forms of smuggling activity deserve to be discussed as well, even if only briefly. For although their contribution to survival in the ghetto was modest, they directly involved the ordinary population of the ghetto.

The smuggling by forced laborers was done in a straight-forward manner. The laborers were taken out daily by the Germans and put to work in military barracks, factories, offices, railway stations and elsewhere outside the ghetto precinct. At times their numbers reached several thousand. The opportunities this gave them to come into contact with Polish laborers allowed them to exchange articles of clothing and small items they could carry on their persons for small quantities of food, which they brought back with them when they were returned to the ghetto in the evening. Usually the German guards at the entrance would not bother to prevent such small amounts of food from being brought into the ghetto. Still, much depended on the good will of the guards, and occasionally searches were made, the food taken away and the workers beaten.

Finally, there were the "lone smugglers." Most of them were people who were themselves at the edge of starvation, who were driven to smuggling as the only alternative to death. They would usually leave the ghetto by stealth, remain illegally for a few days in the Polish district, where they made small transactions by which they procured only enough food to feed their immediate families and themselves. On October 15, 1941, Frank issued the order imposing the death penalty on Jews guilty of being outside the ghetto without permission and on Poles who sheltered them. The decree was strictly enforced and the death penalty inevitable in the case of Jewish violators. In the following month eight Jews were executed under the decree—six of them were women, and from then on the death penalty became an ordinary procedure.

Among lone smugglers, children were a category unto themselves. Children in the ghetto, whose existence was made cruel beyond measure, battled to survive with a tenacity which only the very young, thirsting to live, possess. Lone children, and occasionally groups of children took advantage of every break in the wall and every underground passage in sneaking out of the ghetto. Bands of children gathered at the entrances of the ghetto, and sometimes a guard, out of good humor or in a rare moment of compassion, would allow them to leave. Once on the other side, the children would beg for bread. Polish sources tell us that Poles, especially Polish women, were so moved by pity for these ghetto youngsters that even those who were hostile to Jews would feed the children. One of the croniclers of the Warsaw ghetto, Abraham Levin, noted in his diary on June 7, 1942:

> Many Jews held that . . . the Poles displayed feelings of compassion and goodwill toward the poor Jews, and especially toward the Jewish child beggars. These feelings are still valid . . . It is well know that our beggar children wandering by the dozens and hundreds along the Christian streets receive generous [handouts of] bread and potatoes and are thus able to feed themselves and their relatives in the ghetto."[36]

It was not unusual, however, for guards to conduct a search and, finding a few crusts of bread or a potato, beat the children. There were quite a number of cases, too, of children being shot down by guards while attempting to leave or enter the ghetto. Henryka Lazowert, a Polish-Jewish poetess who died in the ghetto, dedicated an elegiac poem to these children called "The Little

Shmugler." And Leon Berenson, a lawyer who had been famous in prewar Poland for his defense of political offenders, proposed after the war to erect a monument to honor the memory of the war's "anonymous child"—the little smugglers of the Warsaw Ghetto.

Commercial ties between the ghetto and the Polish section of Warsaw did not consist exclusively of smuggling. A certain amount of normal business was transacted as well. The Germans had gone to great lengths to ensure the ghetto's total economic isolation. They not only erected a walled enclosure secured by a mixed guard of German troops, Polish police and Jewish ghetto police, but also concentrated all of the ghetto's import and export commerce, as it were, in their own hands. According to the German economic plan for the ghetto, the sole item Jews were allowed to export in exchange for food and other staple commodities was labor—and Jewish labor existed only to serve the German war effort. The Jews were thereby condemned to total isolation from the Polish free market.

But neither the physical barrier nor the economic prohibitions on trade succeeded in cutting off all avenues of commerce between Jews in the Ghetto and Polish businessmen. A Jewish economist interned in the Warsaw Gehtto described the process by which such commercial ties developed:

> The elimination of the Jews from the economic life of the Government General led to a situation called the "Aryanization" of the economy. The meaning of the mechanical transfer of Jewish business firms to Poles and of the establishment of new Polish businesses . . . [is] that instead of there being hundreds of small wholesalers there have now been created large Polish warehouses . . . Polish companies which were already in existence could now expand their scope . . . . Nevertheless the supplier of Aryan commercial firms in various branches [of business], or of such that became Aryan, was still the Jewish merchant or craftsman. The department store of Jablkowski Bros., for example, is still going to have to buy toys from home-based craftsmen on Zamenhof or Nalewki Streets. The "Charadowsky" Company must strain every fiber to obtain a permit from outside the ghetto. German merchants generally order their stock from Jews. Jewish manufacturers of small wares were the sole suppliers of Polish entrepreneurs, who were forced to resort to Jewish labor just to remain in business.[37]

How was export from the ghetto, the Polish-Jewish "partnership" in this field, managed when the walls surrounding the Jewish Residential Quarter made it seem impossible? It should be established from the outset that legal export by means of the *Transferstelle* (the official and sole German institution for the movement of commodities and wares in and out of the ghetto) accounted, as in the large-scale provision of goods, for only a minuscule percentage of this traffic. Export was largely conducted by smuggling.

JEWS ON THE "ARYAN SIDE"

The anti-Nazi solidarity of the Polish people has earned them the deserved admiration of the world. In view of the unified stand taken by the Poles against the Germans during the occupation, it would be appropriate for us to consider whether the fact that a single enemy oppressed Poles and Jews alike did not lead to increased mutual sympathy and a rapprochement between the two communities, and to a consequent change in the long-entrenched anti-Semitic attitudes among the Polish people. On this issue there are clear differences of opinion between Polish publicists and historians on the one hand, and Jewish writers and memoirists on the other.

The Poles have consistently maintained that there was a conspicuous decrease in Polish hostility toward the Jews during the war, with the result that significant sections of the population were prepared to come to the rescue of Jews. The opinion among Polish writers is that Poles made it a major national enterprise to stand behind the Jews during the occupation and to save them from genocide. These writers are deeply disturbed by the unfavorable image their country has acquired abroad, and especially in the democratic West, in respect to the Holocaust; and they accuse Jews of having consciously conspired to blacken Poland's good name in the eyes of the world. Even Polish writers who were sympathetic and active in rescuing Jews during the war have joined the chorus of blame against Jewish historiography for perpetuating an image of Poles that has "done an injustice to the Polish people."

This Polish literature is essentially apologetic. Certainly the wholesale condemnation of the conduct of Poles during the Holocaust is both unfair and unwarranted. The fact is that there were Poles who made efforts to save Jews and some of them paid for their courageous behavior with their lives. On the other hand it is untrue that the Jews who recorded their experience in the course of the war were obsessed by a desire to chastise the Poles. Actually in the beginning of the war Jewish writing overflows with sympathy for Poland and the Polish people, and it was only when Jewish hopes for assistance were shattered by Polish hostility to Jews that we begin to read criticism of Polish conduct.

The subject is of crucial importance when we consider the efforts made by individual Poles who rescued Jews on their own during the period that begins with the mass deportations and concludes at the end of the occupation. The statements by Poles active in the underground furnish an ample body of contemporary testimony to the existence of anti-Semitism among the Polish people during the war, and even to its exacerbation during the occupation. In a report to London in September 1941, the commander of the AK urged, "Please accept as a fact that the overwhelming majority in the country is anti-Semitic."[38] Knoll, in a memorandum already cited, observed:

> "The whole middle-class continues to pay homage to anti-Semitic ideology and was pleased that the Nazis had solved the Jewish problem in Poland. Thanks to Hitler, the members of the Polish middle class have at one stroke got rid of their unwanted creditors—the Jewish banks and merchants—and, thanks to the mass slaughter of Jews, the scheme of 'numerus nullus' has been achieved in its entirety in industry, labor, commerce and economic life as a whole. By the elimination of the Jews, Gentile 'merchants' suddenly became the owners of many commercial and industrial enterprises, and [Gentile] partners rid themselves of their Jewish associates."[39]

A Polish woman interviewed in connection with a survey undertaken by the Ringelblum Archives, whom we have already quoted in part, has the following to say about Polish attitudes toward the Jews:

> "When all of these advantages will come to an end. One can often hear people saying among themselves, 'Yes sir, what's going to happen when all those Jews break out of those walls, what will they do to us? Its frightening to think of.' Everybody keeps repeating this without thinking, as if a real threat were hanging over them. This psychosis is responsible for the fact that the news about the deportation is being received with a certain degree of relief. It should also be known that the rabble, which has been corrupted as a result of the war, has been spinning out fantasies in which—with an illogicality normal among Poles—blows dealt the Germans are tied in with squaring accounts with the Jews. If you should condemn Poles for their behavior toward Jews, if you should point out that such activity in fact assists the occupier—you can assume in advance that you'll hear the reply that this is in reprisal for what happened on the other side of the Bug.[40] I don't know what happened on the other side of the Bug; certainly it wasn't even a fraction of what is being told about it here at home, because otherwise not a single Pole would have left the eastern districts alive. I think this is a convenient pretext, one way of salving the conscience."[41]

There is a comparatively large body of evidence of this sort contained in Polish sources originating with both Poles who took a viciously anti-Semitic line and those who had reservations about anti-Semitism or were unequivocally opposed to it. Couriers of the Polish Government-in-Exile made no secret of the fact that their contacts in Poland were warning them against making too great a show of support for the Jews in official statements and propaganda, because the public at home did not welcome having the subject brought up.

We might now consider whether Jews writing in Poland during the darkest period of the war were in fact consistently hostile toward the Polish people. In his essay on Polish assistance to Jews during the war, the historian Philip Friedman collects facts and references bearing on the subject which are contained in Emanuel Ringelblum's notes. These he adds to an impressive array of other evidence of Polish actions on behalf of Jews.[42] Nevertheless, when Ringelblum came to make a general assessment of Polish attitudes as experienced by Jews during the war years, he observed:

> Polish "Fascism and its ally, anti-Semitism, have conquered the majority of the Polish people ... The blind folly of Poland's anti-Semites, who have learnt nothing, has been responsible for the death of hundreds of thousands of Jews who could have been saved despite the Germans."[43]

Another Jewish chronicler of Warsaw ghetto Ch. A. Kaplan, wrote in his diary on February 1, 1940:

> The hate propaganda against Jews suited the temper and will of many groups of Poles, and perhaps—the entire Polish populace. For it was as if he were saying: "I have taken away your political independence; but in its place I give you economic independence. Until now all of economic life has been grasped in Jewish hands. Henceforth—it will be transferred into your hands. All of your lives you have been struggling against the Jewish affliction and received nothing. I will show you the way. Under my rule the Jews will be driven from their businesses and you will take their place."[44]

In the following month, on March 28, Kaplan wrote:

> The entire pogrom movement has been deliberately created and arranged by the conqueror, whose policy in occupied Poland has been foundering up to now .... The conqueror has therefore turned to those accursed youths who are ideologically close to him. This element is capricious, lacks any definite outlook, is easily incited and without a stable political orientation. In addition it aspires to violence and pillage. So the conqueror has curried these youths' favor by using the lives and capital of Jews ... and these youths arrived on the scene.[45]

Polish sources themselves indicate that no official Polish help by the underground network was extended to Jews until the late summer months of 1942. It was only exceptional individuals among the Poles who had personal ties with Jews and Jewish families, who made efforts on their own to keep in touch with Jews after their internment in ghettos and to help them to whatever extent they could.

For reasons discussed earlier, attitudes within the Polish underground organization underwent a change, and the means were found to help Jews after the mass deportation from Warsaw in the summer of 1942. The deportations also convinced many Jews in the

ghetto who had previously been hesitant about escaping, to attempt
to reach the "Aryan side" and go into hiding or pass themselves off
as Gentiles for the duration of the war. Just how many Jews were
able to excape what was otherwise certain death is unknown. We
do know that at the time the ghetto was sealed off, a small number
of Jews, and Christians of Jewish extraction who were classified as
Jews by Nazi racial decrees, had chosen to seek survival outside the
ghetto among the Poles. We have little information about this
group, but their numbers could not have been more than a few
hundred. To judge from the few first-hand accounts that we have
received, they had a very difficult time of it and their Jewish origins
haunted them throughout their ordeal. During the mass deportation itself there were many who considered fleeing the ghetto to
seek refuge among Gentiles, and whoever was left behind after the
deportation must certainly have given the matter serious thought.
But for the vast majority of ghetto inmates, this option was closed.
Most of those interned had neither the means to buy a place of
refuge nor Polish friends who would have been ready to help them
at great personal risk. Moreover, their physical appearance and inadequate command of Polish, deprived them of any chance of
successfully disguising themselves as Poles.

From the first wave of Jews attempting to flee the ghetto, many
returned, feeling it was preferable to die with their fellow Jews than
undergo the ordeal of living on the "Aryan side." The German in-
dustrialist Walter Toebbens, who owned a large factory in the
Warsaw Ghetto, claimed that many of his workers who had enough
money to set themselves up in the Polish district of the city were
frustrated in their attempt and came back.[46] But, as we have seen,
approximately fifteen to twenty thousand Jews went into hiding or
lived disguised as Poles in the Warsaw region. A significant
number of them, perhaps even the overwhelming majority, were
native Warsawites, but there were also many who came from small
towns and cities in the Polish provinces. These people, coming
from smaller population centers where they were known locally,
found it easier to escape detection in the populous capital, where
they could lose themselves among the masses.

GENTILES WHO HELPED JEWS

Still, it was virtually impossible for a Jew even to begin his life on
the "Aryan side," not to mention the possibility of spending a
number of years among non-Jews in occupied Poland, without the
active help of Poles. In fact usually more than one Pole, and
sometimes even an entire group of individuals, had to become in-

volved in rescuing a single Jew. We should keep in mind, too, that in Poland and in the East-European territories a person who hid Jews risked his own life and the lives of the members of his household. At the same time all Poles knew—better indeed than did any other occupied peoples in Europe—the fate the Germans had in store for Jews; so that each Pole was individually aware that the life and death of a fellow human being hinged on his decision to proffer or withhold assistance.

Thousands of Polish Gentiles became involved in varying degrees in efforts to save Jews. We know that many Poles—hundreds apparently—lost their lives because of their actions on behalf of Jews.

But the gallant record of those Poles who came to the assistance of Jews does not alter the fact that there also existed a malignant element in Polish society that was responsible for creating a hostile climate of opinion among broad sections of the Polish public concerning the rescue of Jews. The *shmaltsovniks* were a relatively large group in Poland. They operated on an organized basis and made a profession of the betrayal of Jews.

We have already observed that the German invader found it difficult to distinguish between Jews and Gentiles in Poland, and that the fear experienced by Jews hiding out on the "Aryan side" was of being informed on by Poles. Similarly, those who worked to save Jews did so without benefit of support from the great mass of Poles; indeed, they were forced to keep their activities secret from neighbors, friends and, sometimes, even from relatives. The act of concealing or helping a Jew was distinctly unpopular; it was a cause of distress among Poles and often actively opposed by them. One Polish heroine who had taken an abandoned Jewish child under her protection tells of having constantly to change her residence because she was actually driven away by her neighbors, who knew the child was not hers and was Jewish.[47] Many of the accounts of Jewish survivors are replete with expressions of gratitude and esteem for the devotion and courage of the Poles who had helped save them. Most of these stories also tell of the ordeals experienced by Polish benefactors and cite countless instances of Jews being blackmailed or turned over to the German police by Poles.

Mrs. Haiah Elbojm-Dorembus, who smuggled herself and her family out of the ghetto and lived for a time disguised as a Pole on the "Aryan side," tells the moving story of her first approach to a Pole who had known her in the past in order to gain his assistance:

> Fortunately for me, the door to Stach's home was still open. When I walked into the small shack and its serene existence, Stach crossed

himself as if he were seeing a ghost. His wife dropped a spoon she had been drying. The three of us stood dumbfounded.

"Jesus-Mary, you look terrible, Madam Helena!" He was the first to come to his senses.

"Can I spend the night with you?" I whispered. Stach took the bundle out of my hand and offered me a chair. Presently he asked me:

"What do you mean, spend the night? And what'll you do tomorrow, Madam Helena? And where's your husband, your mother, Hilda? The whole family?"

"Listen to me, Pan Stach," I answered, "I'm carrying around a death sentence with me, but I've no right to impose it on others. Tomorrow I'll leave for one of the villages, maybe I'll find work there. My husband's still in the ghetto. My mother, my husband's mother, my daughter—they're no longer alive."

Stach buried his face in his hands and cried.

"You're staying with us," he said after regaining his self-control. "And I'll take your husband in with us too. We are as dust at your feet, and if death strike at *you*, let the devil take us too. Yes, I put my trust in the good Lord to protect us. Look, my left eye is stinging—a sure sign that things will go well with us."[48]

Stach was a simple workingman. Yet he and his family took Mrs. Haiah Elbojm-Dorembus and her kin into their home and shared with them the terrible trails that were to follow. But Mrs. Elbojm-Dorembus tells of disappointments and betrayals as well that she suffered at the hands of other Poles whom she had known before the war. Similar tales of honorable behavior by ordinary Poles are recounted by other witnesses. Thus, Josef Aszhajm tells of a Polish workingman who harbored two Jewish women and a ten-year-old Jewish boy. When asked what he would do if the Germans showed up, he answered that he would rather be killed by them than surrender those to whom he had given sanctuary.[49]

A less inspiring tale is told by another witness, Nina Ekstein, who relates that her brother, Isaac Finkelstein, was betrayed to the Gestapo by a Pole named Szymanski. Her brother was subsequently killed. There were Poles who did help her hide her five-year-old daughter, but their attitude toward her changed after her husband's death and she was forced to flee Warsaw.[50] Maria Fayler-Felinska tells still another story of a change of attitude in a Gentile protector. She was being cared for with great consideration by a Madam Radzynska. In the beginning the son of Madam Radzynska, who was a policeman, helped her as well. Later however, after the son had married a dancer and was in need of money, he began to practice extortion.[51] Helena Fajn testifies that at the same time that she was being helped by Poles, her husband, who had disguised himself as a Pole was betrayed to the Gestapo and killed.[52] Fuks fell into the clutches of a gang of extortionists in Warsaw and was constantly being victimized by them. He moved to Lvov where he was again victimized, this time by the Filerowicz brothers, who were members of the AK. They suspected he was Jewish and repeatedly threatened to betray him to the Germans.[53] Diana Czerska, who came from an assimilated family, relates that her brother, who had managed to keep out of the ghetto and joined the AK, was able to smuggle the family out before the deportation. She tells that even while the Germans were being defeated on the battlefield there were increasing instances of Poles betraying Jews to the German authorities and even ferreting out Jews from the most ingeniously devised hiding places.[54]

There are stories of the altruistic behavior of Poles as well. Basia Folkman, a seamstress, was helped by the owners of a country estate, the Dolski family, who treated her as one of the household.[55] Miriam Friedman, who lived under cover as a Gentile, had a landlady active in the AK, who was aware of her true identity but helped her out of humanitarian motives.[56] Zipporah Fiszer tells about Kazimierz Dzik, a barber, and his lady friend Cesia, who hid thirteen Jews in Praga from whom they received payment in exchange. On the other hand, Colonel Wladyslaw Kowalski hid Jews and applied his entire earnings toward assisting them. Colonel Kowalski would search among the basements of Warsaw looking for Jews who had no place to turn so that he could help them.[57] Throughout, Kowalski acted purely out of a commitment to his fellow men but witnesses also tell us of Poles who hid Jews solely for profit, and who drove them out once they had squeezed them dry.[58]

The Jews who hid among Poles during the occupation belonged to one of three categories:

1. Those who adopted Gentile identities, had acquired the necessary documents and were able to hold down jobs as Poles. They were only occasionally assisted by Poles, and faced the threat of exposure by Polish acquaintances who had known them before the war or suspected their true identities.

2. Jews being concealed by Poles in specially prepared hideaways or in apartments in exchange for payment. Some Poles who offered such protection behaved honorably, asking only for fair payment for services rendered and maintenance. But there were others who would extort and mercilessly rob those dependent on them.

3. Jews receiving assistance from Poles whose motives were purely humane. Their benefactors were often Poles with whom they had special ties before the war—former housemaids, business

partners, colleagues and fellow workers, school friends, and the like. There were not a few cases, too, for former anti-Semites who changed their attitudes during the occupation and came to the assistance of Jews. Jan Mosdorf, for example, experienced such a change of heart, and after having been a leader of the nationalist and pro-Fascist faction in Poland in the prewar period, was interned in Auschwitz during the occupation, and there defended the Jewish inmates.

It would be difficult to categorize the type of person who became involved in saving Jews. According to one study, such people were predisposed to swim against the current. But this thesis does not stand up in view of the evidence. In her list of the occupations of those who assisted Jews, Rachel Auerbach includes "university professors, railway workers, bus drivers, priests, wives of senior army officers, tradesmen, shopkeepers, peasants; especially peasants, who for a single act of charity in bestowing a crust of bread, a liter of milk or a night's lodging were brutally punished, at times shot, and their houses burnt down by the Germans."[59]

Such people therefore came from various social strata, belonged to different professions, and were integrated in the life of their society, in which they fulfilled a variety of functions. As to their motives—a particularly prominent role in saving Jews was played, on the one hand, by people of simple religious faith, and, on the the other, by those brought up in a tolerant liberal tradition or holding liberal and socialist convictions.

But primarily, those who helped Jews during the occupation did so out of a profound personal response to the suffering of their fellow men, and out of their inability to remain uninvolved in a situation in which oppression and murder had run wild.

Judge Moshe Bejski, who during his years of service on the Yad Vashem Committee for Righteous Gentiles had come to know many of these gallant men and women, had the following to say about them in an address he delivered on the subject:

> No study has been made to date on the social origins of Righteous Gentiles who have received the Committee's recognition; they came from every stratum of the population. However, based upon my years' activity on the Committee, it is my distinct impression that most Righteous Gentiles in fact belonged to the less privileged levels of society; prominent among them were simple people without means, the poor who could hardly provide for their own families, but who nevertheless found a way to share their meagre morsel with those they had taken under their protection . . . . When we add to this the fear of the authorities and of anti-Semitic neighbors, of informers and of active collaborators, then we truly know how to appreciate the righteousness of those few who would not hew the general line, and who rose to such

exalted heights among mankind that they came to merit recognition as "Righteous Gentiles" .... There exists no study concerning the motives of those who would not accept the Nazi invader's decree against Jews, and who departed from the accepted pattern of the population at large by choosing, within the limits of their ability, to assist Jews despite the risk involved in doing so. The motives varied, differing in each case and often from country to country. But one motive was surely common to all Righteous Gentiles: for without it the readiness to undertake such work would be impossible: what I refer to is the humanitarian motive that inheres in a humane relation to one's fellow man. Obviously there was also the hostility to the invader and opposition to his brutal conduct toward the Jewish population—but even in such cases the humane motive reigned supreme.[60]

However, as we have already stated, such persons, or the group active within the framework of *Zegota*, were exceptional, and at the other extreme existed a very different collection of human specimens who exploited Jewish suffering and had no scruples about turning Jews over to the enemy—extortionists and informers who, at least with respect to Jews, collaborated with the Nazis.

Just who were these people and how large were their numbers? Polish writers are probably correct in claiming that most of them came from the very lowest orders of society and either lived on the fringes of the criminal underworld or were outright criminals themselves. Affiliated with the extortionist gangs, too, were persons with no criminal past but whom wartime conditions freed from all social inhibiting restraints, allowing them to indulge their overriding desire for easy money and their innate taste for debauchery. But such people were at least no more than a by-product of the war, a wild strain produced by circumstance and the times. However, we learn from the reports of many witnesses that these circles were also joined by rabid anti-Semites for whom such contemptible activities provided an opportunity to give vent to their ideological inclinations.

We have no figures concerning the number of street toughs and informers who made up the gangs that victimized Jews. But there were enough of them around to make life a constant nightmare for Jews living as Poles or hiding in the Aryan part of Warsaw. Polish writers argue, not unreasonably, that the entire Polish nation cannot be blamed for crimes committed against the Jews by a mere handful of thugs. They are also correct in observing that under the occupation it was easier for evildoers than for decent men to flourish. Those who blackmailed and informed against Jews acted under the protection of the Polish and Nazi police, or were at least tolerated by them.

Apart from the hunters, their prey and the occupation authorities, there existed another element whose position must be explained—the Polish public, and especially that segment which made up the powerful underground organization, the so-called "underground state," which operated among the populace. The mere reluctance of most Poles to become involved or forcefully to oppose the extortionists cannot in itself account for the extraordinary confidence and freedom with which these gangs were able to carry on their activities. Naturally they were enthusiastically assisted by the anti-Semitic climate of opinion among the Polish people. In that atmosphere the extortionists were given no reason to feel that their activities in any way struck at Polish patriotism. Moreover, as we have observed elsewhere,[61] the underground took no affirmative action against these gangs, as they routinely did in the case of other types of collaborationists. We can assume that the majority in the underground had no sympathy for extortionists and informers who were battening on Jews; but they were also reluctant to declare war against them, since they were aware that such a move would be unpopular among wide sections of the populace. We need only examine the history of the fruitless efforts by members of *Zegota* to convince underground authorities to take effective reprisals against the extortionists for us to gain a fair idea of the nature of the inhibitions and hesitancies that prevented the Polish underground from taking action.

Ringelblum told in his *Polish-Jewish Relations* about the operations of the *Shmaltsovniks* (blackmails) in Warsaw, and his personal experiences with them: Extortion by *shmaltsovniks* begins the moment a Jew crosses through the gates of the ghetto, or rather while he is still inside the ghetto gates, which are watched by the swarms of *shmaltsovniks*. . . The *shmaltsovniks* walk around in the streets stopping anyone who even looks semitic in appearance. The frequent public squares, especially the square near the central [Railway] station, cafes and restaurants, and the hotels . . . The *shmaltsovniks* operate in organized bands. Bribing one of them does not mean that a second cohort will not appear a moment later, then a third and so on, a whole chain of *shmaltsovniks* who pass the victim on until he has lost his last penny. The *shmaltsovniks* collaborate with police agents, the uniformed police and in general with anyone who is looking for Jews. They are a veritable plague of locusts, descending in large numbers upon the Jews on the Aryan side and stripping them of their money and valuables and often clothing as well. . . .[62]

In tribute to people who were devoted to the mission of rescue, I would like to quote the closing passage of the chapter entitled "The

Idealist" in Ringelblum's *Polish-Jewish Relations*:

". . . There are thousands of idealists like these in Warsaw and throughout the country, both in the intelligentsia and the working class, who help Jews very devotedly at the risk of their lives. Every Jew snatched from the clutches of the bloodthirsty Nazi moster had to have an idealist like this watching over him day after day like a guardian angel. The great majority of these people helped the Jews in return for remuneration, but is there in fact money enough in the world to pay for their self-sacrifice? People who hid Jews for money alone and lacked a strong moral motivation rid themselves of their dangerous ballast sooner or later by turning the Jews out of their flats. The ones who kept the Jews in their flats were those who did so not only for Jewish money. This gallery of Polish heroes could provide subjects for wonderful novels about the noblest of idealists who feared neither the enemy's threats on his red posters nor the obtuseness and stupidity of Polish Fascists and anti-Semites who deem it an anti-national act to hide Jews."[63]

NOTES

1. See: Andrzej Chojamowski, *Kuncepcja polityki narodowosciowej rzadow polskich w latach 1921–1939.* Warsaw 1979, pp. 18–26.

2. See the full list of the members of the Committee in Wladyslaw Bartoszewski, *1859 dni Warszawy,* Krakow, 1982, p. 67, see also & Ringelblum *Kronika getta Warszawakiego,* Warsaw 1983 p. 32.

3. *Documents on the Holocaust,* Selected Sources on the Destruction of the Jews of Germany and Austria, Poland, and the Soviet Union, eds. Y. Arad, I. Gutman, A. Margaliot, Jerusalem, 1981, doc. 86, p. 198.

4. J. Lipski, *Diplomat in Berlin* (1933–1939), London, 1968, p. 411.

5. YVA, 025–15 Antysemityzm, "Informator", no. 2, March 8, 1940.

6. Kaplan, *op. cit.*, p. 206. Ringelblum, *Kesovim fun Geto,* Band 1, Togbukh fun Varshaver Geto (1939–1942), Varshe, 1961, p. 181.

7. M. Weichert, *Yidishe Alaynhilf 1939–1945,* Tel Aviv, 1962, pp. 9–10.

8. Testimony of A. Hartglas and others in *Sefer ha-Zvaot* ("Atrocities"), documents, testimonies, discussions and calculations concerning the Holocaust against the Jews during World War II, vol. 1, eds. Binyamin Minz and Dr. Israel Klausner, Jerusalem, 1945.

9. Wladyslaw Smolski *Zaklete Lata,* Warsaw, 1964, p.

10. Kaplan, *op. cit.*, p. 161.

11. The Warsaw Diary of Adam Czerniakow, eds. R. Hilberg, S. Staron, J. Kermisz, New York, 1979, p. 112.

12. *Ibid.*, p. 112.

13. E. Ringelblum, *Kesovim fun Geto, op. cit.*, pp. 78–79.

14. See footnote 8.

15. Julian Kulski, *Zarzad miasta Warszawy,* Warsaw, 1964.

16. M. Weichert, *Yidishe Alaynhilf, op. cit.*, pp. 13–14

17. *Okupacja, Ruch Oporuw Dzienniku Hansa Franka, 1939–1945,* v. 1, 2 Warsaw 1972, p. 524.

18. Bruno Streckenbach was an SS *Brigadefuhrer,* and chief of the *Sicherheitspolizei* in the Government General. In a discussion concerning security, which took place on May 30, 1940, Streckenbach outlined the powers of the police force in their dealings with the *Judenrats,* and remarked: "After all, it is not possible to starve them to death." See: *Okupacja i ruch oporu w Dzienniku Hansa Franka, 1939–1945,* V.I, *op. cit.*, p. 211.

19. See parts of survey by Waldemar Shoen in *Eksterminacja Zydow na ziemiach polskich w okresie okupacji hitlerowskiej.* Zbior dokumentow, ze-

braliiracawali T Berenstein, A. Eisenbach. A. Rutkowski, Warsaw, 1957, pp. 99–108.

20. *The Warsaw Diary;, op. cit.* p. 210.

21. Kulski, *op. cit.*, p. 134.

22. YVA, 0–25–59.

23. Ludwik Landau. *Kronika lat wojny i okupacji* V.I. Warsaw, 1961, p. 742.

24. Ringelblum, *op. cit.*, vol. 1, p. 167.

25. Kaplan, *op. cit.*, pp. 370–371.

26. Yisrael Gutman, *Yehudey Varsah*, 1939–1943, Tel-Aviv, 1977, p. 76.

27. Ludwik Hirszfeld. *Historia jednego éycia*. Warsaw, 1957, p.191.

28. Arnold Szyfman, *Moja tulaczka wojenna*, Warsaw, pp. 103–104 (My War-time Peripatics).

29. YVA, 0–25–20, *Kronika Okupacji*,

30. Arnold Szyfman, *op. cit.*, p.10. - 25.11. 1940.

31. Emmanuel Ringelblum, *Polish-Jewish Relations During the Second World War*, New York 1976, p. 89.

32. See Rabbi Shimon Huberband, *Kiddush Hashem* ("Sanctification of the Name"), writings from the Holocaust era from the records of the Ringelblum archive in the Warsaw ghetto, 1969, chapter, "Ha-Ukhlusiyah ha-Yehudit shel Pragah bi-Zman ha-Milhamah" ("The Jewish Population of Praga during the War"), pp. 136–144.

33. See except from a memorandum by Roman Knoll, in Emmanuel Ringelblum, *Polish Jewish Relations During the Second World War*, pp. 256–258.

34. Kazimierz Wyka, Zycie na niby . . . , Warsaw, 1959, pp. 197–201.

35. On smuggling, and the class which dealt in smuggled goods, see: M. Passenstein, Szmugiel w getcie warszawskim, (BZIH,) *op. cit.*, Warsaw, 1958. N. 26.

36. Abraham Levin, *mi-Pinckas shel ha-More mi-Yehydia*, (From the diary of a teacher), 1969, p. 74.

37. J. Winkler, Getto Walczy z niewola gospordarcza," BZIH, Nv. 35, 1960.

38. See: Jan Tadeusz Gross, *Polish Society Under German Occupation: The General Gouvernement*, 1939–1945. Princeton, 1979.

39. See extracts from Knoll's memoranda, *op. cit.*, note 45 above.

40. The river Bug divided the Soviet and German areas of occupation in Poland from September 1939 until the outbreak of the Soviet-German war in June 1941. The Poles accused the Jews of welcoming the Soviet annexation, occupying official posts under the Soviet regime, and plotting against the Poles.

41. See the document concerning Polish-Jewish relations published by J. Kermisz in Yalkut Moreshet No. 11, November 1969.

42. Philiip Friedman, *Their Brothers' Keepers*, New York (1978), pp. 111–112.

43. E. Ringelblum, *Jewish-Polish Relations during the Second World War, op. cit.*, pp. 123–124.

44. So Kaplan *op. cit.*, pp. 113–114.

45. Kaplan, *op. cit.*, pp. 209–211.

46. See Toebbens' appeal from March 20, 1943, in Y. Gutman, *Jews of Warsaw*, op. cit, pp. 334–335.

47. See Bogushia, Yalkut Moreshet, No 7, July 1967.

48. Haiah Elbojm-Dorembus, *Oyf der arisher zayt*, Tel Aviv, 1957, pp. 15–16.

49. YVA, 03–2182.

50. YVA, 03–2949.

51. YVA, 03–2316.

52. YVA, 03–670.

53. YVA, 016–450.

54. YVA, 03–1310.

55. YVA, 03–25ɔ2.

56. YVA, 03–1014.

57. YVA, 03–2025.

58. YVA, M1/E–1333, M1/E–959, M1-E–685, M1/E–823, 03–1658.

59. According to P. Friedman, *Their Brothers' Keepers*, New York, 1978, p. 116.

60. Moshe Bejski, The Righteous among the Nations," in *Rescue Attempts during the Holocaust*, ed. Y. Gutman and E. Zuroff, Jerusalem, 1977, pp. 635–636.

61. See chapter on Zegota, in this book.

62. E. Ringelblum *Polish-Jewish Relations . . . op.cit.*, pp. 123–124.

63. *Ibid*, pp. 245.

CHAPTER SIX

Jewish Fugitives Outside Warsaw

For Jewish fugitives from ghettos and camps who sought opportunities for hiding in forests, villages, or in "Aryan" areas of the cities, the prospect of survival crucially depended on the attitudes of the Polish society. In the attitudes which the Poles actually manifested, there was enormous variation. The most typical phenomenon was indifference, as indicated by the refusal to help the victims (usually out of fear), but also by refusal to help the perpetrators of the crimes. But many Poles did help the Jews, unmindful of jeopardizing their own lives; while many other Poles collaborated with the Germans in tracking down the Jews, or else committed a variety of crimes of their own against the latter.

The sources on which this analysis is based include the diaries, accounts and recollections of the Jewish survivors, of the Poles who had some contacts with Jews in hiding, and (to a somewhat lesser degree) of the Poles who merely happened to witness the events of interest.

The record of events has been made on the basis of relatively extensive evidence obtained from qualitatively diverse sources. In terms of numbers, the sources which have been reviewed and verified total nearly 2,000. The file in which their contents are recorded covers about 10,000 events of interest, which occurred in 765 localities scattered throughout the entire area of Government General, the Bialystok district and four Eastern districts of former Poland: Wilno, Nowogrodek, Polesie and Volhynia. Beyond the scope of the study are the territories annexed to the Reich (i.e. Pomerania, Silesia, and the districts of Poznan, Lodz and Ciechanow), because the attempts by the Jews to escape and seek contacts with Poles for the purpose of finding refuge were relatively rare there. The exclusion of the city of Warsaw from the present analysis is also deliberate. The conditions of the Jews hiding in Warsaw were quite different than elsewhere, and therefore the discussion of the problematic of the Jews in hiding in Warsaw is dealt with in a separate chapter.

It may be useful to illustrate our method of ascertaining the facts by contrasting it with other sources. Thus, for instance, the book by the Polish historian Czeslaw Madajczyk "Nazi Policies in occupied Poland," while dealing with reprisals against the Poles who provided Jews with help, mentions the case of the murder of two women in the locality of Giebultow, Miechow county. Madajczyk does say that the women were the wife and the daughter of a Polish farmer who sheltered the Jews, but he neither gives their names, nor tells of any circumstances of the murder, nor indicates his source.[1] However, the information missing in Madajczyk's account is available in the recollections of a Polish resistance fighter, Norbert Michta:

> A farmer by the name of Konieczny hid thirteen Jews in an underground bunker located on his farmland. In April 1944 a detachment of the National Armed Forces (NSZ) from the village of Lubcza killed all the Jews. Konieczny escaped, but the alerted German gendarmerie came and killed his wife on the spot.[2]

Still more information about this event is available in the joint account by Mordechai Herszkowicz and Aharon Matuszynski. The account confirms that the family of Jozef Konieczny sheltered about a dozen Jews in Giebultow, Miechow county. It further says that on May 5, 1944 there appeared in Giebutlow a Home Army (AK) detachment of about fifty men. They are described as having attacked Konieczny's farm, finding and dragging out the Jews, escorting them to a nearby forest, and shooting them there. Some of the murdered Jews are identified as Meir and Rivka Matuszynski with four children, Hinda Herszkowicz with three children, and the teenager Tauba Lejzor. The Home Army men are also said to have murdered Konieczny's family.[3]

The comparison of these three sources permits us to ascertain reliably that about a dozen Jews in hiding were murdered by a unit of the Polish underground. It does not allow us to ascertain, however, whether the murderers were from the Home Army, the National Armed Forces, or from a unit of the National Armed Forces acting under the Home Army's orders. Likewise, the comparison does confirm the very fact of the murder of members of the Konieczny family. But it does not confirm whether or not the latter murder was committed by the same unit of the Polish underground which murdered the Jews, or by German gendarmes alerted as a result of the murder of the Jews.

Next, a member of the Peasant Battalions, Jozef Adamski, recounts:

> In the fall of 1943 our unit helped the units of People's Guard and of Soviet partisans to move to Ludmilowka and Grabowka where the Polish Workers' Party had some backing. In the process, a small girl was found who had been left in the woods all alone. The child turned out to be Jewish. Jozef Adamski (the author refers to himself in the third person) handed the girl over to Mrs. Oldag, a woman from Warsaw then living in our village, who agreed to take care of her. The Peasant Battalions provided Mrs. Oldag with means to support the girl. A few days after she was found she was baptized, receiving the name Barbara. The secretary of the village community Czeslaw Tluscik was her godfather.[4]

However, the circumstances under which the girl was saved are also described by the above mentioned Apolonia Oldag herself. The account of this woman who adopted and brought up the child, rectifies the essentials of Adamski's account. For unlike Adamski, Oldag points out that anti-Semitism and hostility of the peasantry of the Dzierzkowice village toward the Jews was cruel and widespread, to the point where an attempt was made to kill the child. These are her words:

> Let me point out that when the child was found in a pit, she was clothed in a white and warm overcoat. When I received her from the village community's office, the overcoat had already disappeared. It was apparently stolen by one of the peasants. Since she had nothing to wear, I had to begin by cutting two shirts of my husband, from which I sewed for her a dress and several undershirts. In this way I clothed the child.
>
> After a few days, I went to seek a ration of milk for the child. I was turned down everywhere. In the end, I could only get a non-fat milk; I was explicitly told that no peasant will ever give me any good-quality milk for a Jewish child. She was undernourished, and I had nothing to feed her with but buckwheat grits. We had no food. In the village, only the peasants had food, and the peasants refused to give anything to a Jewish child.
>
> Throughout this entire period, the peasants couldn't reconcile themselves with our taking care of a Jewish child. Once several of them entered our house, demanding that the child be turned over to them. I was so terrified that I couldn't move, and I became paralyzed. It took me a long time to recover. Even today, whenever I become upset, my back becomes numb. But the peasants were afraid of us. That is why they didn't turn the child over to the Germans. However, they wouldn't do a thing to help us. In the end, I began to feed the child with meat and tea. This diet restored her health.[5]

Quite often, a source may contain obvious distortions, or even patent fabrications. To make matters worse, fabrications and obvious absurdities appear from time to time in scientific publications, or in recollections of otherwise serious statesmen. Thus, for instance, Zygmunt Walter Janke in his account "Beginnings of resistance in Lodz and its surroundings (1939–1941)" which appeared in the scientific journal "Najnowsze dzieje Polski" (Recent history of Poland) tells the following story:

> Dr. Zbigniew Jaskiewicz led a boy scout team in 1941–1942 whose task was to provide the Jews of the Lodz ghetto with relief. Risking their lives, the boy scouts delivered food and medication over the barbed wire.[6]

In reality, enough is known about the history of Lodz and the Lodz ghetto under Nazi occupation to warrant the conclusion that this team in all certainty never existed, and that no deliveries of food or medication over the barbed wire to the Lodz ghetto ever took place.

For variety, let us cite an example of a different nature: the words of Stefan Korbonski, one of the leaders of the Peasant Party, a man who certainly never revealed any anti-Semitic sentiments:

> Let me limit myself to one simple point. About 300,000 Jews who took the risk, refused to go voluntarily to the ghettos to be executed there, and thus succeeded in surviving the Nazi massacres, owe their survival to the help extended to them by the Polish society.[7]

Throughout the entire period of the Nazi occupation, Stefan Korbonski held top leadership posts in the Polish underground, being promoted towards the end of the war to the post of the Government's Delegate. Given this, he cannot be suspected of ignoring the facts. Yet as soon as he begins to deal with Jewish affairs, he indulges in quoting figures which have no correspondence whatsoever to historical realities, and additionally absurdly misrepresents these realities, when he talks of "going voluntarily to the ghettos to get executed there." Beyond any shadow of doubt, Korbonski was thoroughly familiar with the fact that the vast majority of Polish Jews who survived World War II, owed their survival to their escape to Soviet-held territories at the beginning of the war. The lesson to be drawn from this example is that leading members of the Polish underground need to verify the facts they describe with no less an exactitude than anyone else.

The classification which emerges from the recorded evidence is comprised of the following categories:

A. *Crimes against the Jews*:
1. Participation in raids on the fugitives;
2. Participation in collective murders;
3. Single-handed murders;
4. Capturing the fugitives and handing them over to the Germans;
5. Organized murders committed by Polish underground formations;
6. Informing;
7. Blackmail and plunder.
B. *Forms of help to the Jews*:
1. Sporadic or circumstantial help;
2. Supplying forged documents;
3. Supplying food;
4. Help for pay;
5. Help in hope of converting to Christianity;
6. Help partly for pay, partly benevolent;
7. Benevolent help.

Let us first illustrate the meaning of each of the listed fourteen categories by appropriate examples from selected testimonies.

PARTICIPATION IN RAIDS ON THE FUGITIVES

It was quite common for the rural populace to take part in raids against the fugitives from liquidated ghettos who hid in the forests. Two major forms of such participation are to be distinguished: (1) Peasant participation in raids organized by the Nazi police and gendarmerie shortly after the deportations from local ghettos, in order to capture the fugitives; (2) The forest campaigns which the larger groups of local peasants organized and carried out on their own initiative, without notifying the Nazi police.

In the raids of the former type, the participating peasants would most typically serve the Nazis in the capacity of guides, pinpointing the possible sites in forest areas with which they were much more thoroughly familiar than the Germans. But it often happened that peasants themselves would murder the encountered Jews with pickaxes or scythes. The usual incentive for their participation in anti-Jewish raids was either German instigation or the hope for an opportunity to loot the belongings, clothes or valuables of captured fugitives. In some instances, the Germans would reward the peasant participants with allotments of sugar or salt. But the most common form of reward was simply the division of spoils.

The self-initiated raids of the second type would usually take place no sooner than several months after the largest mass deportations from local ghettos. Accordingly, such raids tended to be aimed at those Jewish fugitives who had already had some opportunity to establish themselves in well-concealed hiding places in the forests. Unaided by anyone, and long after the meager food rations which they could possibly bring with them to the forest had become exhausted, such fugitives for purposes of self-preservation had no alternative save to supply themselves with food stolen from peasant households or fields. Hence the common purpose of the collective raids of the villagers was to kill the Jews in hiding in forests in order to stave off the recurrent farm thefts.

The peasant participation in the anti-Jewish raids carried out by the Nazis is noted in the diary of S. Zieminski, a Polish teacher from Lukow:

> On November 5 [1942] I stopped in the village of Siedliska. I entered the cooperative store. The peasants were buying scythes. I heard the saleswoman say: "They will be helpful during the raid today." I asked about the nature of the raid. "Against the Jews." I then asked: "And how much do you get for a captured Jew?" No one answered. I therefore went on: "For Christ they paid thirty pieces of silver; so make sure that you are paid no less." Again no one replied. But the answer came a little later. While crossing the forest, I heard salvos of machine gun fire. The raid was in progress.[8]

A Home Army member, Dr. Zygmunt Klukowski, notes in his diary under the entry dated November 26, 1942:

> Among the "bandits" there are many Jews. The quotes are in the original: Klukowski means the partisans—the author.) Fearing reprisals, the peasants catch the Jews in the villages, and either kill them on the spot, or escort them to the towns. In general, in their outlook towards Jews people have succumbed to some queer psychosis, to sheer savagery. Like the Germans, they no longer look upon a Jew as a human being, but as some noxious beast which needs to be exterminated by all possible means, like rabid dogs or rats.[9]

Ludwik Landau, a chronicler affiliated with the Home Army, writes under the entry of February 24, 1943:

> Not many Jews will survive the present war. The conditions of the remnant in hiding are difficult. Moreover, by force of circumstances the survivors become entangled into recurrent conflicts with the Christian population. The Jewish gangs which operate in various regions are often blamed for the murders of the local populace and for plunder of their property. In the vicinity of Opoczno, the acts of unavoidable appropriation of foodstuffs from the peasants are said to have been

sufficient to incite the latter to the point of their assisting the Germans in the forest raids, in the course of which even the Jews hiding in the villages were turned over to the Germans.[10]

Our file contains the records of participation of the local villagers in raids on the Jews in 172 localities. Here is a sample of pertinent personal accounts by the surviving witnesses of the recorded events:

Ignacy Goldstein recounts that peasants from the village of Iwanisko and its environs (Opatow county, Kielce district) were being rewarded for their participation in raids with a bag of sugar and one liter of refined alcohol. Later, however, it was the clothes of captured Jews which became the sole reward.[11]

Gitla Kopylinska recounts that in Zambrow region there were a number of Jews hiding in the forest. The peasants were aware of this, but at the beginning showed no interest. Once the Germans announced the reward of one kilogram of sugar for every captured Jew, the local populace began raiding them.[12]

Aharon Kislowicz recounts how the residents of the village of Smoryn near Frampol took part in raids on the Jews hiding in local forests. The raids claimed many Jewish lives.[13]

Abraham Holder recounts the murder of sixteen Jewish fugitives from Jozefow perpetrated by the residents of the nearby village of Lukowa, Bilgoraj county.[14]

Ester Kiterkorn-Grosman recounts the capture of a number of Jews hiding in a forest bunker by the peasants from the vicinity of Markuszow, Pulawy county. The captured Jews were tied up, escorted away and shot. The casualties include Symcha Etinger with daughter Bluma, Mendel Etinger, Toba Szwarc, Icchak Szwarc with wife Lea and daughter, Szewa Rubinstein with daughter Sara, Jona Tajtelbaum, and Dwora Rosenberg. Symcha Etinger's son, eighteen, who attempted to escape, was murdered by blows upon his head.[15]

Mordechaj Goldhecht recounts the details relating to a gang organized by Andrzej Kielbasa from the village of Pilatka near Janow Lubelski. For sometime the members of this gang occupied themselves with tracking down the Jews in hiding and murdering many dozens of them.[16]

PARTICIPATION IN COLLECTIVE MURDERS

No less common were the murders of Jews usually perpetrated by rural groups of relatives or neighbors, whose general purpose was plunder. Here is a sample of cases of this category of anti-Jewish crimes from our records:

A group of villagers for Lukowa, Bilgoraj county, tracked down, robbed and shot Abraham Gutherc who was sheltered by the murderer's neighbor, a farmer by the name of Machen.[17]

In the village of Markowa near Lancut, Przeworsk county, a group of Poles led by Antoni Cyran murdered twenty-eight Jews and looted their belongings.[18]

In the village of Dolmatowszczyzna near Wilno, Janek Achron, twenty-five, organized five persons into a gang which on November 18, 1942, murdered a hiding physician, Dr. Jehuda Barzak, his wife, mother, and son.[19]

In the village of Korzyce near Szydlowiec, Radom district, a group of hiding Jews which included the brothers Mosze and Hersz Cyngiser and Menachem Lepkowicz with wife, were one day attacked with the intention of robbery by a group of local peasants. The Jews put up resistance. In the skirmish, two men were killed: one peasant and a Jew by the name of Pinchas Meir Grynberg. But the remaining Jews had to leave the village.[20]

In the forest near the village of Wygoda, Radomsko county, eighteen Jewish women with their children were murdered with pickaxes by Marian Pawlikowski, Kazimierz Zalinski, Marian Kaczmarek and Stanislaw Piasecki: the former two from Sucha Wies, and the latter two from Strzalkow.[21]

In the village of Zlota Wola near Lagow, Kielce district, the siblings Chana and Heniek Weinryb were murdered by a farmer by the name of Beben from the nearby village of Bardo with the aid of several accomplices.[22]

Several Jews including Chil Rosenblat, twenty-five, from Rakow and Sara Wajnsztok, twenty-two, from Kielce were murdered by three villagers from Stary Rebow near Rakow.[23]

A group of villagers from Rytwiany near Staszow, Sandomierz county, murdered sixteen Jews. Among the victims were the brothers Josef, Baruch and Jechiel Sznyper, the brothers Dan and Moshe Frydman, Shlomo Horn, Pinchas Feferman, and Rachela and Zisel Nisenberg.[24]

Franciszek Uzdowski from Przegaliny near Komarowka Podlaska murdered and looted the belongings of eight Jews to whom he had previously offered shelter. Uzdowski's friends Jan Sadowski, Franciszek Stelmoszuk, Jozef Radczuk and Daniel Bozyk were accomplices in the assault and robbery. The identities of all the victims are known: Gitla Lerner, forty-five, and her five children: Maria, twenty-two, Hanka, twenty, David, seventeen, Hersz, fifteen and Chaim, thirteen; and two young boys from Miedzyrzec Podlaski: Zyfryn and Pomeranc.[25]

In Chelm Lubelski as late as March 1944 (i.e. barely four months before the liberation of the town), a group of local Poles murdered Dr. Langer and his wife.[26]

A group of farmers from the village of Kleszczowka murdered several Jewish fugitives from the nearby Deblin camp. Among the casualties were Natan Tajtelbaum, and Makiwacki from the town of Ryki.[27]

In the locality of Gorajec, Bilgoraj county, a group of local peasants murdered a Jewish teenager by the name of Bemberg who came to the village to collect food for his family in hiding. Jozef Dziwala and Wladyslaw Kaminski from the same village killed a group of Jews hiding in a bunker in a nearby forest.[28]

In the village of Kreznica, Lublin county, Stanislaw Bielak, assisted by his relatives Jan Studniak, Stefan Orzga and Kotowski, murdered Szprinca Feierstein's husband and her sons Net and David.[29]

A teacher by the name of Wdowiak, assisted by several other Poles, murdered the brothers Lwowicz and Jechiel Zylberstein.[30]

SINGLE-HANDED MURDERS

Single-handed murders were no less common than the collective ones. The murderers who acted alone were in most cases peasants whom the Jewish fugitives approached for shelter. As in collective murders, the usual motive of the crime was the intent to ransack whatever money, valuables or clothes could be found on the bodies of the victims. Here is a sample of pertinent cases from our files:

A farmer by the name of Sienkiewicz from a village in the vicinity of Nowe Miasto murdered the parents of Nachman Segal. Sienkiewicz had previously provided the couple with shelter: he murdered them only when they ran out of money and could no longer pay him.[31]

A farmer by the name of Kumin from the village of Smoryn near Frampol murdered and looted the body of a Jew by the name of Yitzhak, a cousin of Aharon Kislowicz.[32]

Kapczuk from Komorowka Podlaska murdered the three year old daughter of Estera Rybak, after extorting a considerable amount of money which he had received for sheltering the child.[33]

A farmer by the name of Nowak from a village in the vicinity of

Bychawa killed Szajdla Biberklajd with family, to whom he had previously offered shelter.[34]

Chaim Pinczewski and his family were sheltered for exorbitant sums of money by the farmer Buczak from the village of Niedzielak. When Pinczewski ran short of money, he decided to seek support from a mill owner whom he had known from before the war. On his way to the mill owner, he was captured by a detachment of Home Army members and shot to death. Upon learning this, Buczak invented for Pinczewski's wife and children a story about the impending German raid on the village, and thus persuaded them to move out of his place. He accompanied them to the shore of Sarna River, where he shot Pinczewski's wife and small son. Pinczewski's daughter, Shoshana, eleven, jumped into the river, swam to the other shore, and survived the war.[35]

Rabajczyk from Jedrzejow murdered Shlomo Garfinkel and Szolowicz to whom he had previously offered a hiding place prepared for them in advance. Rabajczyk committed this crime in order to steal the valuables deposited with him by Szolowicz.[36]

Secemski from Kaminsk near Radomsko received money for supplying food to a bunker occupied by twelve Jews. After a certain time Secemski sealed the entrance to the bunker, causing ten of the twelve suffocate to death. Only two succeeded in getting out of the bunker and escaping.[37]

In the village of Ploskow near Sarnaki, Siedlce county, nine Jews were hiding, for exorbitant payment, in a burrow dug for them by Grzegorczyk on the premises of his farm. After three months Grzegorczyk decided to murder them. His method was to pour boiling water into the burrow, and to wait near its opening with a pickaxe, to make sure that anyone who tried to get out would be chopped down. Of the nine, eight were killed on the spot in this way. The ninth, Eliahu (last name unidentified) from Lowicz, did manage to sneak out, but badly burned, turned himself in to a Nazi police station.

Grzegorczyk's next door neighbor, Teodor (last name unidentified) also killed Jews he had sheltered: among them a young girl by the name of Dvora Silberstein from Sarnaki, and Aharon Szwarcbard from Blaszki.[38]

In the village of Kleczowice near Zakrzowek, Janow Lubelski county, a farmer named Choimski murdered Elka Gewerc and drowned her daughter Chana, six. The victims had approached Choimski for shelter.[39]

In the town of Bilgoraj, one Kolesza murdered Lajzer Wermut

and delivered three relatives of his victim to the German authorities.[40]

Some single-handed murders were committed not with the intent of robbery, but merely for the sake of gratifying the criminal urges of notorious anti-Semites. Murder of this type tended to occur in towns or villages were anti-Semitism had been particularly virulent. The usual victims of such murders were Jewish fugitives encountered by chance. Here are four examples from one town alone: Lezajsk, Lancut county.

Franciszek Borkowski and Marian Kowalczyk murdered Jankiel Kac and his family.[41]

Jozef Owsik killed Maniek Laufer after spotting him by chance in a marketplace.[42]

Lorysz (a son of a forester posted in the vicinity of Lezajsk) murdered a Jew by the name of Hof who had been hiding in a forest guarded by his father. The victim's brother, Moshe Hof, killed the murderer in retaliation.[43]

One Obiszek tracked down and stabbed to death Sender Szank who had been hiding on the grounds of the Lezajsk cemetery.[44]

But in several instances, the Jews in hiding managed to surmise in time that preparations were being made to kill them, and to take precautions by moving elsewhere. Here are two examples:

In the locality of Okrzeja Lukow county, a villager by the name of Bocek, accepted payment in exchange for the promise to provide six Jews with a hiding place. After several days of sheltering them, Bocek assisted by his brother-in-law, robbed and killed one of the Jews, whose name was Firanko. But the remaining five (including the Szlim family) managed to escape.[45]

In the vicinity of Kurow, Lublin county, a farmer, Witkowski, was sheltering Shmuel Chanisman and his son for money. Witkowski's wife, suspecting that Chanisman was wealthy, entreated her husband to kill the two. Both managed to escape.[46]

Our file also contains the common instances of murdering Jews shortly after the liberation, when Jewish survivors were returning to their former residence to reclaim their belongings deposited with their Polish acquaintances. Here are three examples:

In the village of Gruszow, Miechow county, three members of the (Jewish) Sliwa family were murdered immediately after the liberation, out of apprehension that they might reclaim a plot of land which they had owned before the war.[47]

In the village of Kaszalow near Jaroslaw, a local farmer right after the liberation murdered as many as fifteen Jewish survivors, among them Shaul Sznal, his wife and his four children.[48]

In the village of Maciejow, Miechow county, a Jewish survivor, Jankiel Matuszynski, right after the liberation called on Jedrzej Kania, to request back monies he had entrusted the latter to preserve. Kania murdered Matuszynski.[49]

CAPTURING THE FUGITIVES AND HANDING THEM OVER TO GERMANS

Tracking down the Jews in hiding, capturing them, and handing them over to German police or gendarmerie, to Polish "blue" police or to Ukrainian auxiliary police was another very common form of anti-Jewish crime. As a rule, the police would in such cases shoot the Jews delivered into their hands in this way on the spot. Here is a sample of cases from our records:

A Jewish woman by the name of Maurer, with two children, completely exhausted after several months of hiding in the woods, returned to their former home in the village of Kurzyna near Ulanow, Nisko county. Maurer's Polish neighbors apprehended and escorted them to the German police post in Ulanow. All three were shot at once.[50]

In the town of Frampol a certain Poteranski captured two children of Yakov Mordechaj Lichtfeld, and handed them over to the Germans.[51]

On the landed estate of Starzyna near Horodlo, Hrubieszow county, Stanislaw Siemicki captured Mirela Pipler and handed her over to the Germans.[52]

The inhabitants of the village of Potok, Bilgoraj county, captured Moshe Knoch with two children, and delivered all three to the Germans.[53]

Zacharia Lipszyc succeeded in evading pursuit by the German police, only to be captured shortly thereafter and handed over to the Germans by one Kaczmarski from Staszow.[54]

Jozef Gruby from Kock captured Chaim Mancerez and handed him over to the Germans.[55]

In a village near Frampol, two Jewish children of unknown identity came to the farmer Patronski to beg for a piece of bread. Patronski apprehended them and handed them over to the Germans.[56]

A certain Balczuk from the village Majdan Tyszowski, Tomaszow Lubelski county, captured Joel Masmolicz and handed him over to the Germans.[57]

Serkis, Paneczka, and the brothers Woloszyn from Blonie near Tarnogrod were tracking down the Jews hiding in order to hand them over to the Germans. Their victims included two young Jewish girls: Dwora Piliner and Brajdla Honig.[58]

Yitzhak Moro's brother with a seven-year-old son were hiding in a cellar of an abandoned house in Szydlowiec. During the nights, the father would search for food. In April 1944 he was spotted by a local fireman, Posobkiewicz. With the help of two fellow firemen, Posobkiewicz apprehended both the father and the son, and handed them over to the Germans. Both were shot.[59]

In the village of Czaje near Bransk Podlaski, the three Dlugoleski brothers beat up four Jews, tied them up and handed them over to the German police station in the nearby locality Rutki. The four were members of the Krukowski family from Bransk Podlaski: Josef, fifty-three, his son Leib, twenty-one, his daughter Chana, twenty-four, and another son, eight.[60]

In the village of Bojmie, Wegrow county, a peasant of unknown identity was sheltering seven Jews for pay: among them Welwek Rotbart and his sister Lea. Early 1944 the seven ran out of money. The peasant then evicted them all from their hiding place and handed them over to the Germans. The Germans shot all seven on the spot, while the peasant received six kilograms of sugar as his reward.[61]

MURDERS COMMITTED BY POLISH UNDERGROUND UNITS

Organized murders of Jews committed by various underground formations began toward the end of 1942, and occured quite frequently thereafter. They did not stop entirely at the moment of termination of the Nazi occupation, but continued for some time afterwards. The largest number of such murders were perpetrated by the units of National Armed Forces; but some groups of the Home Army also shared this guilt. Obviously most of these units may have belonged to that part of the National Armed Forces which joined the Home Army.

Beginning with December 1942, some Polish underground formations undertook searches for the Jews in hiding. Whenever they discovered any, they would kill them on the spot. Beginning with the summer of 1943, crimes of this type reached a high frequency, due ot the simple fact that the first major armed Polish underground formations appeared in the forests at that time. From then on, we can distinguish between the searches for the Jews hiding in village households, and the murders of accidentally encountered Jews, whatever their place of hiding. Many murders were also committed in the first days after the withdrawal of the German troups, when the Jewish survivors, finally feeling secure, were resurfacing from their places of hiding.

Our file contains cases of murder of Jewish fugitives by Polish underground groups from 120 different localities or forest ranges. Here is a sample:

Eight Jews found a hiding place in a forest bunker near the village of Kamieniec near Polaniec, Sandomierz county. After several weeks their bunker was surrounded by a local unit said to belong to the Home Army. The Jews were ordered to get out of the bunker, and then fired upon. Seven, including Moshe Gladstein, were killed; one, David Sznyper, managed to escape.[62]

In the village of Zarki near Janow, Zawiercie county, a detachment of Jedrusie units encountered a Jewish woman disguised as a peasant girl. After checking her identity, they notified the police station in Zarki. Several days later the "Jedrusie" members learned that the girl avoided capture and was still alive. Thereupon they murdered her on their own, afterwards notifying the gendarmerie in Zarki.[63]

In the village of Zakrzowek, Janow Lubelski county, the following Jews were murdered by a local unit of the National Armed Forces after a lengthy period of time in hiding: Hersz Erenberg with family, Efraim Kon with wife and three sons, Israel Zelig Herson with wife and children, Abraham Broner with four daughters and two grandsons, and the brothers Menashe, Mendel and Abraham Rajs.[64]

Twenty-one Jews lived in hiding near Proszowice, Miechow county: thereof eleven from the Grundman and Stossberg families in the village of Wronce, five in the village of Mniszow, and five including two brothers Serwatko and one Moryles, in the village of Szczytniki. All twenty-one owed a great deal to local members of the Polish Socialist Party who spared no effort to persuade the peasants to provide the Jews with help. It was the local Home Army commander, Kowalczyk (Thomasz) who enjoyed a unique authority among the peasants.

Eventually, however, the influence of the PPS waned, and Kowalczyk was replaced by a new commander, Kociol from Szczytniki. Kociol handed over nine Jews to the Germans. Five other Jews were murdered by Home Army men. Seven escaped.[65]

An underground unit commanded by "Teofil" committed frequent murder of Jews hiding in the vicinity of the village Peclawice near Wolica, Sandomierz county.[66]

In a forest near Staszow, a local Home Army unit murdered a number of Jews, of whom the following have been identified: Chaja

Gladstein with a seven-year-old child, sisters Lonia and Sylwia Frydman, Moshe Kirszenwurcel, Pesach Goldflus, Pinia Monik, and Shlomo Magid.[67]

On February 20, 1943, a unit commanded by "Maniek" from Jozefow murdered thirteen Jews, fugitives from Jozefow, hiding in a nearby forest.[68]

The parents and a sister of Ita Hering were murdered by a Home Army unit operating in the region of Zamosc.[69]

In the vicinity of the village of Biala, Radzyn county, a Jew by the name of Pas (Sara Pas' husband) was murdered by members of the Home Army.[70]

Members of the Home Army murdered Ben-Zion Tiszler who lived in hiding near Zelechow.[71]

Frequent targets of crimes perpetrated by the Home Army and the National Armed Forces were the Jewish fugitives from forced labor camps, especially in the districts of Lublin, Kielce and Cracow where such camps formed a dense network. Here are two examples:

On October 9, 1943, a Home Army unit murdered six fugitives from the Lublin camp for Jewish POWs from the Polish army.[72]

Several Jews were assisted by some Poles in an escape from the Lysa Gora camp near Rzeszow, only to be murdered by a Home Army unit which operated in this region. The relentlessly hostile attitude of this unit towards the Jews frustrated the existing plans to organize further escapes of Jewish inmates of that camp.[73]

Terror from the National Armed Forces and of some units of the Home Army was affecting also the Poles who provided Jews with help. Many of them were beaten up either by Home Army or by NSZ: several were murdered. Here is a sample of pertinent cases from our file.

In the village of Lubliszki, at a distance of four kilometers from Ejszyszki, Lida county, Anna Bikiewicz sheltered fifteen Jews in a bunker. She was a very kindhearted and devout widow with four children, who every Sunday contributed to the church while praying for the survival of her Jewish charges. On February 21, 1943, her house was attacked by a Home Army unit. The Home Army men beat Bikiewicz savagely, demanding that she reveal where the Jews were hiding. She steadfastly refused to tell them anything. But the Home Army men, after searching the house discovered the bunker and murdered its inhabitants. (Only ten out of fifteen were there at that particular time.) Then, they tied Bikiewicz up and set fire to her house. She died in flames.[74]

Eighteen Home Army men quartered in Chmielnik, Stopnica county, appeared in a nearby village, acting upon information that some Jews were hiding with the Kaszub family. The eighteen could not find the hiding place, and therefore proceeded to torture Stanislaw Kaszub, his wife, and his children, demanding that they hand the Jews over. The torture lasted eight hours, but to no avail: the Kaszubs revealed nothing. Through their bravery, eight Jews under their care survived.[75]

Six Jews were sheltered by the Skladowski family in a bunker on their farmland, in the village of Kietlanka, Ostrow Mazowiecka county. A local Home Army unit, upon learning this, captured Skladowski, tied him up to a tree and threatened to beat him up. Skladowski still did not reveal the location of the bunker, but the Home Army men found it anyway while searching the farm. They shot four: Cypa Solarz's (nee Goldberg) mother and sister, Mendel Loffer, and the several years-old daughter of Rywka and Josef Grafe. Cypa Solarz and her brother managed to escape, but the latter was soon captured and murdered by three other Home Army members, a father and two sons by the name of Zakrzewski.[76]

In the locality of Zmudz near Chelm Lubelski, a Home Army unit burned the house of the Sygnowski family as reprisal for their sheltering the Jews.[77]

In the village of Turobowice, Rawa Mazowiecka county, a Home Army group murdered Beniek Goldberg, sixteen, and beat up two Polish women, Wliasz and Adamczyk, who were sheltering the Jews.[78]

In the town of Frampol, Lublin district, the members of the Home Army beat up and for a long time (even after the liberation) continued retributive acts against Stanislaw Sobczak in reprisal for his benevolent sheltering of twelve Jews.[79]

Many recorded murders of the Jews were committed by the units of Polish underground just before or right after the liberation. Here is a sample:

Just before the liberation, the Home Army members tracked down and murdered many Jews hiding in the forests around the locality of Dowgaliszki near Radun, Lida county.[80]

In the locality of Brzozow, Warsaw district, the Home Army men right after the liberation shot a Jewish survivor, Dr. Kuflik.[81]

In Deblin, the Home Army members right after the liberation murdered two Jews who had escaped during the evacuation of Deblin camp inmates to Czestochowa.[82]

Jakub Leski was murdered by the Home Army in Biala Rawska.[83]

Three Jews were murdered by the Home Army in Dzialoszyce.[84]

In the locality of Nowy Kaminsk, the Home Army murdered the sole Jewish survivor from the locality, a bootmaker whose name could not be identified.[85]

Two women by the name of Kasselman (mother and daughter, seventeen) were murdered in Radomsko.[86]

Members of the newly formed local Jewish Committee were murdered by the Home Army right after the liberation in the locality of Zwolen, Kozienice county.[87]

In Lezajsk, Lancut county, the Home Army men attacked two houses into which several dozen Jewish survivors moved after the liberation. Sixteen Jews, including women and children, were killed; several were wounded. Nine survivors lived in a separate house into which a hand grenade was thrown. All perished. On a street of Lezajsk the Home Army murdered a Jewish survivor Nechemia Hof right after he returned to his native town. As a result of these murders, all remaining Jewish survivors moved from Lezajsk to Rzeszow.[88]

INFORMING

Of all crimes committed against the Jews, the most common and probably the most lethal was informing. It assumed epidemic proportions, and it affected as well the Poles who provided the Jews with any help. Informing incurred no risks. Ordinarily, it was sufficient to mail an unsigned postcard to the Gestapo. But many informers acted openly, appearing in person at a station of either the German or Polish auxiliary ("blue") police. This was especially true, when an informer hoped to receive a reward for a Jewish fugitive whom he delivered into German hands. Our records seldom make it possible to identify informers. In most cases they merely ascertain the fact and the identity of the informer's victims. Here is an extensive sampling of cases of informing:

Josef Zajwel and Icek Szer were hiding in an abandoned house in Lezajsk. They were aided by Tosiek Krasinski and Zygmunt Przybylski who supplied them with food. But some of the neighbors notified the Germans. The Germans came, surrounded the house, captured Zajwel and Szer, and shot them.[89]

Ten Jews were hiding on farmland adjacent to the forest near Okrzeja, Lukow county. In the summer of 1943, they were betrayed by the farm owner's son. The Germans murdered them all.[90]

In the town of Gorlice, Cracow district, a Polish woman turned the Meinhardt family over to the Germans: the parents and two children. All four were shot by a single SSman, whose name was Otto. As a result of her guilt feeling the informer went insane.[91]

In the locality of Januszkowice near Jaslo over a dozen Jews were hiding for pay in a cellar of a local farmer's house. The farmer's neighbor happened to be arrested for unlawful hog slaughter. In order to avoid prosecution, he revealed the location of the cellar to the gendarmes. All Jews were shot, along with the farmer who sheltered them.[92]

The owner of the small landed estate Zakrzowek near Cracow was sheltering the eleven people that comprised the family of wealthy Jewish jewelers from Cracow. In this case, it was the landowner's servant who betrayed them. The Gestapo arrested them all.[93]

In the vicinity of the village Wisnicz Nowy near Bochnia a forester tracked down and notified the Germans about a bunker occupied by some ten Jews. The Germans shot them all.[94]

Zareba from the village of Hancza near Kurozweki, Busko county, revealed to the Germans a forest bunker occupied by eight Jews, among them the Basser family from Rakow. All but one who managed to escape were killed.[95]

In Pinsk Majewska turned over Gita Dodiuk to the Germans. The two had been closest friends from their childhood.[96]

In the village of Rutki, Bielsk Podlaski county, a Pole by the name of Skowronek by chance came across an underground bunker hiding Jews. Skowronek notified the police. His victims included: Moshe Orlanski, forty-five, his wife Fruma, forty-two, their daughter Zelda, ten, another daughter, Chaja, seven, Hersh Orlanski, forty-seven, Icchak Jankiel Pribut, thirty-seven, and an unidentified boy of five.[97]

In the village of Hadle Szklarskie near Jawornik Polski, Cracow district, Szeremeta was sheltering Abram and Majlech Bezem for some time in exchange for their promise to cede to him their housing and landed property after the war. But as early as December 1942 Szeremeta turned over the two young Jews to the Germans. In the same village, young Jasiek Mazur recognized Estera Bezem who had "Aryan" identity papers. Mazur turned her over to the Germans.[98]

In the locality of Proszowice, Miechow county, Bajakowski busied himself with observing the local railway station with the aim of tracking down the Jewish fugitives.[99]

In the town of Frampol, Lublin district, Jozef Kaczmarek turned over six Jews to the Germans. They were: Moshe Welczer, his son Michael, Moshe Sztajnberg, Abraham Eli Brik, Szmaj Josef Gajst and a young girl by the name of Nikel.[100]

In the town of Izbica, Lublin district, B. Piotrowska notified the Germans concerning the location of the hiding place of Hedda Arnold.[101]

In the town of Radzyn, Lublin district, a Pole by the name of Kaczka received from Sara Najman her fur as a deposit. A few days later, he turned her over to the Gestapo. The woman was shot.[102]

In the village of Uscimow, Wlodawa county, Mordechaj Frydman deposited his property with a peasant who subsequently turned him over to the Germans.[103]

A Pole by the name of Wojek from the village of Krolowka near Wlodawa supplied two Jewish fugitives from Sobibor with bread in exchange for gold. Once he realized that the two had exhausted their supply of gold, he revealed the location of their hiding place in the forest to the Germans.[104]

In Boryslaw, a Pole by the name of Warchalowski occupied himself with tracking down the hiding places of Jews. He succeeded in detecting a well-equipped bunker beneath the local power station, in which as many as fifty Jews had found shelter. For turning them over to the Germans, he received a reward of 5,000 zlotys and several liters of vodka.[105]

In the village of Wawrzenczyce, Miechow county, a tailor by the name of Latala turned over Rosa Reibscheid's husband to the Germans. As a consequence of his capture, the entire Reibscheid family had subsequently to endure protracted German pursuit.[106]

In a village near Miechow, Jechiel Lejzorek sought refuge with peasants with whom he had been acquainted before the war. But in 1944 they turned him over to the Germans.[107]

In the locality of Zakrzowek, Janow Lubelski county, a Polish woman by the name of Sulowska agreed to take care of the 1½ year-old child of Chaim Gliksztajn. Only a few days lapsed before she turned the child over to the Germans. The child was shot. In the same locality, a shoemaker by the name of Janik turned over Mania Hofman to the Germans. The girl was also shot.[108]

A group of Poles from the village of Sielce near Biala Podlaska notified the German gendarmerie about a forest bunker where the brothers Sznajderman, Chana Tenenbojm, Henoch Kohen, and a young man whose name has not been identified, were hiding.[109]

In the vicinity of Bilgoraj, the Poles revealed to the Germans the location of several bunkers sheltering Jechezkeil Kandel with family, Abraham Tauber with son-in-law, Malka Korenblit, Rachel Goldberg and eithteen other Jews whose names could not be identified.[110]

A group of Poles, each promised ten kilograms of sugar for a delivered Jew, was tracking down and informing the Germans on the location of bunkers in the vicinity of Staszow. They succeeded in the following three cases:

On November 14, 1942, they detected a bunker beneath the local bakery with twenty-four persons, including Joel Sznyper, Goldstein with wife and three children, Moshe Jechiel Kozieniecki, his sister-in-law Fryda Ester Wolman, and others who could not be identified.

On November 17, 1942 the same group of Poles detected another bunker, with Chaim Erlichman, Zalman Szajner, Noach Blustein and others.

On January 10, 1943, the same informers detected a bunker with Mordechaj Zysie Cukier, his wife and two daughters.[111]

Two Poles from Staszow whose names were Stepien and Janik betrayed to the Germans a bunker with twenty-six Jews, including Izrael Weizman with family, Nechemia Wisencwajg with wife and daughter, Lejb Kac with wife and children, Rajzel Lipszyc with her son Zacharia, Josef Gliklich with wife and children, and Estera Mandelzis.[112]

Another resident of Staszow, Sobiesiak, turned over to the Germans three Jewish women whom he had sheltered: Fajga Lipszyc, Chaja Weinberg, and a woman by the name of Milgrom. Fajga Lipszyc managed to escape in time; the two other women were captured and murdered by the Germans.[113]

Late in the spring of 1943 a strong detachment of the gendarmerie surrounded the locality of Szydlow, acting upon the information that Jews were hiding with the family of the teacher Jan Kaczorowski. The Kaczorowski family was murdered and their house burned down.[114]

A man named Moscinski from the village of Zarki, Zawiercie county, turned over a Jewish woman to the Germans. She was subsequently shot.[115]

PLUNDER AND BLACKMAIL

Plunder of Jewish property and blackmail of Jews for the purpose of extortioning ransom were also quite common occurrences. Here is a sample of typical cases of such crimes:

Wicek Mincenty from the village of Zwada near Czestochowa sheltered Gabriel Horowicz's family for some time, then looted their belongings and evicted them from his premises.[116]

The director of the KKO savings bank in Staszow, Rzadkobulski, accepted deposits of money and valuables from the Jews, then later refused to return anything.[117]

In the vicinity of Jadow, Warsaw district, Chana Dzbanowicz left her hiding place in the forest in order to visit the Kalinski family whom she had known from before the war. Mrs. Kalinski fed her and hid her in her garret. But when Mr. Kalinski returned home, he began to scream and told Dzbanowicz to go away. On her way back to her hiding place in the forest she was assaulted by a group of Poles who stripped her of her shoes and sweater.[118] In the same locality, Meir Dzbanowicz was stripped of his jacket during a similar assault.[119]

Bronislaw Kozak and Boleslaw Baniszek from the village of Przybyslawice near Markuszew, Pulawy county, spent their time pillaging the belongings of Jews in hiding. They managed to track down the hiding place of the Laterstein family from whom they demanded ransom under the threat of killing them.[120]

In the village of Ulanow near Sanok, Nisko county, the teachers Michalkiewicz and Patera made it their job to accost Jewish fugitives on the roads with demands of ransom.[121]

Right after escaping from the train to Treblinka in January 1943, Irena Bolkowska and another female Jewish fugitive encountered a peasant who quenched their thirst and advised them to go to Kosow Lacki. On their way there, they encountered another peasant who robbed Bolkowska of all her posessions.[122]

In the locality of Jadow, Warsaw district, Gedalia Finkelman sought refuge from a Pole by the name of Karczewski. The latter, after robbing Finkelman of all his possessions, threw him out of his house. Finkelman did not go far: he was killed but a short distance from Karczewski's house.[123]

After having escaped from the transport to Treblinka, Melech Halber offered a peasant he encountered, a high payment for a ride to Siedlce. The peasant consented, and took his son along to help. On the way, they struck Halber with a pickaxe, intending to kill him in order to loot his possessions. Wounded, Halber managed to evade the entrapment.[124]

Meir Matuszynski had deposited all his possessions with Marian Zelickiewicz from the village of Ksiaz Wielki, Miechow county. In 1943 Matuszynski came to Zelickiewicz to claim his things. Zelickiewicz refused to give him anything or help him otherwise, threatening to turn him over to the Germans if he ever appeared in Zelickiewicz's house again.[125]

In the village of Klimontow, Miechow county, Wojciech Rzepko agreed in August 1942 to take care of the two Rozenwald girls, six and four. Soon afterwards, in the fall of the same year, after cashing in an exorbitant payment from their father, Rzepko forced the two girls to leave his house. Except for a fortunate coincidence, the father would have never been able to reunite with his daughters.[126]

In Cracow, a barber Stefan Zytko tricked Eda Fenik out of her money and then cast her with her child onto the street.[127]

In the village of Bogucin, Pulawy county, Karol Drozd sheltered Estera and Lewi Grosman in exchange for high payment. After a short time Drozd robbed the couple of all their money, and thus forced them to leave his house.[128]

In the village of Kolchowice near Lublin, a local agronomist sheltered a Jew for a payment. When the Jew ran out of money, he was immediately turned over to the Germans.[129]

In Parczew a Polish family in exchange for a very high payment promised to shelter the two sisters Fajgenbaum who were old-time acquaintances. In reality the two women were instantly turned over to the Germans, after their money was taken. Both were shot.[130]

Looting of the corpses of murdered Jews was also a common occurrence. Oftentimes, the sites of mass murders were subsequently scavenged in the hope of finding loot. For example:

Following the murder of the last Jews in the Poniatowa camp, the peasants from the vicinity came to its site with country wagons to loot abandoned belongings.[131]

In the vicinity of Markuszew, the local populace looted the corpses of Jews previously murdered by the Germans.[132]

The sites of the former Nazi camps, in particular of the death camps, continued to be scavenged even after the liberation. For instance, the entire area of the former death camp of Sobibor was dug up by the local populace after the liberation. They hoped to find gold and other valuables there.[133]

SPORADIC HELP AND TEMPORARY SHELTERING

The most common forms of help extended to the Jews, were one-time acts of notifying them in advance about a forthcoming mass deportation or of giving them directions enabling them to bypass German guardposts, or of providing them with food or short-term accommodations ranging from several hours to several days. Circumstantial or short-term help of this type had no effect upon the chances of its recipient's eventual survival, but it protected him/her at the most critical moments right after his/her escape from a ghetto, a transport, or a camp. Here are typical instances of such help as recounted by the survivors:

Helena Dresner recounts: An engineer by the name of Szeliga, was directing drainage works in the estate of Mieszkow near Miechow, which employed Jews. Szeliga warned the Jewish employees in time about forthcoming deportations, and advised them to go into hiding.[134]

Jozef Burzminski [Maksymilian Diamant] recounts: In November 1942 Wladyslaw Prokopec from the village of Lipownica near Przemysl let three Jewish fugitives from a train destined for a death camp (including Burzminski himself), stay in his house overnight.[135]

Renata Fleischer recounts: In Drohobycz a policeman's wife by the name of Szurkowska warned her about the forthcoming deportation, and provided her and her two daughters with shelter underneath the bed for the three days of the deportation's duration.[136]

Stefania Pawlowska recounts: In Lublin, Stefania Srednicka helped her obtain a job in a German hospital as a laboratory manager. It was possible since Pawlowska was equipped with forged "Aryan" identity papers.[137]

Menachem Horowicz recounts: In Jedrzejow, a physician by the name of Przypkowski let four Jews stay for the duration of deportations in a county hospital. In this way the four were saved until the next wave of deportations.[138]

Rajzel Lemska recounts: An unknown Pole let her stay in his house for three days after her escape from a transport to Treblinka.[139]

Moshe Kleinman recounts: A very poor villager extended his hospitality to the entire group of Jewish fugitives from a Treblinka-destined train. Having nothing else to give them to eat, he fed them pea soup. Then, he instructed his fifteen-year-old son to give them directions to Warsaw. The boy accompanied the fugitives for the first five kilometers of the route.[140]

SUPPLYING "ARYAN" DOCUMENTS

Jews who were hiding on the "Aryan" side of a city, and whose physical features were not too distinctly Jewish, could considerably improve their survival chances if they were in a position to avail themselves of appropriate documents. Such documents were usually supplied either by civil servants or by priests, often for pay, but sometimes benevolently, out of humanitarian considerations. Several cases from our files reveal the circumstances under which the Jewish fugitives could obtain the life-saving documents:

Meir Bender recounts: His sister Lea Bender obtained "Aryan" documents from an acquaintance, a farmer from the village of Gutki, Skierniewice county, so that she might replace the farmer's daughter as a laborer in Germany.[142]

Stefania Pawlowska recounts: The village head from Uhrusko, Wlodawa county, provided a Jewish married couple with documents certifying their Polishness and their status of residents of a nearby town.[143]

Blima Hamerman recounts: The parish priest from Boryslaw, Osikiewicz, helped many Jews by equipping them with "Aryan" documents.[144] Anna Wilf corroborates that account, adding that Osikiewicz was in the end caught and sent to Auschwitz.[145]

Szlomo Blond recounts: The Jews received much help from the parish priest in the village of Jackowka near Tlumacz. His name was Tabaczewski, and he was a former anti-Semite. Along with other forms of help, he supplied the Jews with "Aryan" birth certificates. In the end, he paid for it with his life, for he was murdered by the Gestapo.[146]

Jakub Jehoszua Herzig recounts: The secretary of the village council in Frysztak, Krosno county, Stadnicki, helped the Jews by arranging Polish documents and jobs for them on the basis of these documents.[147]

The secretary of the village council in Wysmierzyce, Radom county, Hieronim Sochaczewski, provided the dentist Henryk Rakocz and his family with "Aryan" documents.[148]

SUPPLYING FOOD

Supplies of food were of particular importance to those who were hiding in forests. Usually, the Jews paid for all the food they received. Once their money ran out, however, they had no choice but to appear in the villages surreptitiously in order to pick up some foodstuffs in whatever manner they could. If a Jewish partisan group operated in the vicinity, they would usually use force to obtain food, both for themselves and for the Jews hiding under their protection. But we have recorded the instances in which the peasants supplied the hiding Jews with food benevolently, out of purely humanitarian considerations. Here is a sample of such cases:

In the village Lipnica Gorna near Bochnia, the village dentist Wladyslaw Gorpiel, a rather well-off man, was regularly baking bread for the Jews hiding in the vicinity.[149]

In the environs of Rawa Ruska, a group of Jews hiding in forests were supplied with foodstuffs and otherwise helped by a Polish friend of one of the Jews in the group, Chaim Szpader, and by a Polish peasant woman who baked bread for them. Both Poles acted out of humanitarian considerations.[150]

Feiga Wertman recounts: A woman by the name of Miesiac who lived near the locality of Skalat and was a local forester's wife, cared for the Jews hiding in the forest, by giving them some food from time to time, and by letting them warm themselves and sometimes even stay overnight in her house.[151]

In the vicinity of Jordanow, Myslenice county, Cracow district, the farmer Jan Mirek sheltered the Winstrauch couple in his homestead for ten days. Then, the couple moved to a hiding place in the forest, but for two subsequent years Mirek continued to care for them and to supply them with food. He was a very devout man, and he acted out of religious considerations.[152]

An unidentified resident of the village of Jedrzejowka near Tuczap, Bilgoraj county, supplied food to a group of Jews hiding in the nearby Tuczap forests.[153]

Motke Kitaj was hiding alone in the vicinity of the village of Oldaki near Czyzewo, Wysokie Mazowieckie county. At nighttime, he would slip away from his hiding place in order to get some food from the peasants. Some peasants knew about him and did not intend to harm him, but were also afraid to help him openly. Other peasants were leaving food in such a way as to let Kitaj find it, without his knowing their identity, and thus without risk that he might divulge anything if captured. But there was one exception: a good-natured peasant by the name of Grodski, a father of many children. Whenever Kitaj appeared in his house, he would be seated at the table and fed.[154]

HELP FOR PAY

Many Poles who sheltered Jews, did it for pay, The sums involved varied enormously. Here is a sample of cases from several hundred accounts which refer to sheltering the Jews for payment:

In the vicinity of the village of Wisnicz Nowy, near Bochnia, a poor peasant Feliks Zionkiewicz sheltered a young Jewish girl by the name of Wilner for two years, and some other Jews for shorter periods. The parents of the girl paid Zionkiewicz enough to support his entire family. Nonetheless several months before the liberation Zionkiewicz accepted four additional members of the Wilner family and provided shelter.[155]

In the village of Mogila near Cracow, Adam Kowalski for two years sheltered as many as ten members of the Lieberman family in his Ogrodowa Street house. The Liebermans paid for the service. All ten survived.[156]

In the village of Szewce, Kielce county, a poor peasant named Franciszek Zegaldo sheltered Abraham Ring with wife, the Reiss couple, and Tauba Cytryn underneath his pigsty. Each couple paid 5,000 zlotys per month.[157]

After escaping from a Treblinka-destined train, Icchak Szajman found himself in Zagorz near Warsaw. First, he was directed by the local populace to a 1939 air raid shelter in which he remained for two weeks. Next, he established himself a hiding place in a forest where he was supplied with food by a villager named Kozka. Then, he was cared for and supplied with food by the game-keeper named Ruta and his family. The last several months Szajman spent in Ruta's barn. For all this help Szajman paid 6,000 zlotys.[158]

Relatively unusual were instances of helping the Jews not for pay, but in exchange for their labor. But such cases did occur, and here are some typical examples:

Golda Ryba obtained forged documents in the name of Jadzia Gorska. In the village of Borychow near Wyrozeby, Sokolow Podlaski county, some local farmers hired her as a shepherdess. Her employees treated her well, but the overly inquisitive neighbors began to suspect her of being Jewish. That is why she moved to another village in the same county, Niemirki near Jablonna Lacka, where she continued to work as a shepherdess for Hipolit Dobrowolski.[159]

In Skierniewice, the city hall janitress, Aniela Dabrowska, sheltered the Kuczynski family for 20 months. For her services, the Kuczynskis both paid and produced sweaters, which Dabrowska was selling on the open market.[160]

In a class by itself is the case of Dwora Lencicka. When twelve years old she was hired on the farm of the Zarebski family in the village of Grabce Wreckie, at a distance of twelve kilometers from Zyrardow. Although she was rescued by the Zarebskis, she was also badly exploited, and she continued to work for them without pay for several years after the war.[161]

Also unusual is the case which occurred in the village of Jarocin near Ulanow, Nisko county. Eight Jews, including women and children, were hiding with Polish peasants they had known from before the war. But the men from among the eight were armed, and they used their weapons for the purposes of robbery. They remunerated the Poles who sheltered them by sharing their spoils with them.[162]

HELP IN HOPE OF CONVERTING THE RECIPIENTS TO CHRISTIANITY

The cases of sheltering Jews in the hope of converting them to Christianity were extremely rare in our records. It is otherwise known, however, that a certain number of Jewish children, particularly female, were for this purpose taken up by various convents. Some of the children involved remained in the convents also after the war. But the number of Jewish children reared during the Nazi occupation in convents cannot be estimated, since Church archives continue to be inaccessible. Here are two cases from among the very few of which we know:

The Baptists from the town of Podhajce rescued 22 Jews, providing them with hiding places first in the forest and later in a village. Their attitude towards the Jews under their protection was exemplary. In their motivation humanitarianism was blended with hopes for converting the twenty-two to Christianity.[163]

In Wlodawa, a local priest referred a Jewish girl, Mirka Erlich, for shelter to a Dr. Orzechowski. The Orzechowski family did take good care of the child, but also sent her to study catechism.[164]

HELP ORIGINALLY FOR PAY, LATER BENEVOLENT

Many Jews hiding with Poles for payment faced a difficult predicament once their financial resources became exhausted while the war was still going on. Above, examples were cited of Jews who were murdered, evicted or turned over to the Nazis by Poles who had been willing to shelter them only as long as the latter could pay. But we also have recorded dozens of cases of Poles who continued to shelter the Jews benevolently after the latter used up all their money, or who even began to spend their own money to support their Jewish charges. Here are three examples:

In a village in the vicinity of Wisnicz Nowy near Bochnia the poor peasant family of Marian Wojton sheltered Bluma Wilner, her husband, father-in-law, and brother for over a year in their barn. At the beginning, the Wojtons were paid, but when the funds of the four ran out, they agreed to keep sheltering them without pay. Wojton put the matters succinctly: "My first concern is your surival."[165]

In Blonie, near Warsaw, Hanna Grudzinska sheltered five Jews: Teresa Glezer, Anna Szental, the wife and the daughter of a Lwow attorney, and an unidentified boy of fourteen. In the beginning, the Jews paid Grudzinska fifty zlotys per day, but in 1944 they ran out of money. But Grudzinska agreed to continue to shelter them without payment.[166]

An interesting case is recounted by Abraham Gelblum from Otwock. When the Otwock ghetto was established, Gelblum's father signed away his beer-bottling plant to the Polish butcher Marceli Gorski, whom he knew and trusted. While managing the plant, Gorski shared his profits with the Gelblums. Due to this arrangement, the latter were among the fortunate few in the Otwock ghetto who managed to avoid dire poverty. Later, Gorski convinced his relative Stanislaw Grunt to build a hiding place in his house for the Gelblums. The entire Gelblum family of eight persons moved from the ghetto to that place. Gorski used the profits of the plant to pay Grunt 2,000 zlotys per month for each sheltered Gelblum family member. As the war continued, however, even the profits from the plant could not suffice to cover the expenses. It finally reached a point, when Gorski began to cover them from his own pocket. After the war, the Gelblums wanted to return money to Gorski in deep appreciation for his saving their lives. But Gorski and his wife stubbornly refused, while pleading that they had done nothing out of the ordinary.[167]

BENEVOLENT HELP

Our files contain about 300 cases of benevolent help, usually in the form of long-term sheltering, or in the form of support provided to Jews hiding in the forests. Poles who extended help benevolently came from all conceivable social backgrounds. Their motives were most often religious or ideological, but in not a few cases help was extended out of the sense of personal friendship dating from pre-war times, and sometimes it was a matter of simple kindness based upon the helper's character. On purpose, we chose to present a relatively large number of examples here in order to show what this benevolent help was like, under the conditions when it implied self-imperilment of one's own life.

In the vicinity of the village of Okrzeja, Lukow county, a poor peasant woman by the name of Gurzkowska sheltered for two winter months of 1942/43 the Szlim family, out of commiseration for their children. Fearing her neighbors, Gurzkowska could not continue to shelter them any more: but even then she took the two-year-old daughter of the Szlims and cared for her until the liberation.[168]

In the village of Szarkowszczyzna, Dzisna county, a Polish farmer by the name of Fedorowicz employed Szlomo Estrin until the summer of 1942. Although in principle, Jewish labor was at that time unpaid, Fedorowicz paid Estrin a normal wage. On June 16, 1942, Fedorowicz warned the inhabitants of the local ghetto that deportations were being prepared for the next day. For the duration of deportations, he hid Estrin and another Jewish employee of his, Rafal Cymer, in his own house. In this way, he saved them from transport to a death camp.[169]

Icchak Kleszczelski recounts: After his escape from the ghetto he wandered aimlessly from one village to another. Finally, filthy, raggedy and infested with lice, he dropped by his old Polish friend Wlodzimierz Parzynski from the village of Czeremcha, Hajnowka county, Bialystok district. Parzynski was overjoyed to see him. Well aware of all the perils, he said to Kleszczelski: "If we are to be killed, then both together. You now need someone to help you. And if I don't, who will?" He sheltered Kleszczelski for two years in his bachelor room, protecting him, encouraging him, and supplying him with food which was at times purchased and at other times stolen. Parzynski himself, who worked as a railway engine driver, ate most of his meals at his parents' place.[170]

In the village of Krole Duze near Jasienica, Ostrow Mazowiecka county, a peasant by the name of Till sheltered Rywka Chus, her husband and two children first in his barn, and later in his smoke-house, in a dugout that was 150 x 80 centimeters large. In all this, Till was assisted by his tenant Stefan Stencel who belonged to the Home Army.[171]

Anna Owczarska from the village of Mielno, Opoczno county, sheltered the Jews and was caught. She was sent to Auschwitz together with her husband. She survived, but her husband did not.[172]

Jan Szymczyk and his son Henryk from the village of Potok Rzadowy, Busko county, sheltered two young Jewish sisters in violation of the orders of an organization to which they belonged. Sarcastically, they referred to the murders of Jews by their organization as "intended to get rid of the witnesses before the Soviets came."[173]

A tailor from the town of Zawiercie, Kielce district, sheltered for a certain time Priwa Grinkraut. He eventually managed to obtain for her "Aryan" documents with which she could get to Moravska Ostrava, in search of better opportunities to survive.[174]

Five-year-old Hanka Padoszyn was placed with a villager woman who was supposed to care for her. Instead, the woman in no time made up her mind to drown the child in a river. Although the girl was rescued from drowning, she was turned over to the German police. But a certain Mrs. B. (the wife of the manager of Count Badeni's estates) bribed a German police commander in charge of executing the captured Jews. Because of that bribe Padoszyn was saved and freed. Mrs. B. took care of her, bringing her up as if she were her own child.[175]

Jan Dyrda from the village of Jedrzejowka near Tuczap, Bilgoraj county, helped a group of Jews to survive by hiding in the Tuczap forests.[176]

Stanislaw Wojciechowski owned the estate of Kanie, near Rejowiec, Chelm Lubelski county. Assisted by his wife Zofia and his adult sons Wlodzimierz and Maciej, he sheltered on the lands of his estate six members of the Kohn family: Mosze and Chawa and their children, Zlata, Szymon, Lewi and Rosalia.[177]

Members of the Studist Baptist sect from the village of Stara Huta near Szumsk, Krzemieniec county, were helping the Jews in hiding to survive. They acted out of religious considerations. Their support was a decisive factor in the survival of Mosze Gronek and his two friends.[178]

Henia Niewiadomska recounts being sheltered in Radzymin by the Wasiak family. The family received from her nothing except her gratitude. After the liberation, Niewiadomska married Wasiak junior. In 1966 she emigrated with her husband and their children to Israel, settling in Kibbutz Kiryat Anavim.[179]

Abraham Cukier recounts being sheltered by Jan Kruk in the village of Moszna, Blonie county, near Warsaw. Apart from Cukier, there were two other Jews in the same hiding place: Szmuel Frucht and Szlomo Zalcman. Together, they dug a cellar 2 x 3 meters large, and literally hid in it for two years (Zalcman even longer). Only at nightime could they get out of the cellar to draw a breath of fresh air. All the food was supplied to them by Kruk for free. Kruk refused any remuneration for whatever he did.[180]

Dr. Liebesman recounts: In Stanislawow, a Polish woman by the name of Zakrzewska not only sheltered but also nursed Tusek Safrin who was stricken with typhoid fever after escaping from the hands of the Gestapo. In February 1943 an informer notified the Germans. The officers of the Nazi criminal police (Kripo) who came to arrest him were Polish. Safrin resisted and was shot by one of these Poles.[181]

Aliza Bleiweiss-Nowinska recounts how she, her husband, and her small son were for several months sheltered by the Kawa family in the village of Trzemiesnia, Myslenice county. The family was headed by the widow of the hamlet leader: She had four sons, all of whom behaved in a manner that can only be described as exemplary.[182]

Hanna Lewkowicz recounts how she was wandering aimlessly across farmlands, when she encountered Jozef Przytula, a farmer from the village of Plowowice near Proszowice, a Home Army member who before the war had known her father. Przytula took her to his house and offered her shelter. Przytula's wife who welcomed Lewkowicz with the words: "Whatever happens to us will happen to you too" proved to be particularly affectionate towards her charge. After some time, Lewkowicz became a liaison girl in the Home Army.[183]

There were cases in which intimate relationships developed between the sheltering and the sheltered. In such cases, the motivation to persist in providing help with total disregard for the risks involved was particularly intense. Here are a few examples:

In a village of Kloda, Pulawy county, Yehoshua Rozen was sheltered by a local farmer. The farmer's daughter fell in love with him, and consequently she spared no effort to help him survive.[184]

A Polish woman from Tustanowice near Boryslaw was married to a Jewish engineer named Hecht. She sheltered as many as sixteen Jews, including her own husband, another engineer, Josef Goldsztajn, the Fridlender family from Stryj, and others. Her conduct was dictated by more than the devotion to her husband, for she was strongly affected by innately humanitarian considerations too.[185]

Tadeusz Lasica, together with his parents, sheltered two Jewish female friends, Celina Kaufman and Chedwa Sieradzka for two years. The former eventually married Lasica. The latter recounts: "The conduct of the entire Lasica family toward the two of us was more than exemplary, in spite of difficult financial hardships which they had to endure."[186]

In the locality of Horodlo, Hrubieszow county, the Budniewski couple sheltered Freda Perelmuter from the fall of 1942 right up until the liberation. The reason for sheltering was in this case quite peculiar. In a dream, Mrs. Budniewska saw Freda Perelmuter's deceased mother, who requested her to save her daughter and promised that as a reward for fulfilling her request the Budniewskis would finally have a child after ten years of infertility. And indeed, shortly after accepting Perelmuter for shelter, Mrs. Budniewska became pregnant, which she interpreted, of course, as a sign from heaven that she was being rewarded for her benevolence. That is why Perelmuter got the best care conceivable from the Budniewskis.[187]

In Tarnow, a former servant maid of the Goldfein family, Marysia (last name unidentified) kept in touch with her former employers throughout the entire period of the occupation, encouraged them, sent parcels to the Szebnia camp, and after the liberation helped Mr. Goldfein to recover from the traumas of camp life and to resume his normal daily routines.[188]

Also in Tarnow, Maria Dyrdala-Kielbasa, who before the war had also been employed by Jewish families, did her utmost to save Jewish children. In her endeavors she risked her life constantly.[189]

Jozef Bronislaw Tysik from the village of Wiazownia near Otwock certified the Polishness of Chana Cukierman, thereby making it possible for her to acquire "Aryan" documents which were not forged. With those documents in hand, Cukierman could enlist as a laborer in Germany. While she was in Germany, Tysik wrote letters to her and sent parcels, by which means Chana could allay all recurrently arising suspicions as to her real nationality.[190]

Our files contain cases of Jews receiving help from members of the Polish underground. In most such cases, however, the benefactors were concealing their efforts to help the Jews from their organizational superiors and associates. It sometimes occurred that a Jew sheltered by a member of an underground organization would eventually be recruited by the latter to clandestine work for the Polish underground. But even in such cases, the Jews thus recruited were as a rule concealing their real nationality from all other members of the organization with whom they worked.

Finally, we have recorded several dozen cases of inordinate sacrifice incurred by persons who were helping the Jews benevolently. Here are some examples:

In the locality of Rogozno near Tomaszow Lubelski, Elzbieta Wazna devised a bribery scheme which made it possible to free Chana Szpizajzen from a German jail. Then, she sheltered Szpizajzen for two years at her home. After the liberation, Wazna's neighbors believed that she owned much gold received as remuneration from a Jewess whom she had sheltered during the occupation. There were several attempts to rob her of that gold which she allegedly owned. In the course of these attempted robberies, she was beaten several times. She was thus forced to move from her family home.[191]

A farmer by the name of Wladyslaw (last name unidentified) from a village near Pinczow was a Communist and a member of the People's Guard. In prewar days he had befriended Jews extensively, and during the war he sheltered as many as sixteen of them. Some Home Army members notified the Gestapo that Wladyslaw was a Cummunist. The Gestapo, failing to find Wladyslaw at home, picked up his daughter and tortured her to death. She betrayed none of the sixteen under torture.[192]

In the locality of Omszana near Wlodawa, a poor peasant, Zofia Napierala, for fifteen months sheltered seven members of the Diamant family. Napierala was a widow with four children: her husband had been murdered by the Germans. Yet she treated her Jewish charges, in their own words, "As if she were our own mother."[193]

In the town of Jaslo, Cracow district, a Polish physician, Dr. Julian Ney, applied for and obtained a special permit authorizing him to remain in his apartment which happened to be located in the area designated for the local ghetto. Ney's purpose was to devote himself to providing medical care to ghetto residents. With the assistance of Anna Bogdanowicz, he organized the escape of Sara Diller from the ghetto. Caught in the act by the Gestapo, he died under torture.[194]

Maniek Swierszczak was a gravedigger in the Catholic cemetery of Buczacz. During the deportations from the Buczacz ghetto, Swierszczak prepared bunkers on the grounds of his cemetery in which he placed five Jewish families, including the four members of the Rozen family. A number of times he was beaten, but he betrayed no one.[195]

Rafal Charlap recounts: A priest named Stark, still a young man of about thirty, was doing his utmost to provide the Jews with free forged "Aryan" documents. He called upon his parishioners to extend help to the Jews, and persuaded the Poles he trusted to shelter Jewish fugitives. One of the Jews he saved was a young boy, Jureczek, for whom Stark found a hiding place with a gardener, Josef Mikuczyn. The orphaned boy survived the war there, and was later picked up by his uncle. In the summer of 1941, the Germans exacted from the Jews of the Slonim ghetto a "contribution" of gold. As the deadline approached, the Jews were still ½ kilogram short of the quota which the Germans demanded. In order to enable the Jews to fill the quota, Father Stark organized the collection of golden crosses from his parishioners. When the Germans learned of Stark's activities, they arrested and shot him together with the Slonim Jews, in their mass execution in Petrolowicze.

In the same town of Slonim, the Jews received much help from Dr. Nojszewska, a former nun and the director of the municipal hospital. She sheltered the small son of her Jewish colleague, Dr. Kagan. The Germans were notified and shot her together with the child.[196]

A wealthy and very devout farmer, Bartoda, from the village of Sopaczow, Sarny county, sheltered Sender Apfelbaum, his father, and two unidentified Jewish women. The Apfelbaums were detected by chance, but managed to move away. However, the women remained. The local Ukrainians learned of them, and notified the Germans who shot them on the spot together with Bartoda. But before killing Bartoda, the executioners asked him why he had sheltered the Jews? Bartoda's answer was: "You may take away my body, but my soul will remain clean."[197]

* * *

Obviously, we have succeeded in authenticating merely a fraction—perhaps only an infinitesimal fraction—of the crimes actually perpetrated against Jewish fugitives in hiding. Crimes such as murders, or informing, or turning Jews over to the Germans, were as a rule committed underhandedly. Seldom did the perpetrators want to have any witnesses. In very rare cases would a Jew who accidentally witnessed a crime committed against other Jews be allowed to survive. Also, the Polish witnesses of crimes against the Jews were later seldom willing to testify, if their statements would have implicated their friends or neighbors. As for the perpetrators themselves, they obviously wouldn't reveal their own crimes either. To compound matters, those directly implicated in crimes can usually rely on the solidarity of the people from within the social environment in which they operate. Actually, it is the latter who are often most helpful in covering up the traces.

The instances of participation by Poles in raids on Jewish fugitives have been authenticated as having occurred in 172 localities and the murders committed by Polish underground formations (National Armed Forces and a Part of the Home Army) as having occurred in 120 localities. Beyond any doubt these figures are incomplete: there certainly were other localities in which collective crimes against the Jews were committed, either by groups of local populace or by underground units. Unfortunately, there is absolutely no way of estimating the total number of victims of these crimes in even the roughest general terms. Some Jewish survivors recount that tens and even hundreds of Jews could be either murdered on the spot or turned over to the Germans as a result of one raid in a single locality. The accounts of Icchak Golabek and Icchak Szumowicz which describe the raids in the forests surrounding the town of Zambrow are cases in point. Golabek tells of hundreds of Jews captured by Poles and turned over to the Germans during one single raid of no more than one day's duration.[198] Szumowicz estimates that about 150 Jews who escaped the deportation from Zambrow on January 15, 1943, were subsequently tracked down by the local villagers in a nearby forest and turned over to the Germans.[199]

Similar facts are reported by the survivors from dozens of other localities. The existing evidence does not make it possible, however, to corroborate reliably the raid casualty estimates as given by the authors of the accounts. When totaled, these estimates would reach many thousands who fell prey to raids which Poles either organized or were involved in. Of this, the figure of over 3,000 Jews whom Poles (under varying circumstances) either murdered or turned over to the Germans can be considered reliably authenticated on the basis of the existing sources.

We have studied the files concerning 2652 Jews rescued by help obtained from the Poles. Likewise, we have identified 965 Polish individuals and families outside Warsaw who under many differing circumstances and for specific considerations sheltered Jews or helped them otherwise to hide. We have found that of the 965, eighty persons paid for their deeds with their lives. But again, the existing documentation has undoubtedly failed to record all the acts of help which the Jews received from the Poles. As in the case of the crimes, the actual number of Jews saved by the Poles and the actual number of their Polish benefactors (and of those from among them who made the ultimate sacrifice of their lives) are certainly much higher than the figures presented here. Yet there are reliable reasons to presume that the figures concerning the help to the Jews deviated from the actual realities comparatively less often than the figures concerning the crimes against the Jews. Simply put, the dead can no longer produce information, and the perpetrators of crimes prefer to remain silent. In contrast, the survivors can speak, and they have indeed recounted numerous instances of help received from the Poles. Furthermore, the Poles who did extend such help have had no reasons to be ashamed of their deeds either. This is applicable in cases where the Poles paid for their help to the Jews with their lives. As noted, the actual number of such cases is certainly higher than the figure cited above. It is well documented that the Polish population was subjected by the Germans to brutal terror. Within the framework of that terror, particularly atrocious reprisals were meted out even for minor breaches of all conceivable rulings of the Nazi authorities. Adding the general balance sheet of anti-Polish repression, however, the reprisals for helping the Jews rank rather low in frequency. Informative in this respect is a study of German repression against the citizens of the Polish countryside in the Lublin district, carried out by a Polish investigator, Andrzej Tolpyho. According to Tolpyho, in the Lublin district the Germans destroyed thirty-one Polish villages in 1942 alone (i.e. in the peak year of deportations from the ghettos and of Jewish escapes). Tolpyho concludes:

> Serious discrepancies in available evidence do not permit us to ascertain with precision the actual reasons for the destruction of all the villages. Only in twelve cases is the picture really clear. Of these twelve villages, nine were destroyed in retribution for support for and cooperation with the resistance movement (in one case for cooperation with Soviet partisans), two for helping the fugitive Soviet POW's, and one for sheltering and helping the Jews.[200]

The available documents do not enable us to ascertain either the number of Poles who helped the Jews, and then fell prey to reprisals resulting from their having been informed on by (Polish) neighbors or acquaintance. From various sources it can be inferred that cases of informing on Poles who were helping Jews were by no means rare. For instance, a Polish resident of Kolno, Bialystok district, Czeslawa Kossakowska, confided to her Jewish friend Renata Alter when the latter came to visit her native town after the war:

> The local populace grievously wronged the Jews from the vicinity. They were catching them, looting their possessions, and afterwards turning them over to the Germans. My husband played organ in the church. He tried to save the Jews and sheltered them. Your cousin, Rykower, stayed with us for some time with her family. We also sheltered other Jews. But in the end, my husband was betrayed by our own Polish informers, and the Germans shot him.[201]

In summation, documents reviewed in our study point to a negative balance, in which instances of help to the Jews are outnumbered by instances of crimes against the Jews. To a considerable extent, this negative balance can be accounted for by the policies of the German conquest, which consciously aimed at spreading corruption within as large a fraction of the Polish society as possible. Severe penalties for even the slightest relief offered to a Jew, coupled with rewards for committing crimes against them, did exert a negative influence upon the Polish society's attitudes. Recurrently posted announcements warning of the death penalty for helping the Jews were visible at all the locations in the Government General beginning with September 1942. They were followed by the promulgation of executive ordinances in each of its counties. At the same time, the occupation authorities did everything possible to encourage the Poles to participate in raids on the Jewish fugitives in hiding, and to loot their property. In his recollections, Bronislaw Janik, described situations of this type that occurred in the vicinity of Rokitno:

> It was the ever greedy and vindictive Ukrainian police who undertook to track down the Jews in the nearby forests. Spread out in battle array, the Ukrainians searched the nearby forests in pursuit of victims. The sounds of weapons firing could be heard in Rokitno from dawn to sunset. Within several days, the policemen succeeded in capturing over a dozen Jews in the vicinity of Derc and Masiewicze. They were singing while escorting their captives to the town. Rather than transport them to the headquarters in Sarny, they would shoot them in a nearby quarry.
>
> Most of the Jews in hiding anticipated the raids and took precautions. At nighttime, they were moving towards the forests located at a greater distance, near Dolhan and Okopy. But the Germans intended to spare no one's life. In boldface print, their announcements imposed the death penalty upon anyone who would help Jews in any manner whatsoever. At the same time, the rulers offered one kilogram of salt for the capture and delivery of a Jew to Rokitno. Yes, one kilogram of salt. Such depths of depravity reveal what the Nazi education did to the German nation....
>
> Yet for one kilogram of salt, those creatures in the guise of human beings were stalking the paths of the forests in search of spoils. Pretending to look for mushrooms or blackberries, they were actually peering into forest covers and into all remote corners.[202]

But the rewards for participation in anti-Jewish crimes varied from place to place. Thus the Delegate's Office's Situation-in-the-Polish-Territories Report No. 12/44 for the months of February to June 1944 states:

> In March (1944), the tracking down and the murders of Jews was ceaselessly going on in Lwow. In some instances, the Jews would put up resistance. The police reward for the capture of a Jew from the Lwow camp was 1,000 zlotys. But for the capture of a Jew from the Winniki camp there was a prize reward of 5,000 zlotys plus twenty liters of vodka.[203]

An earlier Situation-in-the-Polish-Territories Report, No. 9, for the months of May and June 1943, added:

> A large numbers of Jews continue to stay in hiding, either in forests or in towns and villages in the midst of the Aryan population. The

Germans chase them relentlessly, organizing raids to capture them. In villages and forests the raids have become virtual manhunts. The Jews who are captured are most often murdered on the spot. Only those whom the Germans suspect of having retained some concealed valuables are imprisoned; or else those whom they expect to divulge the identities of their Aryan benefactors. In the vicinity of Otwock the Germans have encouraged the local toughs to track down the Jews and deliver them to German gendarmerie stations. A Pole who turns up with a captured Jew is first ordered to dig a grave for him. Immediately after his luckless victim is executed, he receives a reward of 200 zlotys plus the clothes and the shoes of the deceased.

The following incident occurred in a Warsaw hospital. A young woman of Jewish origin was about to enter the premises in order to visit her "Aryan" friend. A young hooligan who had apparently known and trailed her, accosted her and demanded a high ransom under the threat of turning her over to the Germans. The woman refused to talk to him and entered the hospital. The youngster then ran to a nearby German Army hospital, where two young Germans pilots became very excited by his news. The airmen called the gendarmerie which quickly dispatched seventeen of its men to the Polish hospital. In the hospital the seventeen, all armed, started a chase after one defenseless woman. They found her soon, and at once bludgeoned her savagely with rifle and pistol butts. A Polish patient who witnessed this macabre scene tried to intercede. Protesting against the sadistic beating of a woman in public, he said that even killing her would be preferable. For this attempt at persuasion he was arrested and handed over to the Gestapo. And the woman, terribly beated and bleeding profusely, was taken away by the seventeen German heroes to jail. And the young man who turned her over to the executioners received 500 zlotys as a reward.[204]

The ratios between the positive acts of help and the instances of crime against the Jews vary from one region to another.

The balance between the acts of help and acts of crime becomes, markedly different, depending on whether a given region was ethnically Polish, or, like Eastern Galicja or Volhynia, predominantly alien. In the latter, the Polish minority was itself a target of brutal persecutions on the part of the nationalists from among the Ukrainian majority. It seems obvious, therefore, that the Poles manifested relatively less hostility towards the Jews, and more empathy towards their tragedy, if, in addition to being oppressed by the occupier, they were persecuted themselves by a chauvinistically inclined alien majority. The same situation applies, in essence, for the region of Wilno, where Poles suffered from harsh persecutions on the part of Lithuanians.

True, in the region of Nowogrodek and Polesie, the Polish population also had a minority status. But the difference was that there it suffered no persecutions from the Byelorussian majority. Unlike the Ukrainians in Western Ukraine (i.e. the Eastern Galicja and Volhynia), or the Lithuanians in the Wilno region, the Byelorussians manifested no particular hostility towards the Poles.

The analysis of the evidence in our records clearly indicates, furthermore, the marked contrast between the heavy involvement of political bodies in the crimes against the Jews, and very little involvement on the part of such bodies in acts of helping the Jews. (It again needs to be stressed that the present analysis does not cover the city of Warsaw.) Among the identified victims of the crimes, a large number were murdered by armed units of the Polish underground, chiefly by the National Armed Forces, but also by some units of the Home Army. Particular cruelty towards the Jewish fugitives in hiding was displayed by the Home Army in the Bialystok region and by the National Armed Forces in the region of Kielce (i.e. Radom district). On the other hand, the meager contribution of the underground organizations to the rescue of the Jews was, apart from Warsaw, confined to Cracow, Lwow and only a few other localities; and even there the extent of this involvement was extremely limited. (The issue is discussed extensively in the chapter dealing with the Council for Aiding Jews.)

Of nearly 1,000 Polish individuals and families who have been identified as providing the Jews with shelter or other forms of help, nearly all acted (whatever their motivation) on their own initiative, rather than within a framework of any organized social or political activity. It is true that their numbers included members of underground organizations. The point is, however, that their activities in support of the Jews were almost without exception unconnected with their underground work. In most cases, their activities in the field of helping the Jews were withheld from the notice of their superiors and associates in a given underground organization, and sometimes even carefully concealed from them. There were even cases in which an underground organization member would be engaged in helping the Jews in direct violation of his/her organization's explicit orders.

It therefore seems logical to conclude that while many of the crimes against Jewish fugitives in hiding were committed by underground organizations, the acts of helping them were for the most part individual, stemming from the personal initiative and good will of the benefactors, and unintegrated within any framework of underground activities.

The attitudes of the local Polish population towards Jewish fugitives in hiding, whether positive or negative, often depended on the attitudes of persons in key authority positions, such as the community head, the hamlet head, or the forester, or of persons who usually enjoy a measure of informal authority among the peasantry, such as the local priest, teacher, or physician. Within each of these occupational groups, we encounter individuals with both friendly and hostile attitudes towards the Jews. The analysis of evidence in our records warrants the conclusion that the attitudes of Poles in positions of authority were shaped to a certain extent by their political opinions and general *Weltanschauung*; but that their actual behavior was influenced less by their opinions than by their character traits: e.g. by the degree of greed, or by the ability to resist temptations, or by cowardice-inspired loyalty towards the occupier, as opposed to courage-inspired readiness to take risks. Here are some examples which present a general description of the attitudes towards the Jewish fugitives in hiding on the part of hamlet heads, foresters, priests and teachers.

THE HAMLET HEADS

In the village of Janowce near Wlodawa, the general assembly of villagers resolved to reinforce the guards in order to track down the Jews and the partisans more efficiently. The hamlet head refused to support the resolution.[205]

In the village of Zylowice near Janow Lubelski, a peasant captured Chana Zylberman with two children. He escorted his captives to the hamlet head, asking him to deliver them to the Germans. The hamlet head refused, invoking religious considerations as his reason.[206]

In the village of Cisow near Proszowice, Miechow county, in 1944 the hamlet head freed two Jewish women captured by the peasants. He warned them to disappear from sight during the daytime, to avoid the danger of their being recaptured by the peasants.[207]

The hamlet head in the village of Szczytnik near Brzesko, Miechow county, Roman Juszczyk, extended himself ever further to help the Jews in hiding. Once, during a raid against the Jews, he encountered a Jewish woman named Fajfkopf, hiding in a field. He helped her to evade capture and thus effectively rescued her.[208]

In the village of Smolewo, Ostrow Mazowiecka county, the hamlet head advised a poor peasant by the name of Kantorowski to shelter the two-year-old daughter of Cypa Solarz, while warning the other peasants that whoever notified the Germans, would be subject to harsh retribution after the war.[209]

The hamlet head in the village of Oleksin near Bransk, Bielsk Podlaski county, Jozef Adamczyk, convened the village assembly to demand from all the villagers that they turn all the Jews detected in the vicinity over to the Germans. Directly from the assembly, accompanied by several other villagers, he went to search the area. That very night, they captured ten Jews. They tied them up and guarded them for several days, until the Germans appeared to take them away. The ten were shot on their way to the village of Klicha. The next day, the Adamczyk group carried out another raid and captured five more Jews who were shot in Bransk. The casualties of Adamczyk include: Estera Oskard, fifty-five, Mordechaj Oskard, five, Ruwen Kozak, twenty, Lea Kozak, ten, Josef Pribit, thirty-five, Pinie Cegielski, twenty-six, Jakow Rotenstein, twenty-one, Lejb Rosen, twelve, Pesie Rosen, twenty, Naftali Awol, sixteen, Szymon Brianski, sixteen, Abraham Dawidowicz, thirty, and Sara Tabak, twenty-five.[210]

THE FORESTERS

In his account, Sender Apfelbaum describes the forester Boleslaw Zawadzki from Andruja near Wlodzimierz, Sarny county, as a truly noble-minded man, always willing to extend help to any Jew who approached him. In one way or another, Zawadzki helped Apfelbaum's father, Mordechaj Weissman, the Sliwkin family, and several other Jews hiding in nearby forests.[211]

Miriam Rozenberg recounts that a forester by the name of Ksiezak from the village of Kiemieliszki, Wilno region, assiduously tracked down the Jews in hiding, in order either to turn them over to the Germans or to kill them himself.[212]

Josef Brojde tells us in his account, that a forester by the name of Kosiak from the vicinity of Bransk Podlaski tracked down and killed thirty-six Jews in hiding.[213]

THE PRIESTS

As the recorded evidence shows, the attitudes of the priests towards the Jewish fugitives varied; and their influence upon the local Polish population reflected this lack of unanimity. Here are a few examples:

In the village of Kreznica, Lublin county, a local priest named Pankowski in his Sunday Mass sermons called upon the parishioners to murder the Jews.[214]

In the locality of Urzedow, Janow Lubelski county, a priest by the name of Swietlik cared for Diana Topiel after she escaped from the Majdanek concentration camp.[215]

In the village of Niechcice, Radomsko county, a priest, Feliks Grela, who had a Ph.D. in theology, expressed in his sermons appreciation for the Nazis, commending them for having exterminated the Jews who, as he put it, "had led the Polish youth astray."[216]

In the town of Wlodzimierz, Sarny county, Father Dominik Wawrzynowicz called in his sermons upon the parishioners to help the Jews. He also preserved valuables which the Jewish owners had entrusted to him.[217]

Gitla Grinwald recounts that in the absence of distinctly Jewish racial features she could pass as a Pole and thus be regularly employed in the village of Kraczewice, first by the Szymanski family, and next by one Kwiatkowski who was the wealthiest farmer in the village and the local Home Army commander. The villagers never even surmised that Grinwald was Jewish. After the nearby labor camp of Poniatowa had been liquidated, the local peasants proceeded to pillage the belongings abandoned on its site. But Grinwald refused to have any part in the plunder. For that, she was commended by the local priest, Kwiatkowski's cousin, who told her: "You did the right thing, for someone had shed tears upon those belongings."[218]

Jentel Kita recounts the following incident which occurred in the village of Lachow, Wysokie Mazowieckie county. Several villagers assaulted a rather well-dressed woman, trying to strip her of her clothes. A priest suddenly appeared, approaching the attackers and asking them why they were harassing a lone woman. They told him that she was a Jewess who had jumped out of a Treblinka-destined train. Upon hearing that, the priest demanded that they leave her alone: he told them that she had suffered enough. The victim of the assault took advantage of his intercession and of the ensuing argument to withdraw speedily. Then the priest also walked swiftly away.[219]

In Lwow, a bigoted woman, Anna Kunc, converted Sabina Kalmus to Christianity and then exploited her badly. For two years' time, Kalmus was forced to support Kunc while the latter idled. But Kalmus was audacious enough to reveal her Jewishness to a priest of St. Nicholas' church who was her confessor. Upon hearing that, the priest called his sacristan, and the two of them beat Kalmus mercilessly.[220]

THE TEACHERS

A number of Jewish survivors recount the village of Czajkow near Staszow, Sandomierz county, as the only one in that area, where they could count on being benevolently received by its Polish residents. Strangely enough, this was due to the influence of a single person with authority: the teacher Irena Circz. She was the moving spirit behind individual acts of help extended to the Jews by the villagers. She also organized aid for a large group of Jews who were hiding in nearby forests. She risked her life in one episode after another. Eventually, the gendarmerie in Staszow began to suspect her of maintaining contacts with the Jews. But even while under investigation, she did not desist from activities on behalf of the Jews.[221]

Somewhat similar is the case of Stefan Stencel, the teacher in the village of Krole Duze near Jasienica, Ostrow Mazowiecka county. He also organized help for the Jews. It once happened that the village butcher, Fruchtel, accepted a pair of Jewish siblings for shelter, offered them a meal, and in the darkness of the night slaughtered them. On Stencel's initiative, Fruchtel was killed in retribution by a local Home Army unit, and his house burned down. The punishment had a deterrent effect: from that moment on, all informing against the Jews in the village and vicinity ceased.[222]

*   *   *

The over-all balance between the acts of crime and acts of help, as described in the available sources, is disproportionately negative. The acts of crime outnumbered the acts of help. To a significant extent, this negative balance is to be accounted for by the hostility towards the Jews on the part of large segments of the Polish underground, and, even more importantly, by the involvement of some armed units of that underground in murders of the Jews. Still, several thousand Jews from our files succeeded in finding shelter and in being rescued because of Polish help. Yet for a Jewish fugitive, the chance of obtaining any help was slight under the conditions of the raging Nazi terror, of the death penalty for anyone extending such help, and of widespread hostility towards the Jews in both the Polish society and its underground organizations. Of the many who sought help, only a few found it. The overwhelming majority of Jews who approached Poles for help fell prey either to Nazi police or gendarmerie, or to rabid anti-Semites in the Polish society and in the Polish underground.

Thousands who sought help but failed to obtain it, unable to cope any longer with all the constant dangers lurking about, were returning to the ghettos already reduced after the mass deportations, or to the newly formed secondary ghettos. It meant that they would be killed eventually, during a later deportation to death camps.

Still more tragic were the instances when Jewish fugitives would come to a German police station to seek death by turning themselves in, after they lost all hope of survival in the forest or elsewhere, or of ever obtaining shelter or any other help from the Poles. This phenomenon was described by the Polish clandestine monthly "Prawda" (Truth) of October 1942. The title of the article was "The ultimate in tragedy":

> Some Jews from Wolomin, Otwock, and other localities around Warsaw who have been hiding for several weeks in the forests, living like wild animals, tormented by hunger and by cold, and downcast in abject despair, are now courting death by turning themselves in to the police. Several instances of such decisions have been reported. In one case, a whole group came. "Please kill us: we prefer to be dead than to live on in this way." The gendarmes happened to be short of ammunition. One of them took a bicycle and pedalled to fetch some. The Jews waited. The gendarme returned with ammunition. The Jews were shot.
>
> In another, an old Jew turned himself in, together with his young and beautiful daughter. They had been well-off once. They still had some jewelry which they indifferently handed to the gendarmes. As usual, they were told to get undressed. With calm and dignity, the girl placed all her clothes on the ground. In an undergarment, barefoot, and proud, she stood upright confronting the executioners. "Is it all right?" she asked. "You have to kneel." They both knelt. A volley of shots resounded.
>
> Our informant talked to the German Platoon commander responsible for their execution. "Her image does not cease to haunt me" he confided. "I keep drinking, but I cannot forget."

Let us close this presentation by quoting from a document which in a very palpable manner shows how slight a Jewish fugitive's chances of survival were. It is the diary of Szlomo Scheiner, who has hiding in the village of Debowka near Pinczow in the house of a Polish farmer named Matias. In this diary, Scheiner recorded nothing but the bare facts which either he or Matias could ascertain:

> On Saturday, January 23, 1943, the Germans found several Jews in a nearby forest. They were shot on the spot.
>
> Next day, January 24, 1943, we observed through an interstice in our hiding place, how the Germans were escorting Berl Natan Zajd from Pinczow with his wife and their two children. They had been captured by peasants whom they approached for shelter.
>
> On January 28 the murderers found the Weiz family.
>
> On February 11, the police arrested a peasant who had previously sheltered a Jewish couple. Next day, the peasant was freed after posting a bond of 10,000 zlotys.
>
> On February 16, the Germans together with the Poles were assiduously searching the entire vicinity. Eighteen Jews were found; all were shot on the spot.
>
> On March 23, Matias had a "visitor." It was Feliks from Boguszyce, a Pole who had once provided us with a shelter. Matias told him that we had moved away long ago to a tiny village near Wislica. Matias doesn't trust Feliks. He purposely entertained him in a room which is still under construction, so as to make it appear credible that there was no

trace of us in the house. In reality, we overheard their conversation in utter suspense. . . .

On April 24, 1943, eighteen Jews were shot in the town of Gacki: among them our former neighbor Gross and Mordechaj Gold with his son Icchak who was our brother-in-law.

On April 22, Icchak Szwager from Wislowicze was captured in Jurkow.

Also on April 22, a dugout was detected in Boguszyce, with twenty Jews in it. Chaim Rot (from the Council of Elders) with family was there.

On May 16, the two brothers Diamant from Pinczow were shot.

On May 24, fifteen Jews were captured in Dziewieszyce near Dzialoszyce.

On May 27, the underground "Jedrusie" organization commanded by"Lobster" shot four Jews around Wislica.

On June 20, seven Jews, including Szmuel Szenker and Herszkowicz, were shot near the mill by some peasants.

On July 11, Heniek Lipszyc and Chuna Gold with wife were captured. They had been hiding in rye in the vicinity of Michalow.

On August 1, four Jews, including Mordechaj Baruch Reinhorn, were shot in Tary.

On August 2, Matias had night visitors: five men from the underground unit of "Lobster," who damanded food. They stayed for several hours. We heard what they were saying: but we had to hold our breaths in total silence, for these Polish "patriots" are no better to the Jews than the Nazis.

On August 21, Abraham Diamant from Pinczow was shot in Zagajew. Two young Jews who were with him managed to escape.

On October 24, five Jews were shot in Mlodzow.

On November 6, seventeen Jews were shot in the Boguszyce forest.

On December 4, the Fiszel family from Pinczow was captured in the village of Zak.

Also on December 4, five Jews were detected in the forest that is close to our place. They were shot at once.

On December 24, 1943, seven Jews were captured in Sadykow: three men and four women.[223]

NOTES

1. Madajczyk, C., *Polityka hitlerowska w okupowanej Polsce* (Nazi policies in occupied Poland), Vol. 2, p.330.

2. Michta, N., *Wspomnienia z nad Nidzicy* (Recollections from over the Nidzica River), p. 179.

3. *Sefer Izkor Miechow* (The remembrance book for Miechow), pp. 274–276.

4. Adamski, J., "Dzierzkowice, Krasnik county". In: *Chleb i Krew: Moja Wies Podczas Okupacji* (Bread and blood: my village during the occupation), p. 23.

5. Oldag, A., account in YVA, 0–3/2557.

6. *Najnowsze dzieje Polski*: materialy i studia z okresu II wojny swiatowej (Recent history of Poland: materials and studies from the period of World War II), vol. 11, 1967, pp. 110–11.

7. Korbonski, S., *W imieniu Rzeczypospolitej* (In the name of the Republic), Paris, Instytut Literacki, 1954, p.257.

8. Zieminski, S., "Kartki z dziennika nauczyciela w Lukowie z okresu okupacji hitlerowskie)" (Pages from the

diary of Lukow teacher in the period of Nazi occupation), BZIM (Bulletin of the Jewish Historical Institute), 27, 1958, p. 109.

9. Klukowski, etal. (Diary from the years of occupation in the Zamosc region), Lublin, 1959, p.299.

10. Landau, L. *Kronika z lat wojny i okupacji* (A chronicle of the years of war and occupation), vol. 2, Warsaw, 1962, p. 223.

11. Goldstein, I., YVA, 0–3/1252.

12. Kopylinska, G., YVA, M-1/E-2164.

13. Kisolwicz, A., YVA, 0–3/3082.

14. Holder, A., account in *Sefer Tarnogrod* (The book of Tarnogrod), p. 420.

15. *Churban Markuszew* (The destruction of Markuszew), p. 330.

16. Goldhecht, M., YVA, 0–3/1658.

17. *Sefer Tarnogrod* (The book of Tarnogrod), pp. 418, 426–430.

18. YVA, M-1/E 1369.

19. Mirska S., YVA, 0–33/567.

20. *Siedlce Izkor Buch* (The remembrance book for Siedlce), p. 640.

21. Przybyl-Stalski, K., *Partyzancki czas* (The partisan times), p. 93.

22. Feferman, D., YVA, 0–3/2977.

23. YVA, M-2/297a.

24. *Sefer Staszow* (The book of Staszow), p. 639.

25. Lerner, I., YVA, 0–33/767

26. Herzig, J. J., YVA, 0–33/194.

27. *Sefer Ryki* (The book of Ryki), p. 465.

28. Bamberg, YVA, M-1/E-1474.

29. *Dos buch fun Lublin* (The book of Lublin), pp. 454–455.

30. *Sefer Staszow* (The book of Staszow), p. 378.

31. Segal, N., YVA, 0–3/2770.

32. Kislowicz, A., YVA, 0–3/3082.

33. Lerner, I., YVA, 0–33/768.

34. *Sefer zikaron Bychawa* (The remembrance book for Bychawa), p.334.

35. *Sefer Staszow* (The book of Staszow), p. 640.

36. Horowicz, M., YVA, 0–3/1316.

37. *Sefer Radomsko* (The book of Radomsko), p. 301.

38. *Churban Siedlce* (The destruction of Siedlce), p. 195; *Izkor Lekehilat Sarnaki* (In commemoration of the community of Sarnaki), pp. 178–183.

39. Erenburg, G., YVA, M–1/E–1563.

40. *Churban Bilgoraj* (The destruction of Bilgoraj), p. 286.

41. *Sefer Lezajsk* (The book of Lezajsk), p. 94.

42. *Ibid.*, p. 95.

43. *Ibid.*, pp. 108–109.

44. *Ibid.*, p. 93.

45. Szlim, E., YVA, M–1/E–1906.

46. *Izkor buch Kurow* (The remembrance book for Kurow), pp. 260–262.

47. Serwatko, I., YVA, M–1/E–620.

48. Welcz, M., YVA, M–1/E–1369.

49. *Sefer Izkor Charsznica*, (The remembrance book for Charsznica), p. 276.

50. Maurer, B., YVA, M–1/E–2495.

51. *Sefer Frampol*, pp. 271–278.

52. *Sefer Horodlo*, p. 120.

53. *Sefer Tarnogrod*, p. 343.

54. *Sefer Staszow*, p. 436.

55. *Sefer Kock*, pp. 233–237.

56. *Sefer Frampol*, pp. 271–278.

57. *Dos buch fun Lublin* (The book from Lublin), p. 550.

58. *Sefer Tarnogrod*, pp. 328–329.

59. *Szydlowiec Izkor Buch* (The remembrance book for Szydlowiec), pp. 489–490.

60. *Sefer Bransk*, p. 312.

61. *Sefer Kaluszyn*, p. 396.

62. Sznyper, D., account in *Sefer Staszow*.

63. *Gwardzista* (The Guard soldier) of May 1, 1944.

64. Erenberg, G., YVA, M–1/E–1563.

65. Cieply, J., YVA, 0–3/3241.

66. Nowicki, A., YVA, 0–3/1620.

67. *Sefer Staszow*, pp. 401, 498.

68. *Sefer Tarnogrod*, pp. 430–432.

69. Hering, I., YVA, 0–16½/470.

70. *Sefer Radzyn*, p. 279.

71. *Izkor Buch Zelechow* (The remembrance book for Zelechow), p. 258.

72. Zyskind, P., YVA, 0–16/447.

73. *Sefer zikaron lekehilat Reisha* (The book in commemoration of the community of Rzeszow), p. 304.

74. Ben-Shemesh (Sonensohn), S., YVA, 0–3/2295.

75. Chmielnik, P., pp. 830–835.

76. Solarz-Goldberg, C., M–1/E–1779.

77. Sztajnwurcel, J., YVA, 0–3/2729.

78. Sztubert, I., YVA, 0–3/2569; Eliasz, J., YVA, 0–3/2721.

79. *Sefer Frampol*, pp. 292–307.
80. Aviel (Lipkonski), A., YVA, 0–3/508.
81. Trachman, H., YVA, 0–3/1328.
82. Ekhajzer, J., YVA, 0–3/2951.
83. Sztubert, I., YVA, 0–3/2569.
84. Serwatko, M., YVA, M–1/E–620.
85. Hempel, YVA, 0–33/950.
86. *Ibid.*
87. Leszcz, C., YVA, 0–33/37.
88. *Sefer Lezajsk* pp. 93, 94, 130; *Sefer Tarnopol*, p. 459.
89. *Sefer Lezajsk*, p. 93.
90. Szlim, E., YVA, M–1/E–1906.
91. Bruk, S., YVA, 0–3/1841.
92. Herzig, J. J., YVA, 0–33/194.
93. Landsman, A., YVA, 0–16/28.
94. Kalpus, J., YVA, 0–3/3284.
95. Mandel-Kolodny, B., YVA, 0–3/2909.
96.
97. *Sefer Zikaron Bransk* (The remembrance book for Bransk), p. 331.
98. Langman, S., YVA, 0–3/816.
99. Blumenfeld, S., YVA, 0–3/3129.
100. *Sefer Frampol*, pp. 271–278.
101. Arnold H., YVA, 0–312984.
102. *Sefer Radzyn*, p. 272.
103. Korn, C., YVA, 0–3/2019.
104. *Wlodawa vehasviva* (Wlodawa and its vicinities), p. 857.
105. Hamerman, B., YVA, M–1/E–2492.
106. Reibscheid, R., YVA, 0–3/2799.
107. *Sefer Izkor Miechow* (The remembrance book for Miechow), p. 276.
108. Erenberg, G., YVA, M–1/E–1563.
109. *Sefer Biala Podlaska*, p. 427.
110. *Churban Bilgoraj* (The destruction of Bilgoraj), p. 271.
111. Horowicz, M., YVA, 0–3/1316.
112. *Sefer Staszow*, p. 432.
113. *Ibid.*, p. 509.
114. Faliszewski, F., *Kartki z przeszlosci ruchu ludowego w bylym powiecie Stopnickim* (Pages from the past of the peasant movement in the former county of Stopnica), Warsaw, 1965, p. 120.
115. *Sefer Zarki*, p. 142.
116. Horowicz, G., YVA, 0–3/2724.
117. *Sefer Staszow*, p. 380.
118. *Sefer Jadow*, p. 254.
119. *Ibid.*, p. 268.
120. *Dos buch fun Lublin* (The book from Lublin), p. 556.
121. Gersten, C., YVA, M–1/E–1496.
122. Bolkowska, I., YVA, 0–3/1595.
123. *Sefer Jadow*, p. 243.
124. *Churban Siedlce* (The destruction of Siedlce), p. 204.
125. *Sefer Izkor Miechow* (The remembrance book for Miechow), p. 275.
126. Rozenwald, W., YVA, M–1/E–1546.
127. Fenik, E., YVA, 0–3/1272; *Sefer Lancut*, pp. 372–373.
128. *Churban Markuszew* (The destruction of Markuszew), p. 327.
129. Krechman, A., YVA, M–1/E–1249.
130. Diamant, I., YVA, 0–3/3153.
131. Grinwald, G., YVA, 0–3/2170.
132. *Churban Markuszew* (The destruction of Markuszew).
133. Feldhendler, YVA, 0–16/464.
134. Dresner, H., YVA, 0–3/2565.
135. Burzminski, J. (Diamant, M.), YVA, 0–3/834.
136. Fleischer, R., YVA, 0–3/2553.
137. Pawlowska, S., YVA, 0–3/3349.
138. Horowicz, M., 0–3/1316.
139. Lemska, R., YVA, 0–3/3500.
140. Kleinman, M., account in *Garwolin Izkor Buch* (The Garwolin remembrance book), p. 199.
141. Stanislaw Wronski i Maria Zwolakowa: Polacy-Zydzi, 1939–1945. Warszawa, 1971.
142. *Sefer Skierniewice*, p. 477.
143. Pawlowska, S., YVA, 0–3/3349.
144. Hamerman, B., YVA, 0–3/2492.
145. Wilf, A., YVA, 0–3/2567.
146. Blond, S., YVA, 0–3/2563.
147. Herzig, J. J., YVA, 0–33/193; and 0/3/1696.
148. Rakocz, H., YVA, 0–3/2342.
149. Kalpus, J., YVA, 0–3/3284.
150. *Sefer Zikaron Rawa Ruska* (The remembrance book for Rawa Ruska), pp. 263–264.
151. Wertman, F., YVA, 0–3/3418.
152. Windstruach, C., YVA, 0–3/2300.
153. Finger, D., YVA, 0–3/2780.
154. *Sefer Zikaron Czyzewo* (The remembrance book for Czyzewo), p. 894.
155. Kalpus, J., YVA, 0–3/3284.
156. Lieberman, J., YVA, 0–3/2987.
157. YVA, 0/3/3390.
158. Szajamn, I., YVA, 0–33/665.
159. Ryba, G., YVA, 0–3/2734.
160. Ziw-Kuczynska, J., YVA, 0–3/3186.
161. Lencicka, D., YVA, 0–3/2310.
162. Maurer, B., YVA, M–1/E–2495.

163. *Sefer Podhajce*, pp. 238–239.
164. *Wlodawa vehasviva* (Wlodawa and its vicinity), p. 763.
165. Kalpus, J., YVA, 0–3/3284.
166. Glezer, T., YVA, 0–3/2538.
167. Gilboa, A., YVA, 0–3/3130.
168. Szlim, E., YVA, M–1/E–1906.
169. Estrin, S., YVA, 0–3/1623.
170. Kleszczelski, I., YVA, 0–3/3262.
171. Chus, R., YVA, 0–3/1398.
172. Dab-Kociol, J., *Moje zycie* (My life), p. 169.
173. YVA, M–2/297a.
174. YVA, 0–3/3283.
175. Padoszyn, H., YVA, 0–33/638.
176. Finger, D., YVA, 0–3/2780.
177. Rodzewicz, R., YVA, 0–3/3056.
178. Gronek, M., *Szumsk: sefer zikaron* (Szumsk: a remembrance book), pp. 84–85; Sztajman, R., account ibid., pp. 41–43.
179. Niewiadomska, H., YVA, 0–3/3438.
180. Cukier, A., *Sefer Pruszkow*, p. 249.
181. Liebesman, YVA, 0–33/914, p. 137.
182. Bleiweiss-Nowinska, A., YVA, 0–3/3271.
183. Lewkowicz, H., M–1/E–548.
185. Goldstein, J., YVA, 0–3/2188.
186. Sieradzka, C., YVA, 0–3/2825; Lasica, T., YVA, 0–3/2859.
187. *Sefer Horodlo*, p.120.
188. *"Wojenne dzieje lekarza"* (Wartime vicissitudes of a physician); recollections YVA, 0–33/195.
189. *Tarnow: Sefer Zikaron* Tarnow: A remembrance book), p. 305.
190. Cukierman, C., YVA, 0–3/2290.
191. Szpizajzen, C., YVA, 0–3/2559; Wazna, E., account in YVA, 0–3/2969.
192. *Sefer Pinczow*, p. 292.
193. *Wlodawa vehasviva* (Wlodawa and its vicinity), pp. 792–800.
194. Diller, S., YVA, 0–3/2531; Herzig, J.J., account in YVA, 0–33/194.
195. Rozen, S., YVA, 0–3/2055.
196. Kaplinski, N., YVA, 0–3/2361.
197. Apfelbaum, S., YVA, 0–3/2882.
198. Golabek, I., *Sefer Zambrow*, pp. 138–140.
199. Szumowicz, I., YVA, 0–3/2311.
200. Tolpyho, A., "Z problemow polityki okupanta wobec wsi w tzw. dystrykcie lubelskim (1939–1944)" (Selected problems of Nazi occupation policies towards the countryside in the so-called Lublin district (1939–1944). *Dzieje najnowsze* (Recent history), 4, 1973, p. 204.
201. Adler, R., *Zyl czlowiek . . . (There lived a man. . .)*, Tel-Aviv, 1969.
202. *Janik, B. Bylo ich trzy* (Three they were), Warsaw, 1970, p. 70.
203. YVA, M–2/226.
204. YVA, M–2/209.
205. *Wlodawa vehasviva* (Wlodawa and its vicinity), pp. 715–717.
206. Goldhecht, M., YVA, 0–3/1658.
207. Cieply, J., YVA, 0–3/3241.
208. Serwatko, I., YVA, M–1/E–620.
209. Solarz, C., YVA, M–1/E–1779.
210. *Bransk: Sefer Hazikaron* (Bransk: a remembrance book), pp. 308–309.
211. Apfelbaum, S., YVA, 0–3/2882.
212. Rozenberg, M., YVA, M–1/E–2530 and 0–3/2857.
213. Brojde, J., YVA, 0–3/3341.
214. *Dos buch fun Lublin* (The book of Lublin), p. 454.
215. Topiel-Czerska, D., YVA, 0–3/1310.
216. Hempel, YVA, 0–33/950.
217. Apfelbaum, S., YVA, 0–3/2882.
218. Grinwald, G., YVA, 0–3/2170.
219. Kita, J., *Sefer Zikaron Czyzewo* (The remembrance book for Czyzewo), pp. 871–872.
220. Lozinska, YVA, 0–33/954.
221. Accounts in *Sefer Staszow* by Gabriel Singer, Szmuel Szaniecki, Nataniel Erlich, Jehuda Feldberg, and Menachem Lipszyc.
222. Chus, R., YVA, 0–3/1398.
223. *Sefer Zikaron Pinczow* (The remembrance book of Pinczow), pp. 278–279.

CHAPTER SEVEN

Zegota: The Council for Aiding Jews

THE PROVISIONAL COMMITTEE AND THE COUNCIL FOR AIDING JEWS

The Council for Aiding Jews, or *Rada Pomocy Zydom-Zegota*, was founded in the autumn of 1942 under the auspices of the Delegate's Office of the Polish Government-in Exile in London. Dr. Adolf Berman, one of the two Jewish members of the Council's administration, went so far as to speak of the organization as having "inscribed its name in letters of gold in the annals of the work of rescuing persecuted Jews from the Nazi killers."[2] An analysis of documentary evidence indicates that the founders and principal active members of *Zegota* had an exaggerated sense of the significance and scope of the activity of the organization. Nevertheless, even after the scope of *Zegota's* achievements has been put into proper perspective, we are confronted with a revelation whose theoretical and practical significance is considerable.

We know that operations to assist and rescue Jews took place in most countries in occupied Europe; even in Germany itself occasional "righteous Gentiles" were to be found. In Belgium, Holland and France political organizations and underground groups made contact with Jewish groups and helped to hide Jews—especially Jewish children; and there were even cases of such organizations and groups, and often individuals, expressing their sympathy for persecuted Jews, notwithstanding the risks they ran in doing so.[3] In Bulgaria various underground groups and, in no lesser degree, individuals in the government and established institutions of the country joined forces and were able to save the Jews of

252

Bulgaria—except, that is, in Macedonia and Thrace which was annexed to Bulgaria during the course of the war.[4] In Italy and territories occupied by Italy there was an increase in the incidence of efforts to save Jews and to disrupt anti-Jewish policies, particularly the deportation to the East; these activities were participated in by persons within the organization of the Facist state and by senior officers in the army, and Mussolini himself took an equivocal stand of the issue of handing Jews over to the Germans.[5] In Denmark the rescue operation undertaken in October 1943, in which the great majority of that country's small community of Jews were transferred to neutral Sweden, involved many Danes and bore the character of a national underground enterprise; it should be noted, too, that this highly energetic undertaking contributed much to strengthening and consolidation the anti-Nazi underground movement in Denmark.[6]

Countries such as Denmark and, to a lesser degree, Belgium and both regions of France experienced relatively mild governments of occupation and were granted limited degrees of self-rule, although under occupation conditions. Satellite states, such as Bulgaria, enjoyed wider independence, and as a consequence had a considerable scope for maneuver.[7]

In Poland, however, the Germans instituted an absolutist regime and a policy of brutal terror from the very start; municipal affairs and welfare excepted—no autonomy whatever was granted to the Government General and the regions annexed by the Reich. In no domain of social existence other than welfare could Jews and Poles meet and work together; nor for that matter did there exist any domain in which the opinion of Poles was sought, or in which they could exert their influence on the situation of Jews. The German occupation regime showed a special interest in augmenting anti-Semitism in Poland, and it went to great efforts to keep the ethnic groups apart. Thus when the ghettos were established, among the justifications given for the policy was that it was intended to prevent Jews from influencing the Polish public and from participating in economic life of the country.[8] Moreover, there can be no doubt that the German were anxious to prevent assistance from being rendered to Jews and rescue operations from being undertaken on their behalf by the population of Poland—a country inhabited by millions of Jews, and one in whose territory extermination camps had been established to which Jews from countries in German-occupied Europe were being transported. On October 15, 1941, Hans Frank, Governor of the Government General, issued an order forbidding Jews to leave the ghettos on pain of death; the same order established the death penalty as well for Gentiles "who knowingly provide Jews with a hiding place." [9] Later, similar orders fixing the death penalty for Poles who aided escaping Jews. and promising grants of wheat to anyone who turned Jews over to the German authorities, were issued on a number of occasions on a district and regional level in occupied Poland.[10] Many Poles were in fact sentenced to death, although many camps sentences were subsequently reduced to internment in jail or concentration.[11] According to current Polish statistics, which still require thorough checking, several hundred Poles were executed for having committed the "crime" of aiding persecuted Jews during the period of the Holocaust.[12] We do not know whether the policy of imposing the death penalty on Gentiles for helping to rescue or hiding Jews threatened by deportation was practiced in countries under German occupation other than Poland.

The wide-spread anti-Semitism among Poles was another factor making rescue attempts difficult; for it created a climate of opinion palpably favorable to Nazi anti-Semitic policy—and this despite the fact that on the whole the Polish people tended toward national solidarity and were strongly opposed to the Extremist Polish groups even took malicious pleasure in the tragedy of the Jews.[13] There were individual members in these anti-Semitic movements who were shocked by the Nazi mass murders of Jews and the implementation of the "Final Solution"; but a considerable part felt no compunctions when the stage of total extermination was reached, and took the view that it was just as well that so desirable an enterprise should be undertaken by others on Poland's behalf.[14]

In an atmosphere, therefore, marked by and anti-Jewish tradition and by indifference or acceptance of the policy of the occupying power toward the Jews, it was not only Jews attempting to escape or in hiding who were in constant danger; the work of rescuing Jews was made extremely difficult, and those involved in it ran no small risk. As we have had occasion to note, the Germans were not especially proficient in recognizing Jews by their facial features and characteristic accent when speaking Polish. Hence the danger of betrayal came often from Polish extortionists and extreme anti-Semites and those involved in pursuing Jews.

The fact that the Council for Aiding Jews–*Zegota* enjoyed the Delegate's official recognition within occupied Poland, and that the organization's documents bore the seal "Council for Aiding Jews of the Delegate of the Government," gave the Council the status of an agency backed by the combined authorities of the major underground organizations in the country. It was a situation without parallel elsewhere in occupied Europe, and official recognition of the Council had the inevitable effect of exerting a moderating influence on the hostility of many Poles towards Jews: for activities on behalf of Jews were not perceived within the Polish underground movement as serving Polish national interests.

The Council had its beginnings in the period of the mass deportation of Jews from Warsaw, when both individual Poles and small Polish groups rushed to the aid of Jews under imminent threat of annihilation. Zofia Kossak-Szczucka, the Polish writer closely associated with conservative Catholic circles, was among those who laid the groundwork for the undertaking. Early in August 1942, when the deportation of Jews from Warsaw was at its height, Zofia Kossak published a proclamation in which she asserted: "Anyone remaining silent in the face of this murder becomes an accomplice to the murder."[15] Polish intellectuals belonging to the Democratic Party were active as well in giving an organized character to the rescue operation; especially prominent among the members of this group was Wanda Krahelska-Filipowicz, whose roots in the Polish socialist movement dated from before the First World War.

The "Konrad *Zegota* Provisional Committee" was established under the Delegate's auspices on September 27, 1942, after the mass deportation of Jews from Warsaw had already been completed. No major organization of the Polish underground appears to have joined. However, the Provisional Committee's membership did include young Catholics of the Polish Renascence Front (*Front Odrodzenia Polski*), and representatives of both the Democratic Party (*Stronnictwo Demokratyczne*) and the Polish Syndicalists.[16]

The Provisional Committee set itself the following tasks: (1) To establish contact with Jewish communities by offering them financial assistance. (2) To provide Jews escaping from the ghettos with apartments and temporary sleeping quarters. (3) To provide the runaways with clothing, food and work. (4) To arrange for the legal status of escaping Jews by providing them with forged identity papers so they could pass as Poles.

Although the Provisional Committee was mainly active in Warsaw, it did manage to make contact with Jews and be of some service to them in other Polish cities, among them Cracow, Lublin, Kielce, Radom and Bialystok. Nevertheless, the scale of its work was minuscule: all told it was able to render assistance to only 180 persons, two-thirds of whom were children. In Warsaw there were as many as ninety people helped by the Committee; but of its work in Brzesc we have the following report: "In Brzesc a permanent branch has been established. One family has received assistance, one person has been brought to Warsaw for permanent residence, emergency financial aid has been given in a few cases." Moreover the whole work of the Committee was carried out by a mere handful of individuals and groups.[17]

The Provisional Committee's own report makes it clear that it had only the most modest means at its disposal, and that the number of its volunteers was far too small for it to be able to expand its operations. If, moreover, we consider that in the period following the Jewish deportation from Warsaw there were as many as 15–20,000 Jews seeking sanctuary in the "Aryan section" of the city and its environs, we can only conclude that the Committee had actually managed to reach fewer than one out of a hundred Jewish refugees in the region.[18]

The Jewish underground active in "Aryan" Warsaw was made up of two organizations, each having its own representative. One was the Jewish National Committee (*Zydowski Komitet Narodowy*, ZKN), whose liaison representative to the Polish underground was Dr. Adolf Berman (Borowski); excepting the *Bund*, it included all of the Jewish political and public groups in Warsaw that supported the Jewish Fighting Organization known as ZOB.[19] The second organization was the Jewish socialist *Bund*, which was represented by Leon Feiner ("Mikolaj"), a lawyer who hailed originally from Cracow. The two organizations worked very closely, and in their dealings with the Polish underground appeared as a unified body, under the guise of the "Committee for Coordination" (*Komisja Koordynacyjna* KK).[20]

Obviously the importance of the formation of a Polish organization dedicated to assisting Jews, and having the official approval of the major forces active in the Polish underground, was well appreciated in Jewish circles. Thus, Adolf Berman wrote:

> It was important to create the broadest possible coalition of parties within the circles offering assistance: first, so that the work of assistance should have the broadest possible scope, in order to increase the opportunities of rendering assistance to Jews by the greatest possible number of aid units belonging to all of the organizations; secondly, to be able to exert influence on all of the movements in the Polish underground as a whole in the struggle against anti-Semitism, extortionist practices, denunciations and the like; third, in order to maintain contact with the outside world, inform, and alert circles abroad, and get the necessary assistance from Jewish organizations for rescue activities and the armed struggle. It was important as well to put pressure on the Sikorski government, on its representation in Poland and on the ZWZ,

the "Union for Armed Struggle," so that they should end their silence
and give real assistance to the Jews and the ghetto fighters.[21]

On October 14, 1942, the following item appeared in *Rzeczpos-
polita Polska* ("The Polish Republic"), the official organ of the Polish
underground organization affiliated with the London government:

> We have been asked to announce to the public that a committee for
> public assistance to Jews who have suffered in the aftermath of the
> bestial persecutions of the Germans is being formed on the initiative of
> a number of organizations from Catholic and Democratic circles. The
> committee will attempt, within the limits of its capacities and of the
> means and possibilities avaliable to it in the conditions of existence
> under occupation, to render assistance to the victims of Nazi
> violence.[22]

The language of the announcement is restrained regarding the nature of the assistance the Committee intended to give. More important, it neglects to mention that the initiative to found the
Committee was undertaken with the sanction of the Delegate.
Nevertheless, the mere appearance of the announcement in *Rzecz-
pospolita Polska* was important, since the item's publication alone
was an indication that an official position, at least of sorts, was
being taken.

On December 4,1942, the Provisional Committee disbanded and
the Council for Aiding Jews was established. The title taken by the
Provisional Committee on being formed would indicate that the
Committee had been conceived as a temporary body meant to function only until such time as a permanent organization should be
established. Nevertheless, the Committee's transformation into the
Council for Aiding Jews seems not to have been accomplished
without some friction. At all events, this is the situation revealed in
the Provisional Committee's own report:

> The leadership of the [Provisional] Committee did not join the
> Council—except for the political representative of the Polish
> Renascence Front, who undertook to serve as temporary delegate act-
> ing as liaison with Delegate (of the Government). . . And the following
> are the reasons for the disbandment of the Provisional Committee: First
> of all a shortage of adequate financial resources, making for an
> ambiguous situation so far as the organizations and persons included
> in the Provisional Committee were concerned. Additionally, there is
> the propaganda campaign being undertaken—without the least regard
> for the means actually at hand—among the Jewish public by official
> elements. (The General Department of the Delegate and the Section of
> Jewish Affairs in the Information Bureau BIP;[23] lack of the possibility of
> coooperation with the representatives of the Jewish organizations (in-
> troduction of political motives into work which is exclusively one of
> welfare).[24]

Hence the Provisional Committee, and particularly its Catholic contingent, was intent on limiting its acativity to saving lives and rendering humanitarian assistance.[25] In consequence its leadership could hardly approve of the Committee's activities being taken advantage of by the elements in the Polish underground in order to propagandize in their own behalf and make sweeping commitments; what is more, the very men who were making use of the operations of the Provisional Committee for the purposes of publicity, especially abroad, had failed to put at the disposal of the Committee the funds necessary for it to continue its work.

Especially vexing to the Committee's Catholic membership was the lack of understanding it encountered in its dealings with Jewish representatives. The source of the problem was the differing conceptions by the two sides concerning the purposes of the Provisional Committee: for the Jews it was the political aspect of the Committee's operations which was highly important, whereas those who had created the Committee had intended for it to concentrate entirely on welfare. The fact, moreover, that both Jewish representatives belonged to Socialist factions—with Berman a member of the Left *Poale-Zion* and Feiner of the *Bund*—could only have sharpened the differences and deepened mutual distrust. In any case, Berman contends that the reason the Catholics finally withdrew from the *Zegota* was that they would not agree to allow Jews to participate in the Council's work or to having them included in the organization's leadership.[26]

At this point we might consider for a moment the more profound, personal motives that led Polish Gentiles to come to the rescue of Jews—an activity which was hazardous in the extreme, and enjoyed no priority in the Polish underground movement; nor was it a popular cause among the Polish masses, so that those who had made it their vocation could hardly have expected to be treated as national heroes.[27]

One of those active in the *Zegota* group was Irena Sendler ("Jolanta"), who had made the rescue of Jewish children her particular speciality. In her memoirs, written after the war, she speaks of the decisive role played by her parental home in unfluencing her course of action. She writes: "My father thought of himself as one of the first Polish Socialists. He was a doctor. We lived in Otwock. His patients were mostly poor Jews. So that neither Jewish customs nor the poverty of Jewish homes were unfamiliar to me."[28] Jan Zabinski, too, was active in *Zegota.* But his efforts on behalf of Jews included more than the work he did in connection with the Council: he and his family rescued and sheltered Jews on their own initiative as well. In this Zabinski was able to make use of his position as director of the Warsaw Zoo—a post which put him at a relative advantage in procuring hiding places and food for the Jews he took under this care. In accounting for his gallant conduct during the occupation he tells us in his memoirs: "I am a democrat and a Pole. My actions were and are the product of the unique spiritual climate absorbed by me in the course of the progressive-humanistic education I received in my parents' home and in the Kreczmar Secondary School where I had studied."[29] About Julian Grobelny (Trojan"), who headed *Zegota* and was a member of the Socialist faction in the underground, we are told, "he was a man of a generous heart who devoted himself unstintingly to saving those for whom death lay in wait at every turn."[30] Miriam Peleg-Marianska was representative for the Jews in *Zegota's* Cracow branch, most of whose members were Polish Socialists. In her memoirs she observes about her colleagues: ". . . from the first moment I sensed what was most essential about these people; they had assumed the burden of working in the Council for Aiding Jews not as a duty, but out of deep conviction and humane feeling.[31]

From the evidence it would therefore seem that there were two principal factors in the lives of these remarkable Polish men and women which accounted in some measure for their choice of affiliating themselves with *Zegota:* (1) Prior acquaintance and intimacy with Jews, and (2) education and progressive political background, which had made them sensitive to the outrage being committed and predisposed them to help the victims.

The individuals who undertook to rescue Jews, not only in Poland but elsewhere in occupied Europe, came from a variety of social backgrounds. They ranged from members of the intelligentsia who were ideologically motivated, to ordinary working people and peasants who were moved to take action out of either emotional outrage or deep religious çonviction. Many were motivated by a sense of personal loyalty to come to the aid of a Jewish friend, or of a co-worker or business associate with whom they had developed personal ties. But in the case of the people active in *Zegota* we are dealing with a commitment that was more inclusive: their conduct was neither the result of a sudden surge of emotion nor determined by a personal tie to a particular Jewish friend or Jewish family, but arose out of the combination of their personal motives and their sense of public and patriotic duty.

The attitude of the leaders of the political underground in Poland toward *Zegota* and its activities is another subject requiring an elucidation of motives. After all, why should the Delegate's Office of the Polish Government have given its blessings to the formation of a group dedicated to helping Jews, and moreover have put the group under its own aegis and, ultimately, even integrated it into the organizational structure of the Polish underground? The claim that in pursuing such a course Polish underground authorities were merely fulfilling their obligations to Polish citizens who happened to be Jewish fails to account for the fact that during almost three years of German occupation preceding the establishment of *Zegota,* the Polish underground had done nothing either to protect Jews or to ease their suffering.

Without doubt at least some of the Polish underground leadership under the command of the London-based government were deeply shaken by the mass annihilation of Jews taking place after the stage of the segregation, economic oppression, forced labor and starvation. The fact that the victims of the mass murders being perpetrated on Polish soil included not only Polish Jews, but Jews who had been brought to Poland for that purpose from all over Europe, certainly added to the horror. Nevertheless, sober political calculation—rather than compassion for the victims—underlay the arguments used to justify official recognition of *Zegota* and the transfer to it of fixed sums of money. Thus in testimony recorded in 1948. Tadeusz Rek, one of the deputy chairman of *Zegota* and the Peasant Party's representative on the Council, observed; "It is my impression that the Delegate of the Government was acting on the basis of political considerations. I know, incidentally, that without London, decisions on matters of principle were no longer taken. The essential motive behind the *Zegota* project was expressed by the motto: It has to be done because the matter is in Poland's best interests."[32]

As news of the mass deportations of Jews from Warsaw reached the West toward the end of 1942, the significance of the "Final Solution" could no longer be in doubt. Public opinion in the free world had become aroused, and pressures were being brought to bear on British and American statesmen. In November 1942, the Polish National Council issued a proclamation to the free nations describing the outrages committed by the German occupation government, and making a particular point of the massacre of Jews being carried out within Polish territory.[33] Requests began pouring in to the Poles from both Jewish and non-Jewish organizations asking them to exert their influence and use whatever means they had at their disposal in order to reverse the terrible fate that was overtaking the Jews. Finally, in December 1942, Anthony Eden read an Allied declaration in the British Parliament which confirmed that mass murder was being committed, and warned the perpetrators that they would be made to account for their deeds.

THE COUNCIL'S MAKE-UP AND ACTIVITIES

Politically, the Council for Aiding Jews was composed of centrist and left-wing parties loyal to the Government-in-Exile in London. However, the members of *Zegota* had not joined merely to represent a particular political faction, but had committed themselves on personal grounds. Tadeusz Rek, for example, reveals in his memoirs that his own movement, the Polish Peasants' Party *(Stronnictwo Ludowe),* which had been less than enthusiastic about the undertaking, was experiencing difficulty in finding anyone within its ranks willing to accept the job of representing it on the Council; it took some time before Rek was approached by his party and his acceptance of the position to be confirmed.[34]

The chairman of *Zegota,* until his arrest by the Gestapo in 1944, was Julian Grobelny ("Trojan"), a member of the Polish Socialist Party (PPS). Serving as his deputies were Tadeusz Rek ("Różycki") of the Peasants' Party, and Leon Feiner ("Mikolaj") of the Jewish Socialist *Bund.* The position of secretary was held by Dr. Adolf Berman, who was the Jewish National Council's representative in the *Zegota* directorate. And the highly responsible post of treasurer was filled by Ferdynand Arczynski ("Marek"), representing the Democratic Party.[35]

During the period of the Provisional Committee, the Young Catholics were represented by Wladyslaw Bienkowski ("Jan", "Wencki", "Kalski"), and it was a member of the same movement who was the only one from the Catholic factions to serve in *Zegota* when it replaced the Committee and the Catholics withdrew as a group. Bienkowski joined the Council as the Delegate's representative to the directorate, a post which he had accepted only temporarily at first, but to which in time he was permanently appointed, becoming concurrently chief of the Jewish Section in the Delegate's Office. Whenever Bienkowski was absent from Council meetings, his replacement as Delegate's representative was Wladyslaw Bartoszewski ("Ludwik)".

In 1944 the directorate of *Zegota* was joined by Piotr Galewski ("Piotr") as represesntative of the left faction of the Polish Socialists (RPPS). There were two others who entered the directorale later as well—Emilia Hiz ("Barbara") from the Democratic Party and Stefan Sendlak ("Stefan"), of whom the latter was the

Council's liaison agent with its branches outside of Warsaw.

The directorate had a team of permanent *Zegota* activists from which to draw upon for its work. The secretarial work, for example, was done by two women members of the Democratic Party, Lawyer Paulina Hausman ("Janina") and Janina Wasowicz ("Ewa"). And in the directorates minutes, as well as the memoirs and testimonies of its members, we find Zofia Rudnicka ("Alicja"), Tadeusz Sarnecki, Irena Sendler ("Jolanta") and others mentioned as working permanently for the Council.

The presidency of the Council had a control board whose members were Adolf Berman, Tadeusz Rek and Leon Feiner. The Council also contained a number of special departments, of which each was responsible for a particular aspect of the organization's work, such as legalization, finance, housing, defense against extortion, information, rescue of children, operations in provincial towns, and provision of clothing.[36]

Of the four major political parties in the coalition of the London based Government-in-Exile—that is to say the Socialist, Peasant Party's, National Democrats or *Endeks*, and Labor Party—only the first two were represented in *Zegota*. Of the two remaining outside the Council, the Labor Party was only a minor faction whose inclusion among the "big four" of the coalition was mostly due to the authority wielded by its leading member, General Wladyslaw Sikorski, who was prime minister. On the other hand, the *Endeks* were a very powerful party with deep roots in Poland's social and political life. They are also the traditional anti-Semitic party of modern Poland, so that their absence from the Council was anything but accidental. Yet, though the *Endeks* refrained from helping the Council in its work, they had done nothing to prevent it from being formed.

Another group conspicuous by its absence from the Council was the Communists. Their failure to participate had nothing to do with ideology, however. The reason for Communist non-participation in *Zegota* was that they had been excluded by the political groups which were subservient to the London Government-in-Exile, and refused either to recognize the P.P.R. or cooperate with it in any underground context whatever—social, political or military.

Hence the Jews—and particularly the National Jewish Committee, which had close ties with the Communists—were constrained to keep their contacts with the P.P.R. secret from both the Delegate's Office and political parties represented in *Zegota*. How difficult it made things for the latter can be judged from Adolf Berman's observation that while he was on the "Aryan side" of

Warsaw he led a threefold underground existence: first as a Jew residing illegally among Poles; then as someone actually engaged in underground work—an activity which was hazardous for Pole and Jew alike; and finally by the fact that he had to keep secret his contacts with one set of Poles in the underground resistance from all of the others.[37]

The Council defined the nature and scope of its activities as follows:

> The Council's function is to succor Jewish victims of the occupier's extermination campaign, and to do so by rescuing (them) from death by legalization, offering refuge, granting material assistance—or, where desirable, finding (them) gainful employment on which to subsist—maintaining funds and distributing grants of money; in sum, activities either directly or indirectly needed in the area of assistance.[38]

But as we shall see, *Zegota* did more than offer immediate assistance: at various times and in particularly critical periods it appealed directly to the Delegate's Office and the political parties to join in the efforts to rescue and assist Jews.

The members of the Council met at regular intervals. According to the Council's official report, twenty-six plenary sessions, thirty-five meetings of the directorate and fifteen of the control board had taken place in the period up to October 1943.[39] And Berman writes that between December 1942 and January 1945 there were sixty-one meetings of the Council plenum, over a 100 of the directorate and over thirty of the control board.[40] The Council had several apartments at its disposal, and a number of "mail drops" at which messages and funds were delivered and picked up.

Zegota was mostly active in Warsaw, where there were the greatest number of Jews in hiding. However, the organization did make efforts to expand its operations to include other regions in Poland. In March 1943 the Council succeeded in setting up a branch in Cracow, from where it was able to reach other parts of West Galicia. It also established a branch in the city of Lwow, and there was work done under its auspices in the region of Lublin as well.

Until May 1943, when the last of the Jews had been removed from the Warsaw Ghetto and the entire area was leveled, the Council had maintained only a very tenuous contact with Jews in captivity. For the most part it concerned itself with Jews seeking refuge on the "Aryan side" of the city, among whom there were Jewish converts to Catholicism, who were categorized as Jews by Nazi racial laws. Only occasionally did *Zegota* agents make contact with Jews in the labor camps, and in some isolated instances they even managed to supply relief, if only of a limited kind, to Jewish camp inmates.

The business of providing Jews with refuge was exceedingly difficult, and fraught with danger for everyone concerned. Because of the punishment awaiting a Pole caught sheltering Jews in his home, *Zegota* agents were constantly confronted by the dilemma of having to decide whether or not to reveal to a Pole with a room or an apartment to rent, that a prospective tenant was Jewish. The advantages gained by deception were that it kept rent within reason and spared the landlord the unpleasantness of living in constant dread of betrayal. But keeping the landlord in ignorance courted disaster in the long run; an unwitting landlord could hardly be relied on to take precautions against discovery, and his tenant, being left to carry the burden of his disguise entirely on his own, might buckle under the strain and give himself away. Nevertheless, with anti-Jewish feeling running high in Poland and the risks involved in harboring Jews being so great, few Poles could be found who would knowingly provide a Jew with shelter.

The very attempt to pass a Jew off as a Pole depended on his physical features and mastery of the Polish language—qualifications which only a part of Polish Jews could meet. But even those Jews who looked Polish and spoke the language well had additionally to be provided with very sizeable sums of money in order to survive. As for those who were unable to disguise their identity, hide-outs had to be arranged where they could be kept out of sight of neighbors, visitors, and even relatives of those whose apartments were being used to conceal Jewish runaways.

The one service which the Council was able to provide on an extensive basis was the regular distribution of financial aid. According to *Zegota's* leaders, payments of survival allowances in limited amounts were made available to all Jews in hiding who were known to either the Council or any of its affiliated groups. The size of the grant varied according to the resources available to the organization at the time it was given, but it averaged out to a monthly allowance of about 500 zlotys. The amount was certainly too small to cover even minimum living costs and constituted, in the words of one of the Council's leading members a "symbolic gesture" from the Polish people to the Jews.[41] And yet, inadequate though the allowance was, to its recipients it had very real value not only as a dependable source of regular income, but as an expression of moral support. Moreover, where there was a special need, as in the case of children, the amount of money was increased; and in emergencies when informers made an immediate change of location necessary, quite substantial amounts were given in a lump sum as one-time grants.[42]

It would be difficult to say exactly how many Jews received monthly allowances from the Council. The estimates range from tens of thousands of Jews with whom *Zegota* came into contact in the cities and labor camps to the figure of 4,000 given be Adolf Berman, which is the one most often cited in the publications on the Council.[43] However, a check of the sources indicates that even Berman's estimate is far too high. The Council's official report on its activities up to October 1943 states that in the early phase of its work it gave financial assistance to between 200 and 300 persons, and that by the end of that period the number of recipients had grown to 1,000 and subsequently to 1000–1500.[44] During the last months of 1943 and the whole of 1944 there was a significant increase in the funds being put at the Council's disposal, and there was also a corresponding increase in the number of beneficiaries receiving monthly allowances. But even so, when we consider that the most *Zegota's* resources ever amounted to was four million zlotys during a very brief span of merely a few months (or quadruple the amount of its October budget)[45] and that the highest monthly sum it had ever received was two million zlotys—and this only on a few occasions—it is difficult to conceive of how the organization could have managed even in the best of times to distribute an average of 500 zlotys monthly to 4,000 beneficiaries. To have done so, the Council would have needed to draw on its entire budget for that purpose alone, whereas the available documents show that the Council paid out sizable sums of money in increased allowances to individuals being given special consideration and to children, and in order to defray administrative costs and the expenses incurred by its other activities, such as the procurement of forged identity papers and the printing of its informational material. We have at hand no document containing a breakdown of *Zegota's* expenses, so that there is no way to determine what portion of its budget the Council actually used for subsistence grants. But it seems likely that although there were very many persons who might have received sporadic financial aid from the Council, the number of individuals benefiting from regular monthly allowances could hardly have reached half the figure of 4,000 even at the height of *Zegota's* activity.

The principal beneficiaries of *Zegota's* aid were the Jews hiding in Warsaw. Ringelbum—whose evidence dates from early 1944, when he and his wife and son shared a hideout with scores of other Jews in one of the suburbs of Warsaw—puts the number of Jews in the city who were dependent on *Zegota's* assistance at 300 families.[46] The most important branch of the council outside of Warsaw was the one in Cracow, whose operations extended into the surrounding region. According to its chairman, Stanislaw Dobrowolski ("Stan"), "Regular material assistance (had reached) hundreds of persons in hiding. In time the number reached over 1000 individuals."[47] But his claim is hardly compatible with the data contained in *Zegota's* report covering the period up to October 1943, which sets the number of persons being helped by its Cracow branch at approximately 100; further, it seem highly unlikely that in the period following October 1943 the number of persons who came under the care of the Cracow branch should have increased by a multiple of ten.

Available lists of persons receiving aid from the Council show a very large turnover in names.[48] It can be assumed that some of the people had dropped out because they had been caught. There were those, too, who stopped receiving allowances because they left Warsaw for towns and villages which were outside the sphere of the Council's operations. One of *Zegota's* cells included in its lists also names of Jews who had never received monthly allowances from the organization at any time, and who testified after the war that they had no need of such assistance and would never have accepted it even had it been offered.[49] And from time to time names were added of Jews who had escaped to Warsaw from labor camps, or who had made their way to the city from provincial towns, and still others who had contacted *Zegota* workers at a very late stage in the organization's activities. It may very well be that the disproportionate number of persons claimed as having received regular allowances from *Zegota* was the result of the inclusion of all beneficiaries in every category of assistance being offered by the Council.

In addition to *Zegota*, there were also Jewish underground groups active on the "Aryan side" of Warsaw, and they, too, offered financial assistance to Jews in hiding. According to the claims of underground operatives working for the Jewish National Committee, that organization distributed regular allowancees to between 5,500 and 6,000 persons; the same sources credit the *Bund* with having given financial assistance in another 1,500 to 2,000 cases.[50] Also the numbers presented by the Jewish organization seem to be very exaggerated. Most of the Jews who received aid from these organizations were themselves members of one of the factions in these movements or had made contact with their representatives. The Jewish underground organizations received amounts of money from Jewish sources abroad, whose contributions were forwarded by the Polish Government-in-Exile in London, and these funds were used by the Jewish underground not only in its financial assistance program for Jewish refugees in hiding, but for such purposes as financing their attempts to reach Jews interned in the camps and purchasing arms for the fighting units in the ghettos. The distribution of subsistence grants was carried out either by Jewish agents able to pass as Gentiles and move about freely, or by trustworthy Poles, some of whom were simultaneously engaged in doing the same work for *Zegota.*

Quite likely the figures claimed by Jewish groups listing the number of people receiving living allowances from them are inflated as well.

For the purpose of this study some 200 testimonies and memoirs of Jewish survivors who had hidden out in the "Aryan" part of Warsaw for varying lengths of time have been examined.[51] In only five cases out of a hundred is there any mention of regular allowances having been received from either *Zegota* or the Jewish underground. There is reason to believe that some of the survivors may have neglected to mention the fact that they were recipients of allowances from underground groups because the conditions under which the underground operated prevented them from knowing who their benefactors were.

The Government's Delegate and the Jewish underground were the principal sources of *Zegota's* finances—with the bulk of the money coming in monthly installments from the Delegate, and smaller amounts being contributed by the Jewish organizations. The secret report sent to London in May 1944 by the Delegate's representative on the Council, Witold Bienkowski, contains a detailed account of the contributions turned over by the Delegate's Office to the Council in the period from January 1943 to May 1944. There is no documentation of this kind for the period following May 1944, because with the outbreak of the Polish revolt in Warsaw in August of that year, the Council's organizational structure collapsed.

Bienkowski's report gives the following breakdown of the sums of money received by the Council:

January 1943	- 150,000 zlotys
February, March 1943	- 300,000 zlotys per month
April, May 1943	- 400,000 zlotys per month
April 1943	- Special grant of 500,000 zlotys[52]
June, July, August	
September, October 1943	- 550,000 zlotys per month
November, December 1943	- 750,000 zlotys per month
January, February,	
March, April, May 1944	- 1,000,000 zlotys per month[53]

In all, *Zegota* was active over a period of twenty-one or twenty-two months, and for the seventeen which are accounted for in Bienkowski's report, the Council's average monthly income amounted to 661,765 zlotys—or about $4,000. Despite the fact that we have no extant official record of the amounts of money received by *Zegota* from the Government between June of 1944 and the liberation in early 1945, Polish sources claim that the Delegate's Office increased its allotments to the Council by one million zlotys beginning in August 1944, when the uprising in Warsaw was at its height. So that it would seem reasonable to assume that the amount received by *Zegota* during at least a few of the months following August 1944 was as high as two million zlotys.[54] However, with the city having become a battlefield and being daily reduced to rubble, it is most unlikely that the Council could have kept up its routine work of distributing regular allowances to Jews concealed at the permanent addresses contained in the organization's lists. Probably the money received by the Council at this time was used as an emergency fund and distributed to Jews being evacuated from the city, and among the small circle of Jewish activists in *Zegota*.

According to the same Polish sources, the Council was supposed to have received six million zlotys, earmarked for aid to Jews, in December 1944 from the Government authority in the underground, and another eight million zlotys in November.[55] These totals greatly exceed the regular allotment. Surprisingly, we find no mention made of the receipt of sums of money on the order claimed to have been sent in the last months of 1944. Rather, the evidence points to *Zegota's* being in very serious financial straits at this time, and we find the Council protesting about the situation to the authorities in the strongest terms. So, for example, on December 15, 1944, the directorate of the Council sent a memorandum to the Delegate calling attention to the fact that there had been a favorable response to appeals made to London for funds, and that Jewish and non-Jewish groups had collected large sums of money to be used for rescuing the last remnant of Jews in Poland. The authors of the memorandum then go on the complain:

> Regrettably, although this aid has long since been sent into the country, addressed either to the Council or the J[ewish] organizations, it has not reached us to date, and the work being done by the Council continues to have the character of a marginal operation which fails to reach the great bulk of needy persons belonging to the most oppressed section of the population in Poland. The situation is being made worse by the following facts: 1. the Jewish organizations in the country have not received the sums that were approved abroad for delivery, and have in fact ceased to finance the activity of the Council during the past

half year; 2. the monthly grant recently approved by His Excellency the Prime Minister and the Delegate—i.e., the same amount as was disbursed before the rebellion, our reference here being only to the routine monthly allowance—cannot now, with living expenses calamitously high and apartment rents escalating due to the destruction in Warsaw, be made to serve as an equivalent of the assistance which was given until August of this year.[56]

And on the 23rd of December 1944 the Council again appealed for urgently needed financial assistance.[57] Clearly then, the millions of zlotys referred to in postwar Polish sources had in fact failed to reach the Council in the critical months of severe distress that preceded the liberation.

We should now consider, if only briefly, the other source of the Council's finances—namely, the funds of the Jewish underground organizations.

In each of the months of July and August 1943, the Jewish National Committee contributed 100,000 zlotys to *Zegota*; in September the amount was increased to 150,000 zlotys. In October the Jewish National Committee and the *Bund* made a joint contribution in the amount of 100,000 zlotys; and in the same month both organizations gave, in addition to their routine contribution, a sum of 140,000 zlotys to the Polish Socialists, for aiding Jews in the provinces. In December 1943, the Jewish representatives on *Zegota's* directorate announced they were putting 500,000 zlotys at the Council's disposal.[58]

Following the arrest in early January 1944 of Adolf Berman ("Borowski"), who had been secretary of both *Zegota* and the Jewish National Committee, stricter security measures were instituted in the Council. The Council's leading members took new aliases, and no clear picture emerges of the size of the Jewish underground's contributions to *Zegota* in the Council's minutes available to us from the time of Berman's arrest to the last of them, dated May 18, 1944.[59] As for the second half of 1944, we know that the Council received no special allocations from the Jewish underground organizations, because the money which had been collected for them abroad, and was thought to have been sent on from London to Poland, had failed to reach them.

The money collected by Jewish organizations abroad for the Jewish underground in Poland was sent from London through Polish underground channels, and the fact that Jewish underground groups had their own independent sources for funds seems to have put a strain on relations between the Delegate and the Council. In September 1943, Adolf Berman was moved to observe at a meeting of the Council that "lately there has been a cooling in the attitude of the Delegate toward the Council. Perhaps, this arises from the fact that the Jewish organizations are receiving sums of money from abroad."[60] And in November 1943, Delegate's Representative to the Council Witold Bienkowski suggested that the differing spheres of assistance work in which the Council and the Jewish National Committee were engaged should be defined. Bienkowski claimed that the principal beneficiaries of the Jewish National Committee's funds were members of the parties affiliated with it, and proposed that all Jews in hiding should receive the same assistance and the same degree of care from the organizations in the underground.[61] None of our sources specify what actually lay behind Bienkowski's criticism, but it may have been inspired by complaints reaching the Delegate from assimilated Jews and converts that persons associated with factions in the Jewish underground were receiving double assistance or sums which exceeded the aid being received from the Council.

At a meeting on October 8, 1943, the Council was informed that a contribution of $25,000 from "an international Jewish organization in America"[62] had arrived in Poland through underground channels, and that the money had been given with explicit instructions for it to be used for assisting Jews living in concealment among Poles. On the Delegate's Office's decision, $2,000 were detached from the amount and handed over to peasants living in the area of Lublin,[63] and the remainder was put at the disposal of the Council.[64] With the arrival of so large a sum, in addition to the significant increase in the joint allocations then being received by the Council, Zegota's economic situation took a more prosperous turn, and the organization was able to expand its operations. According to a Polish source, the Council's budget reached two million zlotys in January, and then declined in the following months to 1.3 million in February and 1.2 million in March 1943. Zegota's straitened circumstances in January forced it to reduce its subsistence grants, notwithstanding the decline which was taking place in the value of money—a situation which drew complaints from the organization's agents in the field who were in direct contact with the people under the Council's care.[65]

The Polish historian residing in London, Kazimierz Iranek-Osmecki, has attempted to estimate the total amount of money forwarded from London to the Jewish underground in Poland, and of the sums given by the Delegate to Zegota, in his highly apologetic book, He Who Saves One Life.[66] His figures are quite high, and greatly exceed the total of allocations and grants recorded as having been received in both the accounts of the Council and those of the

Jewish underground groups. Iranek-Osmecki appears not to have troubled to check his sources in order to determine whether or not all of the decisions to send the allotments were actually acted upon, or, if they were sent, whether the money always reached the people it was intended for. There are cases on record of money sent through underground channels or dropped from the air which was lost *en route*. However, before any conclusions can be reached on the subject, an examination has to be undertaken to determine the sums of money involved, and the dates on which the deliveries were dispatched as well as their ultimate fate.

"LEGALIZATION," OR FORGED DOCUMENTS

One of the principal activities of *Zegota* was to supply false documents to Jews who were either disguised as Poles or were being hidden in Polish homes. Both the Polish police and the various branches of the German police carried out frequent identity checks, entrapments and roundups, and every resident of Poland was required to possess a variety of personal documents. Besides his identity papers, every person had to carry work papers, if only as a guarantee against seizure for forced labor in Germany. As a general rule, a birth or baptismal certificate was the principal document that determined eligibility for any of the others, including identity papers and residence permits.

During the occupation a regular black market in forged documents had developed on the "Aryan side" of Warsaw. The prices of forged documents were fixed according to their type and the degree of "cover" they could provide for their bearer. It was not only Jewish fugitives who were in need of false papers in wartime Poland: the market's clientele also included, members of the Polish underground who were on the occupation authorities' wanted list, public figures seeking anonymity, and persons engaged in any of the variety of illegal occupations and activities flourishing at the time.

There were two principal categories of forged documents being produced—those providing the bearer with a real "cover," and those offering none or only partial "cover." Documents of the first category were naturally in greatest demand and very rare: they bore the names of real persons who had fled the country without the knowledge of the authorities, or had died or been killed without that fact having become known to the Germans. For Jews ideal "cover" consisted of a birth certificate bearing the signature of either a village priest or of a provincial official from a remote region, and made out in the name of either a deceased infant or of someone who had been born in the place indicated on the certificate but had disappeared without a trace. Documents such as these, containing authentic data, were naturally difficult to come by, and were procured only by a very few Jews fortunate enough to have the right connections or to be able to pay for them.

Hence the most common variety of forged documents were those containing fictitious data. These were actually manufactured by printing up blanks in imitation of official forms, and then fitting them out with forged seals and signatures. The results were convincing enough to pass cursory inspection, but could be spotted by officials of policemen experienced in handling documents. Natuarally, if such a document found its way into the office where it was supposed to have been issued, discovery was a dead certainty. It goes without saying that once the forgery was exposed, the bearer of the document fell under immediate suspicion of being a Jew.

Sometimes the underground was able to get hold of limited numbers of authentic blank official forms, supplied to them by office employees loyal to the resistance. But even forgeries carried out on official blanks would not hold up to careful inspection. So that in the case of persons with special priority, the underground made an effort to procure documents which had been legally registered, and to which an official had somehow been induced unwittingly to add his signature. Finally, whatever the degree of authenticity of the form, the forgery was completed by the addition of the bearer's alias, personal data and photograph.

It was advisable for a Jew planning to escape from the ghetto to live under cover on the "Aryan side" to equip himself with a set of false documents beforehand. Many, however—perhaps even most—of those who made their way into "Aryan" Warsaw had fled the Ghetto in haste, having had neither time nor any thought for forged papers. Moreover, the ·problem of the acquisition of documents was, more often than not, an ongoing one for Jews. It was part of the experience of every Jewish fugitive living among Poles to come either under direct threat of an extortionist, or to run into someone to whom he was known before the war, and this on more than one occasion. When this happened he would have to make immediate arrangements for a change of address and another job, and to procure a new set of forged documents as well. The sad fact of the matter was that a Jew living secretly among Gentiles was constantly finding himself in need of acquiring some document, of one kind or another.

The members of *Zegota* took upon themselves the task of obtaining and manufacturing forged documents in bulk for Jewish fugitives. Although the undertaking cost less than others the Council was engaged in, it was very risky work involving a relatively large number of Polish Gentiles who had to be taken into confidence.

In the report covering the Council's activities up to October 1943, the following is said on the subject of "legalization":

> Legalization is a matter of the utmost importance. In this department the Council has contacted an appropriate and well-run bureau which prepares the documents required, such as baptismal certificates, identity papers (Polish), identity cards (Kennkarten), and many other kinds. The Council supplies these documents to all Jews who request them (through the appropriate organizations) [and] brings documents into the field at no charge whatever, although the Council pays the said agency 30-40 thousand zlotys per month. The number of documents supplied by the Council during the period under review comes to a few thousand.[67]

In the chapter entitled "A Jew on the Aryan Side," Adolf Berman gives us a detailed account of what the enterprise involved:

> ... in the early phase, the Council had availed itself of the secret legalization cells in the other underground organizations. But this proved to be inadequate and inconvenient, and the Council therefore organized within its own domain a "factory" for the manufacture of thousands of birth certificates, baptismal certificates, marriage certificates, prewar identity papers, "identification certificates" (Kennkaerten) belonging to the period of the occupation, residence certificates, a variety of work cards, etc. In certain cases—those of the highest priority—the Council also had on hand governmental documents belonging to German institutions, including documents of the SS and Gestapo. These documents were of the highest quality. According to need, documents would arrive blank, and were then filled in, down to the last detail and with a precision that could hardly be matched, mostly to the specifications ordered by the secretariat of the Council, which coordinated the thousands of orders that came in from all of the Polish and Jewish underground organizations, as well as from the assistance cells affiliated with the Council. This "factory" for documents was run by a former mayor of one of the cities in Poland. He had an expert knowledge of this type of work, which he carried out with dedication and good faith. Unfortunately he fell into the hands of the Gestapo and was shot. Those working in the legalization bureau risked their lives day and night. They kept their weapons close by all the time, cocked and ready for use, and not a few died at their posts. The Council gave all of these documents away to Jews at no charge. Thousands of documents were distributed in Warsaw and its environs, and thousands sent out to towns in the provinces, to camps and even to Jews hiding in other cities.[68]

Until the end of 1943, the Council appears to have relied in its legalization activities on the services of an underground cell that specialized in forging documents for various sections of the resistance, among which *Zegota* was the principal client. There exists a document, dating from September 1943, describing the operations of this so-called "bureau"—or, more accurately, clandestine workshop for forged documents—which the Council eventually transferred to the control of the Delegate Bureau. The document includes the following description of its operations:

> This bureau has been collaborating with us for the past eight months, and its services to the Council have been of inestimable value . . . . The bureau employs ten people who are, organizationally speaking, disciplined and also possess a remarkable ideological consciousness . . . . They charge on the basis of cost outlay, so that the price of each document fluctuates form 35 to 80 zlotys. The bureau serves a range of official cells representing all political persuasions (excepting foreign ones);[69] nevertheless it is the Council which is its biggest customer.[70]

By the end of 1943, the Council's enthusiasm for its joint venture with the legalization bureau had perceptibly cooled. In August the directorate of *Zegota* was beginning to feel that "the legalization bureau had its positive and negative aspects," and it appointed one of its members to negotiate with the bureau to try to eliminate the problems.[71] Then, in December 1943, the directorate concluded that "it was apparent that a new, independent cell for legalization must be established, or contact made with other legalization cells.[72]

Finally, in the beginning of 1944, the Council set up a legalization facility of its own, concerning which Mark Arczynski, the Council treasurer, relates:

> . . . in its entirety (six person) it was manned to fit the staff requirements of the Council. In the production process of the forged documents there were six persons permanently employed (for planning and execution) under the management of Leon Weiss ("Leon") . . . Two methods were used to obtain the forms: either authentic forms were obtained for the relevant offices, or examples of authentic forms photographed. The material was run off on the Democratic Party's clandestine printing press at 41 Nowy Swiat Street. There was a special problem in procuring paper and cardboard of the same color and weight [as the originals]. The seals were prepared by expert engravers, who made faithful copies from photographs of the original German patterns. Two of our workers were specialists at forging signatures, to the extent that signatures of German high officials were transcribed without resorting to copies . . . . A separate team was engaged in adding the names of holders of forged documents to the German registers and card files . . . The headquarters on 4, Pius Street was disguised by an antique shop located at the front and a well concealed door leading to a second room. The office, which contained all of the equipment necessary for the work, was always in a state of battle readiness. Our clandestine workers kept submachine guns and hand grenades next to the tools on their workbenches.[73]

Sometime near the end of the occupation, apparently toward the close of 1944, the Gestapo succeeded in learning the identity of the legalization cell's chief, and he and several of his staff were killed.

The Cracow branch of the Council had established a legalization operation of its own. There, *Zegota* was dominated by the Polish Socialists, so that the activities of the Council and the party's local underground cell were very closely linked. In comparison, however, to the Council's legalization work in Warsaw, the operation in Cracow was somewhat less professionally run. For a time the actual work of forging documents was completed in the home of a hairdresser named Wanda Janowski, and Miriam Marianska-Peleg tells us of the highly sophisticated tactics employed by this Polish woman in order to prevent her customers from becoming suspicious of the clandestine work being carried out simultaneously on her premises. The documents that were produced by *Zegota* in Cracow were distributed to both Polish and Jewish fugitives.[74]

From the sources available to us we have no way of determining with any accuracy the number of documents *Zegota* distributed to Jews. The fact that the legalization workshops producing documents for *Zegota* were also forging them for other sections of the underground makes it almost impossible to arrive at any but a general estimate of the total figure for Jews. The report of the Council's activity up to October 1943 speaks in terms of "thousands" of documents, and Marek Arczynski thought that by the time of the outbreak of the Polish rebellion in Warsaw "at the very least 50,000 copies of documents [had been produced], of which at least 80% reached Jews who were under the care [of *Zegota*]."[75] In any case, even without being in a position to verify Arczynski's figures, we can be certain that the Council's work in the field of legalization was extensive indeed.

THE HOUSING SECTION

For a Jew planning to escape to the "Aryan side" the problem of finding shelter among Poles was overwhelming in the extreme. Although much of the business of preparing and distributing false documents was highly dangerous, the element of risk involved in providing shelter for Jews was significantly greater.

There were special difficulties that were connected to the work of providing Jews with housing. Poles who rented rooms or apartments to Jews actually were living with the seeds of their own destruction on their very premises. In the eyes of the occupation authorities, they were guilty of no ordinary, if serious, transgression, but of a captial offense deserving nothing less than death. Nor could they depend, as could others engaged in illegal activities, on the sympathy and help of their fellow countrymen, but had constantly to be on alert for betrayal by their own neighbors and by visitors to their homes. They hadn't even the consolation of belonging to an underground cell in which responsibility and risk were shared, but they and their immediate families had to bear the full brunt of troubles and dangers by themselves.

Most of the Poles who consented to let their premises to Jews did so in return for payments of very large sums of money, and had allowed their expectations of profit to outweigh any consideration of the risk they were running. Although living at the mercy of landlords whose motives were mercenary was hardly a secure arrangement for Jewish fugitives, they often had little choice in the matter. Landlords of this type sometimes did not hesitate to rid themselves of their tenants at the slightest hint of danger, and it was not uncommon for them to squeeze a tenant dry monetarily before turning him out of the house, or even delivering him into the hands of the Germans.[76]

Yet there were a significant number of landlords who rented out their apartments to Jews for money with the honest intention of maintaining their part of the bargain. But just how many of these there were we cannot determine. There were cases also of Poles giving refuge to Jewish friends; and although they may have received money in return, their conduct was principally motivated by their wish to help a friend in trouble.[77] We must keep in mind, too, that there were individual Poles, and even Polish families, who out of pure humanitarian impulse risked their lives in order to shelter Jewish fugitives whom they had encountered by chance and who were perfect strangers to them [78] Finally, there were the orphanages, monasteries and convents where Jewish children found refuge—an important subject we shall return to in another context.

Although *Zegota* had given top priority to the task of providing Jewish fugitives with shelter, its achievements in this field were not very impressive. The Council could not itself buy or rent apartments for Jews. Such a scheme would have required enormous outlays of cash that would have been lost, together with the premises, once the tenants were betrayed. The organization seems, rather, to have acted as an intermediary agent in helping Jews to secure rooms and apartments for rent. But even here the possibilities were greatly limited because of the difficulties experienced by *Zegota* in revealing the identity of tenants to prospective landlords. The Council had several premises available to it where it could put up Jewish fugitives for a few nights; there were also a number of "safe-houses" used by the underground as emergency refuges, but these were obviously unsuitable for use as permanent shelters. There is an entry in the May 6, 1943, minutes of the Council directorate referring to the fact "that the house on Rymarska will be available for use soon in which two apartments have been rented."[79] However, we are not told whether the apartments were to be used by the Council for its own work or as housing. From the testimonies of *Zegota* members we do know that the Council made use of a number of apartments for its routine work.[80]

The Council's own assessment of its achievements in this sphere is contained in its report on its operations up to October 1943:

> . . . the problem of housing is the most difficult to solve. For this reason the Council has invested a great deal of its time and resources in establishing a special housing section; unfortunately, however, [our] assistance here has been minimal.[81]

THE MEDICAL SECTION

There were special problems in providing Jews in hiding with medical attention. A Jewish fugitive who took ill was not only in very serious trouble himself, but greatly increased the difficulties confronting those who gave him shelter. Many Jewish fugitives were unable even to leave their places of refuge in order to seek medical attention, and male Jews who did have freedom of movement were prevented from going to a doctor for fear that the fact of their being circumcised would be discovered during a medical examination.

In October 1943 a number of enlightened Polish physcicians in a variety of medical specialties volunteered to make house calls to Jewish fugitives in need of medical care. Ludwik Rutkowski, the doctor responsible for coordinating the operation, describes the way in which physicians were dispatched to their patients. According to his testimony, he would first receive a request for medical attention through a member of the Council, and then send his son with instructions to the appropriate doctor. Physicians going out on such a house call sometimes took with them, in addition to their instruments and medicines, food, clothing and money for their patients. Rutkowski notes that the number of visits made in any one month ranged from only a few to several score.[82]

CHILDREN'S SECTION

Sometime in mid-1943 the Council directorate became especially concerned about the situation of Jewish children. We know that after the rebellion in the Warsaw Ghetto a number of Jewish children had managed to make their way over to the "Aryan side" on their own, and were roaming about in the streets of the city.[83] Before the rebellion, many Jewish parents had resolved to place their children with Gentiles so that at least their offspring might be saved from death. Members of the left-wing Polish political parties, unaffiliated Poles of good will, and some Catholic groups, all joined in the effort to save the lives of Jewish children. We can assume that many hundreds of Jewish children had reached the "Aryan" section of Warsaw, by one means or another.

A separate section for the care of children was established by the Council in September 1943. At a meeting of the Council's directorate on August 23, 1943, Arczynski reported concerning his contacts with the representatives of S.O.S. (*Spoleczna Organizacja Samoobrony*). The same source reveals that between 700 and 1,000 children had already been placed in various children's homes and conventual institutions. We are also told that these institutions were pressed for money, and that their ability to take more children under their care would depend on their receiving increased financial assistance. It was at this meeting that the directorate decided to create a special children's section.[84] According to the Zegota report from November 1943, we learn that

> . . . recently a special section has been established whose function is to look after orphaned children and other Jewish children in need of care and shelter [either] in institutions or among private families. This work, which has been organized under professional supervision, has begun to progress satisfactorily. The section has succeeded in having about twenty to thirty children accommodated at appropriate locations, and the prospects for continuing the work are good.[85]

Irena Sendler ("Jolanta"), the Polish woman who was in charge of the children's section, records in her memoirs the names and addresses of many women who had sheltered Jewish children until permanent refuge could be found for them. Sometimes the Catholic institutions at which they were placed were actually unaware that the children were Jewish, and the rest made a pretense of not knowing the identity of their charges. Within the institutions the children were classified as orphans or hardship cases. Irena Sendler, who was a social worker in the Warsaw municipality, tells us of the special concern shown for Jewish children by the chief of the city's department of children's welfare, Jan Dobraczynski, who is today a prominent Catholic writer in Poland. Concerning Dobraczynski's activities in helping to rescue Jewish children, Irena Sendler writes:

> Thanks to his sympathetic attitude on the question of rescuing Jewish children and his personal courage, the children were

referred—after he had signed the official form—to Church institutions as Polish children. In order to obliterate entirely all trace [of their origin], the interviews were staged, just as they were in the cases of children being placed with families. First name and surnames were changed, as well as personal histories; dramatic accounts were concocted, altering their backgrounds completely, and securing for them the greatest protection possible in those horrendous times.[86]

By February 1944, the children's section is reported as having taken under its protection ninety-nine Jewish children.[87]

Despite all of the gratitude that was felt by Jewish groups for the efforts being made to rescue Jewish children, there was a stage at which some of them began to grow suspicious of the motives behind the operation. Ringelblum, for instance, wrote in December 1942: "Among some circles a program has been realized lately for rescuing a certain number of Jewish children (a few hundred) by placing them in convents distributed throughout the country. What motives have led the priests to do this? There are three motives. *Pursuit of souls.* First, the Catholic priesthood has always exploited troubled times for Jews, such as pogroms, expulsions and the like, in order to convert older children. This is apparently a point of primary importance, even though the priesthood promises it has no intention of baptizing the children who are being taken under the protection of its institutions." We also find Adolf Berman expressing the opinion that none of Zofia Kossak-Szczucka's efforts were completely free of missionary intention.[88]

THE PUBLIC AND POLITICAL ACTIVITIFS OF ZEGOTA

The government representation on the Council, as well as some of the groups taking part in the efforts to rescue Jews, tried to limit *Zegota's* operations exclusively to the work of rendering direct assistance to Jewish fugitives. However, the Democrats and Socialists active in *Zegota* took the position that it was the Council's duty to make its voice heard on political issues having to do with the situation of Jews still in Poland. They considered it a particular task of the Council to create a climate of public opinion in the country positive to Jews who were seeking refuge among Poles, and they regarded both the working of a change in Polish attitudes and the struggle against the extortion and betrayal of Jews to be the preconditions for the success of the entire enterprise.

The Council adopted an independent stand on a number of issues, and found itself in disagreement, and sometimes at odds, with official authorities of the underground. Among such stands were: (1) its support of assistance to Jewish fighting groups: (2) its insistence that a vigorous campaign be undertaken against informers, extortionists and those who turned Jews in to the authorities; and (3) its opposton to official anti-Semitic statements published by the underground, and its demand that such statements be disowned and condemned.

On several occasions the Council published proclamations to the Polish people, and requested to have them printed in the underground newspapers of the groups represented in *Zegota*. However, there was no unaninimity among the members of the Council about the nature of the public work it ought to undertake. The Delegate's representative on the Council wanted to restrict the organization's activity wholly to assistance operations, and the representative of the Peasants' Party was opposed to having *Zegota* assume a public or political guise in any of its activities.

At a meeting in February 1943, the directorate of the Council decided to make a request to the Delegate that it publish in its own name in the underground press a call to the Polish people "to give assistance to the Jewish community."[89] In the minutes of the directorate's meeting on March 25,1943, we find a proposal "to post public announcements of the verdicts against extortionists."[90] In the same month the draft of a memorandum to the Delegate was read into the minutes of the directorate. The draft sharply criticized the inadequate budget being made available to the Council which could not even cover the organization's essential needs; it also complained about the severity of the regulations which were being imposed by the Delegate on *Zegota* and which prevented the Council from making independent and flexible use of the funds being allotted to it. The text of the memorandum draft includes the following statement:

> The Council calls attention to the fact that the field of its activity is the preservation of thousands of human lives from destruction. Hence the necessity of making every possible effort to rescue those who have been condemned to die by the barbaric occupier and [securing] their escape from the decree of annihilation is not only an obligation imposed on our people by the call of humanity and the dictates of conscience, but also involves the good name of our nation. Moreover, the Council stresses that the proper way of fulfilling those goals which the Council set for itself is also in the interests of the state: for there are advantages in rescuing not only those who have means of their own, but also those who, though at present utterly destitute, will have value to the state in the future as potential workers. . . .

In summation, the memorandum concludes, "if the work, as it has been defined above, is not made possible . . . . thereby putting into question the reason for the Council's existence, then the full responsibility will rest with the Delegate."[91]

Although the memorandum suggests no alternative plan to the aims of the Delegate, the very fact that it makes the point that the Council's work had a political dimension, and was important to the future of Poland, indicates that it had been composed with the assumption that the organization's aims included more than merely humanitarian assistance. On April 28, 1943, members of the Council directorate who had met with the Delegate reported that they had been asked on that occasion "whether the Council was a charitable body or a political one." The reply of the Council member from the Peasants' Party, Tadeusz Rek, was that the organization had a purely charitable character.[92] On July 4, 1943, the Council proposed to send the following telegram to the Polish Government-in-Exile in London:

> The German campaign of annihilation has already swallowed up the overwhelming majority of the Jewish community. The remnant continues to be killed. None of the means being used can, under present conditions of occupation, save those who have remained alive and avert the inevitable decimation that awaits them. The only possibility likely to present itself is an orderly population exchange on the basis of an international agreement. [We] the undersigned Council for Aiding Jews [in Poland] therefore urgently appeal to the Government of Poland to intercede, with all possible speed, with democratic governments [to urge them at least to negotiate] for an exchange of surviving Jews for the many German citizens still living within the territories of the Allied nations.[93]

We have no information revealing who proposed the idea of such an exchange to the directorate, or what circumstances had given rise to the proposal. It may be that the news of small groups of Jewish nationals of foreign countries having left Poland, and of the detention of Jews in the Hotel Polski for the purpose of exchanging them for Germans, had inspired some of the Council directorate with the idea of an exchange agreement of the same sort on a wider scale; the stipulation that the exchange be carried out under international auspices was intended to prevent the exchange from being reduced to a hypocritical game, as had happened in the case of the Hotel Polski affair.[94] It seems more than likely that the idea of an exchange backed by strong international guarantees was put forward either by the Jewish members of the Council directorate, or those close to them. In all events, the directorate as a whole supported the proposal, or at least all of the members gave their approval to it, if for no other reason than their despairing conviction that all of their varied efforts were inadequate to save the small remnant of Jews still alive from being exterminated.

Following its appeal to the Polish Government-in-Exile, the Council came into serious conflict with Polish authorities. We have no explicit statement of the Delegate's objections to the Council's proposal, but they apparently centered around one point: the Delegate was opposed to having the situation of Jews raised as a separate issue before an international forum—that is, to having Jews proclaimed as constituting a group apart, whose fate was distinct from that of the Polish nation as a whole, and which required immediate assistance of a kind different from that being rendered as a matter of course; moreover the Delegate insisted that the situation of Jews must be considered within the framework of the suffering being experienced by the whole nation under the German occupation government, and that the solutions to the problem had to take into account the entire Polish people.

The same attitude was taken by the decision makers in the Polish Government-in-Exile. On more than one occasion appeals from Jewish international organizations had been rejected by the Polish government, national assembly and prime minister on the grounds that no distinction could be drawn between the sufferings of Jews and non-Jews in occupied Poland, and that the "Final Solution" could not be regarded as solely a Jewish tragedy; rather Jewish interests had to be viewed as being inextricably bound up in the fate of the Polish nation as a whole. Only in a few instances were the Polish authorities in London able to reach decisions or make declarations which affected Jews. In the end the directorate was unable to agree on a position, and it was therefore decided to put off sending the telegram until such time as a solution could be agreed upon.[96]

The Council directorate devoted a special session to a discussion of the criticism of its position by the Delegate. At the meeting, the directorate's member from the Democratic Movement, Ferdinand Arczynski, argued that "even if in a purely formal respect he shared the position of the Delegate, he could not in real terms accept [the Delegate's] opinion. The Jews were now an element of Polish citizenry facing the greatest peril, and the contents of the telegram were therefore justified," Tadeusz Rek, from the Polish Peasants' Party, agreed with Arczynski that among Polish citizens it was the Jews who were threatened most, but added that Poles interned in concentration camps faced a similar threat; therefore he proposed a "broadening of the content and application of the telegram to include imperiled Poles." The chairman of *Zegota* and Socialist representative on the Council, Grobelny, was unequivocal in his support of the original text of the telegram. The Bund's representative, Leon Fajner, pointed out that the text of the telegram had been approved at a directorate meeting without anyone, including the representative of the Delegate, having expressed either objections or reservations about its contents; he then went on to insist that under the present circumstances, the Jews (who were, after all, loyal citizens of Poland) regarded the implementation of the exchange program to be the last remaining chance for their survival. And Adolf Berman, although doubting the proposal was realistic, felt that it was the Council's duty to exhaust every possibility that might lead to the rescue of the Jewish remnant in Poland. At the end of the meeting it was agreed that the decision on whether the telegram should be sent would be postponed until the next session of the directorate.[95]

The subject was taken up again on July 23, at which time Tadeusz Rek announced he was opposed to sending the telegram. Jan Binkowski, the Delegate's representative of the Council, explained that he had been moved "to take a negative stand," independent of his personal feelings about the matter, by the position taken by the Delegate after examining the proposal.

A later development in the episode of the telegram is documented in Bienkowski's letter delivered to the Council on July 17:

> . . . . I have forwarded to the Main Office of the Delegate the telegram to the Polish Republic with an appended negative observation [assessment] of my own. It seems to me that Polish citizens of Jewish nationality are not a distinct and privileged community on whose behalf it is possible to conduct negotiations in the international arena in a context separate from that of Polish citizens of Polish nationality. The question of the exchange of Polish citizens for German citizens residing in the territories of the Allies can only be considered within the frame work of a regular process of exchange. [97]

The episode brings into palpable relief the conflicting attitudes of the Council and the senior political leadership of the Polish people; it also shows us how these attitudes affected the members of the Council directorate, and brought to a halt activity aiming at a more comprehensive policy.

One subject constantly appearing on the agenda in meetings of the Council directorate was the ongoing victimization of Jews by informers, blackmailers and betrayers, whose activities had cast a pall of terror over the surviving Jewish remnant in hiding.

The problem of extortionism faced by Jews in hiding was raised at the first meeting of the representatives of the Council. The representatives of the Council received the Delegate's assurances then that "the matter would be attended to by articles in the press, warnings and notices posted in the streets."[98]

In January 1943 the Socialists addressed themselves to the Council directorate in a letter complaining that "repeated incidents are taking place with ever increasing frequency of the exploitation of the tragic situation of Jews by indecent individuals in Polish society. These incidents involve personal possessions being taken that had been given as security for safekeeping, material exploitation, extortion, and, finally, betrayal to German authorities. Under these conditions it has become essential for the Government Delegate to make a public appeal which should also appear in the entire underground press, and which should state that those guilty of the above mentioned acts will be called to account. . . ."[99]

On Frbruary 5 the council directorate warned the Government Delegate that the Jewish community would soon be facing total annihilation, and once again requested that "a call be published asking the public to give assistance to the unfortunate victims from the ghetto, and especially to grant refuge to those people." The Council asked for the publication of that appeal to be accelerated because of the imminent peril awaiting all remaining Jews.[100] On March 4, the Council received a reply to its request; the letter was signed by Bienkowski, the Delegate's representative on the Council and the man in charge of the Jewish section in the civil underground who stated that "because of the impossibility of excepting the Jewish sector from the annihilation campaign, which involves all of the citizens of the Polish Republic, there will be no special call made to the Public in the matter of assistance to Jews." And on the subject of a public appeal against extortionism, the letter went on to say that "the Delegate expresses a completely favorable attitude. . . [but] until now technical reasons have been the cause of postponing the publication."[101]

The council's next appeal to the Delegate is not clearly dated. The memorandum concerns the victimization of a Jewish member of *Zegota* active in the bureaus of the underground, Dr. Alfred, and observes that extortionism was on the increase; it speaks of the war on extortionism as "a most urgent objective, and the extirpation of this shameful evil [as] a matter of honor of our public standing." The council also recalled its earlier communication of the 25th of the month (March, apparently) asking for the posting of public announcements of death sentences carried out against extortionists, and added: "Only the method of street placards setting out the reasons for the sentences having been passed and containing a strong warning to others is likely to produce the required response and bring about the desired practical effects." The communication ends with a demand for imposing the death sentence for extortion as the only effective means of discouraging the practice. [102]

On April 6, 1943, the Council once again felt constrained to appeal for a war on extortionism, "because the evil is spreading in an alarming way, both in respect to dimensions and form. Not a day passes without a whole series of acts of extortion, the possessions of the victim being plundered to the last pennyworth. There is not a family or individual remaining who has not fallen victim to this shameful practice. There have been cases of the same families and persons falling victim to extortion two or three times . . . ."

The same communication spells out the Council's proposal for dealing with the situation: 1. To simplify procedures. 2. To publish immediately by means of placards the fact of a sentence having been carried out. 3. In the event of a sentence not having been carried out, or not yet having been implemented, a number of *fictitious* sentences should at least be announced in placards."[103]

On July 12, 1943, *Zegota's* directorate handed a letter to the Delegate's representative on the Council. Among the points raised in the letter was the directorate's decision at its July 11 meeting to ask the Delegate's representative to inquire at Headquarters for the Civilian Struggle (Komenda Walki Cywilnej) about the progress of extortion trials then being held at the special underground court. The Council requested a list of cases which had been prosecuted to date, and information about the number of sentences passed and the number that had actually been carried out."This material is needed by the Council," the letter goes on to say, "for it has to consider how it may continue to operate under the present calamitous situation of rampant extortionism, which is wholly unabated and urgently requires immediate measures by an official or public agency." [104]

The official reply came on August 9, from the Jewish section of the Delegate's Office. This time the letter was signed by "Ludwik," apparently Wladyslaw Bartoszewski, who worked with Bienkowski and occasionally substituted for him at Council directorate meetings. "Ludwik" wrote that in response to the directorate's request the court had ruled". . . that the Council for Aiding Jews and the *Zegota* Section are not authorized [bodies] entitled to demand from the special courts and other judicial institutions, any report on proceedings being undertaken concerning prosecutions that have been handed over to those institutions, and especially when such proceedings are top secret." [105]

Testifying after the war, Bienkowski stated: "I personally signed 117 death sentences against extortionists throughout the country, eighty-nine of which were carried out. As best as I can ascertain, it seems to me that a total of 220 death verdicts were adjudicated for crimes involving coercion." The Delegate's representative to the

Council furnishes no evidence for his claim, and his figures seem excessively high when considered in the light of the evidence contained in the documents we have on hand. We should recall that in the second half of 1943 the Council directorate had asked for fictitious sentences to be published as a deterrent to potential extortionists; had Bienkowski actually set his signature to the number of death sentences he claimed, it seems likely the fact would have been no reason for the council to complain about punishment being insufficient to curb the alarming increase in the incidence of extortion.

The correspondences in July 1943 on the subject of the penalization of extortionists reveal that, until that time, no more than eight cases of blackmail and victimization of Jews had been brought before the special underground courts, and that only two of these had been prosecuted in full, with the sentences actually being carried out. In September 1943 Bienkowski reported about the sentencing of one of the heads of a gang of extortionists, and there are indications that several sentences were carried out during November and December of that year and during 1944. We can therefore say with some assurance that of the several thousands of death sentences carried out by the Polish underground for the crimes of treason, collaboration and for acts against the national interest, only a few dozen were connected with cases involving extortion. The evidence therefore seems to justify the charge that "failure to punish extortionists was the cause of their acting with impunity and expanding the scope of their criminal machinations. . . ."[118]

A view of the problem of extortion, from the perspective of a Jew who lived on the "Aryan side" of Warsaw, is given by the *Bund* member Bernard Goldstein in his book, *Finf yor in varshever geto* ("Five Years in the Warsaw Ghetto").

"[Extortionism] was a terribly calamity for Jews who lived on the Aryan side. In addition to the prospect of death at the hands of the Gestapo, SS or the Fiends of Hell [Germans in uniform], the Marranos of our time were threatened by an Inquisition run by Polish thugs who made traffic in Jewish lives a profitable venture. These scoundrels came from every level of society. Students would expose their Jewish friends, former classmates from school or university; neighbors identified Jews who had lived in the same building or with whom they shared the same courtyard; businessmen, merchants and shopkeepers identified Jews from whom they had received—as it were 'bought'—businesses and apartments when the latter were forced to move into the ghetto; Polish policemen and officials, armed with authority from their new masters and in the guise of their servants, could now 'rediscover' all of those Jews they had known so well in the past."[107]

We should now consider the Council's response to published charges of anti-Semitism authorized by official underground agencies.

One such publication is the subject of a memorandum sent by the Council leadership to the Delegate on June 30, 1944, in order to alert the Delegate to the existence of a pamphlet originating with the Agricultural Section of the Polish underground and bearing the promising title of *Our New Common Home*. The memorandum quotes a venomously anti-Semitic passage from the pamphlet in which the role played by Jews in Poland's economic life is described as being one of calculated exploitation of the country's population and serving the interests of the enemy occupier. The passage goes on to say of the Jews:

> They owned an appreciable portion of the national property, were active in our economic life, but they did not belong to those parts of Poland which draw their strength and their capacity for renewal from their love and from the sacrifices of the country's sons. With the exception of a minority, they were incapable of either love or sacrifice. *Historical destiny is leading them to their destruction*, and most of them have been wiped out. All that has remained of the vast number of Polish Jews in the areas that have been evacuated for [the use of] others, and these places will have to be seized. . . .[108]

We have available examples of similar anti-Semitic material originating with various sections of the Polish underground; some of the documents were classified as secret and meant for internal distribution only, and some of them—like the pamplet that was the subject of the Council's protest to the Delegate—were published and intended for general circulation among the public. It seems to us that the published material could only have seriously undermined the chances of runaway Jews to find refuge and survive among the Polish population.

When the situation in the Warsaw Ghetto was at its most critical, after the mass deportation of Jews from the ghetto, the *Zegota* Council directorate attempted several times to get key elements in the Polish underground and the headquarters of the Home Army to respond to the urgent appeals for arms being issued by the organization of Jewish underground fighters. These attempts were undertaken by *Zegota* despite the fact that it had been subtly warned on a number of occasions to confine itself to assistance work, and had been required, in cases where clearly earmarked funds were being dispensed by the Council, to confirm by report that the money was not going to be used for buying weapons.[109]

At the end of January, 1943 after the first armed resistance had taken place in the Warsaw Ghetto between the 18th and the 22nd of the month, the Council directorate drafted a general memorandum on the situation to the Delegate. In it the Council asserts that the mass deportation of Jews from the ghetto in January proves that the Germans had begun their final liquidation of the Jews in Warsaw.

"For the moment, apparently because of the armed resistance by the residents of the ghetto"—so the memorandum defines it—the evacuation was interrupted; however, the fate of the Jews of the ghetto was sealed, and it could be expected that the deportation operation would be resumed shortly, and the liquidation of the ghetto brought to completion. In view of the imminent threat, the Council urged that immediate efforts be undertaken to rescue surviving Jews of the ghetto, particulatly individuals who were important for their creative activity in culture and the arts, public figures and thousands of children. To carry out the emergency operation, the Council had need of special funds, and was therefore asking for an additional grant of 500,000 zlotys for the purpose. The memorandum then reasserts that "there is a prevailing opinion, according to which the reason for the relaxation [interruption of the deportation operation] arises from the armed resistance of the Jews, which made an enormous impression on both the Jewish and Polish public. The immediate result of the resistance activities was surprisingly not, as had been predicted, a large scale massacre, but a temporary halt to the murderous deportation." [110]

On January 31, the council directorate addressed a letter to the Delegate in which it again called the Delegate's attention to the Jewish armed resistance that had taken place in January and lavished praise on it. The directorate's request was also aimed at the political groups represented on the council, which were called upon to lend their support to the demands being made by the Jewish fighting organization for arms. [111]

During the Warsaw Ghetto revolt in April and May 1943, the council directorate attempted to convince key elements in the underground resistance to appeal to the entire Polish population to come to the aid of Jews escaping from the besieged ghetto, and urged that such resistance be regarded as a civic and national obligation of all Poles. The Polish underground organizations did in fact publish a proclamation based on the call made by Prime Minister Sikorski to the Polish people in early May of 1943, when he appealed to the nation to come to the assistance of oppressed Jews in Poland. [112]

The activity of the Council in those days was of special significance in face of the discovery of the Katyn graves, and the anti-

Semitic propaganda launched by the Nazis and certain segments of the Polish underground.

On the first anniversary of the Warsaw Ghetto revolt, the Council directorate issued a series of proclamations and appeals expressing praise and admiration for the Jewish fighters in Warsaw and elsewhere. And the text of a decision taken by the members of the directorate April 15, 1944, in connection with the anniversary of the ghetto revolt, contains the following statement:

> ...the battle undertaken by the Warsaw Ghetto under the leadership of the Jewish Fighting Organization against an immeasurably more powerful enemy, as well as the subsequent heroic struggles in the cities and [concentration] camps of Poland (Bialystok, Wilno, Lwow, Czestochowa, Boryslaw, Tarnow, Treblinka, Trawniki), should be granted a place of honor alongside the eternally glorious defense of Warsaw and the other heroic battles for freedom and independence fought by the militant underground in Poland. [113]

And in an appeal marking the anniversary of the Warsaw Ghetto revolt and bearing the same date of April 15, 1944, the directorate once again took up the theme that the Polish public should honor the revolt and armed struggle of the Jews by "intensifying [rescue] operations being undertaken by the entire public in response to the continuing campaign of annihilation by the occupier." [114]

In still another communication to the Delegate (this time addressed as "Prime Minister," in recognition of the appointment by which the Government Delegate was granted the title of Deputy Prime Minister), dating May 1944, the directorate recalls the events in Poland and London marking the anniversary of the Warsaw Ghetto revolt, and goes on to report:

> ...the Council is taking the liberty to transmit to the address of the Government Delegate a part of the information reaching [us] from various regions of the country and touching on the revelation of murders committed by a certain segment of Polish society against Jews in hiding. As we have been informed by the representatives of the KK, an official affidavit has lately been forwarded by the headquarters of the Jewish Fighting Organization (ZOB) to military authorities in Poland on the subject of the shameful murder of thirteen Jewish fighters who were on stand-by in villages in the area of Koniecpol. After an investigation it was found those involved were NSZ or AK units under the command of someone known as "Orzel." Information has reached the Jewish Fighting Organization (ZOB) that in the regions of Czestochowa, Radom and Kielce such units had murdered about 200 Jews in hiding. A memorandum on this has been forwarded to the Jewish Affairs Section of Armed Services HQ. ...There is no doubt that the official military elements have it in their power to eliminate this frightening state of affairs, and the Council for Aiding Jews there-

fore submits its request to the Government Delegate to take decisive steps in this matter in order finally to put an end to these conspiratorial acts of murder being perpetrated by certain despicable elements in the country. [115].

PUBLICATIONS BY THE COUNCIL
ADDRESSED TO THE POLISH PEOPLE

The council for Aiding Jews published a number of proclamations, several of them aimed at the Polish public as a whole and one to German servicemen; it also submitted statements to the underground press. All of these called on various groups and the whole Polish people to come to the aid of Jews and to assist those Jews seeking sanctuary among Gentiles. According to Berman, "The Council established a propaganda section with the purpose of influencing the public, by means of suitable printed matter, actively to cooperate in assisting Jews. The Council brought out four broadsheets—three to the Polish public in twenty-five thousand copies all told, and one in German in five thousand copies supposedly produced by a clandestine German organization. These broadsheets were distributed to homes, posted on the walls of houses in Warsaw and cities in the provinces, and sent to various offices. In addition, the Council produced memoranda for the underground press to report on extermination operations against Jews and on acts of resistance by Jews." [116]

Zegota also helped to put out two publications in 1944 on the Jewish tragedy and Nazi extermination policy. Both publications were the result of initiatives by the Jewish National Committee (ZKN). Nevertheless, as we learn from Janina Wasowicz ("Ewa"), a key figure in the Council, the publications were set and run off on the printing press of the Democratic Party, and the whole undertaking was made possible because of the interest taken in the project by the Democratic representatives to the council.[130]

The first of these publications was called Z Otchlani ("From the Abyss") and was edited by the Polish writer Maria Kann. Z Otchlani was a collection of the works of Polish and Jewish poets written in response to the suffering of Jews in World War II. In her memoirs Maria Kann writes, "I could not sit idly by while hearing the echoes of the revolt in the Warsaw Ghetto." She met with Aleksander Kaminski from the Polish Scout Movement, who was editor of the newspaper *Biuletyn Informacyiny* and maintained contact with the Jewish underground; she informed Kaminski of her intention to write "an appeal to the world about the situation of the Jews." Subsequently, with the collaboration of additional sympathizers, such as Zofia Kossak-Szczucka and Wladyslaw Bartoszewski, material was collected for the anthology. A second work published by the underground was the detailed report of Jankiel Wiernik, a Jewish carpenter who had been deported to Treblinka and had taken part in the revolt of Jewish prisoners at the death camp; Wiernik managed to escape and reach Warsaw, where his story about the camp was published as *Rok w Treblince* ("A Year in Treblinka").[118]

RELATIONS WITH JUS

Zegota faced a completely different series of problems in its policy toward the Jewish welfare organization JUS (*Judische Unterstutzungsstelle*). JUS had evolved at a fairly late stage in the occupation from the "Jewish Self-Help" organization, which were active in the ghettos of Poland under the auspices of the "Joint" and of various political elements, among which were leading personalities in the underground. Jewish Self-Help was integrated within a more broadly-based welfare organization, the NRO (Naczelna Rada Opiekuncza) in which Poles and Ukrainians participated as well, and which enjoyed the status of an official agency under the jurisdiction of the Population and Welfare Section in the administration of the Government General. [119] It was headed by Michael Weichert, a lawyer who had been active as well in the Jewish community before the war in the theater and the arts. Weichert was placed at the head of Jewish Self-Help because of his exceptional skill as a negotiator and his perfect command of German.

Jewish Self-Help was active throughtout the area of the Government General. Indeed, it was the only recognized Jewish organization permitted to operate on a countrywide scale and not restricted in its work to a single ghetto; moreover, it carried out its work in collaboration with Poles. The organization's central office was in Cracow.

In the summer of 1942 the German authorities ordered Jewish "social assistance" to be terminated. The termination of the Jewish welfare organization was carried out in response to the demand of the SS during the height of the campaign of annihilation. Weichert, in his postwar writings on the activities of Jewish Self-Help, claims that he had succeeded in prolonging the process of the organization's dismantlement for some time, for which he had obtained the tacit agreement of Germans who worked in the Population and Welfare Section of the regional governor's administration, and who, for reasons of their own, were interested in the continued existence of the Jewish welfare organization.[120]

The final deportation of Jews from the Cracow Ghetto was carried out in March 1943, when about 12,000 Jews were evacuated from the ghetto and were transferred to the Plaszow concentration camp, located in the area of Cracow. In his memoirs Weichert relates that he had prepared himself to leave for the concentration camp with the rest of the Jews of the ghetto, but was told on the day the transfer was scheduled to take place that he was to remain behind and that the Jewish welfare organization would renew its activities.[121]

Why the Germans should have changed their minds and revived the Jewish social assistance agency at a time when all Jews had been removed from Cracow and the rest of the ghettos in the Government General had either been liquidated or were earmarked for liquidation, is something of a puzzle.

Both *Zegota* and the Jewish underground took a very clear view of the Germans' change of heart. To them it seemed that the Germans had concluded that the existence in the Government General of a Jewish welfare agency which was in contact with organizations outside occupied Europe, and could confirm receipt of assistance shipments to Jews, would counteract the rumors reaching the free world that Jews were being murdered in the Government General and were the victims of a conspiracy aiming at their total annihilation. In addition, it was believed that the Germans had a vested interest in maintaining the flow of aid shipments for Jews. According to the evidence of underground sources, the Germans confiscated the most valuable food items and medicines contained in these shipments, and allowed only a part of the consignments to be distributed among the Jews by the Jewish welfare agency.

Weichert asked to be allowed to meet with Jewish representatives from the underground, and also attempted to get in touch with the Council for Aiding Jews. The representatives of the Jewish underground rejected Weichert's request and advised *Zegota* to do the same and refuse to collaborate with JUS in any way. They also communicated with the outside world through underground channels, and advised that no supplies be sent to JUS since what was involved was really only a German propaganda ruse.

Then on March 28, 1944, *Zegota's* directorate decided that no assistance would be accepted from JUS, and that transfers of medical and food supplies should be returned either in money or kind. And further, it was noted that this decision had been taken after Weichert had announced to the representatives of the Council that he would not be bound by the decisions of the Coordinating

Committee and the Council because he did not recognize their authority as official representatives of the Polish National Council in London.[122] Thus it was that negotiations were broken. Weichert had refused to relinquish his post and turn JUS supplies over to the Council.

After the war, between 1945 and 1946, Weichert was brought to trial in Poland, but the court was unable to establish his guilt beyond a reasonable doubt. Later, in 1949, a public trial was held to once more determine his guilt. Again the court was unable to find unequivocally against him, but did cast doubt upon his conduct and civic integrity during the war. On the other hand many Jewish survivors have claimed that Weichert's actions during the last stage was of a positive character, and he succeeded to provide help and finally to contribute to the rescue of some Jews in camps and in hiding.

NOTES

1. The term "Zegota" apparently had no significance apart from a secret code-name for Jews. According to the testimony of one of the heads of the Council, a man by the name of Konrad Zegota actually took part at the founding meeting of the organization. This testimony is not borne out by any other source.

2. Adolf Berman, "Ha-Yehudim ba-Tzad ha-Ari" ("The Jews on the Aryan Side"), in *Entziklopediyah* shel ha-Galuyot, (encyclopedia of the Galut) Vol. *Varshah*.
I, ed. Yitzhak Grunbaum, Jerusalem, Tel Aviv, 1953, p. 692.

3. See articles by B.A. Sijes. "Several Observations Concerning the Position of the Jews in Occupied Holland During World War II," *Rescue Attempts During the Holocaust Proceedings* of the Second Yard Vashem International Historical Conference, ed. by I. Gutman and E. Zuroff, Jerusalem, 1977, pp. 527–554.

4. See B. Arditi, *Yehudei Bulgariya bi-Shanot ha-Mishtar ha-Natzi* ("Bulgarian Jewry During the Nazi Regime"), Holon, 1962; Chaim Kashles, *Korot Yehudei Bulgariya* ("A History of Bulgarian Jewry"), Vol. III, Tel Aviv, 1970; Nissan Oren, "Hatzalat Yehudei Bulgariya" ("The Rescue of Bulgarian Jewry"), in

Kovetz Mehkarim be-Parshiyot ha-Shoah ve-ha-Gvurah shel Yad Vashem, Vol. VII, Jerusalem, 1968, pp.77–100.

5. On this subject, see, Daniel Carpi, "The Rescue of Jews in the Italian Zone of Occupied Croatia" in *Rescue Attempts*, see note 3, pp. 465–526. Meir Michaelis, *Mussolini and the Jews*, Germat, Italian Relations and the Jewish Question, in Italy, 1922–1945, London-Oxford, 1978.

6. See Harold Fender, *Rescue in Denmark*, N.Y. 1980; Leni Yahil, *The Rescue of Danish Jewry*, Philadelphia, 1969.

7. The changes manifested in the character of the occupying regime with respect to the independent governments which remained in the occupied countries have not yet been subjected to thorough comparative analysis. Lectures and incomplete discussions concerning this important and complex theme can be found in: *Das Dritte Reich und Europa*, München, 1957.

8. See, for instance, remarks by the Governor of the Warsaw District, Dr. L. Fischer, on the reasons to the establishment of the Warsaw ghetto, in *Okupacjai Ruch Oporu w Dzienniku Hansa Franka*, V.1, 1939–1942, Warsaw, 1972, p.335.

9. The wording of the order in: *Ekster-minacja Zydow na Ziemach Polskich*, Zbior dokumentow; Zebrali i opracowali T. Berenstein, A. Eisenbach, A. Rutkowski, Warsaw, 1957, p. 122, doc. No. 52.

10. Eksterminacja. pp. 125–126 a document No. 55. An order by the Director of the Department of Internal Affairs in the office of the Warsaw District Governor to the heads of the municipal and provincial authorities concerning the method of seizing Jews who were hiding outside the ghetto was issued in Warsaw on January 17, 1942.

11. Even Governor-General Hans Frank made a distinction between Jews in hiding, and those who "aided and abetted" the Jews. Frank decreed that the "aiders and abetters" were liable to the same punishment as the Jews, i.e. the death penalty, but "in less serious cases, a prison or jail sentence might be given." See document mentioned in note 9, above.

12. See, for example, Szymon Datner, *op. cit.* In an appendix to the book, a list is given of 105 Poles, including entire families and many children, who were murdered for having hidden Jews. According to the author, the list is incomplete, and is constantly growing. I was informed in Poland in 1978 that the number of Poles who had saved Jews and forfeited their lives as a consequence, had already reached the 400-mark. There is no doubt that there were many cases in which Poles were murdered for aiding Jews, as is confirmed also by the testimonies of Jewish survivors. Nevertheless, the many announcements of aid and rescue of Jews which appeared in 1967–69, did not necessarily present a factual historical picture, but were intended primarily as apologia. After the anti-Semitic drive which took place during the years 1967–1968, the dismissal of Jews from their jobs and from the country itself, and the grave repercussions caused by the campaign, an effort was made to underplay present events in Poland by issuing large numbers of statements concerning the aid and rescue of Jews during the war, and the ingratitude of world Jewry who accused the Poles of anti-Semitism and incurable Jew-hatred. Great caution must therefore be exercised with respect to the wave of books and publications glorifying the endeavors to save Jews during those years. It may be assured, nevertheless, that despite the multitude of these biased publications, a number of other works of real value were also printed which it would have been difficult to publish at an earlier date. Even these books, however, were obliged to conform to the accepted spirit of the times, i.e., they were, to a great extent, one-sided. (See, for example, Bartoszewski's and Levin's important work, *Righteous Among the Nations*, How Poles Helped the Jews, 1939–1945, London, 1969 which is discussed in great length in our book.

13. On this subject, see, YVA, *Zegota* section, 06/48, File II, *Zegota* memorandum which was passed on to a delegate of the underground government on June 30, 1944. The memorandum concerns an official announcement by an office subordinate to the underground which claims that the murder of Jews was their "historical destiny" and prophesied "positive consequences" for Poland. We shall deal with this announcement and its background in detail below.

14. See the book by the Polish literary critic and philospher, Kazimierz Wyka, *Zycie na niby*. On the other hand, Berman, in his work, "Ha-Yehudim ba-Tzad ha-Ari," notes that among the activists on the Provisional Zegota Committee was J. Barski, a Catholic lawyer and communal worker, extremely conservative in his views, who, according to rumor, was an anti-Semite before the war. *Ibid.*,p. 689.

15. See the introduction of Bartoszewski in the original version of *Righteous among the Nations*, (op. cit) *Ten jest Ojczyzny mojej*, Wladyslaw Bartoszewski; Zofia Lewinowna, wydanie drugie, rozszerzone, Warsaw, 1969, p.17.

16. During this first stage, the Committee was composed on a narrow social basis, and its chief members were the founders who belonged chiefly to Catholic circles. Consequently, representatives of leftist socialist circles were not invited to joint the Committee.

17. Material on the organization and

activities of the Provisional Committee can be found in appendices to the book, *Ten jest z Ojczyzny mojej*, *ibid*, documents 61–62, pp.940–42.

18. See: Berman, *"He-Yehudim ba-Tzad ha-Ari,"* op. cit., pp. 685–686.

19. On the organization of the National Jewish Committee, the Coordinating Committee, and the attitude of the Bund to general Jewish self-organization in the framework of the Jewish Fighting Organization, and a general Jewish social and political framework, see, Ysrael Gutman, *The Jews of Warsaw*, 1939–1943, Bloomington Indiana, 1982. pp. 289–291.

20. The Coordinating Committee represented the Jews to the Polish civil underground on a social level, while a united Jewish representation, headed for most of the time by Aryeh Wilner ("Jurek"), worked with the military underground. Wilner was arrested shortly before the outbreak of the Jewish revolt in Warsaw and was replaced by Yitzhak Zuckerman ("Antek").

21. On the problems of relations between the AK and the Jews, and the question of aid to Jewish fighting organizations, see in detail chapter IV of this book.

22. See document no. 60 in the appendices to the book, *Ten jest z Ojczyzny mojej*, op. cit., p. 940.

23. The department of the Delegate's Office was considered, and the post of Delegate became, a high-ranking civilian position in the underground in Poland, or, more exactly, in the area of the Government General (there were separate departments like these in the territories annexed by the Soviet Union, and in the areas occupied by Germany which were annexed to the Reich). The first delegate was Cyril Ratajski, who was succeeded by Jan Piekakiewicz. From March 1943, the post of Delegate was filled by Jan Stanislaw Jankowski. Jankowski was active during most of the period under consideration, and was replaced as late as April 1945, i.e., on the eve of the Armistice. From April 1944, the Delegate was appointed deputy prime-minister by the Polish Government-in-Exile in London.

24. *Ten jest z Ojczyzny mojej*, op. cit., document no. 62, pp. 941–42.

25. A second reason for the disbandment of the Provisional Committee was given as the penetration of "political elements into exclusively philanthropic work," *Ibid.*, document no. 62, p. 942.

26. Berman claimed that "the Catholic communal workers were of the opinion that representatives of the Jewish community rightly served as liaisons between the Committee, the ghetto, and the Jews hiding in the Aryan zone, and represented the interests and demands of the Jewish population, while the Committee was supposed to have a 'purely Polish' character." "Ha-Yehudim ba-Tzad ha-Ari," *op.cit.*, p.691.

27. Extreme circles who. gathered around the NSZ (Narodowe Siy Zbrojne), the military wing of the extreme nationalistic, pro fascist, adopted a fanatically anti-Jewish position, did not balk at killing Jews on their own initiative, and were responsible for the murder of members of the underground with progressive views. On these internal reckonings, see, Jan Rzepecki, *Wspomnienia i przyczynki historyczne*, Warsaw, 1956, pp. 278–180.

28. See chapter of memoirs by Irena Sendler in *Ten jest z Ojcsyzny mojej*, *op.cit.*, p. 131.

29. See memoirs of Jan Zabinski in (BZIH), Nr. 65–66, Warsaw, 1966, pp.198–199.

30. See *Ten jest z Ojczyzny mojej*. *op.cit.*, p. 133.

31. YVA, 03/468, memoirs of Miriam Peleg-Marianska, who was the Jewish representative on the *Zegota* council in Cracow.

32. The memoirs of Tadeusz Rek in BZIH, Nos. 65–66, pp. 185–186.

33. See the Polish version of the declaration of November 17, 1942, in *Ten jest z Ojczyzny mojej*, *op. cit.*, document no. 95, pp. 1006–1007.

34. See Rek's memoirs in BZIH, Nos. 65–66; also a different version of his memoirs in *Ten jest z Ojczyzny mojej*. pp. 118–123.

35. On the composition of the directorate and the *Zegota* instructions, see memoirs and testimonies by the main activists: A. Berman, *"Ha-Yehudim ba-Tzad ha-Ari,"* p. 692; Ferdinand Arczynski ("Marek"), in BZIH, nos. 65–66, pp. 174–175; Witold Bienkowski ("Kalski"),

in BZIH, nos. 65–66, pp.189–190.

36. This detailed breakdown of departments follows the list compiled by Ferdinand Arczynski in the chapter on the *Zegota's* work in BZIH, nos. 65–66, p.175. It seems that not all the departments really functioned as separate entities. The impression is given by *Zegota* protocols that action against blackmailers was not dealt with by a special department; nor is there any sign of a separate department for clothing. On the other hand, there was a special department of health, of which Arczynski himself relates elsewhere. Witold Bienkowski, in his report on *Zegota's* activities up to the end of October 1943, mentions the departments and their work according to a similar order. A copy of Bienkowski's report can be found in the *Zegota* files in the YVA. Also see the printed report, *Ten jest z Ojcsyzny mojej,* document no. 72, pp. 952–960.

37. See, *H-Yehudim ba-Tzad ha-Ari,"* p.691. Dr. Berman adopted the false name, Adam Borowski, and under this name signed most of the documents intended for Polish soil and abroad. However, for greater security, he was forced to use two more assumed names: "Jozef" in Catholic circles, particularly when Jewish children were given into the care and protection of institutions; and "Ludwik," when dealing with the PPR (Communist Party) and its military wing AL.

38. See the programmatic memorandum to the Delegate's Office of December 29, 1942, signed by Grobelny, Berman and Arczynski. YVA, 06/48, File II.

39. See the Council report mentioned above which was compiled on October 23, 1943, and reviews the Council's activities from December 1942 to October 1943 (the report was sent to London), in *Ten jest z Ojczyzny mojej,* p. 953.

40. A. Berman, *op. cit.,* p. 692.

41. The heads of the Council sent an appeal to the Interior Ministry of the Polish Government-in-Exile in London on May 12, 1943, stating that, "the Council for Aiding Jews which began to operate last year, and which is represented by Polish social organizations, has such paltry material resources and patronage at its command—granted to it by the government Delegate for this purpose—that the aid given is purely symbolic in the face of the multiplying tasks and daily-increasing requirements." YVA, 06/48, File 2. Arczynski writes in his list of *Zegoda's* activities in BZIH that, "the monthly lump-sum allowance to each of the needy cases with whom the Council came in contact was at first 500 zlotys. When the number of Jews in need of help began to increase, due to the draining of independent resources as a result of illness, etc., while the Delgate's grant remained the same, the individual grant was gradually reduced to 300 zlotys per month. Taking into consideration the decrease in the value of money, and the high costs of essential foodstuffs, this aid was to all intents and purposes purely symbolic." See, BZIH, document nos. 65–66, p. 178. Also see, YVA, *Zegota* section, 06/48, File 2.

42. A book which deals with the help given to Jews, by a man who did not belong to the small circle of *Zegota* activists but who was, according to his own testimony, connected with the latter, describes the method of dividing the funds and the difficulties involved. Wladyslaw Smolski, *Zaklete Lata,* Warsaw, 1969, pp. 105–115.

43. See, Berman, "Ha-Yehudim ba-Tzad ha-Ari," *op. cit.,* p. 694.

44. See the Council's report up to the end of October 1943, as above. In December 1943, the members of the Council's directorate informed the Government Delegate that a fixed allowance was given to no more than 1000-1500 persons. "This is a mere drop in the ocean." YVA, 06/48, File 2.

45. The Council's report up to the end of October 1943, as above. The report states that during the months of November and December, the Ministry of Health gave the Council a monthly grant of 750,000 zlotys, and that from January 1944, the amount would be increased to 1 million zlotys *Ten jest z Ojczyzny Mojej, op. cit.,* p. 954.

46. On the fate of Ringelblum and those hiding in the bunker, see Joseph Kermish's introduction to the book, Emmanuel Ringelblum, *Polish-Jewish Relations During the Second World*

War, edited and with footnotes by Joseph Kermish and Shmuel Krakowski, Yah Vashem, Jerusalem, 1974, and also New York, 1976.

47. *Ten jest z Ojczyzny mojej, op. cit.*, p.197.

48. An important article on this subject has been published by Teresa Prekerowa "Komorka Felicji", Nieznane Archiwum Rady Pomocy Zydom w Warszawie, Rocznik Warszawski XV, Archiwum Paristwo we Mst. St. Warsawy, 1979. This article, a chapter from a large-scale work on *Zegota* which is now in preparation, gives a detailed description of the activities of the large *Zegota* cell in Warsaw, and was written on the basis of primary documentary material which was not previously known to be in existence.

49. *Ibid.*

50. See, Berman, "Ha-Yehudim ba-Tzad ha-Ari," *op. cit.*, p. 694.

51. In the Yad Vashem archive, there are about 30,000 testimonies, mostly in section 03. During research for this work, the testimonies of Jews in hiding were studied.

52. *This sum was received upon special request by Zegota*, and was designated for immediate aid to escapes from the Warsaw ghetto on the eve of, and during the revolt.

53. See a special secret report on the situation of the Jews in Poland which was transferred by Kalski (code name of Witold Bienkowski) on May 25, 1944, to the Prime Minister of the London Government CSHI 26/27, A9/III.

54. YVA, *Zegota* section, 06/48, File 2. Letter from the *Zegota* directorate to the Government Delegate, December 15, 1944.

55. *Ten jest z Ojczyzny mojej op. cit.*, These data are also cited in the book by Kazimerz Iranek- Osmecki, *He who saves one life*, London, 1968, pp. 235–236.

56. YVA. *Zegota* section, 06/48, File 2. Letter to the Government Delegate, December 15, 1944.

57. YVA, *Zegota* section, 06/48, File 2. Letter to the Government Delegate (the appeal is addressed to the "Prime Minister"), December 23, 1944.

58. The facts were given at a meeting of the Council's directorate; see YVA,

Zegota section, 06/48, File 1, minutes of *Zegota* meetings from 23, 1.43 to 18. 5.44.

59. Berman was released after his captor had been bribed, but was forced to maintain a stricter underground existence, and to change his accommodations frequently. The members of the Council's directorate also commenced a stricter regime of secrecy. See decision of January 10, 1944, to set up a committee of four members of the directorate for "renewed action and conspiracy." YVA, *Zegota* section, 06/48, File 1.

60. YVA, *Zegota* section, 06/48, File 1. Minutes of the directorate meeting of September 27, 1943.

61. YVA, *Zegota* section, 06/48, File 1, minutes of the directorate meeting of November 8, 1943. Bienkowski's comment and his call for a clear definition of separate areas of work came after a discussion on the subject in the presence of the Delegate. On October 28, 1943, two members of the directorate of the *Zegota* Council — Tadeusz Rek and Adolf Berman — were received by the Delegate. The latter asked the Council's representatives to describe the existing division of labor between the Council and the Jewish Coordinating Committee. The representatives explained that there was no formal separation of functions. The Coordinating Committee placed greater stress on activity in the provinces and camps, while in Warsaw, it looked after individuals and families who had not been contacted by the Council, due to the latter's limited financial resources. In reply, the Government Delegate said that a clear separation of roles must be determined by the two bodies, and duplication of aid be avoided. YVA, 06/48, File 2.

62. YVA, *Zegota* section, File 1, minutes of the meeting of October 8, 1943.

63. The *Zegota* directorate was informed that, "the sum of 25,000 dollars had been sent to the Government Delegate by an international Jewish organization in the United States" (contents of the telegram) expressly for Jews hiding in the Aryan zone. At the same time, $2000 was designated to support peasants who had been expelled from the Lublin area. The mass deportation of

peasants from the Lublin area was the most serious item on Poland's agenda during that period.

64. It is not clear who sent this money. We are in possession of a telegram which the Government Delegate transferred to the Minister of the Interior in London, Banaczyk, on December 29, 1943. The telegram described "the political structure of the Council for Aiding Jews and stated that during the year 1943, the Council had received a total of 6,250,000 zlotys. 1) 150,000; 2) 300,000; 3) 250,000; 4) 900,000; 5) 400,000; 6) 550,000; 7) 550,000; 8) 550,000; 9) 550,000; 10) 350,000; 11) 750,000 12) 750,000. Apart from this, the Council was sent a consignment of $23,000 from England. YVA, Zegota section, File of Bernfest documents.

65. See Pekerowa's article, Komorka Felicji", op. cit.

66. Iranek-Osmecki, op. cit., pp. 235–236.

67. See report up to the end of October 1943, as above.

68. Berman, "Ha-Yehudim ba-Tzad ha-Ari," op. cit.

69. Apparently, Communist and pro-Communist organizations are intended, which were not amalgamated within the recognized political framework, and were considered "alien."

70. YVA, Zegota section, 06/48, File 2. Memorandum by the Zegota directorate, September 6, 1943.

71. See YVA, Zegota section, 06/48, File 1. Directorate meeting of August 26, 1943.

72. Ibid., Directorate meeting of December 14, 1943.

73. See remarks by Ferdynand Arczynski in BZIH, no. 65–66.

74. YVA, 03/468, testimony of Miriam Peleg-Marianska.

75. Arczynski, BZIH. No. 65–66.

76. YVA, 03/468, testimony of Miriam Peleg-Marianska.

77. See chapter.

78. Ibid.

79. YVA, Zegota section 03/468, File 1, directorate meeting of May 6, 1943.

80. See the testimonites in BZIH, nos 65–66.

81. Zegota report up to the end of October 1943. op. cit.

82. Tem jest z Ojczyzny mojèj, op. cit.

83. See, for example, the story of a group of Jewish children wandering around aimlessly in the Aryan zone, in the book by Joseph Ziemian one of the activists on the Jewish National Committee The Cigarette-vendors from Three Crosses Square, New York.

84. YVA, Zegota section, 06/48, File 1. Directorate meetings of August 16 and September 4, 1943.

85. Zegota report up to the end of October 1943, as above.

86. Memoirs of Irena Sendler in Bartoszewski, op. cit.

87. YVA, Zegota section, 06/48, File 1. Directorate meeting of February 7, 1944.

88. See Ringelblum, Ketavim ("Writings"), Vol. II. Warsaw, p. 96. Adolf Beman, "Ha-Yehudim ba-Tzad ha-Ari," op. cit.,

89. YVA, Zegota section, 06/48, File 1, minutes of directorate meeting of Feburary 4, 1943.

90. Ibid., minutes of directorate meeting of March 25, 1943.

91. See draft of memorandum signed by "Trojan", WRN representative on the Zegota directorate. A "proposal and decision" concerning the dispatch of the memorandum to the Delegate was accepted at the directorate meeting of March 25, 1943. YVA, Zegota section, 06/48, File 1.

92. YVA, Zegota section, 06/48, File 1. Minutes of the directorate meeting of April 28, 1943.

93. YVA, Zegota section, 06/48, File 2.

94. See also: Abraham, Shulman, The Case of Hotel Polski, New York, 1982. Concerning the case of Hotel Polski, see the article of Nathan Eck, The Rescue of Jews with the aid of Passports . . ." In Yad Vashem Studies, Jerusalem, 1957.

95. See discussion concerning the contents of the appeal in the minutes of a directorate meeting whose date is not given in the material at our disposal. It is clear that the meeting took place between July 7 and 23, 1943. YVA, Zegota section, 06/48 File 1.

96. Ibid. directorate meeting of July 23, 1943. There is no proof that this telegram was transferred by any intermediary to London, and it may be assumed that it did not leave Poland.

97. YVA, Zegota section, 06/48, File 2. Letter of July 17, 1943, from the Zegota

department,i.e., the Jewish Department of the Delegate's Office, to the directorate of the Zegota Council.

98. YVA, Zegota section, 06/48, File 1, meeting of the Zegota directorate of April 28, 1943.

99. See wording of the letter from WRN in YVA, Zegota section, 06/48, File 2.

100. YVA, Zegota section, 06/45, File 5.

101. Ibid., letter from Bienkowski, March 4, 1943.

102. Ibid.,

103. Ibid., memorandum of April 6, 1943.

104. Ibid., letter to the Zegota Department of the Delegate's Office signed by and Marck (Ferdynand Arczynski).

105. Ibid., with codicil of August 8, 1943, signed by Ludwik, Bartoszewski's code name.

106. See Kermish's article, or above.

107. Bernard Goldstein, Five Years in the Warsaw Ghetto, New York (paper edition). pp. 198–200.

108. See detailed memorandum of the Council's directorate concerning the announcement of June 30, 1944.

109. YVA, Zegota section, 06/48, File 2.

110. Ibid., Zegota section, 06/48, File 2, January 1943.

111. Ibid., letter of January 31, 1943. See also further appeal to the Delegate, without an exact date, in the wake of the resistance in January 1943.

112. Ibid., Zegota section, File 5. See proclamation of August 1943. It should be noted that the proclamation was only composed in August, months after the revolt had ended, which indicates that the decision concerning the proclamation was dependent upon many internal considerations. See Sikorski's words of May 5, 1943.

113. Ibid., Zegota section, 06/48, File 2, decision by the Zegota council of April 15, 1944.

114. Ibid.

115. Ibid.; appeal by the Council to the Government Delegate in May 1944.

116. See Berman "Ha-Yehudim ba-Tzad ha-Ari," op. cit., p. 695.

117. See: The testimony of Ewa Wasowicz BSIH, nr. 65–66, 1968.

118. A. Berman, "Ha-Yehudim ba-Tzad ha-Ari," op cit., p. 730.

119. See about RGO: Czestaw Maldajczyk, Polityka III Rzeszy w Okupowanej Polsce, Vol. II, Warsaw, 1970, pp. 103–111.

120. Michael Weichert Yidishe Alaynhilf, 1939–1945, Tel Aviv, 1962. pp. 51–54.

121. Ibid., p. 58.

122. Ibid., see minutes of the meeting of the Council's directorate on March 28, 1944.

CHAPTER EIGHT

The Help of the Polish Government-In-Exile 1943–1944

By the end of 1942, the Jewish leaders in the free world already had a more or less clear recognition of the advances in the Nazi extermination of the Polish Jews. By the time, they already fully realized that what was taking place was not mass pograms but a predesigned and consistently implemented extermination. But they could not yet quite believe that the extermination might turn out to be total. The members of the Representation of Polish Jews still clung to the hope that despite the terrifying bloodshed, a considerable fraction of the Polish Jewry could yet succeed in eluding the Nazis. The "Report of the Activities of the Delegation of Poland Jews during the years 1940–1945" says that "even in January 1943, no one could yet envisage that Polish Jewry would perish in their totality".[1] This explains why the issue of the rescue action comes to the fore when the old preoccupations with arranging Jewish life in a Poland liberated from Nazism continue to be pursued. But it was not long before the final realization that the rescue of the Jewish survivors in Poland must take precedence over any other considerations.

Because of its residence in exile, the Polish Government's position was admittedly sensitive. Still, it controlled considerable resources which could well be diverted for the sake of rescuing at least some of the Jewish survivors. The Polish Government had the power to influence the bulk of the Polish underground and of the Polish civilian population to forward assistance to tens of thousands of Jewish fugitives from the ghettos and the camps who were hiding in forests, in villages, an on the so-called "Aryan" side of some cities. In addition to that, the Polish Government disposed of extensive funds, which could perfectly well be assigned for rescue purposes. In part the funds in question had been taken out of the Polish State Treasury during the September 1939 defeat (and therefore the Jewish taxpayers had contributed to them); they also derived from grants received from the Governments of the United States and Great Britain. The Polish Government had also exclusive control over the clandestine lines of communication with occupied Poland, which could be used for the delivery of financial assistance.

Until the end of 1942, when the vast majority of Polish Jews had already been murdered, the Polish Government did nothing, apart from verbally protesting on several occasions against the extermination of Jewish citizens of Poland, and calling upon the other members of the anit-Nazi coalition to help the Polish Jews. On its own it undertook no attempt to dispatch or to deliver any assistance. But the Jewish leaders were understandably not satisfied with verbal declarations alone. They realized that the only hope for obtaining help in any form lay in mounting pressures upon the Government and upon the London-based members of some political parties. The Representation of Polish Jews decided to take advantage of the fact that a leader of the Peasants Party, Stanislaw Kot, then Polish Envoy Extraordinary in the Middle East, was at that time staying in Palestine. On the initiative of the Representation, represented by Moshe Kleinbaum (Sneh), Stupp and Reiss, a number of meetings with Kot then took place.

During the first meeting, on November 27, 1942, Moshe Sneh (Kleinbaum) informed Kot of the following desiderata of the Delegation:

1. That the Government and the National Council shall enact a decree making anyone taking part in murders of persecutions of Jews liable for criminal responsibility.

2. That the Polish Government shall impel the Allied Governments to undertake retaliatory steps against Germany, and that it shall appeal to the neutral Governments to try to restrain Germany and to convey assistance to Jews who succeeded in escaping from Nazi-occupied Europe. That the Polish Government shall also request certain intervening steps from the Vatican.

3. That the Polish Government shall broadcast instructions, in Polish, intended to neutralize the impact of anti-Jewish propaganda, and to influence the Polish population to attempt to defy the German barbarities. (In the negotiations, Kleinbaum stressed that it was the evidence arriving from Poland which necessitated educational measures of this nature.)

4. That the Polish Government shall call for the Polish clergy to speak up and protest, in the same way as the Western clergy did.[2]

Kot's reply was remarkably evasive. First, he blamed the Jewish leaders, both in Palestine and in the United States, for inactivity. He claimed that they failed to organize protest actions against the German genocide and to mount appropriate pressures upon the Government of the United States. In Kot's view, the Polish Government has done more than enough to mount such pressures.[3]

Kleinbaum summed up the conversation as follows:

> The Government seems to overestimate our influence. You believe, Mr. Minister, that the Jews can do anything. We, nevertheless, believe that the Government can do much more. The Jews operate under political restraints in various countries of their residence. And yet the American Jews did succeed in organizing the mass protest demonstration greeted by special messages from both Roosevelt and Churchill.[4]

The subsequent meetings of the members of the Delegation with Kot took place on December 5 and 13, 1942, and on January 25, 1943. Throughout these meetings, the Delegation members demanded from the Government concrete relief efforts for the benefit of Jewish survivors of extermination. The two chief demands were: to prevail upon the Polish population to supply relief to Jewish survivors, and to make it possible for the Jews to establish direct contact with occupied Poland. Replying to the first demand, Kot argued that the Polish population already is doing a great deal to help the Jews. As for the second demand, his answer was:

> We have already discussed the issue of the contacts with Poland before. I also discussed this matter with Ben Gurion. I said and I reiterate: Yes. Give us the people, and we'll dispatch them. Of course, it requires a preparation: above all else, those people must know what they risk. What is being done in Istanbul is devoid of major importance: nothing beyond interviewing the refugees and reporting to us what they said. Our outpost in Sweden was much more active. But there was a mishap, our people were detained, and the Erickson company suffered badly from that affair. Thus, the only way which remains is from the skies, by parachute. Please, give us the people: we will dispatch them.[5]

The atmosphere of the talks was tense and occasionally hostile. In the course of discussions of the desperate plight of the Jewish population, rapidly facing total extermination Kot could not r84fain from sharply worded attacks on the Polish Jews for supporting both the Pilsudski camp in Poland of the between-the-wars period and the Bolsheviks after the Red Army invaded eastern areas of Poland in September 1939.

The described endeavors had some effects, but they were late in coming. It was not until May 18,1943, or exactly one month after the outbreak of the Warsaw ghetto uprising, when no more than a handful of Jews still managed to survive in the entire occupied Poland, General Sikorski finally broadcast his memorable appeal to the Poles to help the Jews. Schwarzbart commented on the causes of the delay as follows:

> The Polish Prime Minister was apparently afraid to broadcast the special appeal in time to avoid a hostile response against himself and his Government in London by the overwhelmingly antisemitic Polish populace.[6]

But the Sikorski appeal was exceptional. There were no more broadcasts; and the other points agreed upon between the Delegation and Minister Kot were not implemented.

In order to keep the London Government under pressure, the Representation of Polish Jews took advantage of the arrival in Palestine of another Polish cabinet minister, Stanczyk, a socialist who then held the Welfare portfolio. The intention was to discuss with him the matters previously discussed to no avail with Kot. He arrived in the last days of June 1943 and the meeting with him took place on July 1.

The atmosphere during the meeting with Stanczyk was healthier than in the encounters with Kot. The mood of rancor so pronounced in the conversations with Kot was not present. Stanczyk was empathetic concerning the plight of the Jews and his statements were remarkably compassionate. But his views on the prospect of obtaining any concrete help from the Polish Government were devoid of all illusions. He justified it on the ground of the Government's weakness:

> In their plight, the Jews look forward to the Polish Government for help. But this Government resides in exile and has no power which could be used for backing the Jewish demands. This Government itself is in need of help. It must entreat for help, like a supplicant. . . .
>
> In view of these realities, you must mobilize the entire Jewish press of America. You must do everything in your might to exert pressures upon the Governments which united with us are today determined to achieve the war aims, also in regard to the Jews, and also in regard to Russia.[7]

Among the few accomplishments of all the endeavors to obtain help from the Polish Government, of great importance was the meeting of the Polish courier Karski with President Roosevelt. After his return from Poland, Karski became a primary source of information about the extent of the extermination and the conditions of the remnant of Jewish survivors. In a report of August 5,

1943, to the Polish Foreign Minister, the Polish ambassador in the
United States, Ciechanowski, describes how the opportunity of
Karski's meeting with Roosevelt came about.

> First, on July 5, I invited several close friends and advisers of the
> President for a gentlemen-only working dinner in the Embassy. Among
> those who came were the Supreme Court Justice Felix Frankfurter, the
> Deputy Attorney General Oscar Cox, and Ben Cohen, the legal adviser
> of Justice James F. Byrnes who is entrusted by the President with su-
> perordinate powers to coordinate all the Government agencies.
> After the dinner, under the reservation of strict confidentiality. Mr.
> Karski presented his detailed report. He was listened to with keenest
> attention. After he finished, some of the American personalities who
> were present proceeded to question him in depth on various subjects.
> The intensity of the interest he aroused can be measured by the dura-
> tion of the encounter: the dinner began at 8 p.m. and the visitors left the
> Embassy shortly before 1 a.m. Justice Frankfurter was shaken enough
> by Mr. Karski's report to ask me later, on his own initiative, whether I
> wouldn't think it advisable to tell the President of Mr. Karski's ex-
> istence. His idea was to bring the importance and the reliability of Mr.
> Karski's first-hand knowledge to the President's attention, together
> with the suggestion that he might see Mr. Karski in person. Of course, I
> consented with unqualified pleasure. The next day, Justice Frank-
> furter, who had previously postponed his vacation in order not to miss
> the opportunity of listening to Karski, paid a call on the President for
> the sole purpose of telling him about this man, Frankfurter also sent a
> note to Secretary of State Morgenthau, requesting his support for the
> idea of arranging for Karski an audience with the President. . . .
> The report of the meeting with the President is hereby enclosed. It
> has been written by Karski himself with my assistance. I had had
> numerous opportunities to observe the moods of President Roosevelt
> during various encounters, and I can now testify to the fact that never
> before have I seen him as deeply concerned and as totally absorbed as
> during that audience. It could be seen that the President was profound-
> ly impressed by the human side in the attitudes of the Polish nation. He
> told me he hadn't quite envisaged that anything like that could be
> possible. There is no doubt that he now realizes that Poland's role in
> the history of the present war is unique. He stressed it himself, and I
> heard the same from Secretary of State Hull. From all his responses it
> could be seen that his ideas about Poland have matured in a way which
> from our viewpoint is highly advantageous. . . .

Despite its great importance, Karski's meeting with Roosevelt
failed to produce concrete effects in terms of relief for Jews facing
imminent extermination. Instead, the Polish Embassy in Washington managed to exploit this meeting to promote various aims of
Polish politics.

During the same period of time, an idea crystallized to press the
Governments of the anti-Nazi coalition to bomb Auschwitz.
Although it was the largest extermination camp in existence,
Auschwitz was still expanding. As an outcome of the efforts of

Schwarzbart, the Polish army staff officers met their British counterparts to discuss the problem. The conclusion of the meeting apparently was to elicit opinion from the leadership of that part of the Polish underground which was subordinated to the Government-in-Exile. Accordingly, the following cable, signed by Orkan, went on August 24, 1943, to the Government Delegate in Poland:

> The British Army staff is willing to bomb Auschwitz: in particular the synthetic rubber factory and other factories of the same type in Silesia. We intend to plan these raids so as to make it possible to free the masses of Auschwitz inmates. Uttermost effort on your part will be needed to free the inmates and to assist them after they are freed. We also need your help in ranking the objectives according to their priority. This is prerequisite for guiding the aircraft so as to minimize Polish casualties. Let us know your opinion and your conditions. Let us also know whether you can do anything to prepare the inmates for this emergency in advance. It is anticipated that the raid will take place in the season of the longest nights.[9]

The reply of the Polish underground to this cable is not known. But it is known that no raids on either the Auschwitz extermination camp or the roads leading to that camp ever took place.

Evidence of the continuing extermination of the remnant of Polish Jewry's survivors was prevalent throughout all this time. The news promoted the Delegation of the Polish Jews to step up its efforts. The viewpoint of the Delegation can be seen from its successive memo of September 16, 1943, to the Polish Government:

> It now seems likely that there is almost no chance that any aid may reach the Polish Jews from outside. In view of the historically unprecedented tragedy which befell Polish Jewry, we hoped that the Polish Government would at least use its authority and its resources to secure some assistance from the inside to relieve the badly indigent Jewish population.
>
> From the reports which we obtained from persons who recently succeeded in escaping from Poland, we learned that, unfortunately, the compassion and the willingness to help the stricken co-citizens were not a popular attitude among the Polish society, especially in the initial phase of Polish Jewry's tragedy.
>
> On its part, the Government has throughout this time done little to organize any large-scale aid from inside, and to influence the entire Polish population accordingly.[10]

Schwarzbart pursued the matter of relief for the Jews on his own.

A number of futile attempts to persuade the Polish Government to help relieve the Polish Jews were also undertaken by the newly appointed Jewish member of the National Council in exile, Emanuel Szerer.

The Council for Rescuing the Jewish Population in Poland was finally set up by the Cabinet, but not until April 20, 1944. A state authority in charge of rescuing Polish Jews was therefore established twenty-seven months after the Nazis had set in motion the first extermination camp in Chelmno, eighteen months after nearly all the ghettos had already been liquidated and the vast majority of the Polish Jews murdered. At the moment the Council was set up, all that was left was the single pared down ghetto of Lodz, a number of labor camps for the Jews, and tens of thousands of Jews in hiding.

The Council for Rescuing the Jewish Population in Poland was formally established by the Cabinet's resolution of April 21, 1944.

The Six Council members appointed by the Minister of Interior were: Reiss as a representative of the Zionists, Szerer from the *Bund*, Babad from the *Aguda*, and Ciolkosz, Kulerski and Sopicki in the Polish contingent. Dr. Manfred Lachs was appointed to serve as the secretary. Ciolkosz was elected as the chairman, Reiss as the deputy chairman, and Szerer as the honorary secretary of the Council.

Nominally, the funds allotted to the Council amounted to £200,000; thereof one half from the budget of the Interior Ministry, and another half from the budget of the Ministry of Labor and Welfare. In reality no more than a small fraction of these funds actually found their way to the Council's treasury. The rest remained on paper, never to materialize.

The opening session of the Council was convened on May 26, 1944. The Polish Government gave much publicity to this conference, presenting it as an event of great importance. The list of speakers included Minister Banaczyk, followed by all the members of the Council. Polish press and the Polish Telegraphic Agency reported the session in extensive detail.

From the purely Jewish veiwpoint, however, the purpose of the Council was to rescue the Jews. When viewed this way, the realities presented themselves differently from the appearances. The members of the Representation of Polish Jews found that Polish Government officials would again and again postpone the delivery of the sums which had already been assigned to the Council.

The attempts to broadcast appeals calling for the Polish population to forward help to Jewish fugitives were also met with resistance. The decisive importance of such appeals was at once recognized by Lieutenant Jur, a courier who just then arrived from Poland. On June 12, 1944, he was invited by the Council for Rescuing the Jews to deliver a lecture on the conditions in occupied

Poland. Answering Reiss' question concerning the broadcasts, Jur said:

> In my opinion, there is a case for forceful advocacy here. It would help to announce that persons hiding the Jews will be considered members of the Home Organization (he obviously meant the Home Army - the Author) even when they do not belong to it. The promise to count the hiding of the Jews as participation in underground operations will act as an incentive. After all, those who hide the Jews imperil their lives no less so than those who fight in the ranks.[11]

But the suggestion was not accepted by the Polish authorities in exile.

After a few weeks it became increasingly obvious that the Polish authorities were determined to obstruct the implementation of their own resolutions concerning the relief for the Jews. On July 14, 1944, the Representation of Polish Jews finally submitted to the Government of the Polish Republic a memo which spelled all the matters out:

> In the face of the enormity of the tragedy which befell the Polish Jews, the action of the Government has throughout all this time been inadequate and tardy. The attitudes and the behavior of the Government towards the Jews has apparently been guided by two opposite considerations: by concern with the foreign and with the domestic impact of its actions.
>
> For foreign consumption the Government has repeatedly declared that the Jews are to enjoy full equal rights. But for domestic consumption, those declarations have been almost entirely devoid of any binding force. . . .
>
> The same held true later when the problem or rescuing the Jews from total extermination overshadowed all other problems in importance and urgency. For foreign consumption there were announcements that the Government was doing everything its within powers to rescue the Jews. For domestic consumption the Government didn't even do the easiest of the things which we postulated: namely to appoint several Jews to Polish diplomatic outposts in neutral countries so as to let them establish contacts with the Jews in Poland and lead the rescue action from there.
>
> We do appreciate the Government's note of December 1942 to the Allied Governments. Yet even this note was overdue.[12]

Independently from the endeavors of the Council for Rescuing the Jewish Population, various Jewish leaders undertook individual efforts to obtain the help of the Polish Government for the purpose of various one-time rescue undertakings. Among initiatives of this kind belongs the idea of having the Polish underground strike at the camps and arm the Jewish fugitives. On August 10, 1944 Ernest Fischer sent a note on this subject to Schwarzbart:

... I assume that you have entered into negotiations with the Polish Government with a view to their issuing instructions to the Polish Underground to liberate people in Jewish concentration camps as soon as this will be possible, or to supply the inmates with weapons and to protect them in the critical period when the Red Army will advance towards those places while the Germans will be retreating.[13]

Following Fischer's initiative, Schwarzbart sent a note to Mikolajczyk with the request to issue instructions to the air force to strike at the camps. Subsequently, Schwarzbart discussed this matter with Mikolajczyk during their meeting of August 30. Mikolajczyk then told Schwarzbart that the Government had already decided to instruct the leadership of the Polish Underground to attack the camps. He stressed that instructions to this effect had already been sent to Poland. In the now available documents there is no evidence whatsoever that any such decision was ever made, nor that any such instructions to the Polish Underground were ever sent.

Toward the end of 1944/1945 no Jewish leader could any longer delude himself about the Polish Government's support for any measures of providing the Polish Jews with relief that would be more than token. The schemes of Schwarzbart and the hopes of the Representation of Polish Jews were by then totally frustrated.

On July 23, 1945, the Representation dissolved itself. The decisive argument of the dissolution was that the Jewish survivors in Poland had in the meantime set up new representative bodies of their own. By virtue of this fact, the mandates of the Representation members could therefore be considered irrelevant.

NOTES

1. Sprawozdanie z dzialalnosci Reprezentacji Zydostwa Polskiego w latach 1940–1945 (Report of the activities of the Representation of Polish Jews during the years 1940–1945), p.95.
2. Op. cit., p. 54.
3. Op. cit., p. 55.
4. Op. cit., p. 56.
5. Op. cit., p. 80.
6. Schwarzbart, Isaac, The Story of the Warsaw Ghetto Uprising, New York, 1953, p. 12.
7. The Zionist Archive, J 25/2.
8. YVA, M-2/753.
9. YVA, 0-25/94.
10. Report of the activities of the Representation...., p. 128.
11. The Zionist Archive, J 25/89.
12. Report of the activities of the Representation...., pp. 179–182.
13. YVA, M-21/241.

CHAPTER NINE

Jews in General Anders' Army in the Soviet Union

THE ORGANIZATIONAL PHASE

Mustering of the Polish Armed Forces in the Soviet Union (*Polskie Sily Zbrojne w ZSSR*), known as "Anders' Army," began during the latter half of 1941. Until the end of July 1941, the Polish Government-in-Exile in London had not maintained diplomatic relations with the Soviet Union, condemning her as an invader who had conspired with Nazi Germany to seize the eastern portions of Poland during the invasion of 1939. Even the dramatic *volte-face* in the wake of Hitler's attack on the Soviet Union, on July 22, 1941 did not bring about an immediate thaw in Polish-Soviet relations. The Polish Prime Minister in Exile, Wladyslaw Sikorski, maintained that Poland should seek avenues of consultation with the Soviet Union and that she should join the new alignment of forces arising out of the Soviet Union's entering the anti-Nazi camp. The Poles did insist however that any agreement with the Soviet Union be conditional upon an unequivocal Soviet commitment that the Polish state to be reconstituted after the war have its former eastern borders reinstated — that is, the Soviet Union was to rescind its annexation of Western Byelorussia, the Western Ukraine and the Wilna district. The Soviets refused to undertake any such commitment while the tense and exhausting deliberations on the issue resulted in a split amongst the Poles. The official agreement, signed by representatives of Poland and the Soviet Union in London on July 30,1941 contained a clause stating that "The Government of the Union of Soviet Socialist Republics recognizes that the Soviet-German treaties of 1939 relative to territorial changes in Poland have lost their validity."[1]

A prime consideration for Sikorski in seeking an agreement with the Soviet Union was the anticipation of establishing in the Soviet Union a Polish contingent which would be subordinate to the Polish Government-in-Exile in London. The forces that the Poles had managed to muster in the West after the debacle of September 1939, had been almost completely lost in the campaign in France. The Poles attached much importance to a substantial Polish force taking its place alongside the Allied forces in the struggle against Hitler.

In the wake of the debacle, masses of Polish citizens had reached the interior of the Soviet Union, some as prisoners-of-war, some as refugees who had fled before the Germans and some as exiles deported by the Soviet authorities; their number is estimated to have reached a million to a million and a half.[2] A large proportion of these, perhaps even the majority, were interned in Soviet prison camps, where they suffered greatly from degradation, intense hardship and harsh weather. The agreement which was signed in July 1941 stated that "The Government of the Union of Soviet Socialist Republics expresses its consent to the formation on the territory of the Union of Soviet Socialist Republics of a Polish Army under a commander appointed by the Government of the Republic of Poland, in agreement with the Government of the Union of Soviet Socialist Republics.[3]

In a separate protocol appended to the general agreement, the Soviet Government undertook, immediately upon the reestablishment of diplomatic relations, to "grant amnesty to all Polish citizens who are at present deprived of their freedom on the territory of the USSR either as prisoners-of-war or on other adequate grounds."[4].

It is estimated that the number of Jews among the Polish exiles in the Soviet Union reached 400,000,[5] about a third of the total number. Their proportion among the exiles was thus more than triple their proportion among the population of the independent Polish State in the years between the wars. Many of the Jewish exiles were banished and imprisoned under cruel conditions in Soviet prisons and labor camps.

Thanks to the accord reached between Poland and the Soviet Union and the subsequent military agreement,[6] masses of tortured, frail and infirm Polish citizens, Jews among them, were released from the prisons and the camps, whereupon recruiting of Polish military units and the armed struggle of the Poles became possible.

The first Polish units—two divisions plus a support force—were concentrated in army camps in the Saratov region of the Volga. (Staff headquarters were set up at Buzuluk, over 100 km. from Kuybishev; one division was at Tatishtyevo and the other at Tock.) General Wladyslaw Anders was given command. With the opening of the Polish Embassy in Kuybishev, diplomatiic relations between the two countries were normalized. The first Polish Ambassador to the Soviet Union during the war years, Professor Stanislaw Kot, was, until his appointment to this post, a senior minister in the Government-in-Exile, and was regarded as a close friend and confidant of Sikorski's.

From the very beginning of the recruiting, thousands of released Jewish prisoners and exiles flocked to the collection points, acting either on their own initiative or on a basis of orders. For the majority, mobilization signified a guarantee of day-to-day existence and a relatiave sense of permanence, given the war situation.

The first units set up had a disproportionately large number of Jews; according to Anders the Jews at times constituted sixty per cent, and according to Kot, forty per cent. The surge of Jews to the ranks of the Polish Armed Forces aroused suspicion and dismay. In Polish sources one finds complaints to the effect that the Russians intentionally released the Jews from the camps before all others so as to flood the Polish Armed Forces with the "Jewish elememt."

Another complaint was incessantly voiced by the Poles in the matter of the "national reckoning" which they had with the Jews. Anders himself would begin every meeting with Jewish representatives and delegations, and the orders he issued relating to Jews, with the "reminder" that the Poles bore the Jews a severe grievance for their disloyal behavior during the occupation and internment in the prisons and camps.[7]

In his book, *An Army in Exile*, describing the Polish Armed Forces organized in the Soviet Union, Anders begins the chapter on "The Jews in the Armed Forces" with these words: "I was greatly disturbed when, in the beginning, large numbers from among the national minorities, and first and foremost Jews, began streaming to enlist. As I have already mentioned, some of the Jews had warmly welcomed the Soviet armies that invaded Poland in 1939. . . "[8] In documents that were not intended for publication or for public comsumption, General Anders' style is much harsher.[9] Kot, too, writes in his report to the Foreign Minister in London, that "the

Poles feel very bitter towards the Jews for their behavior during the Soviet occupation—their enthusiastic welcome of the Red Army, the insults which they directed towards the Polish officers and men who were under Soviet arrest, offering their services to the Soviets, informing on Poles, and other acts of the sort."[10]

Another claim that recurs in the Polish sources is that the Jews, by and large, are physically inferior and are not suited for active military service. This is what Kot wrote:

> "The liberation of Polish citizens in accordance with the agreement was greeted by the Jews with great enthusiasm. The decent ones among them rejoiced at Poland's achievement, while the inferior element sought to cover up their past behavior by vociferous identification with Poland. It was from this element that large numbers streamed to enlist in the Armed Forces. Not knowing what to do with themselves, they decided that it was obligatory to join the Armed Forces, and once having joined they almost always became a burden. They were found unfit for military service or they were deferred for a time, and meanwhile they would noisily demand that the relief work be continued."[11]

The claim that the Jews were "unfit for military service" undoubtedly had much deeper roots. Amongst the Poles, and in particular amongst the professional soldiers, the opinion was commonly held that the Jews were cowards by nature and were not suited for military service or useful on the battle-field.

The testimonies of Jews who served in the Armed Forces of General Anders and of those who tried to enlist are replete with accounts of many who were rejected because of their Jewish ancestry, and tell of crude injustices done to others who were permitted to serve but denied promotion. These very testimonies reveal the existence of two stages in the recruitment process. During the first stage, which extended from the granting of pardons and the beginning of the organization of the Armed Forces until the end of 1941, a large number of Jews were accepted and they constituted a sizable proportion of the units being formed. However, those Jews who were accepted and remained in the ranks throughout the duration of the war, relate that Jews were often transferred to the support units to the *kolkhozes* in the wake of deliberate "inspections" and re-examinations, or were simply cashiered from the service. During the second stage, when the recruiting was carried out at several centers in Soviet Central Asia, disqualification of Jews, according to these testimonies, was automatic: Jews would try a second and a third time to enlist, and each time they would meet with a flat rejection. Their physical fitness had no bearing on the decision; they were disqualified just because they were Jews. These disqualifications, according to the testimonies, were partly based on restrictions or prohibitions imposed by the Soviet authorities; the principle of collective disqualification was, however, applied not only to Jews but to Ukrainians and Byelorussians as well.

Henryk Dankiewicz, a student of the Warsaw Polytechnic, with an assimilated background, was among the first to present himself for recruiting. He was accepted and sent to officers' training school. In January 1942, the commander of the school singled out "twelve Jews, and one Pole for the sake of appearances" and informed them that they were being expelled from the course since they were not suitable officer material. Some time later, they were transported to a different place and again brought before a recruiting committee. This committee assigned to each of them, without exception, type E classification which meant absolute disqualification. Dankiewicz tried his luck one more time in the city of Tzezar in Uzbekistan, and there too the scene was repeated: all the Poles, without exception, were accepted and the Jews, Ukrainians and Byelorussians were rejected. Dankiewicz finally enlisted in the army organized by the Polish pro-Communists in the Soviet Union; he was given officer's rank and fought later in the Kościuszko division.[12]

Another Jew, Michael Licht, a gymnastics and sports teacher by profession, who had served as N.C.O. in the battle over Poland at the outset of World War II, also presented himself at the recruiting center together with several other Jews who were, in his words "strong as oaks." All of them were disqualified, having been found physically unfit. Licht tried to enlist a second time, and was accepted, making him feel as if he had "finally made it." However, ten days later he was expelled from the service together with all the other Jews. According to his testimony, only Jewish physicians were retained, or those who paid a hundred-dollar bribe to the Polish officers. He also claims that the taking of bribes by the Polish officers was done quite openly.[13]

Another witness, Felix Davidson, an engineer by profession, relates that he did not encounter any particular difficulty on enlisting in the Armed Forces of General Anders. He credits this fact to his profession. He did however have problems in the course of his service: "I asked to be allowed to take a mechanics course, but was rejected because I was a Jew. Anti-Semitism was openly practiced in the Armed Forces of General Anders."[14] Simon Perl, an electrician by profession, was also disqualified. He relates how in the city of Fergana, in Uzbekistan, thousands of Jews, Poles and Ukrainians sought to enlist:

"The scenes familiar from Poland before the war were here reenacted. The Poles were automatically included among the ranks of the army; the Jews were graded type "D" —unfit for active military service — and even those who had already been accepted were expelled for trivial reasons. Finally, my turn arrived to appear before the committee; appearing together with me was Richterman, a swimming champion. Both of us were graded type "D" . . ."

Perl did finally manage to make his way into the ranks of the army with the assistance of a Polish officer whom he had known for many years.[15] Meir Lustgarten, the son of farmers from Western Galicia, relates:

"I was accepted into the army without any difficulty. During the first stage of organization many Jews presented themselves for enlistment; in the beginning they were accepted without any difficulties and there was in fact a Jewish majority in the army. This naturally did not please the Poles who sought ways of getting rid of the Jews, or at the very least of limiting the percentage of Jews accepted into the army. The Polish Command thus ordered all soldiers to appear before a medical board. During the examination most of the Jews were marked grade "D" for physical fitness and were released from the service. This occurred at the outset of the winter of 1941–42. Men were freezing from the cold and nevertheless they were released. . . . From then on, Jews were not accepted into the Polish Army; only Poles were accepted"[16]

Dozens of testimonies checked by the author of this article all present a uniform picture. The directives which ostensibly determined the acceptance of personnel into Polish Army were not applied neither to Jews nor to the members of the other minorities. At any rate, during the later stages of the recruiting no objective criteria whatsoever were applied. It is a fact that during these later stages the Soviets forbade the recruiting of some of the minorities, including Jews. However, it will be seen that this prohibition was not strictly enforced; being open to varying interpretations it served often as a pretext for closing the door to Jews. In any case, all agree that the restrictions imposed by the Soviet authorities did not apply to those Jews who had already been recruited and were serving in the army. Yet, the facts show that not only were new Jewish soldiers not accepted, but also that Jews already serving were systematically and deliberately expelled. In his letter to General Z. Bohusz-Szyszko of April 30, 1942, Kot wrote:

. . . complaints are again being voiced by Jews that a purge is being carried out in the ranks of the army so as to reduce their numbers, and

that those who are healthiest are being released as sick. Is this necessary and does it serve our interests at this time . . . ?[17]

Who then were the Jews who were, nevertheless, accepted into
the army in 1942 or who succeeded in remaining despite the
obstacles and the relentless purges? The impression is that physicians and those trained in the essential professions were accepted,
as well as individuals enjoying the backing of influential Poles. The
Jews who remained in the army were those who were protected by
their superiors or those who simply could not be expelled because
of their excellent service record.

The dominant influence underlying the relationship of the army
command to Jews was undoubtedly the anti-Semitism so deeply
imbedded in the minds of many Poles. This antagonistic attitude
was particularly prevalent among the officer class, and it thus
found expression in army life. In a letter sent from Moscow to
General Sikorski on September 5, 1941, Kot wrote (it was only a few
days after his arrival in the Soviet Union): ". . . I discussed with
General Anders the matter of the Jews. They are generally accepted
into the Army when they apply; after I explained to him the importance of [of recruiting Jews] vis-à-vis America and others, he
promised to stress the necessity of maintaining a friendly relationship with them . . ."[18] Kot often reiterated the political significance
of the conscription of Jews. In a letter to Mikolajczyk[19] on October
11, 1941, he wrote:

> . . . in the future, when we will be dealing with the eastern borders,
> this stream of Jewish recruits will be of considerable political weight,
> particularly when the Ukrainians' systematic hatred of anything Polish
> is taken into account . . .

In that very same letter he notes that "our men in the Armed
Forces, particularly those types like Pstrokoński,[20] are already
anxious to institute a *numerus clausus* in the military institutions."[21]

Of great significance was the conversation between Sikorski and
Stalin which took place in the Kremlin on December 3, 1941. For
the Polish side, both Anders and Kot also attended, and representing the Russians was Foreign Minister Molotov. The discussion
was the high point of Sikorski's much-heralded visit to the Soviet
Union and it was devoted almost entirely to the problems of organization of the Polish Armed Forces and their future. When Anders
dwelt at length upon the difficult conditions under which the
organization was being carried out, and a suggestion was made to
transfer the operation to Persia where more conducive conditions

prevailed, Stalin angrily retorted: "If the Poles don't want to fight, they should leave." To this Sikorski replied: "Mr. President, when you say that one of our soldiers does not want to fight, you insult me." At a late stage in the discussion, Anders submitted details about the size of the force and its distribution at the various collection points:

> ... I am counting on 150,000 people, that is eight divisions together with the army's maintenance forces. Perhaps there are even more of our people, but among them there is also a great number of Jews who do not want to serve in the army. Stalin: Jews are poor warriors. Gen. S.: Many of the Jews who reported are speculators or have been punished for dealing in contraband; they never will make good soldiers. These I don't need in the Polish Army.[22] Gen. A.: Two hundred Jews deserted from Buzuluk upon hearing the false report on the bombing of Kuybishev. More then sixty deserted from the 5th Division a day before the distribution of arms to the soldiers was made public. Stalin: Yes, Jews are bad warriors.[23]

It would appear that all three of these leaders found a common denominator in their assessment of Jews as soldiers. There is also no doubt that Sikorski and Anders carefully weighed everything they said during the course of their discussion with Stalin and they realized the full significance of their words.

The very fact that the Poles were given permission to create an autonomous army within the Soviet Union conferred preferential status and the power of authority. (For many, the chance to be recruited while in the Soviet Union was virtually their salvation.)[24] The Poles realized immediately that they had been granted a position of power and this recognition enhanced their feeling of security and mastery. They did not at first dare to make full use of their freedom fearing that any step contrary to Soviet law and accepted custom would have repercussions. It may be assumed that this was what prevented them from blocking from the very beginning the stream of Jews who sought to enlist in the Army. In discussions with Soviet officers, and in particular in the discussion with Stalin, the Poles sought to sound out the Soviet reaction to imposing restriction on the recruiting of Jews and other minorities. The Poles knew full well that official discrimination against Jews was not acceptable at that time in the Soviet Union. Many surmised—as did the rightist forces in Europe—that a secret pact existed between the Jews and the government and the men in power in the Soviet Union. Stalin's concurring with Anders' and Sikorski's evaluation of the Jews and their ability as soldiers removed any doubt from the minds of the Poles. The Soviet leader in his turn also knew how to exploit the Poles' frankness to his own advantage, as we shall later see.

THE SIGNIFICANCE OF THE SOVIET RESTRICITONS ON THE RECRUITING OF JEWS.

Just a short while after the talks with Stalin and after operative consultations at the military level, Soviet liaison officers informed the Polish Armed Forces authorities in late December that recruiting for General Anders' Army would encompass all Polish nationals of Polish descent, with the exception of Jews, Ukrainians and Byelorussians, who on November 29, 1939 were resident in the territories annexed by the Soviet Union and declared Soviet citizens.

On December 30, Anders sent a telegram to Kot in Kuybishev reporting that two days earlier he had been told by Colonel Wolkowysky, a senior Soviet liaison officer, that "of all the Polish citizens living in the Western Ukraine and Western Byelorussia, only ethnic Poles may be recruited for our Armed Forces.[25] On February 21, 1942, Anders cabled Sikorski stating that the Soviets authorized recruiting of all Polish citizens; from the territories held by the Soviets in 1939, only ethnic Poles were to be recruited.[26] On February 25 Kot asked Anders to clarify the recruitment rights of non-ethnic Polish citizens—whether it was intended to exclude those who were born in the territory taken over in 1939 or was applicable to any individual who was a permanent resident of these territories prior to the outbreak of the war?[27] To this Anders replied: "The Soviet authorities have officially informed me that recruiting encompasses all Polish citizens who until November 29 (1939) were residents of the territories occupied by the Germans [formerly held by the Soviets]."[28]

The Soviet initiative directed towards preventing the Jewish citizens of Poland from enlisting should have helped the Poles to achieve their goal, for it gave them a ready-made answer for the free world: the discrimination was a result of a Soviet coercion and pressure. However, the matter was not that simple. Initially it seems that the Soviet restriction applied only to the members of the other ethnic groups resident in the annexed territories on the date that Soviet citizenship was conferred on all the residents of these territories. As for the Poles in the annexed territories, they too had become Soviet citizens, but the Soviets claimed that they were showing exceptional lenience and making an extraordinary gesture in allowing them to be recruited for the Polish Armed Forces. Consent to this restriction was tantamount to indirect recognition of the

Soviet annexation of Polish territory, and to this the Poles were, of course, vociferously opposed. The Soviet-imposed restriction thus placed the Poles in a quandary, and it is against this background that one should view the anxious questioning by the various Polish authorities concerning the precise meaning of the restriction. It was perhaps not by chance that the Soviets chose the matter of the recruitment for the Polish Armed Forces as a means to undermine the jurisdiction of the Poles over certain categories of Polish citizens living in the occupied territories. It is reasonable to assume that the idea of excluding Jews and other minority groups was broached only after Sikorski and Anders had voiced their anti-Jewish comments in the presence of Stalin and after they had revealed their intentions of disqualifying the Jews as being unfit for "our Army." An episode that occurred the day after the conversation with Stalin, at a dinner given by Stalin at the Kremlin in honor of Sikorski and his aides, is most revealing. Sikorski again raised the issue of the release of prisoners-of-war from Soviet "labour divisions" and complained that the process was too slow and not sufficiently comprehensive. Anders then remarked that he had been officially informed that Byelorussians, Ukrainians and Jews would not be released at all. "Were they not Polish citizens?" he asked in anger. "They have never ceased in fact to be Polish citizens, because your agreements with Germany have been annulled." Stalin then replied, all the while ignoring the basic question that Anders had raised: "What do you need Byelorussians, Ukrainians and Jews for? It is Poles you need, they are the best soldiers."[29]

Naturally, the status assigned to Jewish nationality or religion in this context raises pointed questions concerning the attitudes of the Soviet regime and Communist ideology; however, as in so many other cases, here too pragmatic political interests took precedence over ideological principles. The Polish Embassy rejected both the claim and the interpretation of the agreement as made by the Soviet Foreign Ministry. Kot explained that from the Polish standpoint all citizens, regardless of ethnic origin or race, enjoyed equal rights, and this equality applied both to the amnesty being granted and to the privilege of enlisting in the Polish Armed Forces. Polish law did not discriminate among its citizens, and the military agreement granted every Polish citizen the right to enlist in the Polish Armed Forces.[30] On January 5, 1942, the Soviet Foreign Ministry replied that after studying the arguments put forward by the Polish Embassy with regard to the different categories of citizens, it saw no reason to modify its position. It continued in a lengthy paragraph "explaining" the distinction between "occupation" and the "entry" of Soviet soldiers into the eastern territories of Poland; the gist of the claim was that the annexation of the territories was carried out "as a result of the freely expressed will of the population of those districts."[31] This correspondence between the Soviet Ministry of Foreign Affairs and the Polish Embassy was preceded by an announcement by military circles to the effect that certain categories of citizens were not to be recruited; no protest is known to have been lodged either by military or civilian elements in the Polish camp against the Soviet restrictions imposed in the military sector. Kot emphazises that in the discussion with Stalin on March 18, 1942, Anders did not even hint at the issue of the restrictions on the recruitment of the national minorities.[32]

The documentary evidence and eyewitness accounts indicate that the Soviet authorities did not as a general rule actively interfere in the recruiting process, and they did not enforce rigid adherence to the regulations stipulating rejection of certain of the national minorities. Soviet representatives did sit on the recruiting committees, but only on very rare occasions would they investigate the ethnic background of the potential recruit; for the most part they refrained from taking an active role in the work of the committees.

Numerous testimonies from Jewish candidates for enlistment and from individuals who actually served in General Anders' Armed Forces do not intimate that anyone was rejected on the Soviet representative's intervention or because he was a resident of the annexed territories. Moreover, no difference whatsoever can be discerned in the treatment of the "legitimate" recruits from the western provinces as opposed to treatment of those who, according to Soviet directives, should have been rejected. We have in our possession a list of recruits, both Poles and Jews, drawn up by the military some time between 12–20 of August 1942. This list, unique among the papers found in Anders' files, reveals that of a total of 88 Jews presenting themselves for enlistment, 65 were disqualified and 23 were found fit for service; in contrast, out of a total of 75 Poles, 56 were listed as fit for service. The list also states the grounds for disqualification, but in no case does it note that the Soviet directives were the reason.[33]

A memorandum sent on November 10, 1942, by the Bundists Y. Glicksman and Feinsilber, evacuated with Anders' Army, to comrades in the United States and England, mentions the Soviet prohibition and the attitude of the Polish Armed Forces. A fierce anti-Soviet stance coupled with loyalty to the Polish Government in London were characteristic of the Polish Bundists at that time. In their memorandum Glicksman and Feinsilber state that:

> "The position taken by the Soviet authorities with regard to citizenship has paved the way for discrimination against Jews on the part of Polish anti-Semitic elements. This was most blatant in the matter of recruiting for the Polish Armed Forces. The fact is that the position adopted by the Soviet authorities was instrumental in the exclusion of thousands of Jewish youth who were fit to serve, from the ranks of the Armed Forces. However, a large share of the responsibility for this situation devolves upon Polish military elements."[34]

Ambassador Kot who, as we have seen, attached political significance to demonstrations of concern for Jews, did show a degree of goodwill towards Jews despite his numerous contradictory statements on the subject, and frequently dealt with questions relating to Polish Jews living in the Soviet Union. In a cable to Sikorski of April 10, 1942, he wrote:

> . . . it should be brought to General Anders' attention that the systematic anti-Semitic policy pursued by the General Staff — a policy at which certain officers on the recruiting committee excelled — unwittingly serves the interests of the Soviets, who are seeking to distinguish between Jews and Poles so as to create a precedent which would enable them to take over the territories in the east. . .

Here Kot makes no mention of the Soviet prohibition nor does he claim that it is tying the hands of the Poles; quite the contrary — he emphasizes that Polish officers are cooperating with the Soviets and are carrying our their wishes by getting rid of the Jews.[35]

It is clear, therefore, that the Soviet directives did not have a decisive influence upon the policies and practices of the Poles with regard to the recruiting. The societ directives actually gave the Poles a free hand and served as a ready pretext which was later used to justify to the outside world the low percentage of Jews in the Polish Armed Forces. From a political point of view, the aims of the Poles and the Soviets were diametrically opposed. The Russians sought to emphasize the basic political principle of distinguishing between segments of the population in the east and the other parts of Poland, thus creating a precedent for the future. Whether the Poles were carrying out the order in practice, and preventing Jews from enlisting did not particularly concern the Soviet authorities, although they did fear the possibility of desertion from conscripted units of their own and escape from camps. The Russians attached no importance to the recruiting of Jews from the eastern provinces

— the fact is that at a later stage the Soviet authorities placed no restrictions upon Jews from the various pre-1939 Polish provinces who wished to join the ranks of the Berling Polish Army, which was set up by the Communist-influenced League of Polish Patriots (*Zwiazek Patriotów Polskich*).

Although in Polish military circles there was some difference of opinion concerning the political significance of the Soviet directives, they most willingly adopted the selectivity which was their key feature, adding to it their own brand of discrimination and rejection.

THE "JEWISH LEGION" AND THE "JEWISH UNIT IN KOLTUBANKA"

For a while the concept of a separate "Jewish Legion" within General Anders' Armed Forces in the Soviet Union drew the consideration and the attention of Polish and Jewish sources alike. The idea was independently raised at one and the same time by two individuals active in the Zionist-Revisionist Movement in Poland between the wars — Mark Kahan, a lawyer, and Miron Sheskin, an engineer. Both had been imprisoned in Soviet camps, had been released following the Polish-Soviet Agreement, and had managed to reach the first recruiting centers of the Polish Armed Forces. Only after they met did they band together to try to put their idea into action.

Mark Kahan was sent to the Tolsk concentration center.[36] He found there that relations between the Poles and the Jews were unstable and at times violent fights would erupt. It was this situation which, he says, brought home the need for separating the Jewish from the Polish soldiers; this in turn led to the idea of establishing a "Jewish Legion" within General Anders' Armed Forces. He brought his proposal before General Michal Tokarzewski-Karasiewicz, the commander of the force in Tolsk and an acquaintance of his from the pre-war days of independent Poland. According to Kahan, Tokarzewski showed interest in the idea of establishing a Jewish unit and promised to take up the matter with Anders. Kahan was subsequently summoned to army headquarters in Buzuluk, where he met Sheskin who told him of his meeting with Anders that had been arranged on his own initiative to discuss the possibility of setting up a Jewish unit in the Armed Forces now organizing. After the war, both Kahan and Sheskin claimed that their primary consideration was the potential role that a Jewish military force might play in the envisaged battle for Eretz Israel. Kot notes that the two advocates of the idea regarded the planned unit as a force that would eventually reach the battle theater there.[37] It is indeed quite conceivable the Kahan and Sheskin, both of whom had been active in Zionist-nationalist affairs, did in fact hope that the unit would eventually have a role to play in a Jewish national struggle, even through the immediate stimulus for establishing a Jewish unit arose from the troubled relationships prevailing among the Jews and the Poles within the ranks of the army in formation.

We do not have the written material that Kahan and Sheskin presented nor do we know the precise date of their joint initiative. From Kahan's testimony and the comments of Rabbi Rozen-Szczekacz,[38] a chaplain in the Armed Forces of General Anders who was a close friend of both Kahan and Sheskin, one gets the impression that their plan called for concentrating all the Jews already recruited and those seeking to enlist into one separate unit; all the enlisted personnel and officers of the unit would be Jews, while only the senior military and command positions would be manned by Poles. Since the discussions on the establishment of this separate unit took place some time before Sikorski's trip to Moscow, and on the basis of other indications as well, the assumption seems clear that the idea was first broached during the months of September-October 1941.

After Kahan's arrival in Buzuluk, Anders summoned Sheskin for an additional discussion during which he made it clear that he regarded the "Jewish Legion" plan as essentially political in nature and therefore falling within the purview of Ambassador Kot.[39] Kahan and Sheskin thereupon proceeded to Kuybishev to meet with Kot. The Ambassador put off making a decision pending Sikorski's arrival, apparently because he wished to discuss the matter with him. Some time later Kot returned a categorically negative reply. The Poles utterly rejected the proposal to establish a separate Jewish unit within their Armed Forces in the Soviet Union.

Kahan surmises that the matter of the "Legion" was raised during Sikorski's discussions with Stalin, and that it was at this level that it was rejected. He also assumes that the opposition came from Stalin and that Kot did not dare to defend the proposal in the face of Stalin's *nyet*. [40] However, these assumptions have no basis in actual fact. One can hardly imagine that the Poles attached such importance to the proposal that they saw fit to raise the issue during the summit meeting with Stalin. From the information at hand we can conclude that the Poles were not in the habit of discussing with the Soviets matters relating to the composition and internal structure of their armed forces — this matter was exclusively for Polish determination. The full minutes in our possession of the discussions between the Poles and Stalin and his aides, reveal not a single word of the proposal to establish a Jewish unit within the Polish Armed Forces. One does find references indicating that certain Poles — among whom were Anders and Kot — took note of the proposal to set up a separate Jewish unit, but nowhere is there any indication that the Soviets had formed an opinion on the matter or that Soviet considerations had any bearing whatsoever upon the decision of the Poles.

It is clear, therefore, that the negative decision was taken by the Polish authorities. Kahan claims that some of the senior military staff, including Anders, were in favor of the idea, and that the rejection came from Kot; this version is only partially confirmed. It is apparently true that certain officers in General Anders' Armed Forces did support the idea — for a combination of conflicting reasons. However, Anders and Kot saw eye to eye on the matter, and both were instrumental in its rejection. Kot relates that on October 24, 1941 a discussion was held on the subject at the Embassy in Kuybishev, with the participation of Jewish representatives (of the Bund, undoubtedly including Ludwik Seidenman, the Embassy's adviser on Jewish affairs). Anders also took part in this discussion and it was he who blocked the establishment of the separate Jewish units.[41]

On the other hand, Kahan's assertion that there existed a broad front of Jewish opposition to the plan is substantially correct. According to Kahan,[42] the Jews of Buzuluk belonged to what had been the affluent class in independent Poland and they feared that the establishment of the "Legion" would endanger their rights to Polish citizenship and perhaps also prevent them from recovering their property after the war. It appears that there was a large proportion of formerly wealthy and assimilated Jews in Buzuluk who for personal reasons were not in favor of the idea of separation. The Bundists, who wielded considerable influence in Embassy circles, adopted a position of emphatic opposition to the plan. On October 16, 1941, one of the senior Bundists who chanced to be in the Soviet Union, Lucjan Blit, sent a memorandum to General Anders "concerning the plan to raise military units manned by Jewish citizens of Poland residing in the Soviet Union."[43] Blit notes that he was informed by the army staff that the number of Jewish recruits was above nine percent: that is, it exceeded the percentage of Jews in the population of pre-war Poland. "This fact, which should have given satisfaction to every true patriot, seems to have led to a number of problems of a psychological nature among the organizers and commanders of the various units of our Armed Forces in the territory of the Soviet Union," complained Blit. "The cause would seem to be the anti-Semitic feelings which prevail to various degrees among Polish personnel." Blit claimed that staff officers sought to channel overflow Jewish volunteers into the work units or to establish separate Jewish units in an effort to provide a safety valve for these anti-Semitic feelings. He was informed that these tendencies had gained the support of several Jewish communal leaders who belonged to the extreme nationalist faction. Blit, however, claimed that because the Nazi regime which was enslaving Poland was eager to see a division of the population along ethnic and national lines, the establishment of separate Jewish units would necessarily be interpreted as a political and moral victory for Nazism. The Polish command would be undertaking a heavy responsiblity for which it would be answerable to the whole world should it decide in favor of such units. The Jewish nationalists sought to create a "Jewish ghetto within the Polish Armed Forces," but to do so would run contrary to the interests of the Polish Government and to the sincere aspirations to live together in harmony "which beat in the hearts of the masses of Jewish workers of Poland."

Kot, as was his custom, was guided by diplomatic considerations. He believed that the establishment of a separate unit would serve the Soviet goal of fragmentation and at the same time create an unfavorable stir in the free countries, particularly in the United States. Kot noted that among the initiators and supporters of the idea were "representatives of the Revisionists-Jabotinskyites, the lawyer K. from Warsaw and the engineer S. from Wilna and. . . officers who are known to be anti-Semites are said to be actively supporting the idea of establishing separate Jewish units."[44]

According to Rabbi Rozen, three types of supporters of the idea of a "Jewish Legion" can be distinguished within the Armed Forces of General Anders: 1) Real friends, who sought to assist and aid Jewish national aspirations; 2) A group of officers who supported the old regime and resented Sikorski and Anders; they hoped to win the support of Jewish circles abroad by favoring the creation of the "Legion"; 3) Plain anti-Semites who wanted to rid the Armed Forces of Jews through the medium of the "Jewish Legion."[45]

Anders refers on two occasions to the proposal to establish separate Jewish units. In his book he wrote:

> . . . a series of Jewish communal activists wanted to point up Jewish particularity. The two foremost representatives of Polish Jewry, Alter and Ehrlich, approached me on the matter. After numerous dis-

cussions they admitted that their proposal was unrealistic, for it meant that I would also have to set up Ukrainian or Byelorussian units. I took the position that if we were to continue with the forming of the Polish Army, all citizens without religious or ethnic distinctions could be included.[46]

Anders goes on to quote at length from a letter he received from Alter and Ehrlich, who were the leaders of the Bund. The letter is dated October 31, 1941, and in it, according to Anders' version, the authors advocate one unified military organization in which Jews and Poles alike would be assigned positions on the basis of equal rights. "The primary function of this army must be the waging of the armed struggle on behalf of a free and democratic Poland, the common homeland of all her citizens. . . [47] Anders interprets this letter as a retreat from the position the authors had formerly held and an acceptance of his viewpoint.

The second time Anders dealt with this issue was at a 1967 press conference with Polish journalists. He said:

While we were still in the Soviet Union, several Jewish leaders approached me with the request that separate Jewish units be established. I refused, because in order to be consistent I would have had to establish separate Ukrainian and Byelorussian units too, and this was most undesirable in the Soviet Union. Doing so would have demonstrated the presence of Jews, Ukrainians and Byelorussians in the Polish Armed Forces in the Soviet Union, and the Soviets had tried to prevent that from happening.[48]

There is no basis, of course, for Anders' claim that Alter and Ehrlich had originated the idea of separate Jewish units and that under his influence they had been induced to abandon the proposal. Kot, in his book, deliberately points out every false step made by his rival Anders; in this respect he notes that the General's comments on Alter and Ehrlich "do not, of course, conform to the truth."[49] There are however no grounds for assuming that Anders was wilfully misleading; he was probably just mistaken. Totally lacking as he was in understanding of the postures and ideological variations among the main blocs in Jewish public life in Poland, he could easily have attributed to the *Bund* leaders a stance that was actually quite unthinkable for them. We can, however, safely assume that Anders' claim that he had contact with Alter and Ehrlich was not pure fabrication. In his book Anders praises the leaders of the Bund as loyal patriots of the Polish homeland, while in a note not meant for publication, he prides himself on having thrown these two leaders out of his office.[50] It seems that Alter and Ehrlich were trying to have tension between the Jews and the Poles in the Armed Forces reduced, and in this connection offered several proposals for Anders' consideration. Anders must have confused this intercession with the proposal to set up a separate unit, and it was thus that he came to pen the incorrect version of the facts quoted above.

At a later stage, Kahan was forced to disavow his own proposal. On March 29, 1942, he sent a note to Anders stating that political developments had made it necessary to revise the proposal with regard to the separate Jewish units submitted by Sheskin and himself. "It is not fitting to give priority to specific Jewish interests" he wrote, "since the policies of the Soviets which seek to deprive the Jews of their Polish citizenship and prevent their enlisting in the Polish Armed Forces, also seek to undermine the territorial integrity of the Polish State; this is a situation which calls for greater, not lesser unity." In concluding his declaration Kahan noted that he had sent a similar letter to Professor Kot in Kuybishev. And in fact, Kot did mention in a cable he sent to the Polish Foreign Office in London on March 25, 1942, that Kahan had informed him in writing that he was revoking his proposal concerning the establishment of separate Jewish units "because the Soviets are now forbidding the Jews to enlist in the Polish Armed Forces and they are likely to take advantage of the Revisionists' position and use it to buttress their claim."[51]

In his detailed testimony, Kahan does not mention the letter he sent to Anders and the declaration he transmitted to Kot. On the other hand, in the postscript he wrote for Rabbi Rozen's book, *Cry in the Wilderness*, which was published in 1966, he stated about the "Jewish Legion": "...would this attempt successfully be accomplished, it would change the whole of Jewish history."[52] This statement is a gross exaggeration which bears no resemblance to a realistic evaluation. Kot, on the other hand, in a letter he sent to Rabbi Rozen in 1951, claimed: "Today I am of the opinion that the unrealized Jewish Legion would have been completely drowned in the Soviet camps and that none of it would have reached Poland or Palestine."[53]

Apart from the attempt to create a general "Jewish Legion," there were several local, temporary arrangements in existence whereby Jews were concentrated in special units. D. Katz, a highly experienced electrical technician, relates in his testimony that he chanced upon a reserve unit of this sort which was made up of members of liberal professions (doctors, engineers, lawyers, etc.).[54] He volunteered for enlistment in Yangi-Yul, and in May 1942 appeared before a medical committee; he was disqualified because he was a Jew, while "maimed, crooked, hunchbacked and one-eyed Poles" were assigned fitness grades that qualified them for military service. However, since he was a qualified engineer he was not rejected outright, and was assigned to a company of civilian experts which operated under military cover.[55] Katz's description of the conditions prevailing in the unit is exceedingly bleak. The unit numbered some sixty men, "all of whom were top-notch and dependable both as to age and profession," while most of the officers were coarse Poles who unceasingly demonstrated their deliberate and insulting anti-Semitism. The unit was not issued an adequate supply of food and the men suffered constantly from hunger pangs. They received no blankets, clothing or serviceable tents, and they literally had to sleep on the ground. No one seemed at all concerned that they be equipped at least to the extent that regular soldiers were. In fact no one knew what was planned for the unit: when one of the men asked a senior officer of the division, he was told, according to Katz, that "tests will have to be run, the diplomas checked out, some will be released, and for the rest we'll put up two tents and let them slowly waste away from hunger." Katz noted, with bitterness, that the unit was set up on the assumption that the "army must protect the intelligentsia" particularly in light of the fact that the Nazis were systematically liquidating the intelligentsia of the occupied territory; this "protection," however, was tantamount to torture. At the end of June 1942 the unit was disbanded. Ten or twelve were accepted into the ranks of the army and the rest — "indigent, exhausted men who had been imprisoned in camps and jails and because of their loyalty to Poland and who fervently sought to join the army, were scattered to the wind."

The Jewish unit which did achieve a certain renown was the Jewish battalion stationed at Koltubanka (a village located not far from Tolsk, which was the recruiting center for professional units, such as the men of the armored corps). Kahan claims that the Koltubanka unit was established to serve as a model—or as a small-scale local precursor—for the broader plan for a "Jewish Legion."[56] Kahan says that he was approached by Colonel Leopold Okulicki with the suggestion that a battalion composed of Jewish soldiers already inducted into the army be set up; he was told that if this experiment proved successful it would be possible to set up additional units. A special meeting was held to explain the reason for creation of the unit, and Colonel Jan Galadyk, a Polish officer and devoted friend of the Jews, volunteered to assume command of the Jewish unit. Kahan adds that this offer constituted an unusual gesture on Galadyk's part, since the command of a battalion was generally given to an officer with the lower rank of major. Kahan also claims that relations between the Jews and the Poles within the unit were proper. However, even according to him this idyllic picture was somewhat muddied by the fact that prior to the transfer from Tolsk to Koltubanka, the Jewish soldiers were stripped of their uniforms and were sent to Koltubanka in rags and without equipment. Kahan tends to view this as an isolated episode, the result of ill-will on the part of one particular Polish officer, an apostate Jew who sought in this fashion to demonstrate his antagonism towards Jews; he does not view this as proof of the existence of a definite policy set up by the Polish military command. Kahan argues that the opposite was true, that the Koltubanka experiment was indeed successful and that Kot bore responsibility[57] for the fact that there was no follow-up to Koltubanka as had been planned.

Kahan's version is, however, contradicted on all scores by Rabbi Rozen's description of the general circumstances surrounding the establishment of the Battalion and the conditions in Koltubanka.[58] It will be recalled that Rabbi Rozen had close ties with the original advocates of the "Legion" proposal and he had given his blessing and support to the plan. It also should be noted that Dr. Kahan publicly expressed his agreement with Rabbi Rozen in the postcript he wrote for his book. And yet, according to Rabbi Rozen, the Jewish Battalion was established and sent to Koltubanka at the end of October 1941, i.e. considerably prior to the date when it was decided not to adopt the proposal of establishing a Jewish Legion. According to Rabbi Rozen, before the Battalion was to meet the Jewish soldiers in Tolsk were summarily dismissed from the army in a manner that clearly demonstrated the anti-Semitism of the Poles. All the soldiers were assembled and then officers who in the author's words had themselves just been released from Soviet camps, gave orders to "all those of the Mosaic faith" to step forward. This method of expelling the Jews from Tolsk came to Kot's attention and he complains about it in one of his reports.[59]

According to Rabbi Rozen, the way in which the Battalion was set up resembled nothing more than ghettoization. When Rabbi Rozen protested to Colonel Galadyk of this degrading attitude — an act which placed the Rabbi in personal danger — Galadyk justified the actions by claiming that the Jews "might live happier in ghetto barracks rather than dwell together with anti-Semites and Hitlerites."[60] In the wake of the protest the officers attempted to justify the system.

Rabbi Rozen stated that the Jewish soldiers were made miserable preceding the transfer to Koltubanka. They were, for example, issued boots that were too small and many of the soldiers had to go barefoot as a result. Even Koltubanka itself, after Tolsk, in Rabbi Rozen's words, was merely the exchange of a small ghetto (Tock) for a "larger ghetto" numbering some 1,000 men.[61] In the light of the alarming news from Koltubanka, Okulicki sent Rabbi Rozen "to straighten out matters ... there." According to Rabbi Rozen, Okulicki regarded whatever was happening there as endemic to the Jews, and not as a matter of anti-Semitism in the army.[62] Rabbi Rozen found the Jewish unit in a very low state of morale and fitness. The Jewish soldiers had been forced to dig their own underground dugouts in the rock-hard earth, with the temperature at 40 degrees C. below zero. His first task was to bury the large number of Jewish personnel who had died there. The military kitchen, which was supervised by Poles, often "forgot" or simply refused to issue regular rations to the Jewish soldiers. The officers in the unit were all Jews, but an anti-Semitic Polish captain had command of the Battalion. Colonel Galadyk was in fact stationed at Koltubanka, but as overall commander of the military base and not specifically of the Jewish unit. Rabbi Rozen confirms the fact that Galadyk evinced good will towards the Jews. He had however not come to Koltubanka of his own free will; as a follower of Pilsudski he had been "exiled" to Koltubanka by Sikorski's men. The Jews suffered constantly at the hands of their Polish "comrades-in-arms": "Jewish soldiers were prohibited from passing through the streets where the Polish soldiers camped. ... If a Jewish soldier from Koltubanka did appear there ... he met with both physical and moral degradation in the worst anti-Semitic manner possible."[63] According to Rabbi Rozen, the name "Koltubanka" became synonymous with a "Jewish ghetto" — at army headquarters the mere mention of Koltubanka would elicit cynical smiles, while among Jews it was viewed as a confirmation of their degradation.

News about Koltubanka did reach foreign countries.[64] Rabbi Rozen states that the information was published in the free countries, but he does not indicate how the news was transmitted or when it appeared. But we do know of repercussions arising from the publication of information on Koltubanka, from a cable sent from London by Sikorski to the staff headquarters of the Polish Armed Forces in the Soviet Union, on March 19, 1942. General Anders was asked if a "Jewish Legion had ever been established or was in existence at that time" within the Polish Armed Forces in the Soviet Union; reply was requested by return cable.[65] The answer, sent on March 22 under the signature of General Bohusz-Szyszko, read: "Report that in the Polish Armed Forces in the

Soviet Union there never was nor is there now a Jewish Legion."[66]

Kot's version of the Koltubanka story was included in the report he sent Sikorski for the period September 1941—July 13, 1942. In this report he complains of the army's refusal to accept any suggestions made by the Embassy ostensibly because the Embassy was guided by political considerations and that it was the army's duty to stay clear of politics. In fact, claims Kot, the army provided ample opportunity for very dubious political initiatives, while under the guise of being apolitical:

> In exceedingly severe fashion, the politics of anti-Semitism [has been adopted] and applied first and foremost in Tolsk, the home base of the Sixth Division and the center of reserves. After discussions with several Revisionists who had dreamed of a Jewish Legion and who were popular and influential in army circles back in the homeland, it was decided to separate the Jews and group them in special units. This was carried out arbitrarily on October 7 — upon the order given by a young officer: 'Jews, step out of line." Jewish personnel were then sent to Koltubanka and put under the command of an officer who was known to be an anti-Semite. Jews were subsequently removed from other formations as well, segregated, or discharged *en masse*, no distinction being made between unreliable elements and those whose discharge would provoke a storm of protést that could only be harmful to Polish diplomacy. One of the senior officers at general headquarters[67] vigorously advocated this system which merged the interests of the anti-Semites with the ambitions of the Revisionists.[68]

There is no doubt that Kot's underscoring the collaboration of the Revisionists with the anti-Semites was not just fortuitous. Kot believed that the Revisionists had won the support and the assistance of the *Sanacja* regime and this regime indeed was anathema to him. As a result, he exploited every opportunity to connect the Revisionists with the anti-Semites who were to be found, in his opinion, largely among the supporters of the *Sanacja*. However even if we choose to ignore Kot's tendencious commentary, we must still reject Kahan's apologetic claims. The description of Koltubanka as a partial, or first-stage, realization of the larger plan for a Jewish Legion is not valid; it bears no resemblance whatsoever to the harsh reality as revealed in Rabbi Rozen's book and in the testimonies of others.[69]

One question remains to be answered: what eventually happened to the Jewish Battalion in Koltubanka? Rabbi Rozen claims that when the Polish Armed Forces in the Soviet Union were transferred to Central Asia, in May and June 1942, "the Koltubanka Ghetto was automatically liquidated" and the majority of the

Jews as well as Jewish personnel in other units, were discharged from the Army. However, a small number did manage to remain with the Force in Soviet Asia until August 1942 when they were evacuated with the rest of the Army [to Iran]. Rabbi Rozen does not mention how many of the Jews from Koltubanka managed to remain with the Army nor does he indicate with what unit they served in Central Asia.[70]

However, we have in our possession an additional testimony concerning the final stages of the Jewish Battalion in Koltubanka.[71] Meir Lustgarten (whose testimony was cited earlier) relates:

> Towards the end of the winter of 1942, we all left the camp and were transferred by train to the city of Gusar on the Afghanistan border of Uzbekistan. Several weeks after our arrival, the battalion of Jewish soldiers from the village of Koltubanka also arrived. When the Jewish soldiers were removed from ranks of the Polish Army in Tolsk, the Polish commanders thought that they had rid the army of Jews, that they would disappear. They could not possibly have imagined that these wretched Jews, who had been expelled from the army, would attain a level higher than that of the Poles in the service. The Poles were astounded upon seeing Jews in the uniform of the Polish Armed Forces parading smartly and in unison, all looking fit and well dressed and marching as they sang.

It seems that the situation of the Jewish Battalion in Koltubanka improved considerably with the passing of the time. The change for the better probably came about together with a general improvement in the state of the Polish Armed Forces in 1942; it also resulted from the dismissal of its anti-Semitic commander and the intervention of civilian factors. With the improvement in material conditions, the desire of the Jewish soldiers to demonstrate their ability also grew, and a sort of "Jewish unit patriotism" came into being. (It is here that the positive potential of Jewish units with the capacity for independent development within the Polish Armed Forces, came to the fore.) Lustgarten's testimony shows that Rabbi Rozen's contention that the Battalion was liquidated prior to the evacuation to Central Asia has no basis in fact. However, one cannot determine from Lustgarten's testimony whether or not a purge of the Battalion was carried out in Koltubanka, as was the case in other units of the Polish Armed Forces.

According to Lustgarten, the Jewish Battalion was evacuated by train to Krasnovodsk on the Caspian Sea. From there the soldiers sailed to the port of Pahlevi, Persia, arriving a short time before Passover of 1942. In Iran, the Jewish Battalion was disbanded, for the British refused to transfer a separate Jewish unit to Eretz Israel.[72] Kot for his part relates that he does not know the ultimate fate of the Jewish Battalion in Koltubanka.[73]

ANDERS' ORDERS OF THE DAY CONCERNING JEWS

Further on in his description of the intentions of the military command to create a "Jewish Legion" and separate Jewish units, Kot wrote:

> General Anders put a stop to this harmful trend after the discussion at the Embassy on October 24 (1941) with the participation of representatives of various blocs in the Jewish community. On November 14 he issued an astute order on the treatment of Jews in the Armed Forces. However, in Tolsk he met with very strong opposition; he then issued a follow-up order which contained several paragraphs that are politically touchy. His declaration about 'reckoning' with the Jews in the homeland immediately became widely known in the free countries and the commander of the Polish Armed Forces came to be regarded as an enemy of the Jews.[74]

The two orders of the day to which Kot refers are in our archives. The first was issued in Buzuluk on November 14 and the second, also from Buzuluk, dates from November 30, 1941.[75] Anders' first order gave a decisive definition of the position of the Jews in the Armed Forces and how they were to be treated. The general directives contained in the order were to be obeyed and followed strictly; a "clear, consistent, unambiguous line" was to be pursued in dealing with Jews, on the part of both commanding officers and soldiers in the ranks. He similarly asked that there be an "end to the rumors and the false charges that spring up behind our backs concerning alleged anti-Semitism in the army," rumors that, Anders claimed, originated from foreign sources. In the body of the order, Anders explicitly stated that Jews had the same rights and obligations vis-à-vis military service as all other Polish citizens. Within the Armed Forces, they were to be dealt with "as sincerely and with the same degree of warmth" as all other soldiers and they were to be granted "the same measure of confidence" as everyone else. In order to prevent any misunderstanding, he spelled out the principal directives governing recruitment of soldiers for active service in the Armed Forces. According to these directives, the following were to be recruited forthwith: officers, non-commissioned officers with professional skills, men in the ranks who had seen active service and volunteers who underwent pre-military training and were found fit by the recruiting committee. All others were to be sent to the southern republics of the Soviet Union where the registration of reserve forces would take place. He spelled all this out in refutation of the libel that Jews were encountering difficulty in being accepted into the army. "I order all my subordinate commanding officers to fight relentlessly against any manifestation of racial anti-Semitism." It must also be carefully explained to the soldiers that Poland has always adhered to the principles of democracy and tolerance and any divergence from these principles cannot be countenanced. The Jew will benefit from the same laws that apply to all Poles; drastic action is to be taken against him only "when he does not know how to wear with pride the uniform of a soldier of the Polish Republic and he forgets that he is a Polish citizen.[76]

This order, embodying as it did a clear and forceful enunciation of Anders' position on a whole series of key questions, would undoubtedly have had a decisive impact on recruiting procedure and on relationships within the Armed Forces.

It is clear, from Kot's comments on the subject and from the wording of the original order, that it was Anders who issued the order and not Sikorski, as has been claimed by the Palestine Haganah Weekly that published Anders' second order.[77] Unfortunately, this authoritative and clear-cut order did not remain the sole pronouncement that the Commanding Officer of the Polish Armed Forces in the Soviet Union would make on the matter. Some two weeks later, a second order was issued; the wording of this order and its general tenor virtually cancelled out all that was positive in the first order of the day.

The second order of the day opens with a reference to the previous order.[78] The first had officially presented the supreme commander's political credo on the Jewish question, which he did not care to have misinterpreted by his subordinates. "I well understand the reasons underlying anti-Semitic manifestations in the ranks of the Armed Forces;" these were reactions to the disloyal, and at times hostile, behavior of Polish Jews between 1939–1940. "I am consequently not surprised that our soldiers, those ardent patriots, regard the matter so seriously, particularly since they suspect that our Government and Armed Forces intend to overlook the experiences of the past. When viewed from this vantage point, our defence of the Jews might seem incomprehensible or historically unjustified and even inconsistent." However, explained Anders, the current policy of the Polish Government, tied as it was to the policy of Great Britain, made it imperative to treat the Jews favorably, since the Jews wielded considerable influence in the Anglo-

Saxon world. The soldiers must understand that in the interests of
the Polish Government, the Jews must not be provoked, for any
anti-Semitism was likely to bring about harsh repercussions. "I
therefore recommend that our position be explained to the units in
a suitably discreet manner and that the hot-heads and the quick-
tempered should be particularly warned" that from then on any
overt expression of the struggle against the Jews was totally
forbidden and whoever was found guilty of such would be severely
punished. "However, after the battle is over and we are again our
own masters, we will settle the Jewish matter in a fashion that the
exalted status and sovereignty of the homeland and simple human
justice require."

The differences, indeed, the polar distinctions, between the two
orders are so pronounced that it is extremely difficult to understand how one man was capable of issuing both documents within
the short space of two weeks. The contradictions and vacillations
in Anders' orders do however become more understandable on
comparing Anders' public statements with those he made in closed
sessions with Stalin or wrote for inclusion in his own personal
files.[79] Kot claimed, as we have already noted, that Anders'
retrenchment from the first order and its general orientation was
due to pressure applied by the command staff of the Sixth Division
located in Tolsk. We cannot be certain of the validity of this version, for we know that Kot tended to be suspicious of the Tolsk
command which he regarded as a collection of political rivals
composed of Pilsudskiites. There can however be no doubt that the
sharp about-face in the wording and content of Anders' orders was
prompted by the criticisms voiced by friends and subordinates in
his army. There can also be no doubt as to which version reveals
Anders real feelings and opinions.[80]

In the first order Anders claimed that anti-Semitism was non-
existent in the Armed Forces and that hostile forces had mali-
ciously charged the Poles with hatred of the Jews; for this reason
the Poles should be wary and be responsible in their behavior.
From the second order, it evolves that there actually was rampant
anti-Semitism and the Supreme Commander understood its
causes. He did not demand this time that every manifestation of
anti-Semitism be unequivocally opposed, but only asked that the
hot-heads be held in check and prevented from committing acts of
violence. In the first order, the rejection of anti-Semitism was a
function of a basic attitude stemming from the constitutional and
ideological foundations of the Polish State, while in the second,
opposition to anti-Semitism was but a political stratagem neces-

sitated by momentary circumstances. However, the true reckoning by the Poles would have its day when they would be free to act as they pleased in their liberated homeland.

Kot noted that Anders' second order received exclusive notoriety and gave the Supreme Commander a bad name. However, the fact that Anders' first order was so radically altered under the influence of friends and military subordinates indicates that hostility towards Jews was not the exclusive attribute of the Supreme Commander. The opposite is true: many military personnel would not have taken a position in defence of the Jews even for reasons of expediency. The truth of the matter is that anti-Semitism was general and widespread throughout the Armed Forces and all the Jewish witnesses, regardless of their outlook, education or position testify to this fact; that proves that even the hypocritical approach of the second order remained a dead letter and was not adopted by the Armed Forces. Thus, some of the testimonies tell of attempts to check anti-Semitism "from above," but these attempts were futile.[81] M. Kahan notes in his testimony that the anti-Semitic manifestations increased as the self-confidence and the sense of mastery of the Poles grew,[82] with the consolidation of forces, the acquisition of equipment and the improvement in conditions. This means that not only did anti-Semitism in the Armed Forces not decline, but it actually became progressively worse. One of the witnesses, a doctor, states that "anti-Semitism was expressed in acts of degradation and physical injury."[83] Another witness states that the anti-Semitic treatment of Jews took one form, among others, "of frequent and unjustified demands to do physical labor, of insults, and of the fact that Jewish complaints were not investigated and rectified and no steps were initiated against the parties."[84] However, it is only just to note that there were commanders and officers in various units who did try to protect the Jews under their command, and who, despite the difficulties involved, did adopt an attitude of decency and comradeship towards Jews.

The Haganah Weekly *Eshnab*, edited in Palestine by Liebenstein (Eliezer Livne), published Anders' second order of the day in its issue of June 28, 1943.[85] At that time, elements of General Anders' Armed Forces were stationed in Eretz Israel, and the publication of the order provoked a sharp response from the Jewish community. The "Representation of Polish Jewry" (*Reprezentacja zydostwa polskiego*), with its office in Palestine, was composed of representatives of all the Zionist parties (excluding the Revisionists) and of *Agudat Israel*. They regarded Anders' order of the day as a declaration that "would necessarily give rise to an intensification of anti-Semitic trends and not to their lessening" and approached the prime Minister and Minister of National Defense, Sikorski, on the matter. The "Representation" pointed out that the order stood in direct contradiction to formal and binding declarations made by the Polish Government in London and asked whether the Government intended taking any steps and what conclusions it proposed to draw in the face of the order.[86] The letter to Sikorski was sent on July 5, 1943, the very day on which Sikorski was killed in a plane crash near Gibraltar.

Towards the end of June 1943, Jan Stańczyk, a leader of the Polish Socialist Party and a minister in the Government-in-Exile in London, visited Palestine, and on July 1st he met in Tel Aviv, with a delegation of the "Representation."[87] At the meeting, the secretary of the "Representation," Dr. Abraham Stupp, raised the matter of Anders' order: ". . . I must speak about something very painful. I have before me a paper issued by General Anders in which he explains his position on the anti-Semitic feelings in the Armed Forces." At this point, Stańczyk interrupted Stupp and said: "I am familiar with the contents." Dr. Stupp continued, giving his interpretation on the order's significance. Stańczyk then replied:

> Anders' motives in issuing the order were possibly not as negative as they first appear. Given the prevailing mood, he sought to explain a position that had encountered opposition. He did it in an unsatisfactory manner. Anders is merely a soldier, not a politician. A politician would have done it differently and better. There is no cause to turn this into an international issue. I know that when this becomes known aboard there will be an outcry concerning anti-Semitism in the Polish Armed Forces, and this in turn might bring about an even more severe reaction on the part of the Poles . . . .

Later on, in response to a question, Stańczyk said: "I do not want to deny, and I admit, that an anti-Semitic mood prevails among the population that returned from Russia and in the Armed Forces. I note this in pain, but the fact cannot be changed by decree . . .[88]

On July 12, 1943, that is less than two weeks after the meeting between Stanczyk and the delegation from the "Representation," the "Representation" received a letter from the Polish Consulate in Tel Aviv. The letter stated that in the course of a conversation between Minister Stańczyk and General Anders, the General had denied outright the existence of any such order and "claimed that the text was forged." Stańczyk added for his own part: "I am convinced that this is a product of hostile propaganda which aims at disrupting relations between Poles and Jews."[89]

Among the documents Kot included in his book published in London in 1955, was, as we have seen, Anders' second order.[90] Although it is true that Kot was at that time waging a battle against the General, it is inconceivable that he would have included a spurious document in his book. It is worth pointing out that Anders, in his book, chose to make no mention of the order, although in meetings with Jews he continued to claim that it was a forgery. A meeting was held on September 19, 1943, between Anders and a delegation from the "Representation" at the home of the Polish Consul General in Tel Aviv, Dr. H. Rozmaryn. During the discussion, the engineer Anschel Reiss hinted that "the Armed Forces had been warned not to engage in anti-Semitic tricks, while it had been emphasized that the accounting with the Jews would take place after returning to the homeland." Anders interrupted him at this point and said: "I know that some sort of rag published an order, allegedly coming from me, expressing what you just said. I do not even want to discuss the matter. It is a forgery, no order of this sort ever existed."[91]

Polish sources continued to be concerned over the criticism stirred up by the publication of the order. The Polish Consul General in a report dispatched to the Foreign Minister in London (no date indicated) noted that owing to the commotion that the publication in *Eshnab* had provoked, he had seen fit to arrange a meeting between his deputy, Weber, and Yitzhak Gruenbaum. At the meeting Weber reiterated the claim that the order had never been issued and Gruenbaum was asked to help quiet the excitement. After consulting with the other officials of the Jewish Agency, Gruenbaum agreed to take steps in keeping with the Consul General's request. At the same time, he asked Dr. Rozmaryn to write him a letter confirming that "the document which was published by *Eshnab* and which he (Gruenbaum) had heard about a half-year earlier, was never issued.[92]

An additional reverberation sounded at a meeting held in London on January 13, 1944, between Sikorski's successor as Prime Minister, Stanislaw Mikolajczyk, and two Jewish representatives, Dr. Schwarzbart, a member of the National Council in London, and Dr. Tartakower of the World Jewish Congress. At the meeting, Schwarzbart spoke of what was taking place in the Armed Forces and he cited Anders' order of the day. Mikolajczyk pointed out to him that Anders had explicitly stated that the order was a forgery. To this Schwarzbart replied:

> Yes, I know. However, there are witnesses, among them ministers, who fought against the order when it was issued. We know that one of

the cables referred to the order as a forgery. I have no objection against making such a claim for external consumption, but on the inside, no one should expect me to believe that it was a forgery.

The Prime Minister remained silent and after a while said:"I will deal with this matter also.[93]

It is clear that anti-Semitism was a general feature of the Polish Armed Forces; it had its roots in traditions of the past and in the ideology and political conceptions of Poland in the period between the wars. The various strata in Polish society were not sufficiently perspicacious to study their own history with a critical eye, nor were they able to perceive just how destructive a role anti-Semitism played in the internal life of the Polish republic and how it had served as a vehicle for the penetration of destructive Nazi influences under the guise of anti-Semitism. In the Soviet Union during the Second World War, Jews and Poles came into contact to a much greater extent than in Poland proper where the Jews had been separated from the local population by the walls of the ghetto; in the immigration centers such as London, there was only a handful of Jews and relations there were generally based upon formal attempts at communication, lacking in the elements of spontaneity and frankness.

The political leadership, however, was sensitive to the harmful ramifications of anti-Semitism and it did show an understandable degree of awareness of the negative reactions caused by the Polish hatred of Jews, by public opinion in the free countries and by influential Jewish circles in the West. However, since their attitude concerning the issue was ambivalent and was dictated by an entire array of tactical considerations, it is not suprising that periodic "cracks" in their behavior and pronouncements revealed their true feelings. It should also not be forgotten that the *Endeks*, who enjoyed a position of respect within the broadbased coalition in London, held Jew-hatred as one of the fundamental elements in their ideological and political outlook. And as we have also seen, anti-Semitism was particularly rampant among the officers of the Armed Forces, and this attitude undoubtedly had its reverberations within the ranks as well.

THE EVACUATION OF THE ARMED FORCES OF GENERAL ANDERS FROM THE SOVIET UNION

The total evacuation of General Anders' Armed Forces from the Soviet Union was the outcome of the tensions and suspicions that accompanied all dealings between the Poles and the Soviet authorities.

The suggestion to evacuate part of the force from the Soviet Union was first raised by Sikorski during his discussion with Stalin. Stalin's reaction was most severe, but ultimately he gave his assent for the evacuation of 25,000 men as reinforcements for the Polish troops in the West. Nevertheless, Sikorski opposed evacuating all the troops from the Soviet Union; his basic theory was that Polish soldiers should take part in the battle for the liberation of Poland on all fronts and from all directions. He considered the Soviet front to be of prime importance particulary since the fact that Poles had fought alongside the Soviets would be a trump card in the inevitable bargaining over the eastern borders. The British, for their part, pressed for a full-scale evacuation so that the Polish Armed Forces could reinforce their own points of weakness.

There is no doubt that the Soviets were not unaware of these considerations; with deliberate cunning they bypassed the Polish politicl levels and established direct contact with Anders and his officers, exploiting thereby the commander's extreme personal ambitions. Gradually, Anders achieved a position of independence in both his military and political activity. Anders flaunted this independence before Kot in Russia; he also apparently had the support of the Polish opposition in London, who saw him as a potential rival of Sikorski's.

The Soviets finally decided to rid themselves of the Polish Armed Forces which they now regarded as a political nuisance.

During the two stages of the evacuation, some 114,000 Poles, soldiers and civlians, left the Soviet Union; the Soviet authorities agreed to allow the families of the soldiers and certain groups among the civilian population, such as children, to be evacuated together with the soldiers. In the first transfer, in March-April 1942, some 44,000 (31,500 soldiers and 12,500 civilians) were evacuated; in the second stage of the evacuation, during the months of August-September 1942, more than 70,000 military personnel and civilians left the Soviet Union (close to 45,000 military personnel and over 25,000 civilians).[94] The transports made their way by train to the port of Krasnovodsk on the Caspian Sea, and from there they sailed to Pahlevi, Iran. Thus there came to an end the Polish Armed Forces in the Soviet Union which had been established under specific orders from the Polish Government-in-Exile in London.

The Polish Armed Forces in the Soviet Union never reached the dimensions envisaged by the Poles. Hindering growth were obstacles placed in the way by the Soviets, such as reduction in equipment and supplies, and adverse climatic and sanitary conditions. Evidently the Poles themselves prevented members of

ethnic minorities from joining the army. The force which
numbered 34.000 men in December 1941, grew to 66,000 men in
March 1942[95]. During the very last stages, just prior to the evacuation, there was an additional, hasty recruitment. In total, 72,000
men of General Anders' Armed Forces were evacuated from the
Soviet Union.[96]

The amnesty and the conscription enabled many to rise from the
status of prisoners to free soldiers, from conditions of neglect and
extreme hardship to a framework which provided their basic
necessities; the evacuation meant a chance for salvation and escape
to the free world. When it became known that civilians and
relatives of army personnel would be permitted to join the evacuation, a great stream of people moved from the farthest corners of the
Soviet Union to the exit points in the south.

The numbers of Jews among the evacuees and the attitude of the
Poles and their treatment of Jews during the various stages of the
evacuation. According to Jewish sources, some 6,000 Jews were
among them, one source estimating some 3,500 soldiers and 2,500
civilians.[97] Close to a thousand Jewish children known as *Yaldei
Teheran* (Children of Teheran) were transferred together with a
large camp of evacuated children. In total Jews accounted for about
five per cent of the soldiers evacuated (five per cent of the enlisted
men and one per cent of the officers) and about seven percent of the
civilians.[98]

During the first stage of the evacuation some 700 Jewish civilians
reached Iran.[99] The Polish authorities claimed that the Soviets
made certain that no one to whom the Soviet law of citizenship
applied could leave, and emigration of a much larger number of
Jews was thus blocked. Yet it seems that in at least one case the
NKVD which supervised the transports, forced the Poles, of course,
as a result of their interest and the desire to incite the relations
between the Poles and Jews to take with them a group of Jews whom
they had refused to allow to enlist. During the journey, and even
after arriving in Iran, these Jews were subjected to physical and
mental maltreatment by the Polish officers in charge, who stood
firm in their resolve not to allow them to enlist. The episode became known in the free countries and Yitzhak Schwarzbart queried
it in London. Shapiro, a UP reporter, reported the incident to the
press of the United States, and in the wake of the publications an
investigation was held. The senior officer in charge of the transport,
Lt. Col. Pstrokoński, described the way in which the Jewish group
was added to the transport:

... if my memory serves me right, it was March 25, 1942, we discovered that the Soviet authorities had added to our transport five cars
of civilians, almost all Jews. According to my lists, there were 330
people, including several children. We were not informed about the
coupling on of these wagons. What happened was that at one of the
stations we realized that the cars had been attached and that they were
travelling with us .... [100]

By contrast, Captain Dowiaglo, who was directly responsible for
these Jews and against whom most of the charges were levelled,
states that there were 300 people in the additional cars, ninety per
cent of whom were Jews. Among them, he claimed, were young
children (of pre-enlistment age) and also those advanced in age, but
the majority were young men.[101] A Jewish source decribes the
episode thus:

Before the first units of the Polish Army left Russia, that is on the
22nd of March 1942, 300 Jews of A classification who had been examined by a Russian health board since the Polish committee was no
long functioning, were sent by the *voyenkomat* [the Soviet War Office]
to the place where the division was stationed. However, [the Poles]
ordered them to return to their points of departure. Some of the Jews
requested NKVD intervention and they in turn asked the Polish authorities why these men were not being issued with uniforms and why
they were being sent back. The Polish authorities replied that they did
not have enough railroad cars to transport them. The NKVD immediately supplied cars, and faced with this fact [the Poles] took them
to Persia but did not provide them with uniforms. At the port of
Pahlevi, all the Jews not in uniform were told that they were free to go.
Several Jews then approached the British authorities and asked them to
intervene, and it was only by command of the British authorities that
they all were issued uniforms and inducted into the army.[102]

Anders himself and General Bohusz-Szyszko, his deputy, took
an interest in the evacuation of the Jews. On July 31, Anders and
Bohusz-Szyszko and a Soviet representative, General Zhukov,
signed a protocol delineating which Jews were eligible for inclusion among the evacuees.[103] Paragraph 1 of that document states
that relatives of soldiers who were residents of the Ukraine and
Byelorussia holding other than Polish citizenship would be
allowed to leave only if they could prove a close family relationship with soldiers in the Polish Armed Forces in the Soviet Union.
Paragraph 2 stated that separate lists had to be submitted of family
members who were residents of the Ukraine and Byelorussia and
who were not Poles, and a certification of the authenticity of the
lists had to be supplied by the military command. Paragraph 3

spoke of the prohibition against evacuating Soviet citizens even if they had married Polish soldiers while in the Soviet Union.

Naturally, the very fact that Anders agreed to sign such a document raises questions. In practice, however, Anders went even further than the wording of the document required. At a meeting with several rabbis and Jewish communal workers, and in a note he sent to London, Anders claimed that the Soviet Government "agreed to the evacuation of the close relatives only of those Jews who were serving in the units now stationed in the Soviet Union."[104] In other words: Anders blocked the evacuation of the relatives of those soldiers who had left during the first stage, claiming this was in accordance with Soviet desire. Anders similarly ignored the fact that Jews who were residents of the western provinces and who had not had Soviet citizenship thrust upon them were eligible, from the Soviet point of view, to leave in the same way as any other Polish citizen. In his meetings with Jews and in the reports he sent to London, Anders continued to claim that any attempt to circumvent the Soviet directives would jeopardize the entire evacuation project. On the other hand, he did declare that he had no reason to oppose attempts on the part of Jews to obtain exit permits from the Soviets and that these permits would be honored by the Poles.[105]

A group of Bund activists who had obtained Kot's recommendation for evacuation, met with Anders and asked to be declared Poles for purposes of the evacuation. Anders "categorically rejected" their request. The Bund members related that all those who had stated that they were of Jewish faith were dropped from the transport roster of August 9, 1942. On the other hand, those Jews who declared themselves to be Roman Catholics did leave.[106] As an aside, it is interesting to point out that the Jewish Agency intervened with the Polish authorities to allow these "Marranos" to resume their Jewish identity even while they were in Iran.[107]

In a good many cases, Soviet officers forcibly intervened and claimed that they would have no part in the Polish discrimination policy. One NKVD officer stated that he was prepared to authorize the evacuation of any Jew who could produce two witnesses to testify that he did not fall into the category of those upon whom Soviet citizenship had been imposed.[108] Thanks to the intensive efforts of several Jews, a meeting was arranged between General Zhukov and Bohusz-Szyszko to clarify Soviet restrictions on the evacuation of Jews. According to a Jewish source, Zhukov complained to Bohusz-Szyszko:

General, why do you tell the Jews that we are making it difficult for them to leave? Do you not know that we in fact do not check the lists, that we close one eye to what is going on, and that from our point of view it makes no difference who goes, Ivan, Peter or Rabinovitch?

At the meeting Zhukov also produced the protocol mentioned above and demonstrated that the Polish interpretation of Jewish family relationships did not coincide with the stipulations of the signed document.[109]

In a letter to Kot, Bohusz-Szyszko described the clash with Zhukov and claimed that Zhukov agreed to the arrangement whereby two witnesses would certify that a given individual was a Polish citizen, but he made the Polish commanders responsible for the authenticity of the declaration.[110] The Bundists relate in their memorandum that Bohusz-Szyszko after giving some other arguments admitted to them that the Poles knew that a maximum of 70,000 individuals could be evacuated and thus feared that Jews might occupy places required for Poles and consequently tried to reject Jews by every possible means.[111]

Preserved in Professor Kot's files are reports and surveys of observers and liaison officers sent by the Embassy to the evacuation centers in the various divisions. Jacob Hoffman, the liaison officer attached to the Sixth Division, wrote in his summary:

> The atmosphere at the time the evacuation lists were drawn up was such that even after it was explained to the Jews who bore responsibility for the harsh directives and why they were issued, they still did not believe the explanation. The mood prevailing not only among the men but also among the officers of certain types was near rejoicing over the prohibition to include members of the national minorities.

Hoffman also reports that he was told about one commanding officer who took pride in the fact that he did not include even one Jew in the list of evacuees he had prepared.[112]

The liaison officer who was in charge of the evacuation of the Fifth Division, Witold Misztowt-Czyz, submitted a detailed and angry report of his battle to manage the evacuation of a group of Jews. According to the report, he put together a list of relatives of soldiers who were eligible for evacuation, according to the directives, but Lt. Col. Dudziński, who was in charge of the evacuation of the unit, removed from the list of Polish citizens, members of the following minority groups: 1) those who were by nationality Tatars and Moslems by religion; 2) Jewish apostates who represented themselves as Catholics and as Poles; 3) assimilated Jews who were listed in the census as Poles; 4) a small group of Jews who declared themselves to be Jewish by nationality. The author of the report claimed that the majority belonged to the working intelligentsia and included army veterans, orphans of military personnel, handicapped soldiers and Polish industrialists; "many of them could claim rights earned by their efforts for the Polish cause." Misztowt-Czyz requested the intervention of the army staff.

The problem of the Tatars was immediately settled: they were reinstated on the list. What remained to be solved was the problem of the apostates and the Jews, who numbered 52 families (122 souls in all). General Bohusz-Szyszko favored including them all on the list of evacuees. Bishop Josef Gawlina, the highest ranking religious authority in the armed forces, issued a declaration on behalf of the apostates in which he noted that racial conceptions were foreign to the Roman Catholic Church. Nevertheless, Lt. Col. Dudziński stood his ground and refused to put the names back on the list. Misztowt-Czyz also charges that this same Dudziński removed fifty Jews from the evacuation train even though they had every right to be in the convoy. Misztowt-Czyz concludes that an injustice had been done to Polish citizens who were fully entitled to leave for Iran.

The liaison officer at staff headquarters, the engineer Andrzej Jenicz, drew up a comprehensive summary of the situation in which he included several suggestions of a political nature. He noted the fact that a large number of Jews could be found at those places where the lists of evacuees were being drawn up and where the potential evacuees had gathered. These Jews were incensed at the fact that their rights to be evacuated were being ignored while others were being brought from afar and included in the departing group; Polish soldiers, on the other hand, were angry over the fact that the Jews seemed to be nearby while their own families were far away. Jenicz pointed out in his report that "the behavior of certain army personnel, who acted in an anti-Semitic fashion during the evacuation, contributed to the creation of an ugly atmosphere;" he also pointed out that many of the Jews demonstrated "an aggressive and hostile" attitude. Jenicz described his efforts to have Jews included in the lists, and reported that in several cases he received support from non-military elements. However, his activities brought but meager results. Jenicz states clearly that "the evacuation of Jews from the Soviet Union was unpopular with the Polish public and army and was restricted to the barest minimum, in keeping with the position taken by the Soviet authorities." Jenicz concluded his summary with the following comments:

> Circles in international Jewry will, of course, act upon the advice of our Jews who are embittered because so few were allowed to leave, and

will place all the blame upon the Poles. As far as Polish state interests are concerned it is immaterial whether the blame is laid upon the civilian or the military — the Embassy, general headquarters or division staff. It is quite likely that the Soviet authorities will endeavour to portray the matter in a fashion unfavorable to Polish interests, and that they will do so in the context of the clash over the eastern territories. Soviet propaganda will claim that the Polish authorities did not want to take the Jews, and they will supply the Jews with the appropriate propaganda materials. It won't be difficult for them to obtain. I shall cite as an example the cable which the [Soviet] Commissar for Evacuation Matters attached to the Fifth Division, sent to Bishop Gawlina in Yangi-Yul, stating that the Armed Forces 'were employing racial tactics.' For this reason I advise that the only [correct] approach would be the adoption of a unified front by all elements directly involved in the evacuation and the briefing of all those who must know about the evacuation with one version only, namely that restrictions were applied to the departure of Jews only because of the absolute prohibition imposed by the Soviet Government. If need be, we will be able to produce appropriate material to confirm this claim. All reports giving unfavorable details of the evacuation campaign should be treated as top secret, lest they fall into the wrong hands. The anti-Semitic behavior of certain officers — which has been blown up out of proportions — should be explained as acts of isolated individuals for whom those in charge of the evacuation cannot be held responsible.[113]

It is abundantly clear that the composition of the evacuation lists, the treatment of Jews during the evacuation and the small numbers of Jewish soldiers and civilians among the evacuees all helped to reveal to the free world the anti-Jewish discrimination and the extreme anti-Semitism practiced by many Poles.

According to a Jewish estimate, 3,500 Jewish soldiers were evacuated; according to Anders, 4,000. Even if we accept the Polish figure as the correct one, we are led to an instructive conclusion. Until the end of 1941, the Soviets placed no obstacles before the recruiting of Jews; in fact, according to Polish sources just the opposite occurred — the Soviets deliberately channelled large numbers of Jews to the recruiting centers, and as a result they made up forty per cent of the initial recruits, and some say even more than that. If we may assume that the Polish Armed Forces numbered some 40,000 men until the end of 1941, then the number of Jews was at least 10,000. When the Russians began to place restrictions on recruiting from among the minorities, they also tried, according to Anders, to have the restrictions applied to segments of the force already in existence. Anders claims that he bitterly opposed the Russians on this point, arguing that a law cannot take effect retroactively, and the Russians were forced to accept his position. If all this is true, the queston than arises: where did all the Jews, who by account were allowed to remain in the army, disappear? There can be no doubt of the answer: in addition to the restrictions of the Soviets and the disqualifications by the Poles of new recruits, a drastic purge of existing units must have taken place.

There is no reason to attribute to isolated officers the policy of discrimination in the drawing up of the evacuation lists. The Embassy sought to mitigate the extremism of the Armed Forces and to include a large number of Jews in the lists, in particular the better known Jewish leaders. As we have seen, the Embassy's efforts had disappointing results with the open rivalry between the Armed Forces and the political elements[114] serving as at least a partial cause. Some officers chose to behave in a brutally anti-Semitic manner, making the situation in fact harsher even than the stated policy, and only a few spoke out openly against the dicrimination and sought to intervene to whatever extent they could.

It is very possible that the NKVD wanting to embroil the Poles, sought to utilize for their own propaganda purposes the unrestrained anti-Semitism which was rampant among them. However, we may also assume that even had those circumstances had no connection with the Soviet restrictive regulations, the Russians would hardly have allowed the Poles to carry out their machinations while attributing them to the Soviet authorities. Naturally, as in the earlier stages, those who suffered and were injured in all cases were the Jews.

NOTES

1. See the English text of the agreement in *Documents on Polish-Soviet Relations, 1939–1945*, Vol. 1, London, 1961, pp. 141–142 (hereafter — *Documents*).

2. We do not have reliable statistics of the Polish exiles in the Soviet Union during World War II. The Polish sources give a figure of between one and two millions. The Soviets reported that 350,000-450,000 individuals were transported from Poland to the Soviet Union; see: Wladyslaw Pobog-Malinowski, *Najnowsza historia polityczna Polski, 1864–1945*, Vol.3, London, p. 197 (hereafter - Pobog-Malinowski). Stanislaw Kot, the Polish Ambassador to USRR states that the number of Poles brought to the Soviet Union was over a million and a half, see: Stanislaw Kot,

Listy z Rosji do Gen. Sikorskiego, London, 1955, p. 107 (hereafter - Kot).

3. *Documents*, p. 141.

4. *Ibid.*, p. 142.

5. See Kot, *op. cit.*, p. 163.

6. The text of the military agreement can be found in *Documents*, pp. 149–150.

7. Kot, p. 163.

8. From Anders' Work Calendar of February 4, 1943, Sikorski Archives, General Sikorski Historical Institute, London (*Instytut Historyczny Imienia Generala Sikorskiego*, hereafter—IHGS), Anders' File (hereafter — KGA/24); Minutes of the meeting in Tel Aviv between the "Representation" and General Anders, September 1943, in "Report of the Activities of the Representation of Polish Jewry for the years 1940–1945" (in

Polish), Central Zionist Archives (hereafter — CZA), J25/54/VI, p. 134; Wladyslaw Anders, *Bez ostatniego rozdzialu;* wspomnienia z lat 1939–1946, Wydanie drugie, Newton, 1950, p. 99; English edition: *An army in Exile.* The Story of The Second Polish Corps, London, 1949.

9. In the Anders' File, IHGS, KGA/24, there is a report bearing the title "The Jewish Problem" containing many complaints against Jews — the recurring complaint about the behavior of the Jews during the Soviet occupation, complaints about acts of cowardice, escapes and crimes, phrases such as the "Judaization of the Embassy," "unwillingness of the Jews to work" and others.

10. Kot, *op. cit.,* p. 163. Kot notes in the margin that the text is drawn from the report of the army staff, however in his survey written during the war he did not refer to this fact.

11. *Ibid.,* p. 164.

12. See: Yad Vashem Archives, 03/1298 (hereafter-YVA)

13. YVA, 03/1294

14. YVA, 03/1365

15. YVA, 03/1554.

16. YVA, 03/702.

17. Kot, *op. cit.,* p. 313.

18. *Ibid.,* p. 82.

19. Stanislaw Mikolajczyk was one of the leaders of the Polish Peasants' Party (*Stronnictwo Ludowe*) in the London circle of exiles and Kot's political ally. He was appointed Prime Minister in Exile after Sikorski's tragic death in 1943.

20. Pstrokonski was close to the men in power in Poland in the 1930's and in Kot's eyes was politically unfit.

21. Kot, *op. cit.,* p. 136.

22. The versions of the conversation between Sikorski and Stalin, as recorded by Kot, Sikorski and in *Documents,* are generally identical. However in Kot's version Sikorski's comments about Jews in the Armed Forces are attributed to Anders. It seems clear that Kot, a friend of Sikorski's who thought highly of him as a statesman, sought to clear him of the responsibility for a statement charged with anti-Semitic connotations representing a gross political blunder by means of a

"slightly imprecise" recording of what actually happened. The version in Anders and in *Documents* are identical, with Sikorski appearing as having taking part in the discussion on the Jews. *Documents,* published by the Sikorski Institute, is an official and authoritative publication, thus leaving not doubt that Sikorski actually said what is attributed to him. In this context it is worth pointing out the charges lodged by the Soviets against the Polish officers. Thus, Kot, for examle, records on November 7, 1941 that Volkorisky complained to him that Polish officers who had arrived from London were trading in watches, silk stockings, toothpaste and other such things, and that many officer infected with venreal disease were exploiting the goodwill of Soviet women, see Kot, *op. cit.,* pp. 150–151.

23. The minutes were published in the following sources: Kot, *op. cit.,* pp. 191–208; Anders, *op. cit.* pp. 105–123; *Documents* pp. 231–243.

24. Many testimonies emphasize the fact that the Armed Forces meant a haven for many who had been released from the camps and had neither home nor employment in the Soviet Union, at a time of war and extreme stress.

25. IHGS, KGA/24.

26. *Ibid.,*

27. *Ibid.,*

28. *Ibid.,* cable of 2 March 1942 to Kuybishev.

29. ;Documents, Vol. II. Doc. No. 160, p. 244.

30. *Ibid.,* Doc. No. 163, pp. 250–251.

31. *Ibid.,* Doc. No. 167, p. 259.

32. Cable to Sikorski of 22 March 1942, Kot, *op.cit.,* p. 291.

33. IHGS, KGA/24.

34. IHGS, KOL 25/24.

35. Kot, *op.cit.,* p. 305.

36. See Mark Kahan's testimony, YVA, 03/2863. The great quantity of material on Sheskin in the Anders' File in the Sikorski Archives — a short biography, reports he sent to staff headquarters about the mood in Eretz Israel and in the Hebrew press, particularly in the extreme leftist factions — does not deal with his activities on behalf of the "Legion" and his motivations for undertaking these activities. See IHGS, KGA/24.

37. Letter to the Polish Foreign Minister of 5 Janurary 1942, Kot, *op.cit.*, p. 249.

38. See Leon S. Rozen, *Cry in the Wilderness*, New York—Tel Aviv, 1966.

39. See YVA, 03.2863.

40. *Ibid.*

41. Kot, *op.cit.*, p. 436.

42. YVA, 03/2863.

43. Lucjan Blit, who lived in London, gave the author a copy of the memorandum form his private collection.

44. Kot, *op.cit.*, pp. 164–165.

45. Rozen, *op.cit.*, pp. 79–80.

46. Ander, *op.cit.*, p. 99.

47. *Ibid.*, pp. 99–100.

48. *General Anders — Zycie i chwala*, London, 1970, p. 63.

49. Kot, *op.cit.*, p. 164.

50. IHGS, KGA/24. Anders reports that After and Ehrlich asked for the appointment of Jewish commanders. It is more conceivable that they did ask that Jews be put in charge of separate cultural activities, as this would be in line with the ideological conceptions of the Bund.

51. Rozen relates that when he was in Israel in July 1963, he met with Dr. Kahan and asked whether he had written Kot informing him that he had rescinded his proposal concerning the creation of a "Jewish Legion." According to Rozen, Kahan emphatically denied Kot's contention in this matter. He said that "he had never written such a letter to Kot or to anyone else and he rejected the possibility of having even thought of doing so. He never expressed any doubts about the plan for a Legion." However, there exists a letter in Dr. Kahan's handwriting and signed by him in which he rescinded the proposal, since under the prevailing circumstances he did not believe that there was place for the creation of a Legion. He also noted that a similar letter was sent to Professor Kot. See IHGS, KGA/24.

52. Rozen, *op. cit.*, p. 236.

53. *Ibid.*, p. 231.

54. YVA, M-2/D-11.

55. *Ibid.*

56. YVA, 03/2863.

57. *Ibid.*

58. See the chapter "A Ghetto for the Jews in Totzkoye," Rozen, *op. cit.*, pp. 82–99.

59. Kot, *op. cit.*, p. 436.

60. Rozen, *op. cit.*, p. 87.

61. *Ibid.*, p. 88.

62. *Ibid.*, p. 92.

63. *Ibid.*, p. 93.

64. According to Rozen, it was the Polish journalist of Jewish extraction, Bernard Singer, who transmitted the report on Koltubanka abroad. See Rozen, *op. cit.*, p. 151.

65. IHGS, KGA/24.

66. *Ibid.*

67. The reference is undoubtedly to Colonel Okulicki who was parachuted into Poland after the abortive Polish uprising in Warsaw in 1944 and who became military commander of the Polish underground (*Armia Krajowa*) subordinate to the Government-in-Exile in London. After the war, Okulicki was taken prisoner, tried by the Soviets and executed.

68. Kot, *op. cit.*, p. 436.

69. YVA, 03/702.

70. Rozen, *op. cit.*, p. 216.

71. YVA, 03/702.

72. *Ibid.*

73. Kot's letter to Rabbi Rozen. See Rozen, *op. cit.*, p. 231.

74. Kot, *op. cit.*, p. 436.

75. Copies of the two orders of the day found in the Frisner Collection of the Yad Vashem Archives. The text of the second order is reproduced in Kot's book, pp. 465–466. The text of the second order is also recorded in the "Report of the Activities of the Representation of Polish Jewry for the Years 1940–1945," CZA, J25/54/VI, pp. 118–119.

76. YVA, Frisner Collection, L. dz. 1730.

77. See the text in *Eshnab*, the underground weekly of the Haganah, from June 28, 1943.

78. The second order opens with the following sentence: "With reference to my attached order, L.dz. 1730, from the office of the general staff, Novermber 14, 1941, pertaining to the role of the Jews in the Polish Armed Forces in the Soviet Union, I bring the following to the attention of all subordinate commanders." See Kot, *op. cit.*, p. 465.

79. The reference is to Anders' report "The Jewish Problem," IHGS, KGA/24.

80. It is worth noting that even before the war Anders' name was associated with circles close to the National Democratic Party. Anders was present at an assembly where an attempt was made to bring these circles closer to *Sanacja*. See Jerzy Janusz Terej, *Rzeczywistość i polityka*, Warsaw, 1971, pp. 50–51.

81. YVA, 03/2502.

82. YVA, 03/2863.

83. YVA, 03/2502.

84. YVA, 03/2506.

85. A copy can also be found in the Frisner Collection.

86. Report of the "Representation," CZA, J25/54/VI, pp. 118–120.

87. *Ibid.*, pp. 107–117.

88. *Ibid.*

89. *Ibid.*, p. 120.

90. The text of the order, which was published in the Polish edition of Kot's book, was not included in the English edition.

91. CZA, J25/54/VI, pp. 136–137.

92. IHGS, A.11.755/2, no date.

93. YVA, M-2/754.

94. Pobóg-Malinowski, *op. cit.*, pp. 229–230.

95. According to Pobóg-Malinowski, in the first stage 43,254 individuals left, of whom 30,799 were soldiers, and in the second stage, 70,289 left of whom 44,832 were soldiers. Altogether 70,292—strictly military personnel (p. 241).

96. According to Rozek, 77,000. See Rozek, *op. cit.*, p. 112.

97. Anders spoke of 4,000 Jewish soldiers having been evacuated, CZA, J25/54/VI, p. 38.

98. *Ibid.*, p. 35.

99. *Ibid.*, 37.

100. IHGS, KGA/24.

101. *Ibid.*

102. CZA, J25/54/VI, p. 34.

103. IHGS, KGA/24.

104. *Ibid.*, Anders' cable from August 8, 1942. See also the letter of the Bundists Glicksman and Feinsilber, IHGS, KOL 25/24.

105. The declarations of the group of rabbis and the letters of the Bundists, IHGS, KGA/24, KOL 25/24.

106. IHGS, KOL 25/24.

107. In his response to the petition of the Jewish Agency Representative from November 2, 1942, the Polish Representative stated that in his opinion changing one's name and religion should be viewed as an "'utmost necessity" that should not have led to any repercussions for those involved, *ibid.*.

108. See General Bohusz-Szyszko's review of 19 September, 1942, *ibid.*

109. *Ibid.*, pp. 42–43.

110. Bohusz-Szyszko's letter and analysis of December 2, 1942 addressed to Kot, IHGS.

111. Glicksman and Feinsilber's declarations of October 6 and October 10, 1942, IGHS, KOL 25/24.

112. See Jacob Hoffman's report from Teheran, Septmeber 17, 1942,

113. See Jenicz's 16-page report, Septmeber 22, 1942, *ibid.*.

114. This was emphasized in Glicksman's and Feinsilber's letters from the Bund.

CHAPTER TEN

After the Holocaust

The liberation of Poland from Nazi occupation required six months. The Red Army crossed the Bug River between the 20th and 21st of July, 1944 and advanced into the eastern regions that now form part of the Polist state. By the end of January 1945 Soviet armed forces reached the borders of what had been Poland's western frontier between the two World Wars. By then there were no Jews living in the homes and neighborhoods they had resided in before the war in any of the towns and villages of Poland. Nor had a single one of the approximately three hundred Jewish ghettos established by the Nazi escaped liquidation. About 900 Jews had managed to survive in the former Lodz ghetto: some 600 of these had been permitted to stay in order to clear the grounds and collect what remained of Jewish property and belongings; another 300 had survived by going into hiding, avoided being swept up in the last wave of mass deportations taking place between June and October 1944.[1]

At the time tens of thousands of Jews were still interned in concentration and labor camps in western Poland. However, as Soviet troops advanced, most of these camps were hastily evacuated by the Germans, who led away interminably long lines of camp inmates on death marches during the winter and spring of 1945. For example, 58,000 internees, most of them Jews, were evacuated from Auschwitz during the latter half of January 1945; several thousand remained behind, the great majority of them too ill or feeble to join the march.[2]

How many Jews, then, belonging to the approximately eight hundred Jewish communities that had flourished in Poland before the outbreak of the war in September 1939, were still alive at the war's end? Where did they escape to, and how were they saved? These questions are not easily answered. Our knowledge of these matters is based on only partial data. Even so, we can approximate with fair accuracy the number of Jews who survived. However for our conclusions as to where they had finally found refuge, the circumstances that had resulted in their rescue, and the identity of those involved in saving them from death are of necessity based on only a general evaluation.

Polish survivors can be classified as belonging to one of three major groups:

(1) Jews who had left Poland in the period immediately preceding the war or during the early months of the occupation. We can assume that they numbered about 400,000. Most had either fled or been deported or evacuated to the Soviet Union until the middle of 1944 and during the first days of the German-Soviet war. They remained in exile for the duration of the conflict. Apparently the overwhelming majority of these exiles returned to Poland during the repatriations that took place after the war.

(2) Jews who remained in hiding among Poles by either disguising themselves as Gentiles, or hiding among Polish friends, or being sheltered by Poles in exchange for payment. A number of Jews who had joined partisan fighting units or hidden out in the forests were able to survive as well in Poland.

(3) Jews who had survived in concentration and labor camps. Of these relatively few had survived in camps located within liberated Poland, and the majority had survived in concentration camps scattered throughout Germany and Austria; there were also Polish Jewish survivors in the Theresienstadt camp, near Prague.

The total number of Polish Jewish survivors abroad, in Poland and in concentration camps came to about 380,000.

Jewish survivors were gathered together only gradually. From within the territory liberated by January 1945 between the Bug and the Vistula, about 8,000 Jewish survivors were registered as being concentrated in Lublin.[3] About 3,000 Jews were recorded as residing in Warsaw, most of which had been destroyed.[4] By mid-June 1945, 55,509 Jews were registered by various committees throughout liberated Poland; this figure included all of the Jews who had been liberated in Poland itself as well as a number of Jews who had been released from the camps. In June 1946, there were 240,489 Jews registered with Jewish committees in the major cities of Poland and with the country's regional Jewish committees.[5] This figure included those Jews who had returned to Poland with the great wave of repatriation from the Soviet Union, and would appear to be the highest recorded total for Jewish survivors in Poland.

As a general rule survivors did not return to their prewar domiciles but tended, rather, to simply wander from place to place. There were two main reasons for their transience. The most important of these was the survivors' desperate compulsion to search for living relatives. Although the survivors were well aware of the fate that had overtaken the Jewish people as a whole and their own relatives in particular, they clung to the slender hope that some members of their famililes might somehow have escaped slaughter. The walls in the offices of Jewish committees throughout the cities of Poland were covered with slips of paper containing names and addresses posted by survivors in the hope they would be read by relatives or friends. But it was only on very rare occasions that a searcher, his eyes lighting upon the name of someone dear to him, would raise his voice in a joyous shout that electrified everyone within earshot. Typically, Jews registered everywhere they went; so that there were multiple registrations of individuals, which resulted in a situation making it impossible to establish the precise number of Jews who resided at a particular place at any one time. Those familiar with statistical techniques maintain that the number of Jewish registrees should be reduced by as much as fifteen percent in order to arrive at an estimate of the real number of Jewish survivors in Poland after the war.[6] An additional factor that must be taken into account are those Jews, numbering anywhere from a few hundred to a few thousand, who had assumed Polish names and identities and who had decided after the war to sever their ties with Judaism altogether. To these should be added several thousand Jewish children who had been adopted by Polish families or found refuge in monasteries, convents and boarding schools, and who either remained undiscovered or were not returned during the period in which searches for Jewish children were undertaken and attempts made to ransom them.

The second cause for the migrations of Jewish survivors was their desire to settle in large groups of their own kind, partly out of consideration for their physical safety, partly in response to their deep-seated need to live among their brethren. Thus we find individuals and small groups of Jews relocating from small communities in the Polish provinces to major cities containing large concentrations of Jews. In time, Jews concentrated heavily in Lower Silesia, whose cities had been emptied of their original German inhabitants and repopulated by former camp inmates, some of them Poles, and by repatriates from the Soviet Union. In consequence these cities became new centers of Jewish population in People's Poland.

As we observed earlier, the total of over 240,000 Jews recorded in June 1946 represents the highest figure for the reconstituted Jewish community of Poland after the war. In July 1946, the pogroms that took place in Kielce gave added impetus to the departure of Jews from Poland. In the months following, a mass exodus of Polish Jews took place. By the spring of 1947 all that was left of the Jewish community of Poland were about 80,000 Jews who had chosen, for one reason or another, to remain in the country. When the period of troubles and migrations finally came to an end, this remnant came to be regarded as a permanent segment of the population of the new Polish state. But even the population figures cited for the Jewish community of Poland in the latter years are conjectural. Census figures in Poland did not include data concerning separate religious or ethnic affiliation, so that the exact number of Jews in Poland at the time cannot be accurately established. Moreover, as we well know, after the mass Jewish exodus from Poland during the period of political disruptions following the war, the number of Jews in the country neither remained stable, nor did it increase as a result of natural population growth, In addition, after 1947 there were three more waves of Jewish emigration from Poland; the last of these took place between 1967 and 1968, and was in reality, an officially sponsored expulsion of the remainder of Polish Jewry.

In this brief survey we intend to deal with only the most salient demographic features of Polish Jewry after the war. One of the most striking of these is the greater number of men than women in the community of Jewish survivors in Poland. According to Polish census figures taken before the war in 1931, there were 108.7 Jewish females for every 100 Jewish males in Poland at the time.[7] The registration figures for Jews recorded in July 1946, however, show the Jewish population in Poland to be composed of 54.3% males and 45.7% females.[8] These figures have a direct bearing on the methods of rescue and routes of escape of Jews during the war. On the one hand, Jewish women found refuge more easily among Poles than did men, and fewer difficulties attended their efforts to disguise their identities; women seemed less likely to arouse the suspicious of those in pursuit of runaway Jews, and, even more importantly, the physical examination of women did not reveal their identities as, inevitably, it did in the case of Jewish males. On the other hand, a greater number of Jewish men than women escaped to the Soviet Union and were employed in forced labor at German camps.

Even more impressive is the statistical breakdown according to the age groups of Jewish Holocaust survivors in Poland. In 1945, in Lodz, where the largest concentration of Jews was located at the time, 7.3% of Jews living in that city were children aged fourteen and under; 7.7% were middle-aged and elderly persons over forty-five years of age; 85% ranged in age from fifteen to forty-five.[9] Clearly, the distortion of relative numbers among the various age groups (for every thirteen teenagers and adults in the prime of their life there was only one child and one older person), resulted from the massacres that had taken place during the war; the figures show us as well what the chances of survival were for each of the respective age groups during the war.

A more normal numerical relation among age groups existed among the Jewish refugees who returned to Poland from the Soviet Union. According to the registration figures for this group in the first quarter of 1946, 20.2% of the returnees were children fourteen years old and under, and 14.3% were middle-aged and elderly adults.[10] Hence, not only did the arrival of Jewish repatriates from the Soviet Union dramatically increase the number of Jews in Poland after the war, but they helped redress somewhat the imbalance in the numerical relations among the age groups in the Polish Jewish community. There were also a somewhat greater number of males than females among the repatriates from the Soviet Union; however the distortion in the distribution of sexes among the Jews of postwar Poland was probably due largely to the fact that the overwhelming majority of survivors from the camps were men.

THE CONCENTRATION OF THE JEWISH POPULATION DURING THE LUBLIN PERIOD

The early phases of Jewish self-organization in Poland after the war took place in Lublin, where the provisional capital of the new Polish state had been established. Superficially, the new Polish regime seemed to be composed of the democratic and workers' parties active in Poland between the wars; but in reality the dominant power in the government, both publicly and behind the scenes, was the Communist Party.

In the period between the two World Wars, the Polish Communist Party had been only a small and isolated political movement. Its weakness and lack of popular support arose from the anti-Russian sentiments that ran deep among Poles, and from the fact that the proletarian constituency in Poland was small and under-developed. Nevertheless, Jews, and young Jews in particular, were very strongly represented in the party's ranks. Various sources have estimated that Jews made up as much as twenty-five percent of the Polish Communist Party's membership.[11] The party was able to attract the sympathy of Jews because they saw it as a political force in Poland that disassociated itself from nationalism and rejected anti-Semitism. To those Jews who affiliated themselves with the Communists, only a complete change of regime held out the promise of solving the nation's ills and putting an end to the alienation, degradation and persecution of Jews in Poland.

On the eve of the Second World War, (in 1938) the Polish Communist Party was disbanded, and many of its leaders and theorists subsequently fell victim to Stalinist purges. The party was reconstituted, and renewed its activities in occupied Poland at the beginning of 1942 as the "Polish Workers' Party" (*Polska Partia Robotnicza*, or PPR), a title from which explicit reference to Communism was excluded. In this guise, the party sought to form a broad front of "progressive" forces under its aegis in Poland. But the tactic gained few advantages for the Communists, and the party remained a minor political force, rejected by almost all of the factions in the Polish underground. Only in the latter stages of the war did the PPR gain in strength somewhat as a result of Soviet efforts on its behalf, and because of increased clandestine war activity sponsored by the Communists. The political and tactical errors of the major underground forces directed by the Government-in-Exile in London contributed in no small degree, as well, to the expansion of Communist power in Poland.[12]

In December 1943 the National People's Council (*Krajowa Rada Narodowa*, or KRN) was founded in Warsaw as an underground political body whose membership included representatives of the Communist Party and of radical left-wing groups and factions that had allied themselves with the Communists. One of the participants at the founding of the organization was Pola Elster, a representative of the left *Poale-Zion* Party and one of the very few members of the Jewish underground in the ghetto who lived clandestinely among Poles.

A parallel Polish political force was organized at Communism's center within the Soviet Union. The Union of Polish Patriots (*Zwiazek Patriotow Polskich*, or ZPP) made its first public appearance in the Soviet Union in November 1941, when it was launched by the Soviets to offset the London-based Polish Government-in-Exile. The persons involved in the Union of Patriots actually made no great impression and exerted very little influence on the great mass of Polish refugees in the Soviet Union, of whom there were about 1,200,000 and who may even have numbered as many as one and a half million, according to some sources.[13]

The most prominent personalities active in the Union of Patriots were Wanda Wasilewska, a writer and journalist known in prewar Poland for her leftist views, and Alfred Lampe, the group's ideologist and a veteran Communist of Jewish extraction. Although Jews played a prominent role in the leadership of the organization, it should be noted that they were for the most part people who had rejected their Jewish origins and regarded their personal and social destinies to be bound up with the Polish nation and Polish culture; they looked upon any manifestation of Jewish national aspirations or attachment to the Jewish faith as reactionary and inimical to their philosophy.

The ZPP grew in importance not because of its own activities or any success in converting significant numbers of Polish exiles, but because of the deepening breach between Soviet authorities on the one hand, and the Polish Government-in-Exile and its branches in both the Soviet Union and the underground in Poland on the other. In the summer of 1942, General Anders' Polish army left the Soviet Union after having been consistently kept from joining the line of fighting Soviet forces on the Eastern Front. The conflict and mutual distrust between the Poles and the Soviets exacerbated in the Spring of 1943, with the discovery of the mass graves of Polish officers at Katyn, and the affair ultimately led to a break in diplomatic relations between the Soviet government and the Polish Government-in-Exile in London. Subsequently, many of the functions that had been carried out by the Polish diplomatic mission and loyal Polish emigres in the Soviet Union were taken over by the activists of the ZPP. On May 8, 1943, two weeks after relations had been severed, Soviet authorities officially announced that "the Soviet Union has decided to respond to the request of the ZPP and establish on the Soviet Union's soil, a Polish division named in honor of Kosciuszko."[14] Yet, notwithstanding the Polish national guise the Soviets sought to give to the military force created under its supervision, many officers in the unit were Soviet military men, and responsibility for the political and ideological indoctrination of the ranks was placed in the hands of members of the Union of Patriots.

In July 1944, when Soviet armed forces were about to cross the borders of present-day Poland, the Polish Council of National Liberation (*Polski Komitet Wyzwolenia Narodowego*, or PKWN) was formed.[15] The Council of Liberation was conceived as a supreme national body, or provisional government, in which the

Communist Union of Patriots organized in the Soviet Union, and the PPR and its allies in the underground in Poland, were supposed to be merged. When the PKWN was founded in Moscow a delegation of the KRN was present in the city, and the man placed at the head of the new political body was Edward Osóbka-Morawski, a member of the radical faction of the Polish Socialists. In fact, the appointment of the senior post of someone active in the underground who was not a Communist was made as a symbolic gesture. From the very outset the PKWN presented a contradiction that lasted throughout the majority of the period in which People's Poland was in existence, and whose presence continues to be felt in Poland to this day. It was created by the opposing wills of the Polish Communist emigres who hewed the Soviet line and the Communists and Leftists in the underground whose orientation became, at least to a certain extent, national, and who were inclined to be more receptive to political elements outside the Communist Party, and were ready to cooperate with them. As we shall see, this situation had important consequences for the future of the Jews in Poland.

Naturally enough the PKWN acquiesced to the shift in the Soviet-Polish border, a change that was rejected out of hand by the major Polish political organizations and most of the Polish leadership both abroad and in the underground at home. However, the Soviets and PKWN refrained from publicly instituting a policy and undertaking actions that bore an unequivocally Communist stamp. Desiring recognition by the West, the new Polish authorities began by adopting a provisional policy of concession. Undoubtedly, at least some of the Poles who were joined by Stanislaw Mikolajczyk, the Polish prime minister in exile who took office after the tragic deaths of Sikorski and his supporters, were sincerely convinced that they would be able to establish a democratic government in Poland, and that although the new Polish state would perforce be bound to the Soviet Union by a political alliance, it would nevertheless succeed in preserving its independence and retaining a considerable measure of freedom in conducting its internal affairs.

The PKWN entered Poland on the heels of the Soviet army and established its base at Lublin, from which it operated for a period of about half a year. The "Committee's Manifesto," or the PKWN's statement of its program, drafted when the organization was established in July 1944, announced that "the time for revenge against the Germans is at hand for the suffering and torments, the burnt villages and devastated cities, the plundered churches and schools; for the abductions, the camps and executions, Auschwitz, Majdanek, Treblinka; for the decimated ghettos." Further, it declared: "The Polish Committee of National Liberation, which is setting out to restore Polish statehood, solemnly proclaims the restoration of all democratic rights, the equality of all citizens regardless of race, religion or nationality, [and the restoration of] the freedom of political and professional organizations, of the press and of conscience . . . . The Jews, who were bestially slaughtered by the occupier, will be guaranteed the restoration of the basis of their existence and equal rights as well, both in principle and in practice."[16]

The fourteen initial members of the Polish Committee of National Liberation included Dr. Emil Sommerstein, a long-time Zionist activist who had been a Jewish representative in the Polish Sejm for many years until the outbreak of war in 1939. Dr. Sommerstein was imprisoned in the Soviet Union, but was released shortly before the creation of the Committee of National Liberation and invited to become a member of the new organization. By their appointment to the PKWN of a legitimate representative of Polish Jewry in prewar Poland, the Soviets, and perhaps even the Poles, sought to achieve two goals with one stroke: the inclusion on the Committee of a Jew whose authority no one in Poland or abroad would call into question, who had also been a member of the parliament of independent Poland between the wars.

Among the agencies created to serve the Committee was the Department of Assistance to the Jewish Population. Jewish survivors, both individually and in small groups, began converging on Lublin. Most of them made their way to the city on foot. Although at first their arrival involved them in no physical danger, still they were warned to conceal their Jewish identity to ensure their safety.[17] When Shlomo Hirszhorn, a physician and *Bund* member, began to direct the activities of the Jewish Department in August 1944, there were about 300 Jews in Lublin, of whom only fifteen had been residents of the city before the war (the 1932 census counted 38,937 Jewish residents in Lublin).[18] The Jews lived in public buildings that had been converted into refugee housing centers. The Committee set aside funds for its Jewish Department, but in small amounts which, because of the economic impoverishment of the liberated region, were inadequate to support the refugees. Many of them were ill and in need of clothing, beds and other basic necessities of life.

By September there were already about 2,000 Jews in Lublin and another 2,160 in the provincial towns of the region.[19] A Jewish Committee made up mostly of Zionists was organized in the city;[20] and a series of local Jewis committees were established in various other cities and towns. A public kitchen was set up in Lublin, and a Jewish kindergarden and school; cultural activities and arrangements for religious observance were instituted as well. Occasionally some movable personal property was returned to their original Jewish owners, but in most cases Jews were unable to retrieve their possessions. In Lublin proper Jews were promised the return of two buildings, one of which had served as a Jewish old-age home and the other as a Jewish orphanage before the war; but the transfer was repeatedly postponed.[21] In time, efforts were made to expedite the return and allotment of the public buildings to the Jewish community, but Jews continued to experience great difficulties in retrieving personal property that had fallen into private hands. During the early months complaints were received from the provincial towns that "local authorities were granting no material assistance to Jews"; and information was being received that the security of Jews was being threatened as well.[22]

Efforts were made in Lublin to establish contact with the world Jewish community and the Jewish community in Palestine. In August 1944 Dr. Sommerstein applied by telegram to the Joint in the United States and the Jewish Agency in *Eretz Israel* for emergency assistance for 10,000 needy Jewish refugees. Interviews with Dr. Sommerstein, and articles about Jewish refugees and the Lublin Center appeared in the Jewish press in the United States and Palestine. The telegrams and confirmations that dealt with the subject of assistance for the refugees were routed through Moscow, and the deliveries of aid first began to reach their destination by the end of 1944.[23]

The Provisional Jewish Central Committee was established in November 1944. Dr. Sommerstein was appointed its chairman, and the organization's membership included representatives of a number of Zionist factions, the Communists, the *Bund*, the Jewish Partisans and the Jewish Democrats. At the end of November Rabbi David Kahana arrived in Lublin and there he was appointed to the post of Chief Rabbi of the Polish Army. Also, the Minister of Internal Affairs approved the creation of a religious association of Jewish survivors in Poland.[24] This association provided an officially recognized framework for the activities of Jewish religious movements which had not been included in the Jewish Central Committee (i.e., *Agudat Israel* and the *Mizrahi* movement). The Zionist-Revisionists, too, had failed to get a seat on the Jewish Central Committee, but they managed nevertheless to organize themselves without being granted legal status.

The Polish army which was created in the Soviet Union gathered fresh recruits as it entered Poland. It was joined by about 13,000 Jews; some estimates put the total of Jews in its ranks at 20,000.[25] This force fought alongside the Red Army as it advanced in to occupied Poland. Jews were strongly represented among both its ranks and officers, although many of them hid their identity or at least made no great advertisement of their origins. These soldiers supplied their civilian brethren in Poland with urgently needed food and clothing, and intervened on their behalf with the newly organized agencies; but their most important contribution was to the morale of the survivors, who drew spiritual strength from the mere sight of confident Jewish fighting men who enjoyed the status of bona fide soldiers in a legitimate army.

THE REPATRIATION FROM THE SOVIET UNION

The repatriation of Jewish refugees to Poland from the Soviet Union took place in a number of stages. The entry of the Polish army into Poland involved, in itself, a return to the country of some of the refugees. In addition, the gradual infiltration of Polish nationals, both Jewish and Gentile, past the easily negotiable Russo-Polish frontier accounted for several thousand Jewish returnees, many of them members of Zionist pioneer movements who inaugurated the organized smuggling of illegal Jewish immigrants from Poland to pre-state Israel.[26]

The liberation of Polish territories and the establishment of a Polish provisional government brought to the fore the issue of the repatriation of Polish emigres who had been forced into exile or were imprisoned in Soviet jails, and of ethnic Poles living in the western Ukraine, western Byelorussia and the Wilna District—regions that had been part of the Polish state between the wars, but were now contained within the borders of the Soviet Union. The return of Polish nationals to their homeland became a primary Polish concern because of the drastic reduction in the Polish population. Additionally, settlers were also urgently needed for the German territories that had been newly annexed by Poland and vacated by the original inhabitants.

The problem of the legal and civil status of Jewish refugees from Poland in the Soviet Union proved to be exceedingly complex.

During the early stages in the recruitment for the Soviet-sponsored Polish army, the Soviets showed themselves willing to soften their position on the ethnic requirement. In the initial phase of the organization of this force, it was doubted whether a sufficient number of Poles could be found to complete the rolls of the army's first unit, the Kosciuszko Division. The recruits were not too rigorously screened to determine their ethnic origins, so that many Jews applying for enlistment were accepted. In mid-1944 of a separate Jewish committee within the Union of Polish Patriots (ZPP) in Moscow was established. The membership of the committee included Jewish writers, artists and community leaders; there was even a representative of *Agudat Yisrael*, Rabbi Elhanan Soroczkin, on the committee. The committee was headed by Berl Mark, who was later to direct the Jewish Historical Institute in Warsaw, and Dr. David Sfard.[27]

Support for the return of Jews to Poland was revealed by the Polish Council of National Liberation (PKWN), when the first agreements on exchange of populations were made with the Soviet Republic of the Ukraine, Byelorussia and Lithuania in September of 1944. These arrangements, as well as the discussions held with representatives of the Soviet authorities, concerned permission being granted to Poles and Jews residing in the regions that had been part of Poland, prior to their annexation by the Soviet Union, to settle in the new Polish state.[28] There was a sizable number of Jews living both in the western Ukraine and in western Byelorussia—a minority of them survivors, and many who had had the exceptional foresight to make their way there from deep inside the Soviet Union in the belief that from these western regions they would easily be able to leave Soviet Russia. Approximately twenty to thirty thousand Jews are estimated to have entered Poland as a result of these agreements, which became effective toward the end of 1944 and which became the basis for the population transfers which took place primarily during 1945.

Although these agreements accounted for only a relatively small number of Jewish repatriates, they established an important principle. It demonstrated Soviet readiness to permit the repatriation from the Soviet Union of Polish Jews to their country of origin. The agreements had not included Jews residing in independent Lithuania between the wars. Nonetheless, some Jewish survivors managed to take advantage of the confusion in the early period of liberation and moved into the Wilna District, whence repatriation to Poland was permitted, and there joined Jewish residents of the District who were leaving for Poland.

A full and explicit agreement involving the repatriation to Poland of all Poles and Jews absorbed by the Soviet Union during the war was signed in Moscow on July 6, 1945, about two months after hostilities had ended. This agreement was bound up with the establishment of a new Polish government, called the "Government of National Unity." which was composed also of London emigre elements under the leadership of Mikolajczyk, and representatives from a broad spectrum of the political left and center of prewar Poland. The regime gained the recognition of governments in the West; and, at least in the early days of the Government of National Unity's existence, Moscow seemed to take an indulgent attitude toward it. In the repatriation agreement drawn up between the Soviets and the new Polish government we read "of the right of members of the Polish nationality and members of the Jewish nationality in the Soviet Union to change their Soviet citizenship and return to Poland, and of the right of members of the Russian, Byelorussian, Ukrainian and Lithuanian nationalities who are residing in the territorial regions of Poland to relinquish their Polish citizenship and move to the Soviet Union."[29] The agreement's unequivocal language in guaranteeing repatriation to Poland to any Pole or Polish Jew, irrespective of any views or actions he may have stood accused of by Soviet authorities or police, was regarded as a "victory of the political line of the ZPP."[30] To carry out the repatriation program, a mixed Soviet-Polish commission was created.

The deadline of November 1945 that the agreement had originally set for the registration of repatriates had to be extended a number of times. There had been relatively few Jews among the repatriates returning to Poland after the September 1944 agreements with the Soviet Republics. In the wake of the new agreement, however, Jews made up a substantial part of the bulk of returning Polish nationals. As a result of the July 1945 agreement, 266,027 Polish emigres and refugees returned from the Soviet Union between 1945 and 1949; among them were 165,000 Jews (of whom 157,420 had returned by the end of June 1946, and another 8,000 by the end of 1949).[31] The repatriations following immediately upon the July 1945 agreement did not mark the end of the movement of returning refugees and emigres from the Soviet Union. After the phase of repatriation taking place until the close of 1946 had been completed, the Polish authorities approached the Soviets with a request to allow the return of refugees in certain categories who, for a variety of reasons, had not been included among the original repatriates. The Soviets acceded only in part to the Polish request, with the result that the repatriation of Polish refugees continued, though on a selective basis, between 1947 and 1949. But even after this extension had run its course, there were still Polish refugees remaining in the Soviet Union who had failed to make use of their right to return to their country. To this category belonged mixed marriage couples of whom only one member had been a Polish citizen. There existed categories, as well, of former Polish nationals who were either reluctant or unable to return; among the latter were various classes of prisoners. Following the changes taking place in Poland in October 1956, after Gomulka's return to power, an agreement was concluded to renew repatriations, and as a result 246,370 repatriates arrived in Poland between 1957 and 1959.[32] It should be stressed that in all of the negotiations, and in each of the renewed waves of repatriation, both Poles and Jews holding Polish citizenship, as well as their immediate families, were included in the category of those possessing the right of freely choosing to leave the Soviet Union.

A survey of the data pertaining to the repatriation of Polish nationals from the Soviet Union reveals to us the total number of Polish Jews who took advantage of their right to leave the Soviet Union and (those leaving with General Anders' army included) returned to Poland:

Jewish soldiers and civilians from Polish territories annexed by the Soviet Union who left Russia with the Anders Army	6,000
Jewish officers and troops in the Soviet-sponsored Polish army	13,000
Jews returning to Poland under the terms of the repatriation agreements of September 1944	25,000
Jews returning to Poland under the terms of the repatriation agreement of July 1945	165,000
Jews returning to Poland during 1957–1959	20,000
Total	229,000[33]

These figures cannot be relied upon for an exact estimate of the number of Polish Jews who found refuge in the Soviet Union. We should keep in mind that the data includes several thousand Lithuanian Jews, and couples not of Polish Jewish origin who nevertheless had obtained permission to leave the Soviet Union; included too are the children born to Polish Jewish families residing in the Soviet Union during the war. Moreover, we can assume that several thousand Polish Jews did not take advantage of their right to be repatriated, choosing to remain in the Soviet Union.

But to return to those Polish Jews who chose repatriation, our figures show the greatest wave of Jewish returnees to have occurred after the July 1945 repatriation agreement. The repatriates in this group arrived toward the end of that year and, chiefly, during the early months of 1946. The very high percentage of Jews among the returning Polish nationals during that period was regarded with disfavor by Poles, who came to regard the flow of repatriates into the country as a "re-inundation of Poland by Jews."

The entry of 200,000 Jews into Poland in the years immediately preceding and following the end of the Second World War confronted the new Polish authorities with a complex problem. The Jewish repatriates were totally impoverished; moreover the return of their homes, property and sources of livelihood from before the war turned out to be no easy matter. However, Polish authorities could hardly have ignored their obligations to Jews, who had, after all, been the major victims of the Nazi invaders. It was also clear that the treatment Jews received would be one of the important tests the new Polish government would have to undergo, and would exert a significant influence on the attitude of the West toward the changes being wrought in Poland.

In these circumstances, the massive settlement of Jews in the western territories annexed by Poland recommended itself as a logical solution that was at once convenient and advantageous. The Poles were in any case interested in the rapid settlement of these area in order to replace the natives who had either fled or been expelled; and having Jews settle in Lower Silesia and the Stettin region would also circumvent the problem of the conflicts likely to arise if Poles who had taken possession of Jewish houses, apartments, businesses and other possessions were made to return them to their original owners. Settlement in the new areas seemed to answer to Jewish needs as well. The anti-Semitic agitation and growing campaign of murder directed against Jews returning to their prewar places of settlement began to drive survivors to seek their haven in the cities and towns of the new Polish territories. The movement of Jews to settle in the western territories received further impetus from the strong preference of Holocaust survivors to live among large groups of other Jews. And so, we find trainloads of repatriates now being dispatched directly to the annexed regions.[34]

A summary of the situation is contained in the Central Committee of Polish Jewry's report for the January-June 1945 period:

> The question of where the repatriates should be returned became the major problem of the repatriation. When preparations for repatriation were being undertaken, word was already being publically spread in the Jewish community [and especially among its active members organized in the Union of Polish Patriots] concerning settlement—

following the return to Poland—in the western territories. Operating in conjunction with the political aspect, expressed in the desire to take part in the general governmental undertaking to populate the liberated territories, were also purely practical motives. It was only proper that consideration should be made of the fact that the returning Jews were originally from cities and towns in which they would be unable to settle because of the enormous carnage caused by the war.

Jews were psychologically shattered by the catastrophe which had overtaken them as a result of the Nazi massacres, and they felt drawn to larger communities, where possibilities existed to live in a suitable national and cultural ambience. Considerations of personal security were not without importance, and this, clearly, could be more readily attained in larger communities. For these reasons it was evident that the repatriates had to be directed primarily toward the western territories. Because the Germans had abandoned the region, there were no difficulties about guaranteeing the arrivals with at least a place to live and initial arrangements. The problem of the employment of Jews in developing industry was also relatively easy to dispose of here.[35]

Much as the report goes out of its way to avoid being explicit about facts embarrassing to the government, it does put on record the basic reasons for governmental and Jewish support for concentrating Jewish repatriates in the annexed western regions. Thus it was that Polish Jews, who historically, especially in recent generations, had been concentrated in the central and eastern part of the country, began to settle in cities like Wroclaw [Breslaw], Szczecin [Stettin], Walbrzych and Lignica. On the other hand, the major cities of Poland which had contained Jewish populations numbering in the hundreds of thousands before the war had hardly any Jews remaining. So we find that in 1946 there were only about twelve thousand Jewish residents in Warsaw, 824 in Lublin and 1,036 in Bialystok. Only Lodz, where Jewish institutions had transferred from Lublin and which therefore became the center of Jewish renewal at that time, possessed a sizable Jewish population, numbering 26,538. By contrast there were by then 69,993 Jews living in Wroclaw, and 30,873 in Szczecin. About eighty percent of the Jewish repatriates from the Soviet Union settled in the western territories and Upper Silesia.[36]

THE CAMPAIGN OF ANTI-SEMITIC AGITATION AND VIOLENCE

There were many reasons for the instability and ephemeral character of the postwar Jewish settlement in Poland. But among the major causes of Jewish feelings of insecurity and of the haste with which Jews left Poland were the rise of virulent anti-Semitism and the outbreak of anti-Jewish violence in the country. Official

Polish publications of the period make only occasional and obscure reference to the anti-Semitic campaign unleashed in the country during the early years of the existence of People's Poland, but contain no description or analysis of the event. In the history of postwar Poland this long campaign of pogroms is treated merely as one of many episodes of violence "directed by [the forces of] reaction against the Polish government," and the victims are described as "loyalists of the new regime," who were murdered by "the reactionary foe and fascists manipulated by the wire-puller in London."[37] Obviously this interpretation hardly reveals the true state of affairs.

There exist absolutely no grounds for laying responsibility for the anti-Semitic campaign at the door of the regime or its leaders, who attempted in both word and deed to ameliorate Jewish suffering. Occasionally, complaints were heard from Jews that the government was not doing enough to protect the Jewish community from attack, and there were even accusations that policemen and government officials had actually taken part in the murder of Jews. But on the whole, the government tried to check the resurgence of anti-Semitism and put an end to the attendant wave of murders of Jews, even to the extent of imposing harsh sentences on those involved. We should also keep in mind that the country was in the throes of a power struggle that at times attained the ferocity of actual civil war, and that many government officials died at the hands of the very gangs which were responsible for the murder of Jews. Moreover the political base within the population at large upon which the government relied was narrow and weak, and any public measures taken by the government to defend Jews would not have added to its popularity—this at a time when the new regime was battling for its very existence.

Still, a distinction must be made between the violence directed against the government and its agencies, and the persecution and murder of Jews. The opposition groups, most of whom were affiliated with the factions that went to make up the London government and the major underground organization in Poland during the war, argued that the new regime, having been imposed by the Soviets, was not an expression of Polish national will and would ultimately bring about Poland's total dependence on the Soviet Union.

The major opposition groups either confined themselves to passive opposition by preserving the framework of the Government-in-Exile, which claimed to represent the true interests of the Polish people, or, as in the case of Mikolajczyk and his associates, by trying to gain control from within by a democratic test of strength. However, extremist groups, which had been organized during the war under the guise of the NSZ (*Narodowe Sily Zbrojne*), WIN and other small groups, chose the path of armed opposition, both in keeping with the traditions of Polish history and in the belief that they would in this way succeed in preventing the country from being dominated by a regime which drew its strength and inspiration from foreigners, and from the Russians in particular, who had been conspiring to usurp Polish independence since the end of the eighteenth century. The widespread expectation among the rebels derived from the assumption that the agreements among the major allies are only temporary arrangments, and the first signs of the "cold war" are a beginning of a new conflict and of an inevitable soon-to-come world war.

It was on this point that anti-government sentiment and the struggle against the regime converged to single out the Jews for attack. The Jews were depicted as the regime's supporters, occupying major posts in the government and its administrative apparatus. The extreme oppositionists and fanatical anti-Semites regarded Jews as the new regime's mainstay. This regime, they argued, was in no way Polish but a creation of the Jews working under Soviet tutelage. It was claimed that the leaders of the new government were Jewish, the charge being leveled even at unquestionably Polish personalities, among them General Zygmunt Berling, the commander of the Polish army organized under Soviet sponsorship in the USSR.[38]

It was certainly undeniable that Jews were to be found among the upper echelons of the regime and within the government bureaucracy. By and large Jews had responded favorably to the new regime, which, in contrast to the Polish government between the wars and the major groups in the wartime resistance, had treated them with understanding and, at times, even sympathy. And the regime had accepted a relatively large number of Jews into its apparatus because it encountered difficulties in finding suitable candidates in sufficient number among the Polish intelligentsia, which had been greatly depleted during the war and many of whom either emigrated or had reservations about the government or were openly hostile to it.

In Poland, where the economic, social and educational gap between the upper and lower strata of society was vast, Jews were thought of as belonging, as a group, to the middle class and representing a large reserve of educated individuals. It was natural, moreover, for the government to take into account the fact that Jews made up an element loyal to the regime. For these reasons a certain

number of Jews were able to make their way into the civil service.
Many Jews took up work in the press, radio, literature and cul-
ture-related fields, in which they had excelled and been strongly
represented before the war, and to which many were now drawn
once more. We can question the wisdom of Polish Jews in concentrating in such great numbers, and making their presence so
evident, in sensitive sectors of the country's state apparatus, such
as the foreign service, internal security, university teaching staffs
and the press. But those Jews who occupied positions of responsibility and power were most often either veteran Communists or
committed leftists who set no more significance to their own roots
in Judaism than they did on religious faith in general. They wholly
identified with Polish culture and Polish nationalism, and valued
their commitment to socialism or communism above all else.

In reality, however, the Polish public entertained a greatly exaggerated notion of the numbers and influence of Jews in the
administration of the government and the Communist party.
Although the Polish intelligentsia had been decimated during the
occupation, Jews had suffered even greater losses. Morever, the
majority of Jews who had survived the camps or been repatriated
from the Soviet Union were artisans and laborers, poorly educated
and possessing an inadequate command of Polish, so that they
lacked even the minimum educational requirements to qualify for
places in the government bureaucracy. Only a small number of the
Jewish intelligentsia had survived, either by finding refuse among
Poles, or as in the case of some leftist Jewish intellectuals, as
emigers in the Soviet Union; this group was integrated in Polish
society and felt kinship with it. According to statistics published in
1945 in Lodz (that is, during the government administration's
formative year and in the city which was then the site of the government's major institution), 41% of the city's Jewish males were
artisans, 8.9% laborers, about 3.4% merchants and industrialists;
only 5.3% were clerical workers, exactly the same ratio as in the
liberal professions; 2.9% were studying in school or university.
Only 30% of the Jews in Lodz are recorded as having no occupation, this category being made up of persons either preparing to
leave Poland or whose physical or mental state prevented them
from working. Much the same picture emerges from the occupational statistics for Jewish repatriates in Lodz during the first
quarter of 1946: 35.9% artisans, 10.2% laborers, 5.5% merchants
and industrialists, 5.5% clerical workers, 6.2% in the liberal professions, and 10.1% attending school or university.[39]

In total, no more than a few thousand Jews were employed in the government bureaucracy and other key national sectors, so that in terms of numbers Jews made up as insignificant percentage of the personnel of the new institutional apparatus of the country. The ongoing complaints about Jews inundating the nation's institutions and gaining control of the state were in fact an expression of popular mistrust of the new personalities in the political and administrative organizations of Poland. Additionally, the presence of Jews in administrative and clerical posts in state and municipal institutions, where they had been barred from employment in the period between the wars, was an innovation intolerable to many in Poland who harbored anti-Semitic prejudices.

A few Jewish Communists had entered the upper echelons of the government: Jacob Berman, who was regarded as being in the confidence of Moscow and was close to the Polish president, Boleslaw Bierut; Hilary Minc, who was Minister of Industry and Commerce, and was the architect of the socialist economy of Poland; Roman Zambrowski who occupied a number of key posts in the Communist Party apparatus. But, naturally enough, none of them ever represented themselves as Jews, and the heads of Jewish organizations apparently preferered to deal with Gentile members of the government rather than approach those of Jewish origin. Again, among government ministers and party bosses, Jews were a mere handful, and there was never a single head of state or foreign minister who was of Jewish extraction in People's Poland—posts non infrequently held in democratic countries and, at times, even in countries of the Eastern Bloc other than Poland.

We have no way of resolving the much debated question of whether Polish anti-Semitism increased abated or remained unchanged during the war. However, one thing can be asserted without hesitation: the surfeit of Nazi anti-Semitism that had created the Holocaust had also infected the Polish public and shown elements within it that Jews could be annihilated "with ease and without causing a great stir." The same story is repeated in literally hundreds of Jewish accounts of the period after the war in Poland: A survivor returns to his home town intending to find out about his family home; and when he begins to inquire about the present occupants he is met with threats, curses and most painful of all, told, "Too bad Hitler didn't kill you too!"[40] There were also cases of Jews being received well, and it may well be that the viciousness described in these accounts was confined to a majority of pathological Jews-haters—but there were enough around, and their malevolent voices were clamorous enough to have impressed themselves more deeply upon the memory of Jewish survivors, than did encounters with humane treatment.

Poles and Jews gave very different explanations for the hostility of Jews after the war. Poles charged that the Jews, whom they had rescued from extermination, were, now that in inimical regime was taking over the country, making common cause with Poland's enemies. And Jews, for their part, regarded the emergence of popular anti-Semitism in postwar Poland as an expression of bad Polish conscience: the Poles had, after all, taken an active role in the wartime persecutions of Jews by depriving them of their livelihood and their property; the current outbreak of anti-Jewish outrages and murders of Jews was, accordingly, a reaction to the appearance of surviving Jews bearing witness to Polish guilt during the occupation. Whatever the merits of such an interpretation, it is certainly true that one of the main reasons for the new spate of anti-Semitism and anti-Jewish violence was the fear among Poles that Jewish survivors would demand the return of their homes and property, and of the possessions and assets they had left in the safekeeping of Polish acquaintances.

In conclusion, there were two major motivating factors behind the rise of anti-Semitism in postwar Poland: (1) The claim that it was the Jews who created the new regime and who occupied the highest offices in the government, so that the new regime was Jewish in its very essence, or Judeo-Communist (*Zydo-Komuna*) in the time-worn epithet; and the proof that this was, the case was furnished by the authorities' defense of Jews, and by their official condemnation of anti-Semitism. (2) Opposition to the restoration of Jewish property and to the return of Jews to their former homes and occupations.

The dimensions of the murder campaign against Jews, and the methods employed by the killers, put the entire community of Jews in Poland under a constant threat. It was estimated that between the time the liberation of Poland begun and the summer of 1947 as many as 1,000 Jews had been murdered. A Polish government memorandum dating from the beginning of 1947 states that "according to data on hand," 351 Jews had been murdered between November 1944 and December 1945.[41] Most of these murders took place in the Kielce and Lublin districts. The memorandum classifies the incidents of anti-Semitic incitements and violence into four categories: 1) those in the nature of provocations and pogroms (pogroms following blood libels in which Jews were accused of ritual murder of Gentile children took place in Rzeszow, Cracow, Tarnow and Sosnowiec); 2) blackmail with the purpose of driving

Jews out of a community and depriving them of their possessions; 3) murder and robbery; 4) murder for its ownsake, usually accomplished by throwing grenades into Jewish shelters.[42]

The memorandum attributes these acts to forest-based gangs made up for the most part of members of the NSZ, an organization which had been involved in assults on Jews and in murders of Jews during the occupation,[43] and which was now continuing the custom into the postwar period in the belief that anti-Jewish terror would increase unrest in Poland and would demonstrate that the new regime was incapable of asserting its authority and keeping order in the country. The violence against Jews was also calculated to gain the support and sympathy of population as a whole.

The memorandum asserts as well that "characteristically, the murders are committed in small communities, whereas in the large centers the number of murder victims is minimal."[44] As we have already observed in another connection, it was chiefly the high incidence of anti-Jewish violence in the smaller communities in Poland that was responsible for the movement of Jewish survivors to the major cities, where they concentrated in large numbers. But in 1946, when the outrages against Jews were at a peak, these episodes were by no means confined to small provincial settlements, roads and railways, but took place in the larger population centers as well. The Yidddish-language organ of the Jewish Central Committee in Poland, *Dos naye lebn*, which came out first as a weekly and later appeared several times a week under various guises, published reports of murders and their location and names of the victims in almost every one of its issues. So, for example, in issue No. 8 (March 13, 1946) we read of the murder of four Zionist pioneers in Lodz; in No. 9 (March 20, 1946) of eight Jews murdered in Janow Podlaski and Praszka: and in No. 10 (April 2, 1946) of a Jewish couple killed in Katowice. In this last issue we also learn that Polish President Boleslaw Bierut, in an interview with the former American president, Herbert Hoover, had observed that it was impossible to determine the exact number of Jewish murder victims, but that it was estimated that several hundred Jews had been killed by surviving remnants of illegal anti-Semitic organizations.

Pogroms took place in a number of cities. These were no hit-and-run raids undertaken by small terrorist gangs, but well-prepared and organized assults which were preceded by a campaign of slander in which scores and even hundreds took part. On Saturday, August 11, 1945, a pogrom was carried out in Cracow that began with stones being hurled at the synagogue, after which a mass assult was made on the town's Jewish shelter and Jewish homes. Jews were injured and killed, and their property pillaged. Regular army troops finally put an end to the pogrom. One particularly bloody attack, which ultimately had far-reaching effects on the process of stabilizing and rehabilitating the postwar Jewish community in Poland, took place in the district capital town of Kielce. Before the war Kielce's Jewish residents numbered about 20,000—nearly a third of the city's population; after the war there were only about 250 Jews living there many of them residing in the building of the Jewish Committee, at Planty Street No. 7., where a kibbutz group of the organization of Zionist Youth had also taken up residence. The pretext for the pogrom was provided by an eight-year-old Polish boy named Henryk *Blaszczyk*, who had disappeared on July 1, 1946, and returned two days later with a tall tale about having been kidnaped and held prisoner by Jews who intended to kill him. In investigations undertaken after the pogrom it was learnt that the boy had been sent by his father to a nearby village, where he had been rehearsed in the story that was to inspire the pogrom, it began on the morning of July 4 and was participated in by hundreds of Poles of all ages and belonging to every social stratum.

A few days later a report of the incident as described by eyewitnesses appeared in *Dos Naye lebn:* "... they tell us about how it was conducted; they tell us of how several thousand men, women and children, civilians and servicemen ran amuck from morning until evening, and then even held a festive rally after they had finished the job . . . ." And although the pogrom went on for a full day and in a major population center, not only did no help arrive, but men in uniform had actually lured Jews out of their barricaded homes and turned them over to the mob. Forty-seven persons, among them children who had survived the Holocaust, were killed and over fifty were injured by the rioters.[47]

The Kielce pogrom had a traumatic effect on the Jewish community. It also had wide public repercussions both in Poland and abroad. Polish writers and intellectuals raised their voices in protest against the present massacre of Jews and continuing survival of Nazism in Poland after Nazism had been defeated on its home ground. Both the public figures who supported the Society Against Racism and members of the government took vigorous action to put a stop to the wave of pogroms. It was mainly groups of the political Right and Church leaders who were held to blame for the violence, since they had done nothing to prevent it from taking place, and, after the outrage in Kielce, had failed to respond appropriately.

The blood libel was found to be an effective means of inciting mobs against Jews and was made frequent use of an postwar Poland. Just before the Passover holidays in 1946 the right-wing underground distributed pamphlets containing the warning: "Keep an eye on your child! More and more children are vanishing."[46] There were those in the Jewish community who hoped that the Church might be induced to exert a moderating influence on popular anti-Semitism and reduce susceptibility of Poles to incitements to violence against Jews. Accordingly, the Jewish Religious Association, led by Rabbi David Kahana, decided to meet with the leader of the Catholic Church in Poland, Cardinal Hlond. In May 1946 Michael Zilberberg, secretary-general of the Committee of Jewish Religious Communities, set out for Poznan in order to arrange for a meeting with the cardinal. Hlond remained firm in his reluctance to meet with Jewish religious leaders, although in his reply to Zilberberg he did go so far as to affirm that anti-Semitism had no place in Poland after the war, and to condemn the attacks on Jews. But his assertinos did not take the form of an official public statement, nor did he address himself on the issue to the great mass of Polish Catholics.[47]

After Kielce, demands began to mount for the Church to respond to the outrages against Jews. But for the most part Church leaders avoided taking a stand, arguing that the anti-Semitic episodes were outside the province of religios or Church affairs. Only Bishop Kubina of Czestochowa spoke up openly in his diocese in defense of the Jews and strongly condemned the Kielce pogrom. A week after the pogrom, on July 11, Cardinal Hlond was finally moved, in response to pressures from foreign journalists, to issue an official statement on the subject. Hlond's statement included the following remarks: "The Catholic Church has always condemned killings, and done so immediately. It condemns them in Poland as well, irrespective of whether they have been committed by Poles or Jews, in Kielce or in any other part of the Polish Republic. . . . The course taken by the unfortunate and grievous events in Kielce shows that racism cannot be attributed to them. They developed against a wholly different background, a painful and tragic one. These events are a great calamity that fills me with grief and regret . . . . When Jews were being annihilated in Poland, Poles, though themselves persecuted, supported and hid Jews at the risk of their own lives. Many are the Jews who owe their lives to Poles and Polish priests. Blame for the breakdown in these good relations is borne to a great extent by the Jews. In Poland they occupy positions in the first line of the nation's political existence, and their attempt to impose forms of government completely rejected by the great majority of the people[48] is a pernicious game, for it is the cause of dangerous tensions. Unfortunately, in the fateful armed clashes taking place on the front line of the political struggle in Poland, not merely Jews but incomparably more Poles are losing their lives . . . ."[49]

The situation that existed, therefore, was that the leader of the Polish Catholic Church, whose moral and spiritual authority carried decisive weight among the vast majority of the people of Poland, not only failed to condemn the pogroms and spreading use of the blood libel, but actually elevated the atrocities being committed against Jews to the status of a national political struggle. After having granted political legitimacy to the massacre of Holocaust survivors, he had taken a further negative step by accusing a stricken Jewish community, mourning its dead and troubled by an uncertain future, of taking control of the country's government and conspiring to impose its will in the face of Polish resistance. It was not just ordinary Poles alone, but their spiritual leaders as well who believed that the pitiful remnant of Polish Jewry, compelled to exist on the periphery of a society which was in the throes of revolutionary change and was a focus of global conflict, had actually managed to manipulate events in Poland and exert its influence on the country's political life. Other churchmen as well in Poland refrained from condemning the anti-Semitic violence, and the Vatican's own newspaper, *Observatore Romano*, justified the silence of the Polish Church by claiming that the incidents were "of a political nature" and therefore were outside the sphere of the Church's activity.[50]

In contrast to the Church, a reaction did take place to the Kielce pogrom. In factories and at mass rallies Polish workingmen vigorously demonstrated their revulsion at the killings. But this represented a certain part of the Polish people. The majority was at best indifferent or shared the attitude of the church.

Ultimately the murders, and especially the Kielce pogrom, had a decisive influence in bringing about the mass exodus of Jews from Poland. With it, the almost thousand years coexistence of Jews and Poles on Polish soil came to it's final stage.[51]

NOTES

1. On the last surviving Jews in the Lodz ghetto, see *Pinkas Polin* ("Polish chronicle"), Vol. *Lodz ve-ha-Galil* ("Lodz and the surrounding area"), Jerusalem,

Yah Vashem, 1976, pp. 36–37. Isiah Trunk, *Lodzer Geto*, A Historishe un Sotsiologishe Studie, New York, 1962 pp. 281–308.

2. See Hermann Langbein, *Menschen in Auschwitz*, Wien, 1957. Israel Gutman, *Anashim ve-Efer, Sefer Auschwitz-Birkenau* ("Men and ashes, the book of Auschwitz-Birkenau"), Merhaviah, 1957, pp. 165–176. Halina Wrobel, "Die Liquidation des KL Auschwitz-Birkenau", *Hefte von Auschwitz*, nr. 6, 1962.

3. Michat Szulkin, Sprawozdanie z dziatalnosci referatu dla spraw pomocy ludnosci żydowskiej przy Prezydium PKWN, BZIH, No. 79. Warsawa, 1971, p. 81.

4. *Ibid.*, p. 88.

5. *Tetikayts-Barikht* fun Tsentral-Komitet fun di Yidn in Poyln fun 1 Yanuar 1946 biz dem 31 Yuni 1946. p. 21.

6. See P. Glikson, "Jewish Population in the Polish People's Republic", 1944–1972, Jerusalem, 1973 (draft version), p. 3.

7. See *Tetikayts Barikht, op. cit.*, pp. 7–8;

8. *Ibid.*, p. 7.

9. *Ibid.*, p. 24.

10. *Ibid.*

11. According to an official spokesman of the Polish People's Republic, whose views were markedly anti-Semitic, Polish Communist sources claim that some 22–26% of the Jewish population belonged to the Jewish Communist party between the wars. See Andrzej Werblan, *Szkice i Polemiki*, Warszawa, 1970. p. 161.

12. There is extensive literature containing self-assessments and mutual accusations concerning Polish emigration. In order to understand the various basic concepts, see: J.M. Ciechanowski, The Warsaw rising of 1944, Cambridge, 1974; E.J. Rozek, *Allied wartime diplomacy — a pattern in Poland*, New York, 1958. For the views held by the present-day Polish camp, see: Czeslaw Madajczyk, *Polityka III Rzeszy w okupowanej Polsce*, v. I-II, Warszawa, 1970. Tadeusz Jedruszczak, Antyhitlerowski Ruch oporu w Polsce", in *Roczniki Historyczne* 1977–1978, Warszawa pp. 79–115 (1977), pp. 63–129 (1978)

13. The number is much disputed and the differences in its estimation very large. See: St. Kot, *Listy z Rosji do gen. Sikorskiego*, London, 1955, p. 107; Pobog.-Malinowski, *op. cit.*, p. 197, Krystyna Kersten, *Repatriacja Ludnosci polskiej po II wojnie swiatowej.* Wroctaw . . . ., 1976, pp. 43–44.

14. W dziesiata rocznce powstania *PPR, Materialy i dokumenty*, Warszawa, 1952, p. 228. Kalman Nussbaum, *Helkam shel ha-Yehudim be-Irgun u-vi-Peulot ha-Lehimah shel ha-Tzava ha-Polani be-Brit ha-Moatzot* ("The role of the Jews in the organization of, and activities conneced with, the fight by the Polish army in the Soviet Union"), 1977, (Ph.D. thesis for the University of Tel Aviv).

15. On the PKWN, see: Krystyna Kersten, *Polski Komitet Wyzwolenia Naradowego*, (Lublin 1965)

16. See the text of the manifesto: *W dziesiata rocznice . . ., pp. 387–394.*

17. *Jonas Turkow, In Kamf farn Lebn*, Buenos Aires, 1949, p. 396.

18. Szulkin," Dzialalnosc referatu . . ., *op. cit.*, p. 78.

19. *Ibid.*, p. 79.

20. See the article by Hannah Shlomi: "*Reshit ha-Hitargenut shel Yehudei Polin be-Shelhei Milhemet ha-Olam ha-Shniyah*" ("The beginning of reorganization by Polish Jewry in the final stages of World War II"), Gal-Ed. M. Mishkinsky, Vol. 2, Tel Aviv, 1975, pp. 287–331.

21. Szulkin, *op. cit.*, p. 80.

22. *Ibid.*, pp. 83–84.

23. See article by Hannah Shlomi mentioned above; also article by Y. Bialostocki, "Yidishe Hilfs-Arbet in Poyln", in *Entziklopediyah shel ha-Gluyot*, Vol. 12, Jerusalem, 1973, pp. 439–468.

24. According to the manuscript of memoirs by Rabbi David Kahana.

25. The number accepted by most writers is 13,000. Kalman Nussbaum, in his aforementioned work, however, estimates that there were 20,000 Jewish soldiers in the Polish army established under the aegis of the Russians in the Soviet Union. For the figure 13,000, see Moshe Yishai, *Be-Tzel ha-Shoah* ("In the shadow of the Holocaust"), Bet Lohamei ha-Gitaot, 1973, p. 31.

26. See Yehuda Bauer, *Brihah* (Flight and Rescue), N.Y., 1970, pp. 27–28 ,32.

27. See section for oral documentation, The Oral History Division of the Institute for Contemporary Jewry, the Hebrew University, Files 27 (a and b).

28. Kersten, *Repatriacja . . . op. cit.*, pp.97–99. Bernard D. Weinryb, "Poland", in *The Jews in the Soviet Satellites*, Westport, 1971, p. 241.

29. Kersten, *Repatriacja op. cit.*, p. 98.

30. *Ibid.*, p. 228.

31. *Ibid.*, p. 229 *Tetikayts Barikht, op. cit.*, p. 7.

32. P. Glikson, "Jewish population", *op. cit.*; Y. Bialostotcki, "Yidishe Hilfs-Arbet in Poyln", *op. cit.*, p. 461.

33. This table is based on figures on estimates which occur in most sources and are quoted by the majority of authors.

34. Bernard D. Weinryb, *op. cit.*, p. 267.

35. *Tetikayts Barikht, op. cit.*, p. 13.

36. *Ibid.*, p. 22.

37. See Lucjan Dobroszycki, "Restoring Jewish Life in post War Poland", Soviet-Jewish Affairs, 1973–II, p. 58. See: Kersten, Polski Komitet Wyzwolenia Narodowego,*op. cit.*, 71–73.

38. *Ibid.*, pp. 100–101.

39. *Tetkayts-Barikht, op. cit.*, p. 26.

40. See Shimon Samet, *Bevoi le-Maho-rat*—Masa be-Polin - 1946, ("When I arrived the next day — Journey through Poland 1946"), Tel Aviv. 1946, p.50; manuscript by Rabbi David Kahana; Israel Ben-Dov, Poylisher Antisemitizm in di Yoren 1939–1946", in *Entziklope-diyah shel ha-Galuyot*, Vol. 12, pp. 407–438.

41. An internal Polish memorandum from the end of 1945 entitled "Manifestations of anti-Semitism in Poland and the Battle Against it's" is in the author's possession. The memorandum gives the number of victims in various districts — Warsaw area, 57; Lublin area, 64; Cracow area, 15; Bialystok area, 38; Rzeszow area, 34; Kielce area, 79; Lodz area, 51; Pomorze area, 5; Silesia area, 3. In all, 351.

42. *Ibid.*

43. On murders committed by NSZ, see, for example, an official publication of documents of the archive of the Polish Government-in-Exile in London, *Armia Krajowa [AK] w dokumentach,* 1939–1945, v. 3—IV, 1943–VII, 1943, London, 1976. A document sent to London by the Polish military underground (AK) in June 1944, stated that, "the lower-ranking commanders of NSZ are collaborating with the Germans in liquidating Jews" (p. 490) and leftists. A report of May 25, 1944, stated that members of the underground who belonged to the coalition parties which composed the Government-in-Exile "had expressed reservations about including NSZ in the AK, as "NSZ units collaborate with the Germans in fighting the Commune (Communists), murder Jews and at times attack leftist communal workers" (p. 452).

44. Internal memorandum, see footnote no. 43. above.

45. Many details of the pogrom in Kielce can be found in the Polish-Jewish press of the period.

46. A copy of an announcement in this vein is in the author's possession. Rabbi Kahana discusses circulation of such announcements. See manuscript by Rabbi Kahana in Yad Vashem Archive.

47. See description of Dr. Zilberberg's mission in Rabbi Kahana's work, manuscript in YVA.

48. In announcements printed by the gangs, this claim was expressed very coarsely. Thus, for example, an announcement entitled, "Proclamation to the Jewish Community", which was signed "The Polish anti-Communist Military Organization" (from London, April 4, 1945), reads as follows: "Jews! You have lived through the period of Hitlerite persecutions. Every survivor among you owes his life to the Poles alone. Now, after the entry of the Red Army, you have emerged from your hiding-places for the sole purpose of oppressing and exploiting true Poles; and, most distressing of all, you are handing over to destruction those who, in the most critical moments, gave you a helping hand. Jews! Since you have revealed yourselves to be enemies of the Poles, *we command you* to leave the Piaski settlement within one week, otherwise we shall take suitable measures against you."

49. For the wording of Hlond's statement, see appendix to Rabbi Kahana's manuscript, YVA.

50. For reactions to the declarations by the Vatican Bulletin, see the Polish and Jewish press; Rabbi Kahana's manuscript, *op. cit.*; also Ben-Dov's article on Polish anti-Semitism, *Entziklopediyah shel ha-Galuyot*, Vol. 12, *op. cit.*

51. Yisrael Gutman, *Hayehudim bepolin ahrey milhemet haolom hasheniya* (The Jews in Poland after World War II), Jerusalem, 1985.

SELECTED SOURCES

Unpublished materials

Yad Vashem Archives, Jerusalem (YVA)
— Files of the Office of Dr. Y. Schwarzbart (M–2)
— Collection of testimonies (0–3)
— Collection on Poland (0–6)
— Simon Frisner files (0–25)
— Collection of diaries and memoirs (0–33)
— Alexander Bernfes files (0–55)

Archives of the Central Committee of the Polish Unified Workers'
Party, Warsaw (AZHP AKCPZPR)
— Files of the Delegate's Office (202)
— Files of the Home Army (203)

Archives of the Jewish Historical Institute in Warsaw (AZIH)
— Collection of Testimonies
— The Ringelblum Warsaw Ghetto Underground Archives

Archives of the General Sikorski Historical Institute, London
(GSHI)
— Prime Minister's Office (PRM)
— Army files (A)

Polish Underground Study Trust, London

Central Zionist Archives, Jerusalem

Oral History Division of the Institute for Contemporary Jewry at
the Hebrew University of Jerusalem

Moreshet Archives, Givat Haviva, Israel

Selected books

Ainsztein, Reuben. *Jewish Resistance in Nazi-Occupied Eastern Europe.* New York: Barnes and Noble, 1974.

Anders, Wladyslaw. *Bez ostatniego rozdzialu; Wspomnienia z lat 1939–1946* (Without the last chapter: memoirs from the years 1939–1946), Newton, Wales: Montgomeryshire, 1950.

Arad, Yizhak; Gutman, Yisrael and Margaliot, Abraham (editors). *Documents of the Holocaust.* Jerusalem: Yad Vashem, 1981.

Arczynski, Marek and Balcerak, Wieslaw. *Kryptonim "Zegota"; Z dziejow pomocy Zydom w Polsce 1939–1945* (Cryptonym "Zegota"; From the history of help for Jews in Poland 1939–1945). Warsaw: Czytelnik, 1983.

Bartozewski, Wladyslaw and Lewin, Zofia (editors). *Righteous Among Nations: How Poles helped the Jews 1939–1945.* London: Earlscourt Publications, 1969.

Bauer, Yehuda. *The Jewish Emergence from Powerlessness.* Toronto: University of Toronto Press, 1979.

Bor-Komorowski, Tadeusz. *The Secret Army.* New York, 1951.

Borwicz, Michael. *Arishe papirn.* (Aryan papers). Buenos Aires, 1955. 3 vol.

Ciechanowski, Jan. *Defeat in Victory.* New York, 1947.

Dawidowicz,Lucy. *The War against the Jews 1939–1945.* New York: Holt, Rinehart, and Winston, 1975.

Donat, Alexander. *The Holocaust Kingdom.* New York: Holt, Rinehart, and Winston, 1965.

Friedman, Philip. *Their Brothers' Keepers.* New York: Holocaust Library, 1978.

Gilbert, Martin. *Auschwitz and the Allies.* London: Rainbird, 1981.

Gross, Jan Tadeusz. *Polish Society Under German Occupation: The General Gouvernement 1939–1945.* Princeton, 1979.

Grynberg, Henryk. *Prawda nieartystyczna* (The unartistical truth). Berlin: Archipelag, 1984.

Gutman, Yisrael and Rothkirchen, Livia (editors). *The Catastrophe of European Jewry.* Jerusalem: Yad Vashem, 1976.

Gutman, Yisrael (editor). *Rescue Attempts during the Holocaust; Proceeding of the Second Yad Vashem International Conference.* Jerusalem: Yad Vashem, 1976.

Gutman, Yisrael. *The Jews of Warsaw 1939–1943; Ghetto, Underground, Revolt.* Indianapolis: Indiana University Press, 1982.

Gutman, Yisrael. *Hayehudim bepolin ahrey milhemet haolam hasheniya* (The Jews in Poland after World War II). Jerusalem, 1985.

Hausner, Gideon. *Justice in Jerusalem.* New York: Schoken, 1968.

Heller, Celia. *On the Edge of Destruction.* New York: Columbia University Press, 1977.

Hirszfeld, Ludwik. *Historia jednego zycia.* (The Story of One Life). Warsaw: Pax, 1957.

Iranek-Osmecki, Kazimierz. *He Who Saves One Life.* New York: Crown Publishers, 1971

Kaplan, Chaim Aharon. *Scrolls of Agony; The Warsaw Diary.* New York: The Macmillan Company, 1956

Karski, Jan. Story of a Secret State. Boston: Houghton Mifflin, 1944.

Klukowski, Zygmunt. *Dziennik z lat okupacji Zamojszczyzny* (Diary from the years of occupation of the Zamosc region). Lublin: Wydawnictwo Lubelskie, 1959.

Kot, Stanislaw. *Listy z Rosji do Generala Sikorskiego* (Letters from Russia to General Sikorski). London, 1955.

Krakowski, Shmuel. *The War of the Doomed: Jewish Armed Resistance* in Poland, 1942–1944. New York: Holmes and Meier, 1984.

Kulski, Julian. *Zarzad Miejski Warszawy, 1939–1944* (The Warsaw Municipality, 1939–1944). Warsaw, 1964.

Landau, Ludwik. *Kronika lat wojny i okupacji* (Cronicle of the War years and occupation). Warsaw: Panstwowe Wydawnictwo Naukowe, 1962, 2 vol.

Laqueur, Walter. *The Terrible Secret: An Investigation into the Suppression* of Information About Hitler's "Final Solution". London: Widenfield and Nicolson, 1980.

Luczak, Czeslaw. *Polityka ludnosciowa i ekonomiczna hitlerowskich Niemiec w okupowanej Polsce* (The economic and population policy of Nazi Germany in occupied Poland). Poznan: Wydawnictwo Poznanskie, 1979.

Madajczyk, Czeslaw. *Polityka III Rzeszy w okupowanej Polsce* (Policy of the Third Reich in Occupied Poland). Warsaw: Panstwowe Wydawnictwo Naukowe, 1970, 2 vol.

Mark, Bernard. *Powstanie w getcie warszawskim; Zbior dokumentow* (The Warsaw Ghetto Uprising: Collection of documents). Warsaw: MON, 1963.

Mendelsohn, Ezra. *The Jews of the East Europe Between the World Wars.* Bloomington: Indiana Press, 1983.

Polonsky, Anthony. *Politics in Independent Poland, 1921–1939.* Oxford: The Clarendon Press, 1972.

Prekerowa, Teresa. *Konspiracyjna Rada Pomocy Zydom w Warszawie 1942–1945* (The Clandestine Council for Helping Jews in Warsaw 1942–1945). Warsaw: Panstwowy Instytut Wydawniczy, 1982.

Ringelblum, Emmanuel. *Polish-Jewish Relations During the Second World War.* Edited and footnotes by Joseph Kermish and Shmuel Krakowski. Jerusalem: Yad Vashem, 1974.

Rozek, Edward. *Allied Wartime Diplomacy: A Pattern in Poland. New York* 1956.

Rozen-Szczekacz, Leon. *Cry in the Wilderness: A Short History of a Chaplain. Activities in Soviet Russia During World War II. New York,* 1966.

Tec, Nechama. *When Light Pierced the Darkness; Christian Rescue of Jews in Nazi-Occupied Poland.* New York: Oxford University Press, 1986.

Tenenbaum-Tamaroff, Mordehai. *Dappim min hadleka* (Pages from Fire). Beit Lohamei Magetaot. Israel, 1984.

Terej, Jerzy Janusz. *Rzeczywistosc i polityka; Ze studiownad dziejami najnowszymi Narodowej Demokracji* (Reality and Politics; Selected Studies in the Recent History of the National Democratic Movement). Warsaw, 1971.

Wronski, Stanislaw and Zwolakowa, Maria. *Polacy-Zydzi, 1939–1945* (Poles and Jews, 1939–1945). Warsaw: Ksiazka i Wiedza, 1971.

Wynot, Edward D. *Polish Politics in Transition: The Camp of National Unity and the Struggle for Power 1935–1939.* Athens, Georgia: University of Georgia Press, 1974.

Zuckerman, Yitzhak. *Prakim min hayizavon* (Fragments from the Literary Legacy). Beit Lohamei Hagetaot, Israel, 1982.

Periodicals

Biuletyn Glownej Kmoisji Badania Zbrodni Hitlerowskich w Polsc-BGKBZH (Bulletin of the Main Commission for Investigation of Nazi Crimes in Poland), Warsaw.

Biuletyn Zydowskiego Instytutu Historycznego–BZIH (Bulletin of the Jewish Historical Institute), Warsaw.

Bleter far geshichte (Historical Pages), Warsaw.

Najnowsze Dzieje Polski; Materialy i Studia z Okresu II Wojny Swiatowej (Recent History of Poland: Materials and studies from the period of World War II), Warsaw.

Wojskowy Przeglad Historyczny–WPH (Military Historical Review), Warsaw.

Yad Vashem Studies, Jerusalem.

Yalkut Moreshet (Heritage Collections), Tel Aviv.

Zeszyty Historyczne (Historicel Notebooks), Paris.

I N D E X